Please remember that this is a library book,
and that it belongs only temporarily to each
person who uses it. Be considerate. Do
not write in this, or any, library book.

ISLANDS IN THE STREET

ISLANDS IN THE STREET

Gangs and American Urban Society

MARTÍN SÁNCHEZ JANKOWSKI

UNIVERSITY OF CALIFORNIA PRESS
BERKELEY   LOS ANGELES   LONDON

University of California Press
Berkeley and Los Angeles, California

University of California Press, Ltd.
London, England

© 1991 by
The Regents of the University of California

Library of Congress Cataloging-in-Publication Data

Jankowski, Martín Sánchez, 1945–
    Islands in the street : gangs and American urban society
/ Martín Sánchez Jankowski.
        p. cm.
    Includes bibliographic references and index.
    ISBN 0-520-07434-3 (alk. paper)
        1. Gangs—United States—Cross-cultural studies. I. Title.
HV6439.U5J36   1991
364.1'06'0973—dc20   90-48641
                                                    CIP

Printed in the United States of America
            7 8 9

To my wife
Carmen Carrasquillo
por su apoyo, entendimiento, y los regalos brindados

Will you, surrounded as you have been all these years by all the appurtenances of civilization . . . grasp that the deathlike loneliness of our lives and the misery-laden air of the catacombs we have been breathing for so long have made our eyes terribly clear-sighted? May it not be, in the first moments after your return, that the visions these eyes can now see in the distance will frighten you?

Friedrich Reck-Malleczewen,
Diary of a Man in Despair
(September 1937)

Contents

Preface

Among the meanings given for the word *gang* in *Webster's New American Dictionary* is that of "a journey." The ten years and five months that I have spent on this research project have indeed been a journey. A journey not only through time but also into the lives of gang members and various other individuals who live in the low-income areas of New York, Boston, and Los Angeles. Ironically, it has also been a journey back into my youth, where the actors were different, but the stage and play were quite similar—a journey *Down These Mean Streets,* as Piri Thomas said about his own life in Spanish Harlem. In brief, it has been a journey with many benefits and some costs, a journey that has, irrespective of these emotional highs and lows, allowed me the opportunity to gain an understanding of one of the oldest and most important institutions that exists within the American low-income urban community—the gang. Throughout this journey I have met some wonderful people, whom I shall always remember with fondness, and I have met some not-so-wonderful people, whom I shall also not forget. Though the journey has had some important costs in terms of personal injury and the sorrow I felt for the tragedies that have beset some good people I liked, for me it has been worthwhile.

The origin of this gang project can be located in a study I was conducting in the 1970s on the political attitudes of Chicano youth. At that time, I wanted to compare my findings concerning Chicanos in Los Angeles with Puerto Ricans in New York and Boston. In the process of pretesting the interview schedule in New York and Boston, I noticed that an enormously high number of young Puerto Ricans were involved in gangs, an observation identical to one I had made of Chicano youth in Los

Angeles. It then occurred to me that if one wanted, as I did, to have a sociological understanding of low-income communities in the United States, it would be necessary to understand why the gang phenomenon had persisted in the United States for more than one hundred years. So after completing my study of political attitudes, I embarked on developing a research project that focused on urban gangs. I knew that to develop a full understanding of the gang phenomenon, I would need to spend a great deal of time interacting with gangs. Thus, right from the start I committed myself to what I understood was a multi-year research project. The publication of this book marks the culmination of this ten-year commitment.

Over the more than ten years that I have been involved in this project, I have been the recipient of much support. Of all the things that comprise a book, it is the acknowledgement of support given me that brings me the most pleasure.

First, and foremost, I want to thank those gang members and their families who allowed me the opportunity to experience a part of their lives. Remarkably, all of those that I studied never once tried to influence my analysis of them. I am deeply appreciative of their cooperation. I also want to thank all of those people who in various official and unofficial capacities interact with gangs for allowing me the opportunity to interview them while they were in the process of executing their duties.

In addition to the gang members and the people who interact with them, I am indebted to four of my colleagues at Berkeley: David Matza, Claude Fischer, Ann Swidler, and Mike Rogin. They all read the entire manuscrpt and gave me thoughtful comments that helped me clarify my ideas. Mike Rogin deserves a very special acknowledgement because he tirelessly read two drafts of the manuscript and provided detailed comments on both.

I would also like to thank James F. Short, Jr., and Ruth Horowitz for their detailed comments on the manuscript; and Jameson Doig, who provided me with some insightful comments after a lecture I gave at Princeton.

Now let me turn my attention to the support I received while I was doing fieldwork. First, I would like to acknowledge the financial support that was given to keep me in the field. In this regard, I am indebted to the Ford Foundation, the Weatherhead Foundation, the Joint Center for Urban Studies of M.I.T. and Harvard University Fellowship Program, and the Minority Post-doctoral Fellowship Program at the University of California at Berkeley.

Second, there was the encouragement that emotionally sustained me while I was in the field. For this, I would like to thank Sam Cohn, Julia Sheehan, Andres Jimenez, Maria Martinez, Adriana Jimenez, Troy Duster, Michael Hout, my brother and his family, and the Carrasquillo family. Terry Kemper and Joel Krieger deserve special thanks for their continual support over the full length of the project.

Next, I would like to express my gratitude to Nizam Fatah for his friendship and the opportunity to "hang" at his ICRY office for periodic R & R from the rigors of the street. I would also like to thank J.C., Father Divine, Bobcat, and Crazy Cat. While all of these individuals belonged to gangs, neither they nor their gangs were a part of my study; yet their friendship, like Nizam Fatah's, provided me with some good times and periodic shelter from the storms associated with the fieldwork.

I would also like to thank Lewis Anthony Dexter, whom I was fortunate to have as a professor and friend during and after my graduate training. He provided me with many of the tools that I use to pursue my work, and for that I am very grateful. While he might not agree with some of my conclusions in this study, he will recognize his continued influence.

Although mere acknowledgment of this help cannot accurately portray how much assistance those mentioned provided me with, it is my hope that this acknowledgement will be taken by them as an indication of the fact that they and their deeds remain an important part of my memory.

At this point it is appropriate to state that none of the people or institutions mentioned are in any way responsible for the interpretations found in this book. Simply stated, their help made this a better book. Whatever defects still exist must be attributed solely to me.

Now for two personal notes. I would like to thank my mother and father for their unceasing support of my work, even though they worried, much as they did when I was young, the whole time I was in the field.

Finally, and most especially, I would like to thank my wife Carmen for all the understanding, support, and gifts that she provided me while the study was in progress. Although she was not a part of my life for the entire ten-plus years of the study, she was for a good part of it; and during that time she never once put pressure on me to stop my fieldwork. Nor did she express concern about the dangers of the work, or the time away from home. Remarkably, each time I went to the field, she simply said good-bye in the same manner as if I were on my way to the university to give a lecture. In addition, and more important, during this period she provided me with two sons, Javier and Julian—two gifts that have given me incalculable pleasure. Thus, while this book is dedicated to her, it is in fact a grossly inadequate expression of my appreciation.

Before ending this preface, I would like to say something about my choice of a title for this book. There were many titles that would have been appropriate, but *Islands in the Street* seemed the most suitable. This is because the concept of an island has many of the symbolic meanings that I found fitting for what I discovered about gangs. First, there is the symbolism of being isolated, alone and yet self-sufficient, and this certainly applied to the gang members I studied. Then there is the symbolism involving the relationship between the island and the ocean. In this regard, islands are defined by the ocean they are in, and yet they also give definition to that same ocean. Likewise, gangs are defined by the social environments in which they operate, and yet they give definition to them as well. Finally, the use of the plural form of the word *island* in the title provides the additional symbol of an archipelago. Thus, just as groups of islands form aquatic archipelagos across the seascape, gangs form social archipelagos across the urban landscape.

Introduction

The gang, in short, is life, *often rough and untamed, yet rich in elemental social processes significant to the student of society and human nature.*

Frederic Thrasher, *The Gang (1928)*

Gangs. The word has meant a number of things throughout history, but inevitably most people have used it with a negative connotation. Looking at the history of the word *gang* in the United States, one finds that the term has perennially been used of certain social groups considered to be major social problems of the time. The social science academy's research on gangs has had its own history, and the focus of this research has in turn been influenced largely by what society has considered the major social problems of the period.

In the United States, the history of applying the term *gang* to describe certain groups active in the economy starts with the western outlaws of the nineteenth century. All kinds of gangs were active in robbing stage-coaches, banks, mines, and saloons; some of the more famous were the Doolin, Dalton, and James gangs. There was no question that society, particularly western frontier society, considered these groups a social, economic, and moral problem. They posed a particular threat to social control, and people were concerned with understanding who these men were and what led them to become outlaws. Of course, to most of the residents of those areas in which outlaws were active, it undoubtedly was hoped that answers to these questions might be helpful in aiding the authorities to control them; while to those who resided in areas where outlaws were not active, the answers to the questions simply fueled the ro-

I

mance they had developed with the symbol of the outlaw. A romance, it
might be added, that has carried forward today.

A formalized social science as we know it today did not yet exist, but
various people made efforts to inquire into these questions and report
their findings in books and the tabloids of the day. Interestingly, a problem researchers face today also presented itself to the researchers of the
nineteenth-century outlaws—namely, accessibility to (and the cooperation of) the outlaws themselves. Outlaws, after all, had little reason to
cooperate with a researcher, whose presence had the potential to raise
the risk of their being captured, and most researchers surely judged the
outlaws and their life-style to be too dangerous for field study. In the
absence of direct observation, it is not surprising that the vast majority
of their reportage was based on impressionistic, sensationalized second-
hand accounts.[1] Likewise, it should not be surprising that such reportage
was instrumental in building the outlaw mythology in the United States.[2]

As the nineteenth century moved toward its end, American society was
faced with a new social problem: the social and economic assimilation of
millions of immigrant workers from numerous countries into its cities.
Within this group of immigrant workers, there was, of course, great variation in the quality of jobs secured and the degree of socioeconomic
mobility.[3] Some members of these groups saw an opportunity for socioeconomic mobility in crime and pursued those opportunities.[4] This led
to what has since become known as organized crime—that is, the establishment of organizations designed to operate in various illegal economic
markets. To the general public's alarm, these organizations became increasingly successful, and by the 1920s and 1930s they were often considered the primary social problem of the time, the Great Depression
notwithstanding. Although these forms of collective behavior were business organizations, they were labeled *gangs* by those who studied them.[5]
Thus it was that the word *gang*, originally used to refer to western outlaws, moved with the end of the frontier into the city, from the frontier
wilderness to the urban wilderness.[6]

Although it is true that during this time the term *gang* was associated
with organized crime, an analytic separation was also introduced between organized adult groups and those groups consisting primarily of
young adolescents. This new conceptual framework was adopted out of
an awareness that different individuals and groups experienced slower
rates of integration into the economy, and a concern with identifying
who among the immigrant population were most likely to be potential

recruits for the various organized crime syndicates. Both Herbert Asbury and Frederic Thrasher identified youth gangs as the socialization agents for the graduation of young delinquents to organized crime. Without doubt, the work of Frederic Thrasher was the most important study of gangs at the time. He was the first to treat the gang as an organizational phenomenon, and he focused primarily on adolescent gangs in order to understand both the conditions under which they began and the stages of their development. This approach illuminated the effects of the city on the immigrant community, gangs as an organizational phenomenon, and the process by which certain individuals were socialized into organized adult gangs (organized crime). Thus, Thrasher was both a product of his time and an innovator. His concern for the problems of the time (immigrant assimilation and the antecedents of organized crime) led him to conceptualize the gang in an innovative way. The gang phenomenon for Thrasher was not simply associated with adults; it had a youth component as well.

Because Thrasher's research on the gang was a general survey of all its aspects, his work was not only the most important of the time, it has remained the major influence on gang research ever since. After all, it was Thrasher who asserted: (1) that gangs emerge from poor and socially disorganized neighborhoods; (2) that boys join them because there is a lack of opportunity to do other things; (3) that the boys who do join gangs lack skills and the drive to compete with others for jobs; (4) that gangs are differentiated by age; and (5) that gangs facilitate delinquency. This is only a small sample of Thrasher's observations, and each of them (as well as many others) has been addressed by subsequent researchers, including all those researchers considered to have made important contributions to the theoretical and empirical study of gangs.

As time moved on from Thrasher's publication, *mob* became the term used for organized crime groups, and *gang* gradually became associated with adolescent boys. This trend was owing in part to the desire to separate analytically what Thrasher had identified as two social groupings involved in two related, but distinct, social problems—organized crime and delinquency. Given this new analytic distinction, subsequent research focused on two different aspects of gangs. In the first set of research involving delinquency,[7] some researchers seized on Thrasher's observation that the gang facilitated delinquency and attempted to theorize the nature of the relationship. For example, Richard Cloward and Lloyd Ohlin theorized that limited opportunity structures influence gang involvement and delinquency;[8] Albert Cohen posited that lower-class youths blocked from status within the larger society become involved with gangs to create their own subculture (primarily based on delinquency) in which they can achieve status;[9] Herbert Bloch and Arthur Niederhoffer proposed that gang involvement and delinquency are the result of the process of psychological development among lower-class boys;[10] and Walter Miller argued that gang involvement and delinquency are simply an extension of lower-class culture.[11] What all these theories have in common is that they attempt to explain the gang's role in lower-class youth delinquency.

In addition to theoretical studies on the relationship between gangs and delinquency, a number of researchers attempted empirically to examine (by different methods) how and why the gang facilitated delinquency. These investigations, most notably those of Yablonsky, Short and Strodtbeck, Miller, and Spergel, produced important evidence, as well as theoretical contributions, about the gang's impact on delinquent behavior.[12]

The second set of research focused on Thrasher's contention that gangs are "an interstitial element in the framework of society, and gangland [is] an interstitial region in the layout of the city." Gangs, in this approach, are simply part of the "poverty belt" of communities populated by ethnic peoples who live in the socioeconomic "zone of transition."[13] These researchers' main concern was not with understanding how the gang related to delinquency, but rather with how the gang related to the low-income (primarily ethnic) community. Since the focus of these studies was on the community, the gang occupied only a limited part of their analysis. Although these studies do provide a good deal of rich information about the gang, it is located within the context of understanding the social construction of the communities under investigation.[14]

More recently, there has emerged a series of gang studies combining the interests of both the community and delinquency studies. These studies seek to explain gang behavior and crime as an outgrowth of the persistent and pervasive poverty that has afflicted certain black and Latino communities. Part of a growing number of investigations of what has come to be known as the urban underclass, these gang studies also address an issue raised by Thrasher, that of assessing the role of poverty (particularly the condition of having limited skills to compete in the job market) in stimulating criminal behavior among gang members.[15] More will be said about these important studies later, but in essence, they undertake to explain gang behavior in the context of the more general problems facing people who have been classified as part of an urban underclass.

In all of these studies of gangs, Thrasher's legacy is evident. All these researchers have attempted either to test his conclusions or to provide more current data for them, and most have made significant contributions to that end. However, most studies have more or less ignored one very important area that Thrasher discussed: the analysis of the gang as an organization. Despite all the research that has been done on the gang, the project of the gang itself has not been the primary focus of the vast majority of these investigations. Thus, although researchers have an intuitive understanding that the gang has organizational traits, for the most part, studies of gangs have not closely examined the nature, dynamic, and impact of the gang's organizational qualities.[16] I believe that one of the reasons that society does not understand gangs or the gang phenomenon very well is that there have not been enough systematic studies undertaken as to how the gang works as an organization.[17] We all associate the individual gang member with the organization, but we do not have much evidence at all as to what it is about the organization that makes his/her behavior different from what it would be if he or she were not in an organization. That is to say, what are the micro-dynamics associated with gang organizations. Of course, the primary reason for the paucity of studies with this focus is not simply one of conceptual oversight; it is, interestingly enough, the same problem as that faced by nineteenth-century researchers seeking to study outlaws—namely, the potential danger involved in systematically studying gangs and getting the gangs to cooperate. Through means that are described in some detail later in this introduction, I was able to overcome these two obstacles and systematically observe the internal dynamics and structure of gangs, and how they operate within society. In placing emphasis on the organization, however, the study does not neglect the gang as a collective of individuals. Indeed, one of the important features of this research is the investigation of the interplay between the behavior of the individual and that of the collective (organization). Thus, the present analysis begins the process of distinguishing individual acts from collective ones. This approach will help to explain why individuals come and go in gangs, why certain gangs succeed in their goals and others fail, and why one gang is able to persist and another vanishes.

The Nature of the Study: Setting, Methods, Analysis, and Presentation

The overall goal of the research project was to understand the gang phenomenon in the United States. In order to accomplish this goal, I thought it necessary to understand what was similar in the way all gangs behaved and what was idiosyncratic to certain gangs. In addition, I thought it was also necessary to understand why certain gangs grew, others declined but lingered on, and others declined and died. What follows is an explanation of the research design, the method of data gathering, the method of data analysis and presentation, and some ethical issues related to the research.

Past research on gangs had for the most part focused on gangs in one section of a city, gangs in one city, or gangs of one ethnic group. In order to understand the nature of the gang as an organization and the gang phenomenon in general, I believed it was necessary to undertake a comparative study. This was the only way to understand what gangs have in common with each other and what is idiosyncratic to particular gangs.

The Research Design and the Sample

Because it was deemed necessary for the research to be comparative on many levels, it was first essential to investigate gangs in different cities in order to control for the different socioeconomic and political environments that they operate in. Second, in order to determine if there were any differences associated with ethnicity, it was critical to compare gangs composed of different ethnic groups. Three metropolitan areas were therefore chosen for the study: the greater Los Angeles area, various boroughs of New York City, and the greater Boston area. These three areas were chosen because all three had a long history of gang activity and each had gangs operating within it when the research first began in 1978. In addition, each of the cities had a variety of ethnic groups involved in gangs.

These three cities were also ideal for comparisons because they were so different from each other. Two were eastern cities with certain weather patterns; the other was western with a completely different weather pattern. (Weather has often been thought to have an impact on gang activity, with colder weather restricting activity and warmer weather encouraging it.) Two have a vertical landscape with incredible density, the other is horizontal with incredible sprawl. Lastly, while all are populated with a variety of ethnic groups, each had certain groups in large numbers that the others did not have.

The research sample is divided into two quite distinct groups: those people who participate in gangs (gang members), and those within the general society who have had interaction with gangs. Of the thirty-seven gangs studied, thirteen were in the Los Angeles area, twenty were in the New York City area, and four were in the Boston area. Various ethnic groups are represented in the sample, which includes gangs composed of Irish, African-American, Puerto Rican, Chicano, Dominican, Jamaican, and Central American members. The sample also involves gangs of varying size. The smallest had thirty-four members; the largest had more than one thousand. (See appendix for summary details.)

Because I decided that the sample should include gangs of different sizes and ethnic groups, the selection of gangs began with identifying geographic areas inhabited by different ethnic groups. Once a geographic area had been chosen, information was obtained from either the police or various people who worked in that area as to what gangs operated there, what the major ethnic component of each gang was, and how large an estimated membership each had. Once this information was obtained, a list of gangs within certain ethnic areas of each city was drawn up. The list separated gangs by ethnic composition and membership size. Thus there were gangs composed of one ethnic group and gangs whose membership was ethnically mixed. Within this sample, stratified by ethnicity, I randomly selected ten in each city. It was my intention to study African-American gangs, Latino gangs, Asian gangs, and white gangs, and so gangs representing each of these ethnic groups were chosen. Because I wanted to include gangs of varying membership sizes, I randomly selected gangs from my ethnically stratified list until I obtained a sample representing gangs of different sizes. Since my overall strategy was to study five gangs in Los Angeles and five in New York for two years, then add more, and finally add several Boston gangs, I selected five of the original ten chosen and began my effort to secure their participation.

Before proceeding, it is important to describe the geographic areas the gangs were drawn from. In each of the three cities, there were gangs from working-class families and areas, and from poor families living in areas that sociologists and anthropologists have described as slums. I shall now describe the physical conditions of the communities that the gangs of this study operated in. In New York, there were three types of housing units that dominated the communities I studied. The first was high-rise public housing projects. Because there were often a number of public housing buildings located in one area, there were gangs whose members were exclusively from the housing project itself. These projects are multiple (usually fourteen) stories high, and are composed of units that have a kitchen, a small living room, a bathroom, and from one to three bedrooms. Thirty years ago, these units were inhabited by working-class people of various ethnicities (mostly white), but at the time that research was being done, they were inhabited mostly by Puerto Ricans, Dominicans, and African-Americans.

The second type of housing unit prevalent in the research communities were relatively small apartment buildings, known as walk-ups. These buildings were from three to six floors high and generally came with units having one to four bedrooms, a living room, kitchen, and bath.

Finally, there were single family units, sometimes attached to each other and sometimes separated by a small driveway on one side and possibly a small walk space on the other. These were often duplexes with wrought-iron front porches. They had been built for middle-income families, but in the communities of this study, they were entirely working-class.

Generally, the study covered neighborhoods considered working-class or extremely poverty-stricken. The poverty-stricken neighborhoods were extremely dilapidated and were often referred to as slums. In some of these neighborhoods, there were numerous abandoned buildings. In other neighborhoods, particularly the working-class neighborhoods, there was no appearance of dilapidation, but these neighborhoods often involved only two to four streets, surrounded by neighborhoods of extreme poverty.

The neighborhoods studied in Boston had some physical features similar to those of the neighborhoods studied in New York and some differences as well. There were housing projects in the Boston neighborhoods studied, but they were mostly one- or two-story projects as opposed to the high-rise projects in the New York neighborhoods studied. However, the socioeconomic conditions were not any better than in New York, and neither was the dilapidated condition of the physical structures.

Aside from the projects, two other types of dwelling dominated the neighborhoods of the Boston gangs studied. The first was called "row houses." These houses are attached to each other, are small, and have a high degree of density per unit. The other type of dwelling is what locals call "three and four deckers." These units are houses that have a common entryway and three or four separate units. Each unit occupies one floor and has two to four bedrooms, a living room, bath, and kitchen. These structures were built around the turn of the century for lifelong renters, but recently there has been a move in the Boston area to convert them to high-priced condominiums. In the neighborhoods studied, the residents were still renting and actively resisting developers' attempts to convert their homes into condos. Generally, the neighborhoods studied in Boston were poor or working-class.

The neighborhoods studied in Los Angeles were quite different from those of New York and Boston, at least in appearance. When one goes through the various neighborhoods associated with gangs there, one does not get the impression that one is going through a poverty-stricken area. The Los Angeles neighborhoods were much more varied in appearance than those in New York and Boston. Some of the neighborhoods had single-family homes that had up to four bedrooms or more, and others had a combination of duplexes, triplexes, and bungalows with from one to three bedrooms. Many of the neighborhoods were clean, but others were more crowded and dirty. However, in general, the neighborhoods of Los Angeles were less crowded and dirty than those of New York and Boston. Nonetheless, what the observer would miss when riding or walking through these areas is the crowded conditions in most of the homes. Most of the families that occupied these homes were quite large, and in some cases there were multiple families living in them. Some of these families were related to each other, while others (Latino families) were part of a network system based on the locale the people had migrated from. The consequence of these situations was overcrowding in the home.

As one might expect, having decided what gangs to study, one does not simply show up on their streetcorners and say, "I am a professor and I want to study you." This would be naive and quite dangerous. Therefore, once each of these gangs was chosen, I went to various people active in the community and asked who worked with it. Once I had discovered what individuals or agencies had worked with the particular gang I wanted to study, I contacted them and requested their help in introducing me to the gang. Some of the people who helped me were community leaders, some were social workers who worked with gangs, and some were members of the clergy. I told each of those I contacted what I wanted to do and asked them simply to introduce me to the gang. I specifically told them that I did not want them to feel that they had to endorse me. What each did was to set up a meeting with the leaders of the gang I had chosen. When the meeting was arranged, my contact took me to it and left me there to negotiate my own terms. I believed that this was best, because it allowed me to separate myself from the person who had acted as the liaison.

At the meeting, I explained to the leaders that I was a professor and that I wanted to write a book comparing gangs in Los Angeles and New York (I started this procedure in New York). Most of the gang leaders found this an interesting idea. They were, in fact, curious about how the gangs in the other city operated. Despite indicating an initial interest, they said they would have to discuss it among themselves and the rank and file. Procedurally, I contacted each gang separately and secured a working relationship with it before moving to the next gang on the list. This process took about three months. Five of the ten gangs I initially selected allowed me to begin my association with them. Four of the white gangs in New York (two Italian and two Irish) that I wanted to study refused to allow me access. Believing that I needed to have white gangs for purposes of comparison, I continued my efforts to secure their cooperation. They were not successful, so in the second year of the research project, I began my attempt to secure some white gangs in Boston. I was able to make contact with four Irish gangs in Boston, and all consented to cooperate. Interestingly, a year after I had secured the four Irish gangs in Boston, I recontacted the gangs that had refused to cooperate in New York, and much to my surprise three of the Irish gangs consented to cooperate. However, all of the Italian gangs remained steadfast in their decision not to participate.

The same strategy was used in Los Angeles. The only difference was that instead of targeting white gangs, of which there were few, I targeted Asian and Samoan gangs, of which there were many. I had initial success in securing the cooperation of the Latino and black gangs, but did not have success with the Asian and Samoan gangs.

During the initial stage, the major difficulty with all the gangs had to do with my ethnicity. Since I am not white (the Polish segment of my name coming from my adopted father), I was more readily accepted by the nonwhite Latino and African-American gangs, but had difficulty with the white and Asian gangs. The fact that I was not Asian or Italian prohibited me from gaining access. The Irish gangs were an interesting anomaly. I would have expected that they too would have prohibited me from studying them, since I was not Irish, but because I was not Puerto

Rican (one of their rival ethnic groups) they did not perceive me as a threat and allowed me access.

By the end of the third year of study, I was observing ten gangs in New York, ten gangs in Los Angeles, and four in Boston. From the fourth year of the research through the tenth, thirteen more gangs were added to the original twenty-four, making the total number studied thirty-seven. The new gangs were added to the study for three reasons: (1) some of the gangs in the original sample of twenty had died out as functioning organizations and I wanted to replace them, (2) some of the new gangs were just beginning as organizations and I wanted to study the processes of their development, and (3) some were reported to have a unique quality (in terms of size, the type of businesses they were involved in, or organizational structure) that I wanted to investigate.

There is a good deal of ethnic variety among the thirty-seven gangs. There are African-American, Jamaican, Puerto Rican, Dominican, Chicano, Central American, and Irish gangs, as well as gangs that combined blacks with Puerto Ricans, Chicanos with Central Americans, and Irish with other whites. Whereas Latino, African-American, and white American gangs are included in the study, Asians comprise the major group that is not represented.

Having the gangs consent to my studying them was only the first step in the process of gaining entry into the social confines of their world. In order to have access to these social confines, it was necessary to have the gangs develop both a degree of trust and a degree of acceptance. This was accomplished through two tests that the gangs presented me. The first test was designed to see if I was an informant for the various law enforcement agencies. What nearly every gang did was to undertake some illegal activities over a three- or four-week period in order to see if any of their members were arrested. During this time I was observed closely, and on those occasions that I did not stay with gang members, I was generally followed to where I was staying. With all the gangs, as the time I spent with them increased, and their illegal activities were not reported, they ceased to consider me a threat. However, on one occasion I did have some difficulty. It turned out that a member of the gang, for reasons no one ever discovered, had told the police about some crime that three other members had been involved with. In order to protect himself, he told the leadership that he had heard that I was the one who had informed. The gang confronted and physically attacked me. Sometime later, however, other gang members found out from their informants who had really supplied the police with the information. The leaders contacted me, apologized, and gave me permission to study them. I never knew what action the gang took against the individual who had fingered me; the only thing the members would tell me was that the problem had been taken care of.

The second test involved all of the gangs except the Irish gangs of Boston (for some inexplicable reason). This test had to do with determining how tough I was. While there were variations in exactly how the test was administered, it involved a number of members starting a fight with me. This was done to see how good a fighter I was and to see if I had "heart" (courage). There were some functional reasons for this test. Gang members wanted to know whether I had the courage to stay and fight if we were all jumped by a rival gang, and whether I could handle myself and not jeopardize their flanks. In this test, it was considered acceptable to fight and lose, but it was unacceptable to refuse to fight. This test sometimes doubled as part of my initiation rite. During the period in which the gang was testing me, I would take detailed notes so that I could compare how the gang behaved when they did not trust me with how they behaved when they did. This provided some checks on internal validity.

The two tests described above were not surprising to me, since I had grown up with project gangs and been associated with them while living in Detroit. The fact that I had training in karate did not eliminate the anxiety that such situations create, but it did help to reduce it. Although these tests often left bruises, I was never seriously hurt. Quite remarkably, in the more than ten years during which I conducted this research, I was only seriously injured twice.

The second group of people who were part of the study were those who were not themselves gang members but had had contact with gangs in varying capacities. They included relatives of gang members, people who ran businesses that had contact with gangs, community leaders, politicians, government bureaucrats, law enforcement officials, and members of the media.

Data-Gathering

The research extended over ten years and five months, from 1978 to 1989. There were two methods used in gathering the data. The primary method of data collection for the gangs was participant observation. The basis of the participant-observation method is that the researcher both participates in the activities of and observes those he or she is studying. The advantage of such a method is that the researcher can observe the subjects in their natural environment. In the present study, I basically did what the gang members did for months at a time, traveling between each of the cities and each of the gangs. The primary reason the study took so long was my concern that I spend the time necessary to understand the patterns that existed within each of the gangs.

In terms of my access to gang life, after the initial period of suspicion, mistrust, and testing, gang members forgot (or did not care) that I was conducting research and interacted with me freely and openly. Of course, some of this was facilitated by the composition of gangs, there being a great range in the ages of members.[18] In the gangs under study here, there were members who ranged from ten years old to forty-two. So it was not unusual to see someone who was not in his teens associating with the group. My acceptance was in part the result of spending a great deal of time with the gangs, but also stemmed from the fact that while I was with them, I had found myself in a number of the same precarious situations that they were experiencing and had handled myself according to their expectations. As I experienced what they lived, and as they observed me doing it, gang members simply thought less and less of me as a professor. In fact, the constant comments I heard were: "You don't look like a professor" and/or "You don't act like one."

There were times when members completely forgot I was doing research. New members often had no idea that I was a professor conducting research until they saw me taking notes and asked me why, or someone told them. At other times people were well aware that I was not a member of the gang (mostly because I was not of the gang's ethnicity), but they simply went about their business because I had proven to be no threat or hindrance to them.

In sum, I participated in nearly all the things they did. I ate where they ate, I slept where they slept, I stayed with their families, I traveled where they went, and in certain situations where I could not remain neutral, I fought with them. The only things that I did not participate in were those activities that were illegal. As part of our mutual understanding, it was agreed that I did not have to participate in any activity (including taking drugs) that was illegal.

Basically, I was free to observe and interact with gang members in all the various settings in which they operate. Therefore, if the data presented in this work are biased in any way, such bias should not be attributed to the gangs' lack of cooperation in allowing me access to themselves and their experiences.

I also did not have difficulty in getting those interacting with gangs to cooperate. I believed at the outset of the research that people who felt threatened by the gangs, or people in official positions who might be threatened by the study, would resist my efforts to solicit their cooperation. Much to my surprise and good fortune, they did not. Of the countless number of people that I interviewed, or whose duties (or the duties of those in their offices) I asked to observe, only three refused to cooperate, and none of the three occupied positions different from those who consented to cooperate. The only thing asked of me, to which I consented, was that I maintain their confidentiality.

While participating, I was always cognizant of the fact that I was a researcher gathering data. I went into each day's observations mindful of what previous studies had found, and this helped me establish a focus to that day's data-gathering. However, the fact that I had an agenda that helped to focus my observations did not mean that I had created observational blinders to other important facets of gang life. I was completely open to all aspects of gang activity and recorded it in as much detail as possible. Furthermore, I was careful not to create situations that did not occur as part of everyday life. One strategy I continually employed was to interview members about what they thought before some event occurred, then try to talk to them (and record) while the event was occurring, and finally reinterview them after the event.

I carried two notebooks. One was an 8½-by-11-inch pad and the other was a small note pad that could fit into my pockets. I would record events on these throughout the day or night. I was also aided by the use of two types of tape recorders. One was a medium-sized portable that I used to do interviews with individuals and record some meetings. The other (which I did not purchase until 1982) was small enough to fit into my pocket, and I used it to take notes during the day. These tape recorders were used with the complete knowledge and permission of the gangs. While the use of a tape recorder did inhibit the gang members in the beginning, as time passed they became oblivious to it.

In addition to the notes that I took during the day, at the end of each day I would record an overview of the day's events. This provided me with a context in which to place the specific data recorded during the day. Furthermore, at the end of each week, I would record an overview of what had generally occurred with that gang for the week. This provided me with further contextual information. When analyzing the data ten years later, the daily and weekly summaries proved invaluable in understanding what was occurring with a particular gang during a specific period of time.

The data on the various institutions reported in this work were collected in two ways. First, while with the gangs, I would observe and record the behavior of various institutional agents as they interacted with the gangs. Sometimes the interaction would take place in the gang's environment and sometimes in the institution's (e.g., a courtroom). In addition, at the appropriate time (i.e., a time that would not interrupt their natural interaction with the gang), I would introduce myself to the institutional agents (telling them about myself and my project) and seek to interview them. I promised them that the information I gathered would be kept strictly confidential. Although some of them were reluctant to talk to me during our first encounter, they became more willing to cooperate as time passed. After introducing myself, I would take detailed notes on how they interacted with the gangs to see if they behaved any differently now that they knew I was not a gang member. This data check provided me another opportunity to evaluate internal validity. There were times, however, when various institutional agents did not want to talk to me while they were with the gangs. At such times, I would call and make arrangements to talk with them at a place they decided on.

I spent varying amounts of time with the gangs. In the beginning, I tried to spend a solid month with each new gang. After the initial period, I would spend five to ten days with each gang. In the last three years of the research, I would spend two to three days with a particular gang. Of course, no hard-and-fast line could be followed. If there was something interesting happening with a particular gang, I would stay with it longer. In addition, I would alternate between the East and the West Coast so that I would observe both sets of gangs within roughly the same time period. Moreover, I made every effort to observe the same gang during different seasons of the year in order to observe the effects of weather on gang activity.

Over the more than ten years of research, I attempted to follow each gang for as long as it existed as an organization. There was good deal of variation in the longevity of the organizations I studied. One lasted only eighteen months, whereas others were still in existence when I finished the fieldwork.

Analysis and Presentation of the Data

I began the analysis by establishing topics that would need to be covered in a book about gangs, such as gang recruitment, gang organization, violence, and so on. I then proceeded to read each of my notes (daily notes, daily summaries, weekly summaries) and place them in stacks having to do with each topic I wanted to cover. When notes pertained to more than one topic, I photocopied them and placed each under the additional topics.

My analysis began by taking a topic and reviewing what other researchers had found concerning gangs. Their findings would be written down in hypothesis form and then I would read my notes to determine what my evidence suggested. From the analysis of the notes, I would ascertain what the primary and secondary patterns were. From the content of these patterns, I would create the analytical categories used in the text. The data presented in this study are based on observed patterns of group behavior and what individuals said about them.

Ethics and Research

The research raised some ethical questions. Participant observation provides the researcher with a unique opportunity to observe the subjects of his/her study operating within their natural environment. Because such research is not a controlled experiment, one is not able to control situations, and this presents the researcher with some ethical dilemmas. I observed criminal behavior countless times. The first time such an act occurs, one realizes that one cannot pretend it did not happen because it is being recorded. Before going into the field, I decided that in order to do this research, I would have to remain neutral to behavior that society considered criminal. In addition, because of the sensitive nature of the data, I had to promise the gang members that I would hold all my information in strict confidence and keep everyone's true identity, and that of the gang as well, secret. I remain committed to both of these decisions. It must be obvious, that unless one is able to take this position, sociological research cannot be done on groups such as gangs. If such research is done without witnessing criminal acts, that research leaves out a critical part of the phenomenon.

Furthermore, many people representing official agencies or positions within society talked to me quite candidly because of the explicit understanding that their identities and the information they provided would remain confidential. Here again, I remain committed to such a position.

Finally, there is the question of reliability. Unfortunately, it is not possible to test the validity of my arguments by reanalyzing my own raw data. That is because I would have to reveal too much information about the people I studied, thereby putting them in jeopardy. Even the identification of specific gangs would violate the understanding that enabled me to do this research. However, I have tried to provide as full an account of gang life as possible, making available data for those interested in constructing alternative hypotheses. Ultimately, the reliability of this study must lie in its replication by other researchers, particularly ethnographic researchers.

Data Presentation

In presenting the data, I have also taken to heart one of James F. Short's criticisms of Thrasher's work: that Thrasher did not always present his information in a systematic form that could generate hypotheses for future study.[19] To aid future researchers, I have tried to present the data I collected in a manner that I hope can be used for purposes of retesting. The success of these efforts can, of course, only be answered by future research.

The data presented, often in descriptive form, are generalized patterns that I observed. Where I found idiosyncrasies in relation to generalized patterns, or idiosyncratic patterns, I have identified them as such. The reader should assume that what is being described is a social pattern that was consistently observed unless otherwise indicated. Quotations are employed throughout the text as examples of these observed patterns or idiosyncrasies. I have attempted to provide the reader with information as to how a quotation was recorded. When the quotation came from an interview in which I was using pencil and paper to record it, I have so indicated. In all other cases, the quotation was tape-recorded. I have chosen to do this so that the reader will be aware that a quotation recorded by hand is not completely verbatim. Nonetheless, all quotations taken by hand and reported in the text are very close to verbatim and in no way distort the respondent's language or intentions.

One final point must be made. The anonymity of all those who participated in this study has been maintained. None of the names used to identify gangs are the actual names of the gangs studied. All the names of the individuals used in the text are fictitious as well. However, the information that identifies the age, ethnicity, city lived in, or agency associated with the respondent is accurate.

An Overview of What Follows

Chapter 1 begins the study by presenting a theory of gangs. It offers a brief definition of a gang and then theorizes about what factors affect the behavior of the individuals in gangs; what factors affect the behavior of gangs as organizations; why certain gangs persist and thrive while others decline and die; and finally, why gangs as a phenomenon have been able to persist over time in American urban society.

The subsequent chapters present data on how the elements advanced in the theory get worked out in everyday life. The five chapters of Part I focus on the internal dynamics of the gang within its local environment. Chapter 2 begins the investigation by addressing the most fundamental question: who joins a gang and why? Particular attention is directed toward how the individual decides to join a gang and how gangs recruit. Chapter 3 takes up a question that has intrigued both researchers and the general public: what happens in a gang? In addressing this question, the chapter describes the internal dynamics of gangs, both how gang organizations function and what factors influence organizations to behave in certain ways. Chapter 4 identifies how the organization supports itself and examines both the type of economic activities gang members become involved in and what factors influence whether or not they are successful.

Gang violence—the topic that has occupied most of the general public's attention, thanks in part to the media—is the subject of chapter 5. This analysis of the sociology of gang violence focuses on determining the nature and causes of violence, and how individual members and organizations cope with it.

The final chapter in Part I, chapter 6, examines how gangs relate to their local communities. The central question addressed is what role, if any, the community plays in how gangs operate? Do community members view gangs as so dangerous and destructive that they must be eradicated? Do they see gang participants as misunderstood individuals, legitimate members of the community who must be defended from police abuse and media attack? Or do they simply not think about them one way or the other?

In Part II, I turn from the internal dynamics of gangs in their local milieux to their relations with the world outside their local community. Chapter 7 explores in what ways urban politics and various government agencies affect how gangs operate. Then the analysis turns toward one of the most perplexing questions facing American society: why has the criminal justice system been unable either to eradicate gangs or to control them? Chapter 8 probes the interaction between gangs and the criminal justice system in order to understand its impact on gang operations.

Chapter 9 deals with the continuing debate over whether the media have helped inform the public about the nature of gangs and the social problems associated with them, or have exaggerated the entire issue. Particular attention is devoted to analyzing how gangs and the media relate and assessing the effects of the media on the gang's ability to conduct its business.

The Conclusion makes some final remarks about gangs themselves and the nature of gangs in American society. In so doing, it attempts to clarify the dilemmas and predicament that gangs present to the society.

Chapter One

A Theory of Gang Behavior
and Persistence

*To this war of everyman, against everyman, this also is consequent; that nothing can be unjust. The notions of right and wrong, justice and injustice have there no place. Where there is no common power, there is no law: where no law, no injustice. Force, and fraud, are in war the two cardinal virtues.
... It is consequent also to the condition, that there be no propriety, no commission, no mine and thine distinct; but only that to be every man's, that he can get: and for so long, as he can keep it.*

Thomas Hobbes, *Leviathan* (1651)

The inhabitant of the United States learns from birth that he must rely on himself to combat the ills and trials of life; he is restless and defiant in his outlook toward the authority of society and appeals to its power only when he cannot do without it.

Alexis de Tocqueville, *Democracy in America* (1835–39)

The behavior and persistence of gangs in American society remains a perplexing problem. It is especially so given the great resources that law enforcement officials have used in their efforts to control gangs, not to mention the number of social programs that have been developed to assist youth in poor and lower-class communities. The sociological literature on gangs offers a number of theories, but a close look at each of these indicates that they are really theories about delinquency and not theories about gangs per se. They are therefore sociological theories of crime rather than sociological theories of the gang. This has influenced what each has focused on, and it has produced similar and limited explanations concerning the behavior of gangs and why they persist. Thus, regardless of whether these theories are, as Ruth Kornhauser has eloquently formalized, social disorganization theories, control theories, or cultural deviance theories, they share a similar logical foundation.[1] They all rest on the assumption that gangs emerge from poverty and persist because poverty persists. The same can be said for some of the newer conceptualizations arguing that both gang behavior and the persistence of gangs can be explained by the emergence of an underclass in the United States.[2] For most of these theories, the gang persists simply because socially disorganized poor communities have developed a culture that has spawned these deviant behavior patterns and made it difficult for formal social institutions to institute control.[3]

Although these theories can account for the gang as an instrument facilitating delinquency, they are inadequate for understanding: (1) the behavior of individuals in gangs, (2) the behavior of the gang as a collective, and (3) why some gangs persist and thrive while others (or the same gang at another time) decline and die. It is precisely the questions of why some members of poor communities join gangs and some do not, why some gangs succeed and others fail, and why gangs persist in a society that has unlimited power and resources to enforce control that must be accounted for if we are to begin to understand, not simply the crime associated with gangs, but the more general gang phenomenon in the United States.

The theory of gangs advanced here is composed of three elements: the kind of individuals who become gang members, the types of organizations they become members of, and the linkages of their organizations to the broader community.

Nearly all other theories of gangs emerge from the assumptions associated with theories of social disorganization.[4] According to these theories, poor economic conditions have caused social disorganization to the extent that there is a lack of social control. The lack of social controls leads to gang formation and involvement because young people in low-income neighborhoods (slums) seek the social order (and security) that a gang can provide.[5] However, in the theory I am proposing, gangs emerge not as a result of disorganization and/or the desire to find order and safety, but as a consequence of a particular type of social order associated with low-income neighborhoods in American society. Low-income areas in American cities are, in fact, organized, but they are organized around an intense competition for, and conflict over, the scarce resources that exist in these areas. They comprise an alternative social order. In this Hobbesian world, the gang emerges as one organizational response—but not the only one—seeking to improve the competitive advantage of its members in obtaining an increase in material resources. While portions of this theory are similar to other theories of gangs, the central premise of my theory differs significantly from most others, including those associated with underclass theory, in that they attend too exclusively to the social environment (emphasizing social disorganization) and focus insufficiently on the interrelationship between the gang as an organization and gang members as individuals. In other words, to understand the gang phenomenon and gang behavior, it is necessary not only to understand the deprived socioeconomic conditions that gang members come from but to go beyond those conditions and focus on the dynamics between individuals in gangs, gang organizations, and the institutions of the outside world.

Inequality, the Quest for the Good Life, and Defiant Individualism

Gang members, virtually all of whom come from low-income neighborhoods, have, to varying degrees, developed what I shall call a *defiant individualist* character. Throughout the text, I use the term *character* rather than *personality* to refer to a group of personal traits structured in such a manner as to constitute a psychological system. My use of this concept is similar to that developed and used by Erich Fromm. "The concept of social character," Fromm observes, "does not refer to the complete or highly individualized, in fact, unique character structure as it exists in an individual, but to the 'character matrix,' a syndrome of character traits which has developed as an adaptation to the economic, social, and cultural conditions common to that group."[6] Elsewhere Fromm says:

> In studying the psychological reactions of a social group we deal with the character structure of the members of the group, that is, of individual persons; we are interested, however, not in the peculiarities by which these persons differ from each other, but in that part of their character structure that is common to most members of the group. We call this character the *social character*. . . . [Thus although] there will be always 'deviants' with a totally different character structure, the character [structures] of most members of the group are variations of this nucleus, brought about by the accidental factors of birth and life experience as they differ from one individual to another.[7]

The advantage of this concept is that it accepts and incorporates the interconnectedness of individual personality traits and the social environment they interact with. The defiant individualist character is composed of seven attributes, which I shall now identify and discuss.

The first is an intense sense of *competitiveness*. Gang members display a very competitive attitudinal impulse that is most often seen in physical aggression but is present in other areas of their behavior as well. This competitiveness emerges from the scarcity of resources in the low-income community. Since poor communities have scarce resources, so do the families that live in them. It is experience within the family that lays the seeds of competitiveness. Members of families in many of the low-income neighborhoods of America must compete for portions of the family's overall material resources. Because parents have to work and families are often large, children also have to compete for parental affection, which may thus be one of the most contested commodities within families. Finally, because families in low-income neighborhoods have difficulty securing adequate housing for their needs, space is at a premium and is another provision for which siblings compete. This competition is over both physical and psychological space (privacy). These conditions teach the individual about the need to fight for scarce resources.

The competitiveness within low-income families is the initiator of the second trait to be found in defiant individualism and that is a sense of *mistrust* or *wariness*. Competition within the family may plant the seeds of mistrust, but it is nurtured by the competition individuals engage in and/or observe as they interact with others in their community. They learn that trust is not simply a given, but something to be calculated. In his classic *The Moral Basis of a Backward Society,* Edward Banfield found the trait of mistrust to exist among the southern Italian villagers he studied, and it became part of his concept of "amoral individualism."[8] However, one of the differences between my defiant individualism and Banfield's "amoral individualism" is that Banfield perceived "amoral in-dividualism" to prohibit organization, whereas the individualism I en-countered does not.

The third trait has to do with *self-reliance*. Because there are few re-sources in the family or the community, individuals learn that they must be self-reliant. This is true even if the family is dependent on public assis-tance, because public assistance is not sufficient in most cases to meet the expenses or needs of its recipients. In addition, public institutions (like the welfare department), public ideology, and members of the commu-nity reinforce the belief that individuals should be self-reliant; and that assistance of any type is limited and has reciprocal costs. In essence, it is believed that it is personally more beneficial to rely on oneself.

Self-reliance, however, influences another trait, which is *social isolation*. Since self-reliance is valued and trust is something that must be calculated, individuals become less emotionally attached to others. It is believed that becoming emotionally attached (and this would include attachment to women) can reduce one's self-reliance, reduce the options available to the individual, and increase the chances of being personally (emotionally) hurt. Thus, for the individual, the remedy is to become a social island.

Self-reliance and social isolation, along with life in poor neighborhoods, stimulate the fifth trait, which is the *survival instinct*. Life in low-income neighborhoods is quite competitive for the limited resources that exist within them. This competitiveness leads many of the people in these neighborhoods to assume the character of predators trapping prey. Young people often observe, confront, and negotiate with people whose competitive mode has led them to view young people as prey. There are drug dealers, who sometimes intimidate young people into buying drugs whether they want them or not. There are drug addicts, who use the threat of bodily harm to rob people (including young people) in order to satisfy their habits. There are pimps, who are constantly asking young people either to buy some sex or to become employees in the sex business (prostitution or sex movies). Finally, there are the armed robberies and the shootings between rival factions competing for some object, which inform the young person of the ominous nature of his or her world and trigger the instinct to survive.

While all the experiences mentioned above nurture the survival instinct, it is the unfortunates or "failures" within the young person's world who solidify it. The derelicts on the street, the women and men dependent on public assistance, and the men and women (including possibly their fathers and mothers) who have taken jobs in secondary or informal labor markets that lead nowhere represent to many young people those who have succumbed to the environment. All of this leads to a determination among some of the young not to succumb, but to survive. Some, of course, will succumb, but in the beginning stages of development (that is, among some young people) the goal is to fight, to survive, to overcome. The competitive, isolated struggle to survive in a hostile human environment, "and which is worst of all, continual fear and danger of violent death," results in a life that is "poor, nasty, brutish, and short," evoking the "state of nature" depicted in these words by Thomas Hobbes.[9] Although Hobbes is considered sociologically naive about the bases of social cohesion, defiant individuals, like Hobbesian men, come together and organize on the basis of wariness, fear, and mistrust.[10]

As the young person becomes older, experiences within the community and knowledge about the outside community lead to the seventh trait, a *Social Darwinist worldview*. This more formal view of the world is developed as the young person in the low-income neighborhood compares his or her environment with that of the outside world. This comparison elicits some striking similarities for these young people. They see that competitiveness, illegality, and predatory behavior are all operative in the larger society—not only tolerated, but in some respects encouraged as well. The bottom line for them is that many successful people outside their community have operated, a little less crudely perhaps (though not necessarily), in a similar fashion to those in their own community. It is therefore reasonable for these young people to conclude that this is the natural order. Comparisons with the world outside of their community thus produce another critical element of their belief system. They have seen what people in the more affluent neighborhoods have, and they want it too. Therefore, when they analyze how the people who are considered successful were able to achieve their goals, they come to the conclusion that many acted exactly the same way that members of their community act. Hence their assumption is that if they are to be successful (survive, as it were), they will need to operate this way as well.

Ultimately the desire to be successful and have the good life gives rise to the last trait, and perhaps the one the public sees the most, a *defiant air,* signaling these individuals' clear idea of what they want (and what they do not want) and their defiance of those who would try to prohibit or inhibit their attempts to realize it. As Paul Willis noted among working-class youth in England, they realize all too well that certain types of jobs (assuming they can even get a job) and a certain type of life-style await them if they do not manage to break out of their situation.[11] This desire for the new order (their coveted life-style) and resistance to the old (what awaits them in the old life-style) fuels the flames of resolve and defiance toward those who would challenge them.

There are two sides to the defiant air: the public and the private. On the public side, there is the behavior that confronts authority and power with few indications of deference, fear, or remorse. Often, for example, an individual will continue to defy someone regardless of the amount of abuse or pain he or she absorbs. The private side is more subtle, of course. It is the resolve that individuals have to continue despite the obstacles and abuse they encounter, the resolve to resist any suggestion that they are not up to the challenge. There have been some studies of gangs that suggest that many gang members have tough exteriors but are insecure on the inside. This is a mistaken observation. Although it may be somewhat disconcerting, in the vast majority of cases, the nut that has a hard shell has a tough kernel too—that is, the individual believes in himself and has strong resolve.

It should be pointed out that there are variations in defiant individualism, and these variations are linked to ethnicity. Individuals from different low-income communities will all exhibit defiance, but because people operate within different cultural contexts, there are variations in the ways individualism is manifested. For those who live in Irish and Chicano communities, where the cultural milieu (the community's norm) often requires one to give something back to the community, the individual must not ignore this value, because if one does, one will have difficulty operating within that community. In the case of Chicanos, the cultural context often emphasizes that one should identify with and be loyal to one's family and community. Of course, for Chicanos the family unit itself serves to protect its members from others in their community whom they do not trust. In addition, community solidarity is often used to protect residents from people on the outside who are not trusted. Therefore, an emphasis on family, clan (as in the case of Samoans), or community is itself a manifestation of the mistrust that nourishes defiant individualism. The important point to emphasize here is that an individual who operates within these cultural contexts must take into account the issues of family and community in calculating what will be best for him or her (risks/costs). Consequently, what sometimes may appear to be aspects of a gang member's behavior that do not fit what would be expected of an individual motivated by defiant individualism, such as attempts to incorporate family and community concerns, are in fact expressions of defiant individualism as shaped by a particular cultural environment.

In this regard, both culture and emotions are things a successful individual must calculate. In a multi-ethnic society like the United States, culture is an object that people are often called on to maintain and a form of action that influences the ways individuals think and behave. In the context of culture as object, the gang may simply be one of the institutions that identifies and attempts to preserve ways of life associated with a particular traditional culture. In the context of culture as action, the gang as an organization rationally attempts to pursue goals considered appropriate or desirable within its cultural context, as do its members as individuals. In this way, culture influences what is considered rational, but does not wholly determine it.

Likewise, emotions are something that gang members work to control. This is because emotions can be either a resource or a sign of vulnerability, depending on the situation. Thus, individuals must rationally assess the situation before deciding whether to express certain emotions, and to what degree.

Finally, and most important, the level of defiant individualism in individuals is a composite of the observed traits mentioned above as a function of the number of these traits that any one individual exhibits and the observed intensity with which he or she demonstrates them in everyday behavior. Hence, while most members of low-income communities will share some of these traits (such as competitiveness and mistrust) by virtue of their experience within this shared environment, gang members will more generally display nearly all of these traits (larger composite number) and to a much more intense degree (more intense display over greater time). What is most important to understand is that this is not because they have joined gangs but because of their particular experiences before they joined. Thus, far from simply reinforcing these traits, the gang, if it is to survive, must itself cope with and try to control them.

Defiant Individualism, Life Chances, and the Organization

Before proceeding, I would like to clarify some ambiguities in the use of the term *gang*. Although *gang* has been used to label a range of group behavior, this study treats organization as a necessary, though not sufficient, defining feature of gangs. As studied here, a gang is an organized social system that is both quasi-private (not fully open to the public) and quasi-secretive (much of the information concerning its business remains confined within the group) and one whose size and goals have necessitated that social interaction be governed by a leadership structure that has defined roles; where the authority associated with these roles has been legitimized to the extent that social codes are operational to regulate the behavior of both the leadership and the rank and file; that plans and provides not only for the social and economic services of its members, but also for its own maintenance as an organization; that pursues such goals irrespective of whether the action is legal or not; and that lacks a bureaucracy (i.e., an administrative staff that is hierarchically organized and separate from leadership).[12] When the characteristics mentioned above are absent, or nearly so, the group of individuals who socialize in a city may be called a gang by some, but the chances of their exhibiting the kinds of behavior and having the kinds of political and economic influence described in this study are slight.[13]

In addition to the characteristics noted above, a gang is an organization composed of individuals who possess defiant individualist characters—that is to say, a gang is organized defiant individualism. The present definition may not include all the attributes necessary to constitute an "ideal type" in the Weberian sense of the term, but it will enable researchers to differentiate gangs from other formal associations in low-income areas, such as "crews," which are small groups (usually fewer than ten and generally around three to five individuals) organized solely for the purpose of committing crime. The definition also aids in distinguishing the gang from a group of people involved in collective behavior who lack the formal infrastructure to be a gang. Such a group, which may be a pre-gang association, is simply involved in ad hoc collective behavior (as in the term *ganging*).

Since the defiant individual is a loner, an island, the obvious question is: given the nature of this Hobbesian world, and the defiant individualist characters it has produced, how is it possible for these individuals to join a gang, exhibit solidarity with each other, and operate as an efficient organization?

To begin with, not all those who possess defiant individualist characters join gangs. Whether an individual with a defiant individualist character decides to join a gang or not depends on calculated decisions on the part both of the individual and of the organization.[14] In the case of the individual, the decision to join a gang is based on the belief that it is best for him or her at that particular time to be a gang member. Because the decision has been made in a calculated manner, gang members resist outside attempts to convince them that gang membership is detrimental to them—they have already considered that possibility. This is not to suggest that in considering their options they have not miscalculated, and that they will not later tell some interviewer that they regret their bad judgment. It is simply to say that at the time when they made that judgment, they considered their options.

In sum, individuals with defiant individualist characters believe at the time of their decision that the gang is capable of providing them with a number of advantages that they would otherwise not enjoy at all, or would enjoy only in part. They believe that through the business dealings of the gang, or the contacts they are able to establish while in the gang, they will be able significantly to improve the quality of their lives (primarily in respect to money and status, but some include power). In essence, they believe that their "life chances" have been enhanced. By this I mean that they assume that the probability of there being greater opportunities to improve the quality of their lives has increased.[15]

Now take the case of the organization. The gang deliberately does not have an open-door policy on membership. It cannot allow every individual who wants to be a member to join. Decisions concerning membership are dependent on assessments of its needs by the organization (both leaders and rank and file). Criteria include the optimal number of members needed to maintain: (1) the prestige of the gang; (2) the efficiency of its operations; and (3) the level of services to its members considered adequate. For a variety of reasons, some of which are discussed below in relation to organizational structures, gangs are not always capable of assessing these needs in the most sophisticated ways, and their judgments are not necessarily sound. Nonetheless, they do undertake some degree of assessment in deciding how many members to have, whom to recruit from, and whom to accept from among the recruits.

The act of becoming a member is thus a two-way negotiation between the individual representing himself and the individual representing the organization. The interaction of these two evaluations determines the size of a particular gang (that is, the number of members compared to other gangs) and the extent to which individuals of a particular neighborhood are involved in gangs (that is, the proportion of individuals from a particular neighborhood who are active).

The ability of the organization to hold its members is dependent on its capacity to provide them with services, which may include entertainment, protection, financial assets, and material possessions. The organization's ability is dependent on its economic efficiency—that is, its ability to cope efficiently with scarcity. The organization's capacity for efficiency is dependent on its proficiency in planning activities, mobilizing its resources (including human resources), creating new resources, executing its plans successfully, and controlling its market (degree of monopoly).

The gang's ability to be an efficient organization is contingent on its capacity to establish legitimacy in its authority structure. Authority is established through the construction of leadership structures and the roles assigned, either formally or informally, to both leadership and rank and file. There are three basic structures that establish authority within gangs, which I have labeled the vertical hierarchical form, the horizontal/ commission form, and the influential form. In chapter 4, I discuss each of these forms in substantial detail; here it suffices to say that within the first form, power is distributed among the leadership in a hierarchical manner; within the second form, power is dispersed relatively equally among a number of people; and within the third form, power is centered in an unlimited way in an extremely small number of people (two to four).[16]

Legitimacy within each of these authority structures is established in two ways: by the rank and file's calculation of the difference between what they expect of leaders and their assessment of their performance, and by the organization's ability to establish an accepted process to manage leadership change.

The ability of the organization to institute legitimacy is dependent on its capacity to manage the members' defiant individualism and create cooperation through obligation. In the case of the former, the organization must be flexible in its relationship with individual members. While it is true that as an organization, it must impose some degree of discipline, it must not try to control members to any great extent. Rather, it must allow them freedom to pursue some of their own personal goals, including economic goals. Failure to do this will lead the members (precisely because of their psychological characteristics) to quit the organization, and the gang will become ineffectual and/or dissolve.

Obligation on the other hand, can be accomplished through (1) interest incentives, where the individual member feels he receives some type of return for his cooperation;[17] (2) moral incentives, where the individual believes that his participation in the organization is basically an agreement between him and the other members, and that as long as he continues to be a member, he must uphold his side of the agreement; and (3) organizational rules, where obedience occurs as a result of the members understanding and accepting a set of rules as being necessary for internal order, or through fear of punishment.[18]

Organization, Community, and Societal Institutions

Having an organization that has strong internal cohesion and efficiency is not sufficient to ensure its ability to survive. The final element necessary not only for the health of the gang (i.e., the ability to operate an efficient and prosperous organization) but for its survival is for the organization to be integrated into both the local and the larger community. By local, I mean the neighborhoods the gang operates in.[19] It is necessary for every gang to be integrated into its local neighborhood or community. The gang must be accepted by local residents as an integral part of their community. This is done in two generalizable ways. First, gang members must not only avoid antagonizing the residents, they must also persuade the residents to consider them "their own." Members must be respectful in their interactions with residents of the community. They must avoid preying on residents, insulting them in conversation, or harassing them in any way.

Secondly, they must be attentive to the needs of both individual residents and the general community. By this, I mean they should provide residents with help when the occasion arises. This help can be in the form of protection, manpower when physical strength is required for a particular task (such as moving, carrying groceries, or unloading), giving financial assistance, or providing shelter when necessary.

If both of these requirements are met, the gang will receive the support of the community, on which it must depend if it is to be protected from rival predators (other gangs) and the police. The gang's dependency on the support of its own community is thus similar to that described by E. J. Hobsbawm for what he calls "social bandits": "It is important that the incipient social bandit should be regarded as 'honorable' or non-criminal by the population, for if he was regarded as a criminal against local convention, he could not enjoy the local protection on which he must rely completely."[20] Of course, having said that, I do not intend to equate the gang with Hobsbawm's social bandit, for a number of characteristics make them different. For example, social bandits tend to be more charismatic than average members of a gang; social bandits assume the stature of heroes in the community and gangs do not; social bandits tend to have very little formal organization compared to gangs; and social bandits tend to be more overtly political in their outlook.[21] Rather, the gang must assume a role closer to the concept of a militia, because that role allows greater opportunity for the gang to integrate itself into the local neighborhood. In this role (that of a militia), the gang responds to the community, as opposed to trying to take a lead in setting the agenda for the community.

The gang's ability to integrate itself into the immediate area in which it operates is likewise not sufficient to create for itself an optimal environment in which to grow. In order to maximize its capabilities, and increase the probability of its longevity, it must have linkages with a number of important institutions within the broader society. These linkages with the world outside its immediate environment have the potential to provide the gang with material possessions, the opportunity to secure certain political advantages, and/or an environment with less risk.

There are essentially three sets of institutions that gangs find useful in establishing links. They include the various branches of government that operate at the local level, the assorted units of the criminal justice system that gangs have contact with, and the diverse elements of the media. Each of these institutions is located in a position that makes it strategic for it to be either helpful or detrimental to the gang's operations, and ultimately to its survival.

The ability to establish these linkages is a function of two sets of interests, those of a particular gang and those of the individuals representing the various institutions. It is obvious why a gang would want to establish a positive relationship with each of these institutions, but less so why these institutions might want to form a relationship with the gang. The answer lies in the fact that the people who operate within each of these institutions periodically determine that a relationship with gangs may be beneficial either to their ability to carry out their personal responsibilities or, more generally, to their organization's ability to execute the function it is charged with.

Linkages between gangs and other institutions are established on the basis of exchange relationships. There are essentially two ways in which a mutually beneficial relationship can be arranged. There is the direct approach in which representatives of one of the parties initiates contact with the other and proposes an exchange. The probability of establishing such a relationship is related to the type of service needed, the resources each party has to provide, and the track record of each in providing either the specific service requested or services in general. Owing to the ad hoc nature of these relationships, they are usually more unstable and temporary.

There are other times when an exchange relationship can be established incrementally through the processes involved in natural interaction. By this, I mean that through their natural dealings with each other, the two parties (gang and institution) establish a formal exchange relationship. These exchange relationships usually involve agents of institutions that have consistent contact with gangs, such as agencies providing social services and the branches of law enforcement. Because these relationships emerge from the everyday interaction of the two parties, once established, they tend to become increasingly stable and persistent.

The theory holds that the more linkages a gang has with government, the criminal justice system, and the media, the more likely it is to secure its goals and persist. Gangs unable to secure such linkages are usually those already experiencing some degree of organizational decline, and for these gangs, decline will accelerate and survival will become more tenuous.

To summarize, the theory holds that gang behavior, as well as gang (organizational) persistence, is a function of: (1) inequality, and individual responses to reduce inequality; (2) the ability of the gang (both leadership and rank and file) to manage the desires and behavior of people with defiant individualist characters; (3) the degree to which a collective of individuals has been capable of developing a sophisticated organization to carry out its economic activities; and (4) the extent to which it has been able to establish ties to institutions belonging to the larger society. The operations and rate of survival of gangs will vary greatly, but these variations can be accounted for in terms of the interaction of these four elements.

Part One

The Gang
and Its Environment

Chapter Two

Gang Involvement

Now it is thought to be the mark of a man of practical wisdom to be able to deliberate well about what is good and expedient for himself, not in some particular respect, e.g. about what sorts of thing conduce to health or to strength, but about what sorts of thing conduce to the good life in general.

Aristotle, *The Nicomachean Ethics*

We are looking for a few good men.

U.S. Marine Corps Recruiting Poster

In chapter 1, I argued that one of the most important features of gang members was their defiant individualist character. I explained the development of defiant individualism by locating its origins in the material conditions—the competition and conflict over resource scarcity—of the low-income neighborhoods of most large American cities. These conditions exist for everyone who lives in such neighborhoods, yet not every young person joins a gang. Although I have found that nearly all those who belong to gangs do exhibit defiant individualist traits to some degree, not all those who possess such traits join gangs. This chapter explores who joins a gang and why in more detail.

Many studies offer an answer to why a person joins a gang, or why a group of individuals start a gang. These studies can be divided into four groupings. First, there are those that hold the "natural association" point of view. These studies argue that people join gangs as a result of the natural act of associating with each other.[1] Their contention is that a group of boys, interrelating with each other, decide to formalize their relationship in an attempt to reduce the fear and anxiety associated with their socially disorganized neighborhoods. The individual's impetus to join is the result of his desire to defend against conflict and create order out of the condition of social disorganization.

The second group of studies explains gang formation in terms of "the subculture of blocked opportunities": gangs begin because young males experience persistent problems in gaining employment and/or status. As a result, members of poor communities who experience the strain of these blocked opportunities attempt to compensate for socioeconomic deprivation by joining a gang and establishing a subculture that can be kept separate from the culture of the wider society.[2]

The third group of studies focuses on "problems in identity construction." Within this broad group, some suggest that individuals join gangs as part of the developmental process of building a personal identity or as the result of a breakdown in that process.[3] Others argue that some individuals from low-income families have been blocked from achieving social status through conventional means and join gangs to gain status and self-worth, to rebuild a wounded identity.[4]

A recent work by Jack Katz has both creatively extended the status model and advanced the premise that sensuality is the central element leading to the commission of illegal acts. In Katz's "expressive" model, joining a gang, and being what he labels a "badass," involves a process whereby an individual manages (through transcendence) the gulf that exists between a sense of self located within the local world (the here) and a reality associated with the world outside (the there). Katz argues that the central elements in various forms of deviance, including becoming involved in a gang and gang violence, are the moral emotions of humiliation, righteousness, arrogance, ridicule, cynicism, defilement, and vengeance. "In each," he says, "the attraction that proves to be most fundamentally compelling is that of overcoming a personal challenge to moral—not material—existence."[5]

Most of these theories suffer from three flaws. First, they link joining a gang to delinquency, thereby combining two separate issues. Second, they use single-variable explanations. Third, and most important, they fail to treat joining a gang as the product of a rational decision to maximize self-interest, one in which both the individual and the organized gang play a role. This is especially true of Katz's approach, for two reasons. First, on the personal level, it underestimates the impact of material and status conditions in establishing the situations in which sensual needs/drives (emotions) present themselves, and overestimates/exaggerates the "seductive" impact of crime in satisfying these needs. Second, it does not consider the impact of organizational dynamics on the thought and action of gang members.

In contrast, the data presented here will indicate that gangs are composed of individuals who join for a variety of reasons. In addition, while the individual uses his own calculus to decide whether or not to join a gang, this is not the only deciding factor. The other deciding factor is whether the gang wants him in the organization. Like the individual's decision to join, the gang's decision to permit membership is based on a variety of factors. It is thus important to understand that who becomes a gang member depends on two decision-making processes: that of the individual and that of the gang.

The Individual and
the Decision to Become a Member

Before proceeding, it is important to dismiss a number of the propositions that have often been advanced. The first is that young boys join gangs because they are from broken homes where the father is not present and they seek gang membership in order to identify with other males— that is, they have had no male authority figures with whom to identify. In the ten years of this study, I found that there were as many gang members from homes where the nuclear family was intact as there were from families where the father was absent.[6]

The second proposition given for why individuals join gangs is related to the first: it suggests that broken homes and/or bad home environments force them to look to the gang as a substitute family. Those who offer this explanation often quote gang members' statements such as "We are like a family" or "We are just like brothers" as indications of this motive. However, I found as many members who claimed close relationships with their families as those who denied them.

The third reason offered is that individuals who drop out of school have fewer skills for getting jobs, leaving them with nothing to do but join a gang. While I did find a larger number of members who had dropped out of school, the number was only slightly higher than those who had finished school.

The fourth reason suggested, disconfirmed by my data, is a modern version of the "Pied Piper" effect: the claim that young kids join gangs because they are socialized by older kids to aspire to gang membership and, being young and impressionable, are easily persuaded. I found on the contrary that individuals were as likely to join when they were older (mid to late teens) as when they were younger (nine to fifteen). I also found significantly more who joined when they were young who did so for reasons other than being socialized to think it was "cool" to belong to a gang. In brief, I found no evidence for this proposition.

What I did find was that individuals who live in low-income neighborhoods join gangs for a variety of reasons, basing their decisions on a rational calculation of what is best for them at that particular time. Furthermore, I found that they use the same calculus (not necessarily the same reasons) in deciding whether to stay in the gang, or, if they happen to leave it, whether to rejoin.

Reasons for Deciding to Join a Gang

Most people in the low-income inner cities of America face a situation in which a gang already exists in their area. Therefore the most salient question facing them is not whether to start a gang or not, but rather whether to join an existing one. Many of the reasons for starting a new gang are related to issues having to do with organizational development and decline—that is, with the existing gang's ability to provide the expected services, which include those that individuals considered in deciding to join. Those issues will be treated in chapter 4, which deals with the internal dynamics of the organization. This section deals primarily, although not exclusively, with the question of what influences individuals to join an existing gang. However, many of these are the same influences that encourage individuals to start a new gang.

Material Incentives

Those who had joined a gang most often gave as their reason the belief that it would provide them with an environment that would increase their chances of securing money. Defiant individualists constantly calculate the costs and benefits associated with their efforts to improve their financial well-being (which is usually not good). Therefore, on the one hand, they believe that if they engage in economic ventures on their own, they will, if successful, earn more per venture than if they acted as part of a gang. However, there is also the belief that if one participates in economic ventures with a gang, it is likely that the amount earned will be more regular, although perhaps less per venture. The comments of Slump, a sixteen-year-old member of a gang in the Los Angeles area, represent this belief:

Well, I really didn't want to join the gang when I was a little younger because I had this idea that I could make more money if I would do some gigs [various illegal economic ventures] on my own. Now I don't know, I mean, I wasn't wrong. I could make more money on my own, but there are more things happening with the gang, so it's a little more even in terms of when the money comes in. . . . Let's just say there is more possibilities for a more steady amount of income if you need it.

It was also believed that less individual effort would be required in the various economic ventures in a gang because more people would be involved. In addition, some thought that being in a gang would reduce the risk (of personal injury) associated with their business ventures. They were aware that if larger numbers of people had knowledge of a crime, this would increase the risk that if someone were caught, others, including themselves, would be implicated. However, they countered this consideration with the belief that they faced less risk of being physically harmed when they were part of a group action. The comments of Corner, a seventeen-year-old resident of a poor Manhattan neighborhood, represent this consideration. During the interview, he was twice approached about joining the local gang. He said:

I think I am going to join the club [gang] this time. I don't know, man, I got some things to decide, but I think I will. . . . Before I didn't want to join because when I did a job, I didn't want to share it with the whole group—hell, I was never able to make that much to share. . . . I would never have got enough money, and with all those dudes [other members of the gang] knowing who did the job, you can bet the police would find out. . . . Well, now my thinking is changed a bit 'cause I almost got hurt real bad trying something the other day and so I'm pretty sure I'll join the gang 'cause there's more people involved and that'll keep me safer. [He joined the gang two weeks later.]

Others decided to join the gang for financial security. They viewed the gang as an organization that could provide them or their families with money in times of emergency. It represented the combination of a bank and a social security system, the equivalent of what the political machine had been to many new immigrant groups in American cities.[7] To these individuals, it provided both psychological and financial security in an economic environment of scarcity and intense competition. This was particularly true of those who were fifteen and younger. Many in this age group often find themselves in a precarious position. They are in need of money, and although social services are available to help during times of economic hardship, they often lack legal means of access to these resources. For these individuals, the gang can provide an alternative source of aid. The comments of Street Dog and Tomahawk represent these views. Street Dog was a fifteen-year-old Puerto Rican who had been in a New York gang for two years:

> Hey, the club [the gang] has been there when I needed help. There were times when there just wasn't enough food for me to get filled up with. My family was hard up and they couldn't manage all of their bills and such, so there was some lean meals! Well, I just needed some money to help for awhile, till I got some money or my family was better off. They [the gang] was there to help. I could see that [they would help] before I joined, that's why I joined. They are there when you need them and they'll continue to be.

Tomahawk was a fifteen-year-old Irishman who had been in a gang for one year:

> Before I joined the gang, I could see that you could count on your boys to help in times of need and that meant a lot to me. And when I needed money, sure enough they gave it to me. Nobody else would have given it to me; my parents didn't have it, and there was no other place to go. The gang was just like they said they would be, and they'll continue to be there when I need them.

Finally, many view the gang as providing an opportunity for future gratification. They expect that through belonging to a gang, they will be able to make contact with individuals who may eventually help them financially. Some look to meet people who have contacts in organized crime in the hope of entering that field in the future. Some hope to meet businessmen involved in the illegal market who will provide them with money to start their own illegal businesses. Still others think that gang membership will enable them to meet individuals who will later do them favors (with financial implications) of the kind fraternity brothers or Masons sometimes do for each other. Irish gang members in New York and Boston especially tend to believe this.

Recreation

The gang provides individuals with entertainment, much as a fraternity does for college students or the Moose and Elk clubs do for their members.

Many individuals said they joined the gang because it was the primary social institution of their neighborhood—that is, it was where most (not necessarily the biggest) social events occurred. Gangs usually, though not always, have some type of clubhouse. The exact nature of the clubhouse varies according to how much money the gang has to support it, but every clubhouse offers some form of entertainment. In the case of some gangs with a good deal of money, the clubhouse includes a bar, which sells its members drinks at cost. In addition, some clubhouses have pinball machines, soccer-game machines, pool tables, ping pong tables, card tables, and in some cases a few slot machines. The clubhouse acts as an incentive, much like the lodge houses of other social clubs.[8]

The gang can also be a promoter of social events in the community, such as a big party or dance. Often the gang, like a fraternity, is thought of as the organization to join to maximize opportunities to have fun. Many who joined said they did so because the gang provided them with a good opportunity to meet women. Young women frequently form an auxiliary unit to the gang, which usually adopts a version of the male gang's name (e.g., "Lady Jets"). The women who join this auxiliary do so for similar reasons—that is, opportunities to meet men and participate in social events.[9]

The gang is also a source of drugs and alcohol. Here, most gangs walk a fine line. They provide some drugs for purposes of recreation, but because they also ban addicts from the organization, they also attempt to monitor members' use of some drugs.[10]

The comments of Fox and Happy highlight these views of the gang as a source of recreation.[11] Fox was a twenty-three-year-old from New York and had been in a gang for seven years:

> Like I been telling you, I joined originally because all the action
> was happening with the Bats [gang's name]. I mean, all the foxy
> ladies were going to their parties and hanging with them. Plus
> their parties were great. They had good music and the herb [marijuana] was so smooth. . . . Man, it was a great source of dope and
> women. Hell, they were the kings of the community so I wanted
> to get in on some of the action.

Happy was a twenty-eight-year-old from Los Angeles, who had been a gang member for eight years:

> I joined because at the time, Jones Park [gang's name] had the best
> clubhouse. They had pool tables and pinball machines that you
> could use for free. Now they added a video game which you only

have to pay like five cents for to play. You could do a lot in the club, so I thought it was a good thing to try it for awhile [join the gang], and it was a good thing.

A Place of Refuge and Camouflage

Some individuals join a gang because it provides them with a protective group identity. They see the gang as offering them anonymity, which may relieve the stresses associated with having to be personally accountable for all their actions in an intensely competitive environment. The statements of Junior J. and Black Top are representative of this belief. Junior J. was a seventeen-year-old who had been approached about becoming a gang member in one of New York's neighborhoods:

> I been thinking about joining the gang because the gang gives you a cover, you know what I mean? Like when me or anybody does a business deal and we're members of the gang, it's difficult to track us down 'cause people will say, oh, it was just one of those guys in the gang. You get my point? The gang is going to provide me with some cover.

Black Top was a seventeen-year-old member of a Jamaican gang in New York:

> Man, I been dealing me something awful. I been doing well, but I also attracted me some adversaries. And these adversaries have been getting close to me. So joining the brothers [the gang] lets me blend into the group. It lets me hide for awhile, it gives me refuge until the heat goes away.

Physical Protection

Individuals also join gangs because they believe the gang can provide them with personal protection from the predatory elements active in low-income neighborhoods. Nearly all the young men who join for this reason know what dangers exist for them in their low-income neighborhoods. These individuals are not the weakest of those who join the gang, for all have developed the savvy and skills to handle most threats. However, all are either tired of being on the alert or want to reduce the probability of danger to a level that allows them to devote more time to their effort to secure more money. Here are two representative comments of individuals who joined for this reason. Chico was a seventeen-year-old member of an Irish gang in New York:

> When I first started up with the Steel Flowers, I really didn't know much about them. But, to be honest, in the beginning I just joined because there were some people who were taking my school [lunch] money, and after I joined the gang, these guys laid off.

Cory was a sixteen-year-old member of a Los Angeles gang:

> Man I joined the Fultons because there are a lot of people out there who are trying to get you and if you don't got protection you in trouble sometimes. My homeboys gave me protection, so hey, they were the thing to do. . . . Now that I got some business things going I can concentrate on them and not worry so much. I don't always have to be looking over my shoulder.

A Time to Resist

Many older individuals (in their late teens or older) join gangs in an effort to resist living lives like their parents'. As Joan Moore, Ruth Horowitz, and others have pointed out, most gang members come from families whose parents are underemployed and/or employed in the secondary labor market in jobs that have little to recommend them.[12] These jobs are low-paying, have long hours, poor working conditions, and few opportunities for advancement; in brief, they are dead ends.[13] Most prospective gang members have lived through the pains of economic deprivation and the stresses that such an existence puts on a family. They desperately want to avoid following in their parents' path, which they believe is exactly what awaits them. For these individuals, the gang is a way to resist the jobs their parents held and, by extension, the life their parents led. Deciding to become a gang member is both a statement to society ("I will not take these jobs passively") and an attempt to do whatever can be done to avoid such an outcome. At the very least, some of these individuals view being in a gang as a temporary reprieve from having to take such jobs, a postponement of the inevitable. The comments of Joey and D.D. are representative of this group. Joey was a nineteen-year-old member of an Irish gang in Boston:

> Hell, I joined because I really didn't see anything in the near future I wanted to do. I sure the hell didn't want to take that job my father got me. It was a shit job just like his. I said to myself, "Fuck

this!" I'm only nineteen, I'm too young to start this shit. . . . I figured that the Black Rose [the gang] was into a lot of things and
that maybe I could hit it big at something we're doing and get the
hell out of this place.

D.D. was a twenty-year-old member of a Chicano gang in Los Angeles:

I just joined the T-Men to kick back [relax, be carefree] for
awhile. My parents work real hard and they got little for it. I
don't really want that kind of job, but that's what it looked like I
would have to take. So I said, hey, I'll just kick back for a while
and let that job wait for me. Hey, I just might make some money
from our dealings and really be able to forget these jobs. . . . If I
don't [make it, at least] I told the fuckers in Beverly Hills what I
think of the jobs they left for us.

People who join as an act of resistance are often wrongly understood
to have joined because they were having difficulty with their identity and
the gang provided them with a new one. However, these individuals actually want a new identity less than they want better living conditions.

Commitment to Community

Some individuals join the gang because they see participation as a form
of commitment to their community. These usually come from neighborhoods where gangs have existed for generations. Although the character
of such gangs may have changed over the years, the fact remains that
they have continued to exist. Many of these individuals have known people who have been in gangs, including family members—often a brother,
but even, in considerable number of cases, a father and grandfather. The
fact that their relatives have a history of gang involvement usually influences these individuals to see the gang as a part of the tradition of the
community. They feel that their families and their community expect them
to join, because community members see the gang as an aid to them and
the individual who joins as meeting his neighborhood obligation. These
attitudes are similar to attitudes in the larger society about one's obligation to serve in the armed forces. In a sense, this type of involvement
represents a unique form of local patriotism. While this rationale for
joining was present in a number of the gangs studied, it was most prevalent among Chicano and Irish gangs. The comments of Dolan and Pepe
are representative of this line of thinking. Dolan was a sixteen-year-old
member of an Irish gang in New York:

I joined because the gang has been here for a long time and even though the name is different a lot of the fellas from the community have been involved in it over the years, including my dad. The gang has helped the community by protecting it against outsiders so people here have kind of depended on it. . . . I feel it's my obligation to the community to put in some time helping them out. This will help me to get help in the community if I need it some time.

Pepe was a seventeen-year-old member of a Chicano gang in the Los Angeles area:

The Royal Dons [gang's name] have been here for a real long time. A lot of people from the community have been in it. I had lots of family in it so I guess I'll just have to carry on the tradition. A lot of people from outside this community wouldn't understand, but we have helped the community whenever they've asked us. We've been around to help. I felt it's kind of my duty to join 'cause everybody expects it. . . . No, the community doesn't mind that we do things to make some money and raise a little hell because they don't expect you to put in your time for nothing. Just like nobody expects guys in the military to put in their time for nothing.

In closing this section on why individuals join gangs, it is important to reemphasize that people choose to join for a variety of reasons, that these reasons are not exclusive of one another (some members have more than one), that gangs are composed of individuals whose reasons for joining include all those mentioned, that the decision to join is thought out, and that the individual believes this was best for his or her interests at the moment.

Organizational Recruitment

Deciding whether or not to join a gang is never an individual decision alone. Because gangs are well established in most of these neighborhoods, they are ultimately both the initiators of membership and the gatekeepers, deciding who will join and who will not.

Every gang that was studied had some type of recruitment strategy. A gang will frequently employ a number of strategies, depending on the circumstances in which recruitment is occurring. However, most gangs use one particular style of recruitment for what they consider a "normal" period and adopt other styles as specific situations present themselves. The three most prevalent styles of recruitment encountered were what I call the fraternity type, the obligation type, and the coercive type.

The Fraternity Type of Recruitment

In the fraternity type of recruitment, the gang adopts the posture of an organization that is "cool," "hip," the social thing to be in. Here the gang makes an effort to recruit by advertising through word of mouth that it is looking for members. Then many of the gangs either give a party or circulate information throughout the neighborhood, indicating when their next meeting will be held and that those interested in becoming members are invited. At this initial meeting, prospective members hear a short speech about the gang and its rules. They are also told about the gang's exploits and/or its most positive perks, such as the dances and parties it gives, the availability of dope, the women who are available, the clubhouse, and the various recreational machinery (pool table, video games, bar, etc.). In addition, the gang sometimes discusses, in the most general terms, its plans for creating revenues that will be shared among the general membership. Once this pitch is made, the decision rests with the individual. When one decides to join the gang, there is a trial period before one is considered a solid member of the group. This trial period is similar, but not identical, to the pledge period for fraternities. There are a number of precautions taken during this period to check the individual's worthiness to be in the group. If the individual is not known by members of the gang, he will need to be evaluated to see if he is an informant for one of the various law enforcement agencies (police, firearms and alcohol, drug enforcement). In addition, the individual will need to be assessed in terms of his ability to fight, his courage, and his commitment to help others in the gang.

Having the *will* to fight and defend other gang members or the "interest" of the gang is considered important, but what is looked upon as being an even more important asset for a prospective gang member is the *ability* to fight and to carry out group decisions. Many researchers have often misinterpreted this preference by gangs for those who can fight as an indication that gang members, and thus gangs as collectives, are primarily interested in establishing reputations as fighters.[14] They interpret this preoccupation as being based on adolescent drives for identity and the release of a great deal of aggression. However, what is most often missed are the functional aspects of fighting and its significance to a gang. The prospective member's ability to fight well is not looked upon by the organization simply as an additional symbol of status. Members of gangs want to know if a potential member can fight because if any of them are caught in a situation where they are required to fight, they want to feel confident that everyone can carry his or her own responsibility. In addition, gang members want to know if the potential gang member is disciplined enough to avoid getting scared and running, leaving them vulnerable. Often everyone's safety in a fight depends on the ability of every individual to fight efficiently. For example, on many occasions I observed a small group of one gang being attacked by an opposing gang. Gang fights are not like fights in the movies: there is no limit to the force anybody is prepared to use—it is, as one often hears, "for all the marbles." When gang members were attacked, they were often outnumbered and surrounded. The only way to protect themselves was to place themselves back to back and ward off the attackers until some type of help came (ironically, most often from the police). If someone cannot fight well and is overcome quickly, everyone's back will be exposed and everyone becomes vulnerable. Likewise, if someone decides to make a run for it, everyone's position is compromised. So assessing the potential member's ability to fight is not done simply to strengthen the gang's reputation as "the meanest fighters," but rather to strengthen the confidence of other gang members that the new member adds to the organization's general ability to protect and defend the collective's interests. The comments of Vase, an eighteen-year-old leader of a gang in New York, highlight this point:

> When I first started with the Silk Irons [gang's name], they
> checked me out to see if I could fight. After I passed their test, they
> told me that they didn't need anybody who would leave their
> butts uncovered. Now that I'm a leader I do the same thing. You
> see that guy over there? He wants to be in the Irons, but we don't
> know nothing about whether he can fight or if he got no heart
> [courage]. So we going to check out how good he is and whether
> he going to stand and fight. 'Cause if he ain't got good heart or
> skills [ability to fight], he could leave some of the brothers [gang
> members] real vulnerable and in a big mess. And if [he] do that,
> they going to get their asses messed up!

As mentioned earlier, in those cases where the gang has seen a prospective member fight enough to know he will be a valuable member, they simply admit him. However, if information is needed in order to

decide whether the prospective gang member can fight, the gang leadership sets up a number of situations to test the individual. One favorite is
to have one of the gang members pick a fight with the prospective member and observe the response. It is always assumed that the prospective
member will fight; the question is, how well will he fight? The person
selected to start the fight is usually one of the better fighters. This provides the group with comparative information by which to decide just
how good the individual is in fighting.[15] Such fights are often so intense
that there are numerous lacerations on the faces of both fighters. This
test usually doubles as an initiation rite, although there are gangs who
follow up this test phase with a separate initiation ritual where the individual is given a beating by all those gang members present. This beating
is more often than not symbolic, in that the blows delivered to the new
members are not done using full force. However, they still leave bruises.

Assessing whether a prospective gang member is trustworthy or not is
likewise done by setting up a number of small tests. The gang members
are concerned with whether the prospective member is an undercover
agent for law enforcement. To help them establish this, they set up a
number of criminal activities (usually of medium-level illegality) involving the individual(s); then they observe whether law enforcement proceeds to make arrests of the specific members involved. One gang set up
a scam whereby it was scheduled to commit an armed robbery. When a
number of the gang members were ready to make the robbery, the police
came and arrested them—the consequence of a new member being a police informer. The person responsible was identified and punished. Testing the trustworthiness of new recruits proved to be an effective policy
because later the gang was able to pursue a much more lucrative illegal
venture without the fear of having a police informer in the organization.

Recruiting a certain number of new members who have already established reputations as good fighters does help the gang. The gang's ability
to build and maintain a reputation for fighting reduces the number of
times it will have to fight. If a gang has a reputation as a particularly
tough group, it will not have as much trouble with rival gangs trying to
assume control over its areas of interest. Thus, a reputation acts as an
initial deterrent to rival groups. However, for the most part, the gang's
concern with recruiting good fighters for the purpose of enhancing its
reputation is secondary to its concern that members be able to fight well
so that they can help each other.

Gangs who are selective about who they allow in also scrutinize whether the individual has any special talents that could be useful to the collective. Sometimes these special talents involve military skills, such as the ability to build incendiary bombs. Some New York gangs attempted to recruit people with carpentry and masonry skills so that they could help them renovate abandoned buildings.

Gangs that adopt a "fraternity recruiting style" are usually quite secure within their communities. They have a relatively large membership and have integrated themselves into the community well enough to have both legitimacy and status. In other words, the gang is an organization that is viewed by members of the community as legitimate. The comments of Mary, a 53-year-old garment worker who was a single parent in New York, indicate how some community residents feel about certain gangs:

> There are a lot of young people who want in the Bullets, but they don't let whoever wants to get in in. Those guys are really selective about who they want. Those who do get in are very helpful to the whole community. There are many times that they have helped the community . . . and the community appreciates that they have been here for us.

Gangs that use fraternity style recruitment have often become relatively prosperous. Having built up the economic resources of the group to a level that has benefited the general membership, they are reluctant to admit too many new members, fearing that increased numbers will not be accompanied by increases in revenues, resulting in less for the general membership. Hackman, a twenty-eight-year-old leader of a New York gang, represented this line of thought:

> Man, we don't let all the dudes who want to be let in in. We can't do that, or I can't, 'cause right now we're sitting good. We gots a good bank account and the whole gang is getting dividends. But if we let in a whole lot of other dudes, everybody will have to take a cut unless we come up with some more money, but that don't happen real fast. So you know the brothers ain't going to dig a cut, and if it happens, then they going to be on me and the rest of the leadership's ass and that ain't good for us.

The Obligation Type of Recruitment

The second recruiting technique used by gangs is what I call the "obligation type." In this form, the gang contacts as many young men from

its community as it can and attempts to persuade them that it is their
duty to join. These community pressures are real, and individuals need
to calculate how to respond to them, because there are risks if one ignores them. In essence, the gang recruiter's pitch is that everyone who
lives in this particular community has to give something back to it in
order to indicate both appreciation of and solidarity with the community. In places where one particular gang has been in existence for a considerable amount of time (as long as a couple of generations), "upholding
the tradition of the neighborhood" (not that of the gang) is the pitch used
as the hook. The comments of Paul and Lorenzo are good examples. Paul
was a nineteen-year-old member of an Irish gang in New York:

> Yeah, I joined this group of guys [the gang] because they have
> helped the community and a lot of us have taken some serious
> lumps [injuries] in doing that. . . . I think if a man has any sense of
> himself, he will help his community no matter what. Right now
> I'm talking to some guys about joining our gang and I tell them
> that they can make some money being in the gang, but the most
> important thing is they can help the community too. If any of
> them say that they don't want to get hurt or something like that, I
> tell'm that nobody wants to get hurt, but sometimes it happens.
> Then I tell them the bottom line, if you don't join and help the
> community, then outsiders will come and attack the people here
> and this community won't exist in a couple of years.

Lorenzo was a 22-year-old Chicano gang member from Los Angeles. Here
he is talking to two prospective members:

> I don't need to talk to you dudes too much about this [joining a
> gang]. You know what the whole deal is, but I want you to know
> that your barrio [community] needs you just like they needed us
> and we delivered. We all get some battle scars [he shows them a
> scar from a bullet wound], but that's the price you pay to keep
> some honor for you and your barrio. We all have to give some-
> thing back to our community.[16]

This recruiting pitch is primarily based on accountability to the community. It is most effective in communities where the residents have depended on the gang to help protect them from social predators. This is
because gang recruiters can draw on the moral support that the gang
receives from older residents.

Although the power of this recruiting pitch is accountability to the community, the recruiter can suggest other incentives as well. Three positive incentives generally are used. The first is that gang members are respected in the community. This means that the community will tolerate their illegal business dealings and help them whenever they are having difficulty with the police. As Cardboard, a sixteen-year-old member of a Dominican gang, commented:

> Hey, the dudes come by and they be putting all this shit about that I should do my part to protect the community, but I told them I'm not ready to join up. I tell you the truth, I did sometimes feel a little guilty, but I still didn't think it was for me. But now I tell you I been changing my mind a little. I thinking more about joining. . . . You see the dudes been telling me the community be helping you do your business, you understand? Hey, I been thinking, I got me a little business and if they right, this may be the final straw to get me, 'cause a little help from the community could be real helpful to me. [He joined the gang three weeks later.]

The second incentive is that some members of the community will help them find employment at a later time. (This happens more in Irish neighborhoods.) The comments of Andy, a seventeen-year-old Irish-American in Boston, illustrate this view:

> The community has been getting squeezed by some developers and there's been a lot of people who aren't from the community moving in, so that's why some of the Tigers [gang's name] have come by while we've been talking. They want to talk to me about joining. Just like they been saying, the community needs their help now and they need me. I really was torn because I thought there might be some kind violence used and I don't really want to get involved with that. But the other day when you weren't here, they talked to me and told me that I should remember that the community remembers when people help and they take care of their own. Well, they're right, the community does take care of its own. They help people get jobs all the time 'cause they got contacts at city hall and at the docks, so I been thinking I might join. [He joined three weeks later.]

The third incentive is access to women. Here the recruiter simply says that because the gang is a part of the community and is respected, women look up to gang members and want to be associated with them. So, the pitch continues, if an individual wants access to a lot of women, it will be available through the gang. The comments of Topper, a fifteen-year-old Chicano, illustrate the effectiveness of this pitch:

> Yeah, I was thinking of joining the Bangers [a gang]. These two homeboys [gang members] been coming to see me about joining for two months now. They've been telling me that my barrio really needs me and I should help my people. I really do want to help my barrio, but I never really made up my mind. But the other day they were telling me that the *mujeres* [women] really dig homeboys because they do help the community. So I was checking that out and you know what? They really do! So, I say, hey, I need to seriously check the Bangers out. [One week later he joined the gang.]

In addition to the three positive incentives used, there is a negative one. The gang recruiter can take the tack that if a prospective member decides not to join, he will not be respected as much in the community, or possibly even within his own family. This line of persuasion can be successful if other members of the prospective recruit's family have been in a gang and/or if there has been a high level of involvement in gangs throughout the community. The suggestion that people (including family) will be disappointed in him, or look down on his family, is an effective manipulative tool in the recruiting process in such cases. The comments of Texto, a fifteen-year-old Chicano, provide a good example:

> I didn't want to join the Pearls [gang's name] right now cause I didn't think it was best for me right now. Then a few of the Pearls came by to try to get me to join. They said all the stuff about helping your barrio, but I don't want to join now. I mean I do care about my barrio, but I just don't want to join now. But you heard them today ask me if my father wanted me to join. You know I got to think about this, I mean my dad was in this gang and I don't know. He says to me to do what you want, but I think he would be embarrassed with his friends if they heard I didn't want to join. I really don't want to embarrass my dad, I don't know what I'm going to do. [He joined the gang one month later.]

The "obligation method of recruitment" is similar to that employed by governments to secure recruits for their armed services, and it meets with only moderate results. Gangs using this method realized that while they would not be able to recruit all the individuals they made contact with, the obligation method (sometimes in combination with the coercive method) would enable them to recruit enough for the gang to continue operating.

This type of recruitment was found mostly, although not exclusively, in Irish and Chicano communities where the gang and community had been highly integrated. It is only effective in communities where a particular gang or a small number of gangs have been active for a considerable length of time.

The Coercive Type of Recruitment

A third type of recruitment involves various forms of coercion. Coercion is used as a recruitment method when gangs are confronted with the need to increase their membership quickly. There are a number of situations in which this occurs. One is when a gang has made a policy decision to expand its operations into another geographic area and needs troops to secure the area and keep it under control. The desire to build up membership is based on the gang's anticipation that there will be a struggle with a rival gang and that, if it is to be successful, it will be necessary to be numerically superior to the expected adversary.

Another situation involving gang expansion also encourages an intense recruitment effort that includes coercion. When a gang decides to expand into a geographic area that has not hitherto been controlled by another gang, and is not at the moment being fought for, it goes into the targeted area and vigorously recruits members in an effort to establish control. If individuals from this area are not receptive to the gang's efforts, then coercion is used to persuade some of them to join. The comment of Bolo, a seventeen-year-old leader of a New York gang, illustrates this position:

> Let me explain what just happened. Now you might be thinking, what are these dudes doing beating up on somebody they want to be in their gang? The answer is that we need people now, we can't be waiting till they make up their mind. They don't have to stay for a long time, but we need them now. . . . We don't like to recruit this way 'cause it ain't good for the long run, but this is necessary now because in order for us to expand our business in this area we got to get control, and in order to do that we got to have members who live in the neighborhood. We can't be building no structure to defend ourselves against the Wings [the rival gang in the area], or set up some communications in the area, or set up

a connection with the community. We can't do shit unless we got
a base and we ain't going to get any base without people. It's that
simple.

A third situation where a gang feels a need to use a coercive recruiting
strategy involves gangs who are defending themselves against a hostile
attempt to take over a portion of their territory. Under such conditions,
the gang defending its interests will need to bolster its ranks in order to
fend off the threat. This will require that the embattled gang recruit rapidly.
Often, a gang that normally uses the fraternity type of recruitment will
be forced to abandon it for the more coercive type. The actions of these
gangs can be compared to those of nation-states when they invoke uni-
versal conscription (certainly a form of coercion) during times when they
are threatened and then abrogate it when they believe they have recruited
a sufficient number to neutralize the threat, or, more usually, when a
threat no longer exists. The comments of M.R. and Rider represent those
who are recruited using coercion. M.R. was a nineteen-year-old ex–gang
member from Los Angeles:[17]

> I really didn't want to be in any gang, but one day there was this
> big blowout [fight] a few blocks from here. A couple of O
> Streeters who were from another barrio came and shot up a num-
> ber of the Dukes [local gang's name]. Then it was said that the O
> Streeters wanted to take over the area as theirs, so a group of the
> Dukes went around asking people to join for awhile till everything
> got secure. They asked me, but I still didn't want to get involved
> because I really didn't want to get killed over something that I had
> no interest in. But they said they wanted me and if I didn't join
> and help they were going to mess me up. Then the next day a cou-
> ple of them pushed me around pretty bad, and they did it much
> harder the following day. So I thought about it and then decided
> I'd join. Then after some gun fights things got secure again and
> they told me thanks and I left.

Rider was a sixteen-year-old member of an Irish gang from New York:

> Here one day I read in the paper there was fighting going on be-
> tween a couple of gangs. I knew that one of the gangs was from a
> black section of the city. Then some of the Greenies [local Irish
> gang] came up to me and told me how some of the niggers from
> this gang were trying to start some drugs in the neighborhood. I

didn't want the niggers coming in, but I had other business to tend to first. You know what I mean? So I said I thought they could handle it themselves, but then about three or four Greenies said that if I didn't go with them that I was going to be ground meat and so would members of my family. Well, I know they meant business because my sister said they followed her home from school and my brother said they threw stones at him on his way home. So they asked me again and I said OK . . . then after we beat the niggers' asses, I quit. . . . Well, the truth is that I wanted to stay, but after the nigger business was over, they didn't want me. They just said that I was too crazy and wouldn't work out in the group.

This last interview highlights the gang's movement back to their prior form of recruitment after the threat was over. Rider wanted to stay in the gang but was asked to leave. Many of the members of the gang felt Rider was too crazy, too prone to vicious and outlandish acts, simply too unpredictable to trust. The gang admired his fighting ability, but he was the kind of person who caused too much trouble for the gang. As T.R., an eighteen-year-old leader of the gang, said:

There's lots of things we liked about Rider. He sure could help us in any fight we'd get in, but he's just too crazy. You just couldn't tell what he'd do. If we kept him, he'd have the police on us all the time. He just had to go.

There is also a fourth situation in which coercion is used in recruiting. Sometimes a gang that has dominated a particular area has declined to such an extent that it can no longer control all its original area. In such situations, certain members of this gang often decide to start a new one. When this occurs, the newly constituted gang often uses coercive techniques to recruit members and establish authority over its defined territory. Take the comments of Rob and Loan Man, both of whom were leaders of two newly constituted gangs. Rob was a sixteen-year-old gang member from Los Angeles:

There was the Rippers [old gang's name], but so many of their members went to jail that there really wasn't enough leadership people around. So a number of people decided to start a new gang. So then we went around the area to check who wanted to be in the gang. We only checked out those we really wanted. It was like pro football scouts, we were interested in all those that could help us now. Our biggest worry was getting members, so when some of the dudes said they didn't want to join, we had to put some heavy physical pressure on them; because if you don't get members, you don't have anything that you can build into a gang. . . . Later after we got established we didn't need to pressure people to get them to join.

Loan Man was a twenty-five-year-old member of a gang in New York:

I got this idea to start a new gang because I thought the leaders we had were all fucked up. You know, they had shit for brains. They were ruining everything we built up and I wasn't going to go down with them and lose everything. So I talked to some others who didn't like what was going on and we decided to start a new club [gang] in the neighborhood we lived in. So we quit. . . . Well, we got new members from the community, one way or the other . . . you know we had to use a little persuasive muscle to build our membership and let the community know we were able to take control and hold it, but after we did get control, then we only took brothers who wanted us [they used the fraternity type of recruiting].

In sum, the coercive method of recruitment is used most by gangs that find their existence threatened by competitor gangs. During such periods, the gang considers that its own needs must override the choice of the individual and coercion is used to induce individuals to join their group temporarily.

The Type of Coercion Employed

In order to induce individuals to join, two types of coercive tactics are used: physical intimidation and psychological intimidation. Psychological intimidation is the preferred form of coercion because it has the least risk of creating resentment in the prospective recruit. Resentment is something that all gangs try to avoid because it leads to a lack of unity, which in turn leaves the organization in a state of instability. The first step in psychological intimidation is to threaten the prospective recruit with bodily harm. Most of those who are wanted in the gang just become defiant when confronted in this way. This usually necessitates a second step: threatening one of the prospective member's family. This type of intimidation occurred when a gang in New York wanted a particular individual and his friend to join quite badly. Both had been members of gangs before, but were asked to leave when they became drug addicts. The gang that wanted to recruit them was involved in an intense fight with two rival gangs and needed people who could fight. Therefore, it approached the two men about joining and both declined. The leadership decided to harass them into joining for a short time by constantly following both their sisters. As the gang leader said to the other officers:

> You watch, they'll join for the short run we asked because they'll want to protect their sisters. . . . Hell, they know we won't do anything to their sisters, but if we're hanging around them and the Movers [the rival gang] jumps us, their sister will get hurt because the Movers will think they're our ladies . . . so I guarantee they'll join.

The tactic worked. Both of the individuals joined until the fighting between the gangs was over.

Physical intimidation is the other form of coercion used to secure new members. It includes inflicting physical pain on the individual or a member of the individual's family, as well as destroying the individual's property. Although effective, this strategy involves the risk of creating resentment and defiance of the organization, and gangs therefore try to use it judiciously.

Who Does Not Join a Gang?

Who does not become involved with a gang, and why? There are two answers. First, individuals who see no personal advantages in participating in a gang do not become involved. These individuals can be separated into two distinct groups. The first is those who possess all the characteristics associated with defiant individualism, but have decided that participation in a gang is not to their advantage at the present. Most of these individuals are involved in a variety of economic ventures (usually illegal) that they hope will make them rich and do not perceive any advantage to becoming involved with the gang's activities, but the vast majority of them will become involved with a gang at some time in the future. The comment of Cover, a seventeen-year-old who lives in New York, illustrates this point:

Right now, man, there ain't no reason for me to join the Black
Widows. I got some good business going and I'm making some
decent money. If the police don't mess me up, I can get some good
cash flow going. So right now there ain't any incentive to join, you
know what I mean? Now I ain't saying that I won't join sometime, 'cause they gots some good business going themselves. But
right now I want to keep with what I'm doing and see where it
goes. [He joined the gang one year later.]

There are also those who not only see no advantage to becoming involved in a gang, but also see significant disadvantages: the risks of being
killed or imprisoned associated with gang life are too great in their view.
They want to get out of the area they live in, but they have developed a
strategy for doing so that does not involve the gang. Some of these people
will seek socioeconomic mobility through sports, placing their hopes for
a better life in their ability to become professional athletes. Ironically,
however, there is probably less likelihood of their achieving such mobility through sports than through becoming involved in some illegal type
of business venture.

Others from low-income neighborhoods who seek socioeconomic mobility but do not want to join a gang are those prepared to take the risk
that investing their time and money in some type of formal training (formal education or the trades) will produce mobility for them. The comments of Phil, the eighteen-year-old son of a window washer in Los Angeles, represent this group:

No, I don't want to join any gang. I know you can make money
by being in, but frankly I don't want to take the risks of being
killed or something. I mean some of the dudes in the gang make a
whole lot of money, but they take some big risks too. I just don't
want to do that. I want to get out of this neighborhood, so I'll just
take my chances trying to get out by studying and trying to go to
college. I know there are risks with that too. I mean even if you go
to college don't mean you going to make a fortune. My cousin
went to college and he started a business and it failed, so I know
there is risks that I won't make doing it my way, but at least they
don't include getting shot or going to prison.

The individuals in both these groups (those seeking mobility through
sports and those who seek it through training) possess some of the characteristics associated with defiant individualism, but not the full defiant
individualist character structure. Why some people from low-income
areas have only a few of the characteristics of defiant individualism

and others have them all has to do with a number of contingent factors related to exactly how each individual has experienced his or her social environment.

The second answer to the question of who does not become involved in gangs and why has to do with the fact that gangs do not want everyone who seeks membership. They will reject people if they are not good fighters, cannot be trusted, or are unpredictable (cannot be controlled), as well as if the gang itself already has too many members (in which case additional members would create difficulties in terms of social control and/or a burden in providing the services expected by the membership). Take the comment of Michael, the eighteen-year-old son of a street sweeper in New York:

> Sure, I wanted to join the Spears and I hung out with them, but they never invited me to formally join. You have to get a formal invitation to join, and they didn't give me one. They just told me that they had too many members right now, maybe sometime later.

What Happens to Gang Members?

What is the tragectory of the individual who is involved in gangs? Thrasher and most of the subsequent studies on gangs believed that individuals who were in gangs simply matured out of them as they got older.[18] However, evidence from the present study suggests that the real story is more complicated. I found there are seven possible outcomes, some of which are not necessarily exclusive of each other. First, some people stay in the gang. As of this writing some individuals in their late thirties were still members of gangs. What will happen to them is open to question.

Second, some members will drop out of their gangs and pursue various illegal economic activities on their own.

Third, a number of gang members will move on to another type of organization or association. Many of the Irish will join Irish social clubs. Others will move to various branches of organized crime.

Fourth, there will be individuals who move from gangs and become involved in smaller groups like "crews" where they can receive a larger take of the money they have stolen than if they were in a gang.

Fifth, some will be imprisoned for a considerable part of their lives. While this will negate their involvement in the gangs of the streets, they will remain involved in the prison gangs.

Sixth, there will be those whose fate will be death as a consequence of a drug overdose, a violent confrontation, or the risks of lower-class life.[19]

Seventh, a large number will take the jobs and live the lives they were trying to avoid. While this may appear to be what Thrasher and others have previously reported, it is hardly accurate to think of it as "maturing out of the gang."

What do these future paths mean for the gang? Gangs are composed of individuals with defiant individualist characters who make decisions on the basis of what is good for them. On an individual level, this means that gang members will often come and go throughout long periods of their lives. Take the comment of Clip, a thirty-six-year-old member of a Los Angeles gang:

> I've been in gangs since I was fifteen. I joined and then quit and joined again. I did different things, I been married twice, but I come back to the gang 'cause there is always a chance if you get some business going, you can make some big money and live in leisure. That's been my goal and always will be.

On the aggregate level this means that coming and going is merely an integral part of the organizational environment.

Conclusion

Who joins a gang and why have been central concerns of many studies having to do with gangs. One set of studies concentrates on delinquency, asking why individuals are inclined to engage in illegal acts. Another incorporates gangs into a larger analysis of community. Neither approach directly addresses the gang itself. If one begins not from delinquency or community but from the defiant individualist character of gang recruits, one sees that defiant individuals make rational decisions as to what is best for them. Although previous studies have argued that all individuals have the same reason for becoming involved with gangs, prospective members in fact have a variety of reasons for doing so. However, this chapter also shows that the varying motives of defiant individuals do not suffice to explain who joins a gang and why. Gang involvement is also determined by the needs and desires of the organization. The answer to the question of who joins a gang and why depends on the complex interplay between the individual's decision concerning what is best for him and the organization's decision as to what is best for it.

Chapter Three

In the Organization

He would get back again into the Organization. Again peo-
ple would be afraid of him. Again clever men would be al-
ways at hand to make plans for him, to provide him with
money for doing daring things, to protect him, to praise his
recklessness, his strength and his . . . Mother of Mercy! What
Luck! . . . such was his eagerness to qualify immediately for
readmission to the Organization.

Liam O'Flaherty, *The Informer* (1925)

Chapter 2 identified many reasons why both young and adult males join gangs. This chapter addresses the question of what the gang does with this group of disparate individuals to transform them into cooperative members, and ultimately into a working organizational unit. This question has attracted considerable attention among sociologists interested in gang behavior and has generated two basic schools of thought concerning gang organization. The dominant body of research concludes that gangs are not cohesive units. These studies argue that gangs are loose associations of individuals that have little in the way of a defined leadership and a shifting pattern of role expectation.[1] In other words, gangs have few of the properties associated with the concept of an organization; they are either pre-organizational associations or simply primitive organizations. On the other hand, a few studies have found gangs to be quite cohesive. They argue that gangs have a relatively well-defined leadership with differentiated roles.[2] This chapter begins the process of detailing and analyzing the leadership structure of gangs, the roles associated with such structures, the tactics used to create unity and cohesion, the process of leadership change, and the internal politics of gangs. This analysis enables a better understanding of what gangs look like, why they look the way they do, what types of behavior exist within a gang, and why gangs behave the way they do. In essence, this chapter explains how the gang as an organization operates.

63

The Formal Structures of Gangs

In order to function as efficiently as possible, gangs establish organizations with particular structures. There are three basic elements to a gang's organization. The first has to do with formal leadership structures in which leadership categories are labeled and assigned a degree of authority. The second has to do with the definition of roles and duties for both the leadership and the rank and file. The third involves the codes that each collective creates and enforces in an effort to engineer order.

In this study, three distinct models of gang organizational structure were observed, with each model represented in each of the three cities studied. The first model I have labeled "vertical/hierarchical."[3] Within such a structure, leadership was divided hierarchically into three or four categories or offices, with authority assigned to each. Gangs organized in this way usually had a president, vice president, warlord, and treasurer. Authority and power were related to one's place in the line of command. The president had the most power, followed by the vice president, then the warlord, and then, if one existed, the treasurer. There were two gangs that I studied that adopted a variation on this structure by creating a leadership position called a "godfather" or "supreme godfather," whose place in the authority/status queue was above that of president.[4] Within the vertical/hierarchical organizational arrangement, each leadership position entailed a number of official roles. First, the president was in charge of all the gang's operations. He had authority both to plan for the gang's future and to develop short-range goals and strategies for achieving this future. The president also was in charge of administering rewards and punishments within the gang. The vice president, more often than not, was charged with the duties of running meetings and coordinating the communications network. Sometimes the communications network simply involved word of mouth, but generally it involved the telephone or a small, remote-communication system similar to the walkie-talkie systems used by the military. Most of the communications equipment was purchased from people who sell military matériel on the black market. Generally, the vice president in this type of structure acted as the president's chief of staff (similar to the position of the chief of staff to the president of the United States), coordinating much of the gang's business. However, in very large gangs, there tended to be intense competition for leadership and thus more political infighting for power. In such situations, the vice president sometimes functioned as the leader of the opposition, since in most cases he had competed for power and lost to the presidential incumbent. When the vice president was the opposition leader, he assumed few formal duties, because the president (and his advisers) viewed him as a competitor who aspired to be the leader and therefore could not be trusted as a member of the inner circle.

Next in the vertical/hierarchical chain of command was the warlord, whose general duty was to command the gang where force was thought to be required. The warlord sometimes designated who or what was to be attacked, but more often he decided only how the attack was to take place. Some gangs limited even this aspect of the warlord's duties by having the president, vice president, and their closest friends decide the battle strategy and then authorize the warlord to execute that strategy. When this strategy-establishing facet of the warlord's duties had been seriously limited, it was usually for two reasons. First and foremost, the warlord was generally someone who in the past had sought, or presently was vying for, the leadership of the gang. Therefore, in an effort to reduce that person's influence and prestige, the president instituted a set of duties that essentially limited the warlord's intraorganizational authority to the task of executing strategy. Secondly, sometimes the person chosen as warlord had fighting skills that the gang needed but lacked the savvy to be the strategic architect of collective action. In such a case, the warlord's formal duties would have been restricted in a way that did not offend him (because, practically speaking, the gang needed him for the job), but also did not allow the gang to suffer as a result of having someone less competent commit members to a particularly ill-conceived action. Finally, the warlord was usually charged with the duties of maintaining order at formal meetings and, when necessary, dispensing punishment to those members that the gang, or gang leadership, had designated.

The last in the chain of command was the treasurer. Most gangs did not have a treasurer, either because they did not need one or because the president and vice president wanted complete control over the organization's finances. However, there were times when a treasurer did exist. When such was the case, the treasurer's duties were to collect and manage the gang's finances. For a treasurer, the act of collecting generally involved the garnering of dues from the rank and file. Having collected the money, it was the treasurer's responsibility either to hide the money or deposit it in the gang's bank account. The treasurer was also in charge of keeping the financial records of the gang, dispensing cash to those designated to receive it, and reporting on the financial status of the organization. Usually gangs that employed a treasurer were those that had accumulated a good deal of capital (either legally or illegally) and the person chosen as treasurer possessed the necessary skills to manage the assets.

The second model of gang organization was what I shall call the "horizontal/commission type."[5] Such gangs usually had officeholders, but unlike in gangs employing a vertical/hierarchical structure, none of the offices were ranked in hierarchical order. Within this type of organization there were usually four officers who shared roughly "equal" authority over the members. Responsibility in terms of duties was usually divided among the officers, and who was assigned what task was worked out within the group. Sometimes, but not often, certain officers would assume certain tasks based on a claim to some expertise. However, in most instances, the duties assumed were interchangeable. What the horizontal organizational structure resembled most was a ruling commission or council.[6] When observing this type of leadership organization, one finds that it takes much longer to arrive at a decision because a consensus has to be worked out before going to the rank and file. The point to emphasize is that power and authority are shared among the leadership, as are the duties associated with that leadership. This is significantly different from the "vertical/hierarchical" model discussed above.

The third form of leadership organization was what I shall call the "influential" model.[7] In this model, the formal leadership operated under the guise of informality, by which I mean that there was an understanding among the gang members that leadership needed to exist and that the present leadership was legitimate, but there were no written formal duties assigned to the leaders and no titles were assigned to the leadership positions. Within this type of system, two to four members were usually considered to be the leaders of the group. I have called these people the "influentials" because they did not have specific titles, yet when important decisions concerning the direction and goals that the gang should undertake were up for the collective's consideration, their influence was so great that the gang rarely decided on a policy different from what they were advocating. Their authority, then, was based, more than in any of the other structures of gang leadership, on a form of charismatic authority.[8] Here it is important to point out that the charismatic authority present among these gangs was different in two ways from that described by Max Weber. First, where Weber associates such authority with one person who displays attributes that are "supernatural, superhuman, or at least specifically exceptional powers or qualities," the gangs utilizing the "influential model" almost always had a number of leaders (usually two to four) who were recognized as having special qualities.[9] A question that arises is whether it is possible for more than one leader to rule with charismatic authority over one domain. In other words, is it possible for there to be plural charismatic leadership rather than just one charismatic leader? For the gangs using the "influential" model of leadership, the answer is yes. Here one finds that all of the "influentials" had special qualities that were the bases of their legitimacy.

Secondly, Weber describes attributes "not accessible to the ordinary person, but regarded as of divine origin."[10] None of the members of gangs organized according to this third model believed that the "influentials" of the group possessed attributes that were so special that they were of "divine origin" (their defiant individualist characters would not allow for this). In fact, the gang members believed that they themselves possessed many of the same attributes, but they did recognize that the leaders (the "influentials") either had more of these attributes or had them at a much higher level. A good example of this would be a pick-up baseball or basketball game, where most of the players have certain attributes that allow them to compete in the game, but a number of individuals have certain skills at a much higher level, and these individuals usually are deferred to while the game is in progress. Thus, because individual gang members recognized that leadership was necessary if they were to realize their interests through the gang, they were willing to give authority to certain individuals with special qualities as long as those individuals were able to provide the benefits that the general membership thought them capable of delivering.

Within this model, when new leaders were necessary, the gang attempted, as Weber points out, to "search for a new charismatic leader on the basis of criteria of the qualities which will fit him for the position of authority. . . . In this case the legitimacy of the new charismatic leader is bound to certain distinguishing characteristics; thus, to rules with respect to which a tradition arises. The result is a process of traditionalization in favor of which the purely personal character of leadership is reduced."[11]

In sum, while those who lead a gang under this model did not have any specific titles accorded to their authority, their influential roles within the group had assumed a sufficiently predictable pattern to establish a stable leadership structure.[12]

Adopting an Organizational Structure

This section examines what factors influence gangs to embrace one particular type of organizational structure over others. Two general factors influence the type of organizational model gangs adopt: the short- and long-term goals of the gangs; and the economic, social, and political conditions in which gangs find themselves.

The Appeals of the Vertical/Hierarchical Model

Although the vertical/hierarchical organizational model was used by gangs in all of the cities studied, it was used most by the New York gangs. Two factors influenced the New York gangs to prefer this structure. The first had to do with the long- and short-term goals that the gangs had set for themselves. The gangs in New York based most, if not all, of their legitimacy on the overall goal of improving the social and economic conditions of their members. In order for the gangs to pursue their quest for greater revenues to share with their members, they had decided on a vertical organizational structure because they had found that it provided more control and was more efficient. In the gang's quest to accumulate material resources, there was a constant desire to extend its control over more territory. This was done to increase the possibilities for greater economic activity and/or to create buffer zones to protect areas already controlled by the gang. Whatever the case, when such expansion occurred, gangs acquired new members from the newly annexed areas. Then, in order to maintain organizational control and efficiency, it was necessary to change some of the organizational structure. The change that occurred most often was the division of the gang into branches (although in New York such branches are often referred to as "clubs"), each with its own set of officers.[13] However, despite the appearance of decentralization, an effort was made by the original gang leadership to create an understanding among the various branch or club leaders that they were subordinate to the central leadership and had to answer to them. This met with varying degrees of success. Thus, as an organization grew (and, contrary to popular belief, growth is not very fast), most people in the gang organization understood that the best way to maintain control over the organization was for there to be a vertical/hierarchical structure.

This preference was exemplified in a discussion that a large number of the Blades gang had about the status of a rival gang. One of the members,

Dandy, was complaining about being punished by the gang leader, and, in the process, was calling into question the whole idea of having a hierarchical type of leadership. He got little support from his fellow members. Another member, Mean Stuff, asked him if he wanted the gang to end up like the Robins (a gang that had been their arch rivals). Dandy, who was relatively new to the organization, asked what he meant. Mean Stuff said that the Robins had been a large and formidable competitor of their gang, but that a number of the Robins thought it would be better not to have a strong leadership. So they voted to have a loose association of groups that answered only to their own group leaders. After they changed their structure, they couldn't get all the groups to agree on a joint program, and so when other gangs like the Blades wanted to take over some of their territory, they had to let them do it because they did not have the necessary organization or leadership to resist effectively. Mean Stuff went on to say that nobody wanted to belong to any of the Robins' groups now because they had no money to do things for their members. Not even their community liked them, because they could not protect it. He would not like to belong to their type of organization, Mean Stuff said, because "in New York if you ain't organized with good tight leadership, you ain't nothing and you won't be nothing." At this point, nearly everybody listening chimed in to say that they would not like to be involved in that type of organization either, which promptly and emphatically ended the discussion.

In numerous other discussions with gang members in New York, a dominant preference emerged for a hierarchical leadership structure because the gangs felt that it was only with this type of structure that they could maintain the organization necessary to compete with the other organizations in New York, including the police. In other words, there was an understanding among gang members that part of New York's social environment was an "organizational culture" that stressed the importance of being well organized if a group wanted to compete successfully for the available resources. This understanding was greatly influenced by the success that the Italian Mafia has had in accumulating capital for its members in New York (as well as other places). A number of Mafia qualities appealed to the gangs. First, Mafia organizations allowed poor people, especially young adults, to become financially well off—that is, to become economically mobile.[14] Second, the Mafia provided a service to the communities in which it was based in that it saw to it that crime did not take place there—in other words, it created crime-free zones in its neighborhoods. Third, it was able to do this through the development of a "rational" (in Weberian terms) organization and a defiance of the law. In the first three years of the present study, a majority of the New York gang members that I was associated with said they wanted to work their way into the Mafia's organization. When it became clear that there were too many recruits and not enough openings, not to mention that the Mafia was, for the most part, ethnically limited (Italian/Sicilian), the gang members were forced to abandon their idea of joining.[15] However, because the Mafia operated in defiance of the law, and operated successfully, most gangs looked to it as the prototype organization to emulate and often one would find gangs in New York not only trying to organize themselves to imitate what they thought the Mafia looked like but also copying Mafia leadership categories like "godfather."

The Appeals
of the Horizontal/Commission Model

The horizontal/commission model represents a transitional phase in gang development. If a gang no longer desires to maintain the vertical/hierarchical structure, it often moves to a horizontal structure as a temporary compromise between those who want the vertical organizational structure and those who want to decentralize. Alternatively, the horizontal structure also can be the secondary stage in a gang's development from a very loose association to a vertical/hierarchical structure. What type of transition this model represents depends on the goals (both short- and long-term) that the gang has established for itself.

Chicano gangs in Los Angeles often used the horizontal organizational model. Their decision to take on this structure emanated from their goals, as well as from some important cultural traits. Chicano gangs in general tended to downplay the goal of accumulating a great deal of capital. This is not to say that they were not interested in accumulating money, only that they did not emphasize it as much as did the gangs in the East. They tended to emphasize goals related to protecting their neighborhoods and families. Because they did not emphasize financial gain, they did not see the need to maximize the efficiency of the organization, and thus did not want to adopt a vertical/hierarchical structure. Their logic was that they could protect themselves, their families, and their communities without having as structured an organization as the vertical/hierarchical model offered.

The second reason why Los Angeles Chicanos did not adopt a vertical organization was that cultural constraints inhibited an organizational movement in that direction. To begin with, there is a strong emphasis on the family in Chicano culture. Because Chicano gangs tended to be much smaller than the other gangs studied (some with as few as twenty members), and to be composed of a significant number of people who were related (brothers, cousins, uncles, etc.), there was considerable difficulty getting members to submit to the authority of one person.[16] Throughout my research, I observed many attempts by Chicano gangs to transform their organizational structure into a more hierarchical form. The usual result was failure in the first few attempts. Finally, if there was consistent pressure for some type of change, the horizontal model was adopted as a compromise. An example of this took place in the Pearls gang. A number of the members wanted to change the way the gang was organized because they felt that the gang's difficulty in selling drugs had to do with the fact that there was little leadership. They also complained that it was becoming more difficult to control all the groups in the gang (called *klikas*) because there was no coordinating body. At a meeting that included representatives from all but one of the *klikas*, however, none of the leaders would agree to changing the structure. As Cat-Man, one of the *klika* leaders, said, "Why should I want to follow someone who was not from my barrio?" To the members of these *klikas*, where they lived was their barrio and they were not about to let someone from another barrio have any authority in their neighborhood. There were two issues at stake. The first was that the gang members' expectation of themselves, and their perception of their families' expectation of them, was that they should be capable of protecting their own barrio. Thus, because protecting their barrio was related to their perceptions of honor as a man,[17] a change in organization also had cultural ramifications. Ultimately, resistance to organizational change was associated with cultural values.

The second issue was the fact that even though they were all members of the Pearls, a gang that included a number of barrios, they simply did not trust all the people in the gang as a whole. The farther away another member of the gang lived from them, the less trusting they were of that person. Also there was less trust (not that there was no trust) of members who were not part of one's immediate or extended family. Chicanos emphasize family loyalty (which is strengthened by the fact that extended family subgroups often live on the same or adjacent blocks) so strongly that the combination of family living patterns and territory tends to reinforce suspicious feelings about those from different barrios.

In the discussions of reorganizing the gang from a loose association of *klikas* to a vertical organization, the major stumbling block was the fact that the new leadership would be composed of relatives from the various *klikas*. One example is provided by the Titans. The Titans were considering a change in organizational structure, but nobody would agree to change because nobody could agree on who would be the leaders. Juan, who was proposing the change, nominated Tino for one of the leaders, but Roberto, Tino's cousin, said, "Why should I follow Tino? He is just my cousin, and I am as good as he is." The other objections raised had to do with age. The *klikas* in Chicano gangs tend to be age-bound, with most members being within three years of each other's age. While gangs in other cities and involving other ethnic groups also practice age differentiation in their organizations,[18] Chicano gangs tend to have more stratification by age than other gangs.[19] Given that the *klikas* in the gangs were often age-graded, the younger members did not want to have an older person leading their group, and the older members were not about to have someone younger be their leader. Allegiance to family and status based on age, both of which are emphasized in Chicano culture, therefore inhibited most of the Chicano gangs studied from moving toward a more vertical/hierarchical organization with clearly defined authority and roles. Nonetheless, conditions made some type of change in organization necessary for a number of the gangs.

Three situations caused gangs to adopt a horizontal/commission type of leadership structure. The first had to do with their ability to defend themselves and their territory from rivals. The RRs were a Chicano gang that had operated for about fifteen years, and their defined territory encompassed about fifteen square blocks. The RRs included about ten *klikas,* organized along geographic and age lines. For three years, rival gangs had been making raids into their area, stealing things, selling narcotics, trying to pick up their women, and insulting their elders as they rode by in their cars. In addition, in the last two fights that the RRs had had with the Zebras, they had been soundly beaten. The situation had become worse: the Zebras had been riding into their neighborhood recently and beating up RR members. At an emergency meeting called by the leadership of the RRs, Johnny, one of the members, said that something had to be done, but that nothing could be done given the type of leadership structure that now existed. Johnny said that the reason things had gotten so bad was that there was no communication or leadership. The real problem was that nobody was willing to give up the autonomy of their *klika* in order to correct this. Then Diego said that he fully agreed, and that if nothing were done the whole gang would soon be just a memory, and not a very good memory in the eyes of the community. At this point, Hector suggested that the gang choose a president and vice president and a commander-in-chief of the gang's forces. This was met with stiff resistance from three leaders of individual *klikas,* each of whom said that their "homeboys" would not follow anybody into battle unless they were a part of the decision. Jorge, one of those opposing the proposal, said that he was not about to go into battle whenever some so-called president told him to, and that he knew that none of his homeboys would either. The risks were too high to take the word of a single leader, or even of two leaders. The debate intensified into a very heated argument. Jesse and Philip, the leaders of two other *klikas,* interjected and offered an alternative to the two positions being argued. They proposed that the gang create a ruling body of about six members, elected by their respective *klikas,* with the authority to commit the *klikas* to tasks that the committee thought necessary. Some gang members were against this new proposal, but everyone finally agreed that the commission type of organization was worth trying. Within the week, the RRs elected six representatives from their *klikas* to form a board of control for the gang. This arrangement may seem surprising since four of the ten *klikas* appear to be unrepresented. However, the members of these four were very young in age and were associated as "peewees" with the older *klikas* in their barrio. They agreed to give their authority temporarily to elected representatives of their parent *klika* until the crisis was over and the gang had regained its strength.

The second situation that caused a movement toward the horizontal/ commission form of leadership structure stemmed from the difficulties some gangs experienced in achieving their economic goals. The T-Men, a Los Angeles Chicano gang that had existed for about eight years, had been having a hard time meeting the desires of its members. In particular, the gang was having difficulty securing drugs for all its members. At one of its meetings, it was discovered that some *klikas* were getting supplied with what they needed for their own consumption, plus an extra amount to be sold to prospective buyers, while others were not getting any drugs.

The reason for the discrepancy in the supply had to do with the fact that there were about four sources of supply and each source was tied to one of the *klikas*. During the meeting, it came to light that it was not a matter of any one *klika* holding out on the others, but rather the lack of communication and direction that had led to the problem of supply and distribution. At the meeting, the gang also came to the realization that it could have made a great deal of money through the sale of drugs had it been more organized, because a number of *klikas* reported that they could have expanded their sales had they known of a reliable supply. At this juncture, it was decided that the way to rectify this problem and capitalize on new opportunities was for a group of leaders to be established who would coordinate things for the gang as a whole. While no one was completely happy with having a formal group of leaders, a commission type of structure was established by unanimous consent.

The third situation is the reverse of the others. In the first two, there was a movement from a loose structure of smaller groups with a number of influentials as leaders toward a more formal leadership style with a board or commission. In the third situation, gangs started with vertical/hierarchical structures and moved to horizontal/commission type configurations. One case involved a gang in New York. There was dissension within the ranks of this gang concerning the performance of the present leadership. Many members thought that the leaders were not representing the interests of the gang very well, that they had done an inadequate job of raising revenues, that they had unwisely committed the gang to a war with two other gangs, and that this had resulted in their having lost some of the territory they once held. A number of gang members defended the present leadership, saying that it was because certain dissenters wanted to be the president and the warlord themselves that they were complaining. They went on to say that there was no reason to replace the present leadership. At this point, Elfy said that his group did not trust the present leadership's ability to make decisions. Tempers were quite high and Dump, one of Elfy's friends, warned that if the present leadership were not replaced, his group would drop out. Jockey and Time also said they would have their groups drop out of the gang. Dipper, a supporter of the present leadership, pleaded with Dump, Elfy, Jockey, and Time not to jeopardize everything that the gang had been able to gain by pulling out. When this did not persuade any of the dissidents, who still were going to pull out, Log, the leader of a group that was neutral in this particular argument, suggested that the gang change the leadership structure to include representatives of these other groups. A long argument followed about how people would be chosen for the commission, but it ultimately was worked out and a commission was formed. Thus, in this situation, a horizontal/commission leadership structure was adopted as a result of a crisis in confidence concerning the present leadership that forced a change in leadership structure in order to save the gang as an organization. The new structure, therefore, represented an organizational compromise to solve an internal political problem.

In sum then, all three situations highlight the peculiar nature of this form of gang leadership structure. The horizontal/commission model is, as an organizational form, not the preference of most gangs, but rather the one that acts as the palatable compromise between the decentralized "influential" model and that of the highly structured vertical/hierarchical design. It rarely surfaces out of a gang's predilection for the horizontal/commission structure.

The Appeals of the Influential Model

The third form of leadership structure is that which I have called the "influential" model. This model is found most among Irish and Chicano gangs, but for slightly different reasons. For the Irish, it is necessary to understand that gang membership is only temporary. Much as Thrasher argues, the Irish gang represents a transitional phase between adolescence and adulthood.[20] Membership is thus seen as a time to prove oneself as helpful and loyal to both friends and community. Through this process, gang members establish their status not only within the gang and the community, but also among the Irish social clubs that are the next institutional step in their development. In their minds, the establishment of status within the community, and, even more important, in the social clubs, is imperative to making the necessary contacts to get a job later in life. Therefore, because gangs are viewed as a way to build resources through friendships, leadership tends to be established as an aspect of the close friendships being developed.

Within the Irish gangs studied, the leaders were usually those who exhibited traits admired by others in the group. These traits were most often: (1) symbolic loyalty to one's friends, which is used by the organization as a functional mechanism to artificially bond individuals who do not really trust each other; (2) loyalty to the community; (3) ability and willingness to fight, which is equated with courage and conviction; (4)

willingness to devote most of one's time to the gang; (5) an outward display of generosity to others; and finally (6) some connection with the Irish social clubs. While most gang members had these traits, those who assumed leadership positions (the influentials to whom the others deferred) were those who possessed them to a greater degree and who outwardly displayed them with more symbolic force. In short, the leaders were those who demonstrated a certain charisma, something special that members recognized as separating them from the others in the gang. Thus, those who became the most influential within the gang and formed its leadership did so as a result of a natural process of group consensus.

In addition to the fact that the "influential" model fits nicely with the goal of establishing and maximizing friendships, another important factor in the Irish gangs' tendency to adopt this particular leadership design was that the Irish social clubs had created the social conditions that encouraged it. It is important to point out that all of the Irish gangs studied were associated with the adult Irish-American social clubs. Because the Irish-American social clubs already had leadership, there was no need to reproduce a strong leadership structure at the gang level; most of those in the gangs would eventually graduate to the social clubs. In addition, if there was something that affected the whole community, for which there was a need to request help from the gangs, the Irish social clubs would usually take the lead and direct the gangs. We shall see an example of this later (in chapter 6); for now, it is necessary only to point out that the linkages between the gangs and the social clubs allowed the Irish gangs to be less hierarchical in their leadership style, while nonetheless remaining able to compete with other gangs.

The influential model also was used by many of the Chicano gangs. There were three reasons for this. First, Chicano gangs tended to have small memberships, and thus there was no perceived need for a more formal leadership structure. Secondly, most Chicano gang members believed that those who become leaders (and who I have called influentials) should and would emerge from the group in a natural way. As Gato, a sixteen-year-old gang member from Los Angeles, said:

> You don't have to choose leaders; there is no need for that in this gang. Those that lead just do it naturally. I mean they just are the dudes who have always shown that they know what's happening and know what to do; and everyone has seen them do their number [perform] before.

In essence, a large number of Chicano gangs in Los Angeles were like the Irish gangs and relied on individual charisma. The third reason why many of the Chicano gangs preferred the "influential model" of leadership has to do with the issue of authority itself. In a large number of the cases observed, those who objected to the vertical and horizontal structures did so because they were familially related to the present leadership and would not accept the idea that their cousin, brother, or some other relative should/would assume a formal title of authority over them. They were willing to defer to a relative, which the "influential" model was designed to allow, but they were not willing to give one of their relatives some formal title of control over them. Their objection was essentially an extension of familial rivalry.

There is, however, another reason why Chicano gang members have objected to other structures of gang leadership. Chicano gang members were prepared to give authority to a number of influential people, not because they were required to, but because they wanted to. In this way, they felt that they were participating in allocating authority and not simply involved in having to acquiesce to an established authoritative procedure.

Lastly, just as in the Irish gangs, a large number of leaders in Chicano gangs preferred the "influential" leadership structure. As Sock Man, an eighteen-year-old Chicano gang member, said:

> I ain't about to accept some dude as leader just because he won 50 percent of the vote. I only follow those that have shown me that they deserve it. . . . I would quit any gang that had a president and whole lot of officers, and I would really get out if these officers were elected, because any *pendejo* [jerk] can get elected something.

This was an interesting statement because Sock Man was the leader of a Chicano gang and would have been elected president if the gang had adopted a more hierarchical structure. However, he preferred to have his leadership legitimized as a function of his emergence as the consensual choice. He simply wanted to be a "natural" leader or at least one of a group of "natural" leaders. This was preferable to him (as well as to other Chicano gang leaders) because the process by which leaders (or influentials) simply emerge out of the group carries with it the prestige that they are special vis-à-vis the other members and this enhanced his power. Furthermore, leaders who emerge and are influential by virtue of their possessing certain charismatic characteristics are also able to avoid the structural obligations to other members that the other leadership models entail. Sock Man, like many other "influential" leaders, was therefore attracted to this particular leadership model because it gave him psychological prestige and power without the burden of a great deal of accountability.

In sum, there are two reasons why the influential model of gang leadership structure is adopted. First, in a large number of cases, because the gang was small, the conditions were such that a more structured and sophisticated leadership form simply was not needed. Second, there was, among the memberships of a number of gangs, a certain intrinsic appeal to a leadership style that relied a great deal on charismatic skills to build an identification with and a bond between leaders and followers. The attractiveness of the "influential" model was that the leaders appeared more personal, more involved in a friendly relationship with the rank and file. This gave the rank and file the impression that the organization was more flexible and thus allowed more freedom to the individual members.

Social Control in the Organization

There has been some debate in the sociological literature on whether or not gangs have a cohesive organization. All but one of the gangs I studied had a great deal of cohesiveness, brought about through a conscious organizational effort to establish formal mechanisms for internal social control. Regardless of the type of leadership structure adopted, each of the gangs studied employed three mechanisms to create and maintain internal organizational control: formal codes, a collective ideology, and social conflict. It should be emphasized that while strategies for organizational control varied among the gangs studied, all these mechanisms were present to some degree in each of them, and without them the gangs would have ceased to exist as organized units. All the gangs that had withered away had lost these mechanisms of internal social control.

Internal Codes

In his 1928 study of 1,313 Chicago gangs, Thrasher reports that the gangs he studied tended to have a code of behavior for themselves.[21] In some of the research that followed Thrasher, gangs were described as rather loose associations of individuals who were unable to develop codes (or by-laws) to regulate their behavior.[22] In a more recent study, Horowitz reports that the gangs she studied did have rules, but she does not devote much analysis to these rules.[23] So there remains a question as to the extent of the existence of rules and their importance. For all the gangs in the present study, social codes (or groups laws) not only existed, they played an important part in maintaining group control.

Among the thirty-seven gangs studied, twenty-two had codes regulating the behavior of their members.[24] These codes pertained to three areas. One group of codes regulated the behavior of the general membership, including both leaders and the rank and file. These regulations defined what was appropriate behavior in conflicts among members. Not one gang studied forbade its members to fight with one another, but at least 70 percent (twenty-six) had formal codes that broadly outlined what members could do in a fight with other members. Most of these codes restricted aggressive behavior between members to hand-to-hand action. This meant that fights between members could not involve the use of knives, guns, or kung-fu sticks. An example occurred one night in the clubhouse of a New York gang. An argument between two Puerto Rican gang members, Horse and Dagwood, led to a very intense fight between them. The other members of the gang just stood on the sidelines watching, but after Horse was thrown to the floor, he pulled a knife and lunged at Dagwood. At this point, five members of the gang, who, according to the informal gang code, had stayed neutral, broke their neutrality and grabbed Horse. They took the knife away and led him to the president of the gang, where he was severely punished. If Horse had kicked Dagwood or bounced his head against a hard surface until he was half dead, that would have been all right, but the use of a weapon was strictly forbidden in the gang's codes, and punishment was automatic.

If there is an area where most gangs try to regulate the behavior of their members, it is that of personal relations between members and the female relatives and lovers of other members. There is no area more sensitive, and none that can do more to destroy the unity of the gang. Thirty-one of the thirty-seven gangs studied had codes prohibiting a member from harassing a female relative of another member. In addition, all of these gangs had codes prohibiting members from physically or sexually abusing the female relatives or lovers of fellow members. Furthermore, it was forbidden for a member to attempt to have sexual relations with another member's lover unless that member had given prior consent.[25]

In this type of code, men have the right to consent to trade women, but women have little voice in the decision-making process. Despite these codes, there were innumerable times when members did, in fact, harass women who were either relatives or lovers of other members. Like the codes of the larger society, there was both flexibility and leniency in enforcing the codes governing gender relations. However, if a member was accused by another member of violating a code, an ad hoc committee was often established to hear the case. If the committee found the accused member guilty, he would be punished.[26] Punishment varied depending on the type and severity of the offense. Less severe crimes included those involving verbal harassment and attempts to establish relations with another member's lover. The more severe crimes included any type of physical harassment. The less severe the crime, the more likely the member would be to receive probation and/or be required to do maintenance work around the clubhouse for some specified period of time. The more severe the crime, the more likely the member would be to receive physical punishment, some of which was quite severe itself.

In addition to the codes regulating relations with women, gangs also have codes regulating the behavior of their members while they are in the clubhouse. This is done because members often become intoxicated with alcohol and/or drugs, and when this occurs there is a tendency for benign play to escalate into violent behavior. Thus most gangs prohibit violence of any kind in the clubhouse. These codes, then, protect not only the members who come to the club, but also the property. Punishment for violating these codes usually involves loss of privileges associated with using the clubhouse and/or a physical beating.

There are three other areas in which gangs use formal codes. The first has to do with the consumption of drugs. The vast majority of gangs (including all the gangs in New York) had no restrictions as to the use of marijuana, cocaine, some amphetamines, and alcohol, but they did have codes strictly prohibiting the use of heroin. The rationale for heroin prohibition is that the addict has allegiance only to the drug, and this undermines the gang's effort to build allegiance to, and trust in, the organization.

On the other hand, many of the gangs in Los Angeles did not prohibit heroin use. To explain the reasons for these varying policies concerning drugs, it is necessary to reiterate the differences between the gangs in New York and some of the Chicano gangs of Los Angeles. New York gangs are organized around the general principle of providing their membership with a more comfortable and enjoyable life. They understand that in order to accomplish this, they must generate money, and so they are intent on building efficient organizations for that purpose. Everyone in the New York gangs knows that it is impossible to trust a heroin addict, so heroin use is prohibited. The comments of Kite, a twenty-year-old member of a New York gang, are representative:

> No one wants to have anybody who is on heroin in their gang because you need to be able to trust one of your gang brothers and everyone knows that the heroin addict owes his soul to the pusher. The only thing you can count on from a junky is that he will find a way to score, and you can't run an efficient organization with people like that.

On the other hand, many of the Chicano gangs in Los Angeles are not organized with the same goal in mind.[27] Instead, many of them are organized primarily around providing entertainment. The comments of Chopper, a sixteen-year-old member of a Chicano gang in Los Angeles, illustrate this:

> Most of the *vatos* [gang members] joined to kick back and have fun. So yeah, we take drugs and have a good time. If the leaders couldn't get us some drugs, we wouldn't stay. What fun would that be? Hey, we want to party, take some drugs, have some women and have a good time.

To the Los Angeles gangs, taking drugs is a way of separating themselves from others in the community, a way to make a statement that they are not going to follow the rules of a society that asks them to conform, but offers them only inferior jobs in return (a time to resist). The comments of Sub, a seventeen-year-old member of a Chicano gang, are representative of this position:

> Everybody takes drugs because it's fun. . . . There is a lot of Anglo people who say why are they doing that? I say fuck them! Why should we follow their rules? All they say is follow our rules, behave yourself, don't make trouble. Then what do they do? They say if you're a good Mexican and obey the rules, you can have a job cutting our lawn. So I say fuck them! I am not going to follow their rules like a lot of other people in this community.

There were some Latino gangs (most often Central American) that were organized to accumulate money and they prohibited the use of heroin. In addition, some Chicano gangs had changed their priorities and wanted to be more business-oriented, and they began to establish codes prohibiting heroin use as well.

The Irish gangs were closer to the Chicano gangs in that they were not attempting to build organizations that would strive to accumulate large sums of money. Rather, they tried to provide their membership with recreational pleasures, including drugs. What distinguishes them from the Chicano gangs is that while they use cocaine, their members have not been attracted to heroin. Thus they do not need to establish codes to prohibit its consumption.

Certain gangs developed codes to guard against the leadership abusing its power. The gangs that had either a vertical/hierarchical or a horizontal/commission structure to their leadership generally adopted codes for this purpose. Such codes served to prevent the organization from disintegrating rather than to protect individual gang members. This may seem odd, but the fact is that if the leaders became dictatorial, the individuals comprising the gang, with their defiant individualist characters, would rebel and quit rather than be subjected to this type of abuse. Codes regulating this relationship thus acted as a legitimizing mechanism.

Gangs also established codes that specified what kind of offense merited a particular kind of punishment. This helped the gangs maintain the leadership's legitimacy in the event that those being punished charged that the punishment prescribed by the leadership was too harsh. Here again it was found that the gangs that specified punishments for particular offenses were those that employed a vertical/hierarchical or horizontal/commission type of leadership structure. Those that followed the influential model did not see the need to have such codes, because everyone (by consent) had given all the power to those recognized as the influential leaders. In essence, the "influentials" had been given the authority (and they used it) to administer the punishment they thought appropriate.

Some gangs also had codes dealing with leadership changes, but such codes were associated only with gangs with horizontal/commission or vertical/hierarchical leadership structures. Essentially these codes gave some detail to the procedure to be followed when a leader was to be removed. The gangs that decided to have such codes wanted to facilitate a more fluid transition.

Informal Codes

At this point I shall turn to the informal codes that play a large role in gang life. These codes assume the form of unwritten laws—that is, they define "expected" actions that members perform by gang custom.

It is important to draw attention to two areas where informal codes were found. First, among most gangs, it was customary to avoid taking any action that could be construed as demeaning to another member. Such behavior was thought to be particularly dangerous to the organization because it always produced intense antagonism and aggression between members. Thus gangs generally adhered to an informal code of being respectful to fellow members.

Informal codes also operated in the area of dress. Twenty-five of the thirty-seven gangs that I studied had some informal code concerning appropriate dress for the membership. The Chicano gangs dressed alike. They mostly wore T-shirts and khaki pants with their hair cut medium length and swept straight back. Sometimes they would wear handkerchiefs tied around their heads.

For a period of time in the present study, the Puerto Rican, African-American, and Dominican gangs in New York wore what they called their "colors." Basically, the colors consisted of blue jean jackets cut off at the arms, with the gang's emblem sewn on the back. In addition, the gang members usually wore blue jeans with chains as belts, metal wristbands, and engineer's boots. Owing to increased police harassment of those who wore colors, however, the gangs stopped wearing them.

The African-American gangs in Los Angeles also had a dress code. Those belonging to the various Crips gangs would wear something with the color blue in it, usually a blue cap. Those who were members of the Bloods gang would wear something red, usually a cap or handkerchief.

Originally, two of the Irish gangs studied wore a kind of uniform consisting of loose white or green nylon jackets. One of the gangs, Black Rose, wore a black rose emblem on the front of the jacket; the other gang, Green Street, had a shillelagh (an Irish cudgel) emblem on the back. Both of these gangs also subsequently abandoned their colors. Two other Irish gangs did not have any specific dress codes, but all members nonetheless dressed in T-shirts, sweat shirts, or flannel shirts with blue jeans. Even if one of the members had money and could afford fashionable clothing, the unwritten code was that such attire was inappropriate.

Dress codes changed over time, a good example being the Chicano gangs in Los Angeles. In previous times, gang members wore Pendleton shirts and khaki pants, and sometimes even wore stocking caps, which served to identify them because, given southern California weather, a wool shirt or stocking cap is out of place. Even earlier, the *pachuco* (predecessor to the contemporary *vato loco*) made the zoot suit famous. The primary objective of most of the dress codes, not only for Chicano gangs, but also for gangs in general, was to use clothing to establish a collective identity. Clothing, through the medium of the dress code, assumed the symbolic role of a uniform. It acted to identify those wearing such clothing with a certain group. Gang members honor these informal codes, which become powerful organizational customs.

In sum, formal and informal codes are established with a dual purpose in mind: to maintain internal control and to create a mutual bond among members. Through adherence to codes, it is hoped, the gang organization will increase its efficiency and ultimately its effectiveness.

Ideology

Every gang studied employed ideology as an organizational resource. By ideology I mean a logically connected set of beliefs that provide the members with (1) a picture of the world, (2) an interpretation of that picture, and (3) a justification for its superiority over other pictures. Ideology serves two interconnected functions in gangs. First, it attempts to explain how the world functions on a broad societal level; second, it creates a set of moral principles that will solidify the group.

Most of the gangs studied attempted to articulate an explanation of why their members should be in the gang. They began by picturing American society as structured in such a way that certain groups are discriminated against and kept by other groups from enjoying all the benefits of the society. Nearly all the gangs believed that their ethnic group had been denied access to conventional opportunities that would allow them to live more comfortable lives.

Gangs differed with respect to the groups each identified as responsible for their predicament. Chicano gangs blamed Anglos (whites) and viewed African-Americans and Asians as competitors. African-American, Puerto Rican, and Dominican gangs in New York also viewed white society in general as the cause of their plight and saw certain working-class white ethnics (like Irish and Italians) as competitors. The Irish gangs regarded liberal, upper-class WASP society in particular, and upper-class white society in general, as the cause of their difficulty and identified most nonwhite groups as competitors.

Gang members understood social life as being organized around two sets of groups: the ones that preyed on their particular ethnic/racial group (through some form of exploitation) to accumulate the big things in life, and the others that preyed on them for the material scraps that remained.[28] They believed that if they were to survive, the only course was to organize themselves.

The gang thus builds on the defensive and wary aspects of what I have called the defiant individualist character in order to establish an ideological rationale for committed involvement. This is illustrated by the comments of Whale, a twenty-two-year-old member of an African-American gang in New York:

> Take the white society in this city, they just keep you poor by giving you bad schooling, you know, giving you no skills, paying you low wages, and then not letting you live in certain areas. You see they get the good things in life because they get profits from paying you low. And then when you do get some money, they don't let you live in any area but the one they say you can live in, which is not where the better houses are—you know, the bigger and cleaner houses. So most of the big things in life they keep for themselves and then the scraps they let us niggers and spics fight with the spaghetti and potato heads [Italian and Irish] for. So all the brothers [gang members] know if you don't belong to an organization at least some of the time, you just a sittin' duck for their organizations.

Jinx, who was nineteen years old and one of the "influentials" in an Irish gang from Boston, said:

> Hell, everybody knows that those Brahmin assholes try to squeeze every penny from you, they worse than the Jews 'cause at least the Jews sometimes do some humanitarian deed. But those blue bloods just go ahead and pay cheap wages and then walk around thinking they're hot shit. So you never get enough money to get a decent house and then they get together with them pointy head bastards from Harvard and draw up plans to let niggers to live in our area so they don't live in theirs. Ain't that something! All the boys know that those rich bastards and the pointy heads just letting us and the niggers and spics fight over shit jobs. So the only way you can protect what you got from all of those bastards is to

be organized and fight 'em all, otherwise you're going to be left nothing.

Silk was a twenty-four-year-old member of a Chicano gang in Los Angeles:

> Los Angeles. Take a look at the west side of L.A. and then look at the south and east and that ought to sum it up. . . . You know how the rich Anglos stay rich? I tell you. They got business organizations, neighborhood organizations to keep us out, and the police to harass us. They are all organized. So they take all the good stuff and let us and the Asians and blacks fight it out for the rest. So if you want to get ahead yourself, you got to be in an organization yourself. You don't have to be in all the time, but you got to for some of the time. 'Cause if you don't, they be on you like vultures.

There was another ideology that existed in gangs, which I will call the "organizational ideology." It was created by the gang for organizational purposes and nothing more. Both the leadership and the members understood its function and everyone attempted to spread it to some degree. Specifically, this ideology focused on the issue of unity and dealt with the question of identity. Gangs find themselves having to socialize a group of people who have certain attributes that are useful for a gang, but nearly all these individuals also possess certain qualities that are potentially divisive. The gang must mediate many of the attributes of the defiant individualist character, the most fundamental being the feelings of suspicion that are so dominant among most gang members. This was accomplished by attempting to foster the attitude that all the members of the gang were brothers—what R. Lincoln Keiser has called "brotherhood ideology."[29] The strategy was that if members could come to think of themselves as brothers, they would be likely to develop more respect for fellow members and ultimately more empathy with the gang as a whole. There was not one gang studied that did not attempt to socialize its members to identify as a brotherhood. The Chicano gangs, who actually call fellow members "homeboys," have most success in this, a good part of the reason being that many of their members are famScially related. None of the other gangs has succeeded in socializing members to think of each other as brothers.

Although Keiser reports the existence of a brotherhood ideology in the Chicago gang he studied, I observed no such ideology in the belief systems of the vast majority of gang members I studied. What the organization has generally been able to do is to get most of its members to pay lip service to the ideology. Thus what I most often encountered were expressions of solidarity in the context of a brotherhood ideology that was largely symbolic.

It is interesting that gangs (as organizations) attempted to utilize a concept having to do with family, because most gang members would not really trust their own biological brothers to the degree that they attempted to get members to trust each other. Many researchers have heard gang members refer to being part of a brotherhood and have accepted it, but this feeling generally does not exist in gangs.[30] Everyone that I talked to understood that the brotherhood ideology existed. They realized that members did not really look on one another as brothers, at least not with the intensity that the brotherhood ideology intended, but that the ideology nonetheless acted as a kind of bonding agent. The comments of Sonic, a sixteen-year-old member of a New York gang, illustrate this:

> Well, we brothers in the Lord Squares, or we try to be. You see, we're brothers in the sense that we're in a gang, but that don't mean that you don't watch yourself. 'Cause if you don't stay alert, there sometimes be trouble with your brothers, you dig? But having brotherhood in the gang keeps us together and that's good, you dig?

Internal Social Conflict

Georg Simmel was one of the first sociologists to assert the benefits of hostility in permitting the maintenance of relationships in times of crisis.[31] In his study of social conflict, Lewis Coser elaborates on the "group-preserving functions of conflict." One of the topics he develops is Simmel's safety-valve theory of conflict resolution, proposing that the availability of safety-valve institutions allows frustration and aggression to be displaced onto substitute objects, which has the potential for preserving the group.[32]

Although there are areas in which internal social conflict helps maintain control in a gang, the process is slightly different from the psychological venting function Simmel and Coser identify. One way social conflict helps to establish control in a gang is that it allows the gang to legitimize itself as an organization. Often one will observe the breakdown of the brotherhood ideology and the eruption of a fight among members of the same gang. When this occurs, other members of the gang, acting as representatives of the gang organization, intercede to mediate the conflict. In so doing, the organization is seen by most members as helpful and legitimate. Because most members have defiant individualist qualities, internal conflict is present a great deal of the time, so the gang as an organization acts as a binding and controlling agent among individuals—the constant conflict (or threat of it) thus creates more organizational control.[33]

Another way social conflict aids internal control has do to with the gang's ability to provide venting mechanisms for frustration. Mediation aside, gangs have two ways of dealing with internal conflict. First, gang leaders may defuse the conflict by providing a scapegoat outside the gang itself. Frequently another gang is blamed for an internal problem. The scapegoating action is simply a frustration/aggression-venting function.[34] The second approach elaborates on the first. Here, leaders of the gang not only provide the members involved in a conflict with a substitute object on which to vent their frustrations, but also commit the organization to take some form of collective action against the designated object. Usually the substitute object is a contending organization. When this type of collective action occurs, it tends to build group cohesion and reestablish internal social control. Thus the gang organizations are able to use internal social conflict as a resource for cohesion and survival.

Gangs: Democratic or Dictatorial?

In his study of the social bases of politics, Seymour Martin Lipset analyzes the factors that support or undermine the liberal democratic systems of the west.[35] Lipset believes that certain institutions in society are private governments, and that the way they operate internally is an important factor in influencing the social conditions that either support or undermine liberal democracy. In *Union Democracy,* Lipset seeks to understand the "conditions which govern the internal political life of one major type of private government"[36] by taking up the question of whether the private governments of trade unions are democratic or oligarchical.[37] If there is competition among them, Lipset argues, even oligarchies can help support a democracy. The gang has often been thought of as a monolithic institution in which physical force (who is strongest) is the primary criterion in gaining and maintaining power within the organization.[38] However, the gang, as an important institution in low-income communities, also resembles the private governments described by Lip-

set. In this section I shall show how gangs operate as private governments. Information as to whether gangs are generally democratic or
dictatorially oriented is important because it will both provide a better
understanding of the internal operations of gangs and help explain why
gangs behave the way they do in their external relations with people from
within (chapter 6) and outside (chapters 7, 8, and 9) their communities.

In determining whether gangs are dictatorial or democratic, the analysis will focus on two factors: how the leadership interacts with the rank
and file (that is, the rules by which it maintains its leadership position
and how it deals with dissent) and the process of leadership succession.

Whether a gang operates internally in a democratic or dictatorial manner
depends first and foremost on the type of leadership structure the gang
has established. The organization found to be the most democratic is that
which utilizes the "horizontal/commission" leadership model. Under this
model, power and authority are held evenly by various members of the
leadership. One should remember that the gang that adopts this type of
model is usually involved in an internal power struggle that forces it to
accept this model in a last-ditch attempt to hold the gang together. Because
it is the compromise position between a very loose structure of leadership
(the "influential" model) and a very structured leadership (the "vertical/
hierarchical" model), it should not be surprising that the "horizontal/
commission" model turns out to be the most flexible and the most determined in its efforts to reduce conflict/tension by encouraging all who
are involved in intra-gang conflict to participate.

An example of participation within this type of leadership structure
involves the Royces, a Puerto Rican and African-American gang from
New York. The Royces, like other gangs adopting the horizontal/com-
mission leadership structure, handled dissent emerging from the rank and
file in a politically prudent manner. On one particular occasion, Head,
an eighteen-year-old member, opened a general meeting by making a
blistering attack on the leadership commission's decisions concerning some
recent drug business. In leveling his attack, he challenged the competence
of the commission to lead. Interestingly, instead of disciplinary action
being taken against Head, commission members listened intently, and
when he was done, they said that they would revise how they were presently distributing the drugs and submit the plan to the rank and file for
approval. The reason the leadership took such a compromising position
is that they, as a group, did not know if Head was speaking for himself or
representing an entire branch that included a member of the commission.

If he were representing the views of an entire branch, then to censor and/ or discipline him would risk his branch rebelling against such action by threatening to quit the organization. If this were to occur, and it did in a significant number of similar cases, it would create a legitimacy crisis in the leadership and cause these gangs to cease operations for varying amounts of time.[39]

There is little doubt that gangs utilizing this form of leadership structure are the most democratic, and they are democratic by comparison with most voluntary associations. The horizontal/commission model is one that allows for democracy because each of the component parts has roughly equal power. This is very similar to the balance of power associated with the American political system.[40] What the commissioners did was organize and coordinate activities. In addition, commissioners rarely decided something important on their own. Most of the significant business was voted on by the members who attended meetings. Such gangs, therefore, had a double democratic safeguard. In addition to possessing checks and balances at the leadership level, operationally they resembled the direct democracy associated with the New England town meeting.[41]

This type of structure encouraged participation, and in the overwhelming majority of cases observed, policy initiatives (goals and operations) affecting the general membership were brought before the entire gang for approval. A simple majority was all that was required, but in nearly every case, an effort was made to reach a consensus among all the major factions within the organization. Ironically, these gangs allow for, and are tolerant of, dissent, not out of a commitment to democracy, but because they fear that any action to stifle dissent will only lead to major cleavages within the organization. Yet regardless of the motives generating these actions, the actions themselves are democratic.

While the democracy inherent in this type of leadership structure had its virtues, it had its costs as well. One of these was that the leaders rarely led, for they were impeded by the convention of having to get approval from the membership. Simply stated this leadership structure lacked the organizational discipline that gangs operating under the other two leadership structures had. This put a gang using the horizontal/commission structure in a precarious situation when dealing with other gangs and the police, or even simply conducting business. Most of the time it was difficult to motivate the entire gang to act collectively to achieve a goal, with the result that gangs operating with such a structure were usually short-lived. It should be recalled that in nearly all of the cases studied, the horizontal/commission structure was adopted as a compromise between those factions that wanted a vertical/hierarchical structure and those that wanted an "influential" model. Thus the horizontal/commission structure was not adopted out of commitment to the model, but as a last resort to save the gang itself. When a commission-structured gang did collapse, it either was incorporated into the structure of a rival gang (much like a takeover in the business world) or broke into factions that reorganized into a new gang or gangs utilizing one of the other two leadership structures.

The next most democratic organization was the vertical/hierarchical structure. As reported earlier, the gangs that embraced this structure were usually large, and they needed a consensus of the membership to achieve the most rational type of organization for operating the gang's expanding business. Thus, because there was a strong hierarchy in place, one's initial sense might be that this model of organization was the most dictatorial. However, this was not the case because of the complicated internal politics (i.e., dealing with gaining and maintaining of power) of this leadership structure.

These organizations were hierarchical and did have specific roles associated with each office. Leaders, however, were nearly always those who possessed a number of rather sophisticated political skills. Many of the traits that make for a good leader are the same as those described by Machiavelli.[42] Three of the more important, although by no means the only ones, are the talent to plan and successfully complete creative business ventures, the ability to build coalitions, and the capacity to mobilize political resources built up over time. Such calculating political strategies that make a person a potential leader are part of the defiant individualist character that all gang members possess, but one fact that must be emphasized is that an extended period of time is required for a gang leader to rise to power. It is not a quick process. A future leader must get to know the politics of the gang and spend enough time to develop political support from various factions within the group. Even if a person were to distinguish himself in a fight or in making money for the gang, this would not be sufficient to catapult him to power. He would need to have developed a power base within the organization (through making contacts) in order to gain office. An example involves the Savage Profits, a mixed Puerto Rican and African-American gang in New York. During the time of the study, this particular gang had over three hundred members, one of whom was named Snake. Snake was seventeen years old and had been in the gang for three months. One afternoon, Snake told another member, Bambi, that he wanted to become president of the gang. Bambi told him that there was no doubt that he (Snake) could become a leader of one of the gang's fourteen chapters. However, Snake said that he was not interested in becoming a chapter president, he wanted to be president of the whole gang. Bambi listened and just shook his head in disbelief. In the ensuing two weeks, Snake began participating in most of the gang's activities, including meetings, social events, business, and fights. He worked very hard to do an exemplary job at what he was told to do. Throughout this time, he made an effort to meet people and to discuss the future prospects of the gang. At every opportunity, he would criticize the present leadership for not doing things as well as it could, but he would always do so within the confines of a select faction. Snake told me that the only way to take power was to develop supporters in a number of factions—that is, secure a number of political allies (resources) throughout the gang. After about six months, Snake raised several issues at a general meeting that affected the gang as a whole. Through this calculated effort, he became well known throughout the gang. Over the next year, he worked hard to talk to as many different factions as he could. His efforts were very similar to the activities that occur within the caucuses of the major political parties in the United States. Ultimately, the incumbent president was sent to prison, and at the next general meeting Snake offered his name for the presidency. Because of his political work, he had gained the support of a wide and varied number of factions, and he was elected president. Interestingly, Snake had made political deals with a number of the factions that eventually supported him. He promised two factions a large supply of drugs to sell. He promised four others access to larger amounts of the gang's collective cache of stolen goods that they could resell. Finally, to two others, he promised additional amounts of the gang's collective revenues to finance some new business projects they wanted to launch. It had taken two years, but Snake had done what was necessary to achieve his goal.

The example of Snake is not unique, with respect to individual, gang, or situation. Over the two years that it took Snake to become president, this same process was played out by six individuals in five different gangs.[43] Four were able to secure political power; two were not. However, it must be emphasized that during the more than ten years of this research, no one became a member of the ruling elite in vertical/hierarchical-structured gangs without political maneuvering.[44]

Being a good politician was important if one wanted to become a gang leader, but once a person had become the leader, three factors were necessary for maintaining power. First, as has been pointed out in other research, the leader of a gang cannot maintain his position on the basis of power alone.[45] Above all, he must be able to meet the needs and desires of the rank and file members. If he does not do this, he ends up with a lot of disgruntled members, who almost always call for a change in leadership. As an example take the case of Blade, a twenty-four-year-old African-American gang member in New York. It took him about fifteen months to gain power and become president of his gang. During the first seventeen months of his presidency, he increased the gang's territory a modest amount (one square mile); he built a new clubhouse and increased social events for members; and he increased the gang's treasury (which included increasing the amount of the profits distributed to members). In short, he had been a very successful leader and enjoyed the support of the vast majority of members. However, this success was not sufficient for him to maintain his position. In order for that to occur, he was required to do other things. First, he had to consolidate his support by establishing what Lewis Dexter has called a "court"—that is, a group of loyal supporters and advisors who act as confidants and agents to the leader.[46] Interestingly, after Blade had been elected to office, the first thing he did was establish a close relationship with about eleven members. Some of these people were both active and important in the organization, others were merely active. Each of these members developed a strong loyalty to Blade. For his part, Blade tended to many of their needs and desires. He saw to it that they had spending money, access to the most attractive women, and drugs when they wanted them. In turn they developed a strong bond with Blade and acted as his confidants and agents. As confidants, they provided him with information concerning the rank and file's attitudes about certain issues, what factions were discontented, and who was attempting to wrest power away from him. As agents, they were constantly asked to bring Blade's policies to the rank and file—that is, they were charged with selling the membership on a particular policy or getting them to act on it. In essence, it was loyalty that provided both the energy and the cohesiveness of Blade's court (or any gang leader's court). Thus while the loyalty that was established between Blade and his court, and more generally between other gang leaders and their courts, was strong, it was not everlasting. According to Lewis Dexter, such loyalty may be corrupted if a president, a king, or a corporate executive does not recognize that courtiers are self-interested entrepreneurs whose expectations must continually be met.[47] In a real sense, this was what eventually led to the demise of Blade's court and ultimately to his removal from the presidency of the gang. Blade was unwilling with some of his court, and unable with others, to meet their expectations concerning favors. This resulted in a loosening of the loyalty bonds and to a general disintegration of the group's ability to function as an effective court. Without a court to represent his interests within the organization, Blade became politically vulnerable to those who were vying for his position, and ultimately he was outmaneuvered and voted from office.

Some leaders of vertical/hierarchical gangs attempt to build a staff to take charge of various duties like maintenance of the clubhouse or other property of the gang. The staff is different from a court in that it is task-oriented and not really loyal to the leader; it simply performs its tasks no matter which leader is in power. Leaders who establish small staffs do so in order to improve the efficiency of the organization and thereby increase the rank and file's support for them. However, most leaders are politically astute enough to realize that they cannot count on their staffs to represent their interests within the rank and file because staffs are not driven by loyalty to the leader.

There are two additional things that leaders of vertical/hierarchical-structured gangs must do to maintain power. First, they must be prudent in dealing with dissent from the rank and file. The leader of a vertical/hierarchical gang uses prudence differently from the ways leaders of a horizontal/commission type gang do. Where leaders in horizontal/commission structures employ prudence in relation to compromise activity, leaders of vertical/hierarchical gangs employ prudence in relation to acts of political manipulation and maneuvering.

With individuals who possess defiant individualist characters, it is inevitable that there will be dissent. When dissent occurs during a general meeting, it is particularly delicate to handle. The leader has to show flexibility without appearing weak. Take the case of Stick, a twenty-two-year-old Puerto Rican who was the leader of a gang in New York. On one occasion when the gang was discussing whether to use gang funds to renovate an abandoned apartment building (for use by fellow members or people from the community who did not have housing), two members, Rabbit and Heat, objected to the use of collective resources for this project. They did so, not because they believed it to be a foolish business venture, but because they were confidants of Coffee, who wanted to become president of the gang and saw this as an opportunity to challenge Stick. The challenge voiced by Rabbit and Heat was particularly delicate for Stick because he had already pledged the gang's revenues to the building's owner, and Rabbit and Heat had been especially aggressive in calling Stick's decision a waste of gang revenues. Stick listened to the entire criticism and later told me that he did so in order to avoid being seen as disrespectful to either of the two individuals or the position they were expounding because he did not know how many of the rank and file held the same views. When Rabbit and Heat finished, Stick and one of his court whispered to each other for about a minute. Then Stick got up and gave reasons why he thought it was a good business venture. After he finished, he offered some modifications to the proposal. Stick said that he would use gang revenues to buy the building materials for renovation, but instead of hiring professional carpenters, he would ask for volunteers from the gang to help make the necessary repairs and this would eliminate labor costs. He then said that when the renovations were completed, the gang would ask those staying in the building to make donations (a form of rent) to reimburse the gang treasury for the purchase of the house and materials. Stick followed this by saying that he thought this was a good idea, but that the gang should vote on it and if he lost, then the whole deal was off. However, he added that if the majority of the gang voted for the proposal he had just outlined, then everyone should abide by it. Having said this, he asked Rabbit and Heat if they would agree, and they said yes. As it turned out, the gang approved the proposal, and Rabbit and Heat were forced to honor the decision. Stick's action also had been effective in neutralizing Coffee's attempt to create a crisis over his leadership abilities. In sum, Stick's actions had encouraged dissent (because he had made compromises) for the future, but this, in turn, had legitimized him as a strong and tolerant leader.

The second way that leaders of vertical/hierarchical gangs maintain their positions is by being prudent in their administration of punishment. Leaders must know when they are required to punish delinquent members and how much punishment is enough to preserve their authority. The general rule among the astute gang leaders was to punish mostly individuals who violated the gang's codes of conduct (both formal and informal). When such violations occurred, leaders were protected from criticism because they could rationalize their actions as part of their duty to enforce the codes. In gangs where there was ambiguity because no specified punishments existed, fifteen of the seventeen leaders followed over the ten years of this study brought each case before the general membership to decide if punishment should be administered and what the severity of that punishment should be. As an example, take the case of Cool Cat, a president of a New York gang. He was told by one of his confidants that another member of the gang, Scarface, himself a confidant of a competitor of Cool Cat's, had deliberately sabotaged one of the gang's drug ventures in order to make Cool Cat look bad. There was a great deal of discussion among Cool Cat's court as to just how this should be handled. However, Cool Cat proposed to bring it up at the general meeting. Most of Cool Cat's courtiers wanted him to mutilate Scarface. They argued that it was foolish to bring it up at the general meeting because there would be a split vote and, once that happened, there would be no way to punish Scarface. In their opinion the only way to punish Scarface was to do it "unofficially" before the meeting. Despite the advice of his court, Cool Cat brought the matter before the general membership. Later, he told me why he did not punish Scarface before the meeting. He said that if he had punished him and it had gotten back to the rank and file, it would be the kind of information that his competitors could use to say he was a bad leader. Because Scarface's actions were an attempt to discredit Cool Cat rather than a violation of gang codes, Cool Cat was reluctant to punish him without the consent of the gang, so he decided to bring the matter up before the entire gang in order to protect himself. The gang voted to punish Scarface.

Let me now turn to the least democratic of the gang organizations. The "influential" model is not only less democratic than the others, it is actually dictatorial. Authority within this model of gang structure is associated with the charismatic properties of the leaders. Weber is correct in saying that the "personally legitimated charismatic leader becomes leader by the grace of those who follow him," which implies some type of choice, but there are no formally defined rules governing the process, and this has undemocratic consequences.[48]

To begin with, in gangs that utilized this model, there was no way to determine how a particular leader who had some degree of charisma at one time, and who subsequently lost some of it, could be removed from having a significant influence within the gang. Since formal procedures were lacking, there were no checks on the influential leaders, and this usually produced unilateral decisions at the top.

For several reasons, dissent within this type of structure was usually minimal. First, because there generally is more than one influential leader in any one gang, it is difficult to determine whom to direct dissent at.

Second, because "influential" leaders do possess attributes that the gang members believe are extraordinary, there is group pressure to obey the authority of the "influentials." The result is that members with grievances tend to be either reluctant and/or guarded in expressing them.

Because of the oligarchical nature of the "influential" model, punishment could be administered in a more indiscriminate manner than in the other two forms of gang organization. The Snow Tigers in Boston offer a good example of how punishment is often administered in an "influential" gang. Stoney and Doke were rumored to have committed a number of robberies in the area adjacent to the gang's official territory. The police, irritated by the crimes, decided to pick up the two "influential" leaders of the Snow Tigers (Boots and Dirt) on suspicion of burglary charges. After being released, Boots and Dirt ordered Stoney and Doke picked up. The robberies had been undertaken by Stoney and Doke as individual projects to raise money, not as part of the gang's official operations, and Boots and Dirt were furious that Stoney and Doke's personal business had affected the gang. They claimed that Stoney and Doke should not have committed so many robberies, that their greed had caused the police to harass the organization. After Stoney and Doke were picked up, they were beaten severely (at the direction of Boots and Dirt), suffering numerous lacerations on their backs, ribs, and legs. As opposed to gangs utilizing the other two models of leadership, the gangs with an influential structure made no effort to offer due process. "Influential" leaders did not have external group pressure to establish due process. They believed, and their rank and file reinforced it, that the leaders spoke for the whole group because they embodied the spirit of the group. Since such leaders possessed attributes that all the members both identified with and strived for, the rank and file established a strong bond with them and generally supported their decisions. Thus, in the case of Stoney and Doke, many members did not know why they had been beaten, but they felt that Boots and Dirt must have had a good reason for ordering it done. The comments of Frame and Tape are typical of those heard from other members. Frame, who was nineteen years old and had been a member of the gang for one year, said:

> Stoney and Doke must have had it coming. They had to, because Boots and Dirt wouldn't have dealt with them that way. They [Boots and Dirt] just don't beat people up for no reason at all.

Tape, who was seventeen years old and had been a member of the gang for three years, observed:

I've known Boots and Dirt for three years and they wouldn't
bump people up [beat people up] for no reason at all. . . . They
must have their reasons, and whatever they are, it was to make
things good for the gang.

Leadership Change and the Problem
of Succession

For those interested in the question of whether or not gangs are democratic, there is no issue more central than leadership change (or the problem of succession). In the case of gangs that utilize a vertical/hierarchical
leadership model, leadership change sometimes was regulated by codes
(quasi-constitutions) that directed the process by which succession would
occur. Some gangs were quite formal in this regard and wrote down when
there should be change and how it should be done. In other gangs, the
procedures for leadership change took a cultural form—that is, members
honored the traditional way in which leadership change has been handled, despite the fact that there was no written document spelling out
how it should occur. In the gangs with agreed-upon procedures, one
observes a relatively smooth transfer of power, and they thus rarely experience a long disruption in operations.

Having a procedural code for leadership succession can be enormously
helpful, but only if leaders and would-be leaders abide by it. As one might
expect, incumbents are always tempted to disregard these rather crude
formal procedures and retain power. Only three of the gangs studied
(among those that operated with a vertical/hierarchical or a horizontal/
commission model) had the experience of having the incumbent leadership refuse to relinquish power, and all those gangs completely disinte-
grated a short time later.

All of the other gangs had a relatively smooth power transition, for
two reasons. First, the leadership understood that just because they had
been removed from office did not mean that they might not be voted back
into office at a later time. In fact, eight former leaders who were voted
out of office returned to lead again. Second, and most important, those
who thought about not abiding by the rules realized that failure to do so
would result in the organization itself dissolving, because almost everyone in the gang distrusted everyone else and such an action would have
fueled those feelings.

Succession for the gangs that operated under the "influential" model
was slightly different from that in the vertical and horizontal models. Of

course, this might be expected, since leaders were not elected. However, although leaders were not elected, both the leaders and the rank and file understood that the leaders held power as a consequence of the rank and file's consent. Thus, when issues related to succession emerged, the rank and file were integrally involved. The issue of succession would emerge when one of the present group of influentials left the group (because he wanted to, imprisonment, death, etc.), or when one or more influentials had been ineffective in providing for the well-being of the membership. In such situations, either the rank and file would suggest a new person, or a new person would, through his actions, emerge as an influential. If the incumbent influentials fought the newly emerging ones, the gang would lapse into a period of infighting. If these internal tensions could not be mediated by all the influentials involved, the gang would die out.

Some Summary Remarks

It seems appropriate to begin by entering the debate among sociologists as to whether gangs have strong, cohesive organizational structures or ones that are weak, loose, and constantly changing.[49] What this chapter posits is that the gang is able to take a disparate group of individuals who possess defiant individualist dispositions and incorporate them into a functional organization. Gangs do this through a variety of interactions that occur within particular forms of leadership structures. As has been demonstrated, members who join (or remain) in a gang behave differently depending on the type of leadership structure in operation ("vertical/hierarchical," "horizontal/commission," or "influential") and the role expectations associated with that particular authority structure.

One might ask, are there gangs that have no structure at all? The answer is that those gangs with very limited structures are in a state of withering away. Without some type of formal structure that recognizes the legitimacy of leaders and gives them a mandate to lead, gangs find it impossible to function effectively. Therefore, if gangs fail to build and maintain a cohesive structure, they simply dissolve as organizations. The idea that gangs generally are loose associations, with little in the way of a cohesive leadership structure, is simply not accurate.[50] Those groups that do have loose associations are not a gang as I have defined it—they are simply loose associations that could be groups in a pre-gang state. More important, groups that have loose organizations will not be able to operate efficiently or for any long period of time.

Evidence presented in this chapter describes some correspondences between ethnicity and the types of organization gangs adopt. For instance, Chicano and Irish gangs employ the "influential" and "horizontal/commission" types of leadership structures more than the "vertical/hierarchical" form. There are Chicano and Irish gangs that do use the "vertical/hierarchical" structure, but the "influential" and "horizontal/commission" forms are adopted more often because they fit better into the cultural environment of many Chicano and Irish neighborhoods.

Most important of all, any conclusions drawn about the nature of gang organizations cannot overlook the interplay that exists between the defiant individual and the organization. No matter what organizational model a gang chooses, it must attempt to mediate the interests of the organization with that of the individual. The relationship between the defiant individual and the organization is an uneasy one. Gang organizations (both leaders and rank and file) are always cognizant of not offending the defiant individual's sense of autonomy. If a gang is unable to meet the individual's material and social expectations and/or encroaches on the individual's sense of autonomy, then the individual gang member's response is either to start internal divisions or quit. The organization can tolerate neither choice on a large scale.

The question of democracy in a gang is important in that it provides information concerning some of the internal dynamics of the various gang organizations and highlights how gangs with different leadership structures have dealt with the question of participation. Adoption of a particular structure or a change from one structure to another is an effort to integrate the interests of the individual with those of the organization. Failure to create a balance will lead to a disequilibrium, and the gang will decline. Since democracy is used as a balancing instrument to strengthen gangs, it is ironic that the more democratic gangs (horizontal/commission form) also tend to be the least effective. This would suggest that there may be a limit to how democratic an organization like a gang can be without hindering the effectiveness of its operations.

The strongest organizational structure for achieving a gang's goals was the vertical/hierarchical, followed by the influential, followed by the horizontal/commission. It must be understood that gangs can, and do, move around on this continuum depending on a number of contingent factors discussed in this chapter. It is therefore possible, if one spends enough time, to observe one gang operating under each of these structures at different periods in its history.

Chapter Four

Gang Business: Making Ends Meet

Cunning and deceit will serve a man better than force to rise from a base condition to great fortune.
Niccolò Machiavelli, *The Discourses* (1517?)

As we have seen, gangs must meet many of the needs and desires of their members. Thus gangs, like other organizations, undertake a number of economic activities. These, like other gang activities, can only be understood within the context of the interrelationship between the needs, goals, and opportunities of the defiant individualist, those of the organization, and those of the community in which a gang operates.

The Individual and Entrepreneurship in Gangs

If there is one theme that dominates most studies of gangs, it is that gangs are collectives of individuals who are social parasites, and that they are parasitic not only because they lack the skills to be productive members of society but, more important, because they lack the values, particularly the work ethic, that would guide them to be productive members of society.[1] However, one of the most striking factors I observed was how much the entrepreneurial spirit, which most Americans believe is the core of their productive culture, was a driving force in the worldview and behavior of gang members.[2] If entrepreneurial spirit denotes the desire to organize and manage business interests toward some end that results in the accumulation of capital, broadly defined, nearly all the gang members that I studied possessed, in varying degrees, five attributes that are either entrepreneurial in character or that reinforce entrepreneurial behavior.

The first of these entrepreneurial attitudes is competitiveness. Most gang members I spoke with expressed a strong sense of self-competence and a drive to compete with others. They believed in themselves as capable of achieving some level of economic success and saw competition as part of human nature and an opportunity to prove one's self-worth. This belief in oneself often took on a dogmatic character, especially for those individuals who had lost in some form of economic competition. The losers always had ready excuses that placed the blame on something other than their own personal inadequacy, thereby artificially reinforcing their feelings of competence in the face of defeat.[3]

Gang members' sense of competitiveness also reflected their general worldview that life operates under Social Darwinist principles. In the economic realm, they believed there is no ethical code that regulates business ventures, and this attitude exempted them from moral constraints on individual economic-oriented action.[4] The views of Danny, Arrow, and Lobo provide three good examples of this Social Darwinist outlook. Danny was a twenty-year-old Irish gang member from Boston:

> I don't worry about whether something is fair or not when I'm making a business deal. There is nothing fair or unfair, you just go about your business of trying to make a buck, and if someone feels you took advantage of him, he has only himself to blame. If someone took advantage of me, I wouldn't sit around bellyaching about it, I'd just go and try to get some of my money back. One just has to ask around here [the neighborhood] and you'd find that nobody expects that every time you're going to make a business deal, that it will be fair—you know, that the other guy is not going to be fair, hell, he is trying to make money, not trying to be fair. This is the way those big business assholes operate too! The whole thing [the system] operates this way.

Arrow was an eighteen-year-old African-American gang member from New York:

> Hey, man, what do you mean by ethics? Ethics don't pay bills, money pays bills, and I'm hustling to get money. There ain't nobody interested in ethics, morality, and all that shit—the basic line is, did you make money or not? Fuck those guys who lose and then complain, everybody knows that if they won and I or somebody else lost they wouldn't be saying nothing. Hey, it's dog eat

dog, and if you ain't up to it, you get eaten, simple as that! And look at the corporate businesses, they ain't moral or ethical, they never have been and they ain't about to be either, 'cause they only know that they want money. Since nobody complains about them, nobody will complain about us.

Lobo was a twenty-year-old Chicano gang member from Los Angeles:

I act like they do in the big time, no different. There ain't no corporation that acts with morals and that ethics shit and I ain't about to either. As they say, if it's good for General Motors, it's good enough for me. . . . It boils down to who is smarter, you either take somebody or get taken, and General Motors, General Dynamics, all those big cats know that shit. They take the government's money—that's really mine and yours—for some type of ride. Check this man, they sell a two cent bolt to the government for thirty dollars and don't blink an eye. They get caught, but they ain't sorry, they're just sorry they got caught. Who talks ethics and morality to them? They keep doing it because that's the rules, so when I do my business, I just do it and if somebody gets hurt, then they get hurt 'cause that's just the way it is.

The second entrepreneurial attribute I observed is the desire and drive to accumulate money and material possessions. Karl Marx, of course, described this desire as the "profit motive" and attributed it primarily to the bourgeoisie.[5] There is a profit-motive element to the entrepreneurial values of gang members, but it differs significantly from Marx's analysis of the desire to accumulate material and capital for their own sake, largely divorced from the desire to improve one's own material condition. Nor is gang members' ambition to accumulate material possessions related to a need for achievement, which the psychologist David McClelland identifies as more central to entrepreneurial behavior in certain individuals than the profit motive per se.[6] Rather, the entrepreneurial activity of gang members is predicated on their more basic understanding of what money can buy.[7] The ambition to accumulate capital and material possessions is related, in its initial stages (which can last for a considerable number of years), to the desire to improve the comfort of everyday living and the quality of leisure time.

This desire, of course, is shared by most people who live in low-income neighborhoods. Some of them resign themselves to the belief that they will never be able to secure their desires. Others attempt to improve their life situation by using various "incremental approaches," such as working in those jobs that are made available to them and saving their money, or attempting to learn higher-level occupational skills. In contrast, the entrepreneurs of low-income neighborhoods, especially those in gangs, attempt to improve their lives by becoming involved in a business venture, or a series of ventures, that has the potential to create large changes in their own or their family's socioeconomic condition.

The third attribute of entrepreneurial behavior prevalent in gangs is status-seeking. Mirroring the dominant values of the larger society, most gang members attempt to achieve some form of status with the acquisition of possessions. However, most of them cannot attain a high degree of status by accumulation alone. To merit high status among peers and in the community, gang members must try, although most will be unsuccessful, to accumulate a large number of possessions and be willing to share them. Once gang members have accumulated sufficient material possessions to provide themselves with a relative level of comfort or leisure above the minimal, they begin to seek the increase in status that generosity affords. (For philanthropic purposes, accumulating cash is preferable to accumulating possessions, because the more money one has, the more flexibility one has in giving away possessions.)

The fourth entrepreneurial attribute one finds among gang members is the ability to plan. Gang members spend an impressive amount of time planning activities that will bring them fortune and fame, or, at least, plenty of spending money in the short term. At their grandest, these plans have the character of dreams, but as the accounts of renowned business tycoons show, having big dreams has always been a hallmark of entrepreneurial endeavors.[8] At the other end of the spectrum are short-range plans (also called small scams) that members try to pull on one another, usually to secure a loan. One member will say, "Can I borrow a few bucks until I get paid?" What he is really saying, however, is, "Can I have so-and-so-many dollars, or any amount to that figure, and if you need some money later yourself, and if I have some, I might give it to you." Once a member has been scammed by another in this way, future requests for "loans" usually elicit some type of respectful refusal.[9] Another common small scam begins with one gang member collecting money from several others for the purpose of obtaining drugs, usually cocaine. Later he returns and claims that he gave the money to the drug dealer, who then ran off with it. Everyone suspects that the gang member used all the dope himself or pocketed the money, and they usually greet the tale with a great deal of hostility, but punishment is seldom administered. The vast majority of small scams within the gang (among members) are tolerated because all the members recognize that they are all continually running scams, and scams, therefore, are considered within the realm of acceptable behavior. But nine of the gangs I studied (14 percent) viewed running a scam on another member to be unacceptable, because it destroyed a sense of group commitment, and severe punishment was administered to those found guilty of being involved in the scam.

Gang members also engage in intermediary and long-range planning. A typical intermediary plan might concern modest efforts to steal some type of merchandise from warehouses, homes, or businesses. Because most of the sites they select are equipped with security systems, a more elaborate plan involving more time is needed than is the case for those internal gang scams just described. Long-range planning and organization, sometimes quite elaborate, are, as other studies have reported, at times executed with remarkable precision.[10]

Finally, the fifth entrepreneurial attribute common among gang members is the ability to undertake risks. Generally, young gang members (nine to fifteen years of age) do not understand risk as part of a risk-reward calculus, and for this age group, risk-taking is nearly always pursued for itself, as an element of what Thrasher calls the "sport motive,"[11] the desire to test oneself. As gang members get older, they gradually develop a more sophisticated understanding of risk-taking, realizing that a certain amount of risk is necessary to secure desired goals. Now they attempt to calculate the risk factors involved for nearly every venture, measuring the risk to their physical well-being, money, and freedom. Just like mainstream businessmen, they discover that risk tends to increase proportionally to the level of innovation undertaken to secure a particular financial objective. Most of these older gang members are willing to assume risks commensurate with the subjective "value" of their designated target, but they will not assume risks just for the sake of risk-taking.

The Source of Entrepreneurial Attitudes

Gang members' entrepreneurial attitudes and behavior can be traced to four distinct sources. First, there are those psychological traits associated with the defiant individualist character into which nearly all gang members have been socialized. Two aspects of defiant individualism that directly relate to entrepreneurial attitudes are: (1) the lack of trust that

gang members have of people in general, and (2) the more general acceptance of the Social Darwinist position that only the fit survive. Their lack
of trust in people leads them to become self-reliant and confident that
they can and must do things for themselves. An example is Circus, a
seventeen-year-old African-American gang member from New York:

> Dig, I don't know if you can trust people, but there ain't no way
> that you should trust them. I mean I trust myself, I defend and
> depend on myself, then I got nobody but myself to hold me back
> or fuck me up . . . what's more, I can do things better on my own
> than with other dudes who ain't as talented as me. You dig?

The belief that only the fit survive, in turn, lays the foundation for the
proposition that one should exploit those opportunities that are present
themselves, even if in doing so one hurts other people. The ethic of survival at any cost is somewhat tempered by feelings of attachment (in a
number of cases) to family, community or neighborhood, and some other
gang members. Nonetheless, despite some exceptions, gang members
generally consider most people as competitors. Take Sweet Cakes, a fifteen-year-old African-American gang member in New York:

> Look, everybody gets certain chances in life and you got to take
> advantage of them. Those who get ahead are just more better than
> those that don't. If you mess somebody up by taking advantage of
> your opportunities, that's just the way it is. You can't worry about
> it because you were the best this time and you know that if you
> don't stay competitive, you're done forever . . . no, I wouldn't
> mess with my community that way, but the rest of the folks is all
> fair game.

A second source of entrepreneurial attitudes arises from the tensions
between mainstream American consumer culture and the scarcity of resources in low-income neighborhoods. In all social classes, we have seen
in the postwar period a gradual but consistent increase in the degree to
which young Americans believe money to be a necessary tool for social
interaction. After decades of being courted by American businesses, which
correctly saw the potential for vast profits in the youth market, children,
teenagers, and young adults have come to accept the premise that having
cash is necessary to purchase the goods and services that make life worth
living. Activities that do not require cash, the consumerist message reads,
are not satisfying. As a result, kids of all ages, especially teenagers, feel
the need to have at least some pocket money available at all times.[12] This

need becomes a sense of urgency for those kids from low-income areas where there is a scarcity of financial resources. The reality for these kids is the need to struggle for the resources that are available and this acts to stimulate creativity. Without creativity, a youth from a low-income or working-class neighborhood would not be able to secure the money that American culture has established as a high priority. It is this need to be creative in order to secure money that has been one of the underlying elements in building the "entrepreneurial spirit" among gang members. The comments of Mano, a fifteen-year-old Puerto Rican gang member in New York, are representative:

> Let me put it like this. There ain't a lot you can do without some green stuff [money] so if you want to have some good times, you got to get it . . . hell, yes, it's tough out there, that's why you got to be creative in how you go about raising your cash. Those who ain't creative will be paupers, man! Can you digest that? I sure couldn't.

Another credo of American business culture has also stimulated gang members to think like entrepreneurs: the belief that one can improve oneself with one good idea. In talking to gang members, I repeatedly heard the refrain that all one needs is one good idea, and that what separates successful people from failures is that the former are able to cultivate the necessary contacts to operationalize their big idea. In their search for the big idea that will produce the desired wealth, gang members often generate what in effect are a number of small ideas that take on the character of "conning." Understood in this context, "conning behavior," which has often been misunderstood as the effort of weak-minded and/or parasitic hucksters, is an idiosyncratic variant of the general entrepreneurial spirit. Stake, a twenty-year-old African-American man in a New York gang:

> Yeah, man, what you need in life, no matter who you are, is one, not two, not three, but one good idea that you can get working. You do that and you got yourself some easy life, dig it, man . . . well, yeah, sometimes you be running some deal down on a dude, but sometimes you get ideas that you got to try out to see how good they are. You know like some experiments that people do. And dig, some experiments they be a job on people [take advantage of people], but that's just the way it is. Hell, medical experiments are just researchers doing a job on some poor sucker, and

then they tell him it made a difference to society. What do you call that, science, or a con? It's all the same. It's just some people don't want to see it; or they too stupid to see it.

Finally, gang members' entrepreneurial spirit is both stimulated and reinforced by the desire to resist what they perceive to be their parents' resignation to poverty and failure. As small boys, many gang members were keenly disappointed that their parents had not been successful at becoming self-made people who lifted the family out of poverty. Instead, what they observed was their parents' hopeless inability to do anything that would improve the family's material conditions. What stuck in their minds most vividly was their parents' vulnerability: their objective vulnerability in selling their labor on the market and their feelings of being vulnerable. Here are two representative comments.

Dark, an eighteen-year-old member of an Irish gang:

> A few years ago I would be pissed at my old man 'cause he didn't do things like save his money and move from the projects. He just seemed to be unwilling to have a desire to improve himself so that my mother and us kids were better, you know? . . . Later I could see that he didn't have much of a chance, given that he was just a worker. I resented that, not him, but the situation. But you know, after I talked to him, I was more pissed at the way he felt than anything else. He felt like he had no control over the situation; and I said to myself, I'll do everything I can not to let the fuckers make me feel like that. And I hustle all the time trying to develop projects to get money.

Face-Man, a sixteen-year-old Puerto Rican gang member:

> No, my pop didn't have a chance to make it, 'cause if you're a laborer you don't have any power on the job market. What can he offer that's different than seventy thousand other laborers? Get my point? So he couldn't get out of this hole that we live in or help the rest of us too much. . . . He always was feeling nervous about keeping work or getting it. You could always see him worrying about it. This was a lesson to me, and I said I ain't going to lay down and feel vulnerable to these motherfuckers! So I work hard on my various deals.

Winners and Losers in Entrepreneurial Activity

Most members of gangs, then, have a fairly strong entrepreneurial spirit and engage in a variety of economic activities. Of all the entrepreneurial traits discussed, the one most crucial to an individual gang member's economic success or failure is his pattern of risk-taking. The prevailing view among the public is that nearly all gang activity involves a high degree of risk, but in truth gang members are like other economic actors, making choices among low-risk, moderate-risk, and high-risk ventures. Risk can be defined as the level of jeopardy in the potential loss of material assets, personal freedom, or physical well-being. While the economic environment in which gang members act is a dangerous one, some activities are far more or less risky than others. My observations indicate that gang members who were not successful economically were those whose risk-taking profile fell at either extreme of the spectrum. To be sure, some low and high risk-takers had some successes, but their cumulative efforts were unsuccessful. A good example is the story of Jumbo, an eighteen-year-old member of an ethnically mixed New York gang. Jumbo was always trying to come up with and sell his ideas for making a fortune. He would constantly propose new ideas that had the potential to deliver great profits to himself, those that would help him, and the entire gang, if he could persuade the leadership to commit resources and manpower. During the five years that I studied Jumbo and his particular gang, he had been able to secure gang participation only three times: twice during the first year of his involvement and once only recently for a rather small project. Of Jumbo's numerous entrepreneurial projects involving non-gang members, only a small fraction were successful.

Although each of Jumbo's successful efforts had yielded him several thousand dollars, most had involved high risks. Many of the participants were caught by law enforcement authorities, physically injured, or both. On six occasions, Jumbo had been arrested by the police; he had gone to jail twice. He had also been shot three times and beaten severely four times. Take one episode as an example. Jumbo had decided that a great deal of money could be made distributing cocaine. He was able to get the gang's support in the initial stage, which was to carry on some form of negotiation with the branch of the Mafia in charge of wholesale drug supplies for his area. He made contact, and the Mafia was in principle interested in his offer to have the gang act as the local dispensing agent. In listening to Jumbo's sales pitch, I was struck by how organized and professional it was, but I was also struck by the risks that he took in negotiating with the Mafia, which clearly had more bargaining power. Once the agreement in principle had been made, Jumbo raised the ante by asking for a commission that was so high that everybody (both the syndicate's men and his own) laughed, though members of his own gang did so in a somewhat uneasy manner. Once it became clear that he was serious, the syndicate made a counterproposal that cut his opening figure by seven-eights. Jumbo balked at the figure and said he would not make the deal.

After the meeting, he told the leadership of the gang, who were quite angry with him, that he wanted to skip the Mafia as a source and open a drug mill (drug factory) himself. The gang leaders admitted that his idea had the potential to earn big profits, but they were not interested because too many risks were involved. At this juncture, Jumbo said he would do it on his own. In the following weeks, he was able solicit eighteen people to help him, only three of whom were from the gang. They started to make "treated marijuana" (marijuana spiked with other drugs) and some synthetic LSD. The operation lasted about three weeks, until three of the workers were shot at (no one was actually hit) and the place of business was fire-bombed. Jumbo and another participant escaped with second-degree burns. The money and time that Jumbo had invested in this project were considerable and the potential return was great, but the risks proved too high and the project ended in failure. Yet although his losses repeatedly outran his gains by an overwhelming margin, Jumbo persisted in undertaking high-risk projects, judging the prospects of high returns worth the dangers. However, for Jumbo, as well as others, such ventures generally end in bodily injury and/or loss of time and money.

At the other end of the risk-taking spectrum is Toga, a twenty-year-old member of an Irish gang. On one occasion, he had the idea that he could make good money by stealing car radios and selling them. He found a person who would buy the radios from him and then proceeded to look for radios he could steal. After one week, he had become proficient enough to have stolen ten radios. As he became more efficient, he was making several hundred dollars a month from this project. Because the word had spread that he had been relatively successful, he was able to persuade a number of people that a larger operation would be extremely profitable, and they agreed to join him. Before the new group was to start, however, Toga said that they needed to get some equipment that would help them break into cars that had sophisiticated alarm systems. All of the new members of the group agreed to invest in the new equipment, which cost several hundred dollars. Having secured this new equipment, the larger group went to work, and within a month they had accumulated more than one hundred radios. The man Toga had been selling the radios to now declined to buy them, saying that the operation had gotten too big, and that he would not be able to move that many radios fast enough. Toga then asked if he knew of anyone who would buy in quantity, and the buyer agreed to check around and get back to him. Toga described this conversation to his group, telling them not to worry, that they would start making money as soon as he and the new buyer were able to make a deal.

By now the place where the group was storing the radios was so crowded that they had to rent a small space in an adjoining building. This required still more capital. Toga received a message from his first buyer that he had found a new buyer who could handle the volume. But when Toga was told that the new buyer was part of the syndicate, he became uneasy. He could not decide whether to go ahead and meet with this new buyer or try to find another one. He told his group that working with the syndicate would present some risks to all of them and their operations. Maybe they were being set up by the syndicate, he said, and maybe the syndicate would take all their radios or expect them from now on to work for it. While Toga was tying to decide what to do, the number of radios was rapidly increasing—there were now over eight hundred in storage. Toga finally made a date to meet the syndicate's representative, but then decided not to go, believing, as he told me, that there were too many risks. So he contacted his old buyer and asked him whether he knew of someone else. His old buyer told him that he had blown it: there was no one else who could deal in such volume.

Needless to say, the other members of Toga's group were frustrated and angry. They had endured personal risks and invested money and time, and all they had to show for it was several rooms filled with stolen radios they could not peddle. Toga's reluctance to take a chance resulted in the failure of the enterprise, and he was given a generous amount of time to return some of their money to his confederates. Though Toga generated more ideas, he found it difficult to get other gang members to participate, and the gang as an organization would not do so. Over the eight years that I observed Toga, he continued to exercise a caution that consistently resulted in missed opportunities and failures.

In contrast, the successful gang entrepreneur tends to assume a moderate risk profile. He is likely to pursue a strategy where risk is present, but has been reduced to a moderate level through careful planning: selection of the type of activity, location, strategy for executing the task, protection from being apprehended. Like a mainstream businessman, the successful gang entrepreneur calculates the risk factors, the probability of the venture failing, and the odds of misfortune of various sorts. A good example of this type of gang entrepreneur is Grisly, a nineteen-year-old gang member from New York.

Grisly decided that he would steal stereos and televisions from apartments and then resell them. Before he began this venture, he made contact with two people who bought stolen objects and he entered into an agreement to sell to both of them. As he said to me: "The smart thing to do is find more than one buyer, in case one of them is picked up by the police, or if one of them can't buy what you have 'cause they just don't have the money or they can't move them. If you do that, you keep moving your stuff." Then he talked to a number of people in the gang to see if they were interested. He offered them a percentage of the amount obtained from the buyer. He then had each of them look at buildings that might have easy access. They also checked out what kinds of locks the apartments had and avoided all those with police locks. They discussed various techniques for ascertaining if people were home before they burglarized a place. They also worked out a warning system to minimize the risk of being caught. Eventually, Grisly decided not to become involved in the burglaries himself, but to buy the stolen objects from those who did and then sell them to his contacts. After accumulating a significant amount of money from this, he moved on to more extensive projects. Because Grisly was well organized and attentive to details, his plans were successful, and most of the gang members wanted to be involved in his projects. In Grisly, then, we see the successful gang entrepreneur who selects enterprises that require some risk but takes steps to ensure that he does not lose everything if the business fails. Because he also works to minimize the risks for his associates, he has little difficulty in recruiting accomplices.

What Does Entrepreneurship Mean for the Gang?

The fact that most gang members have entrepreneurial attitudes and, to varying degrees, act on them, presents the gang with an interesting situation. On the one hand, this entrepreneurial spirit is a valuable resource for strengthening the organization's treasury. On the other hand, leaders in most gangs recognize that entrepreneurial attitudes and actions pose a potential source of dissension within the ranks. To minimize the chances of gang members working for themselves or competing with other members, leaders have developed two strategies to control entrepreneurial behavior and direct it toward the organization's common good. One approach is to have gang members commit themselves to projects developed in some type of official capacity by the collective membership of the gang, or a subset of the leadership, in order to promote the economic well-being of the organization. Members are persuaded to devote a portion of their time, energy, and expertise to those economic ventures that will build the gang's treasury. The other strategy is to encourage members' individual entrepreneurial activities and then require members to donate a portion of their earnings to the treasury. While gangs would like members to see this donation as similar to religious tithings, given out of organizational loyalty, members nearly always consider it a form of income tax.

Organizational Economic Activity: Investing

Although gangs include a large number of individuals who are oriented toward being economically active, if a gang hopes to remain a vital organization, some type of collective effort is needed. Thus, like other organizations, gangs are constantly discussing how to make money. These discussions involve decisions concerning the investment of time, money, and resources.

Investment begins for gangs when the leaders ask members to invest some time in the pursuit of collective economic rewards. While this may seem like a reasonable request, it must be made with prudence because most members have a number of economic projects they are either planning or involved in, and they are reluctant to invest time in an effort that will not provide as large a return as many other self-managed ventures would. Therefore, the leadership must provide material and social incentives for participation. The material incentives vary by gang. New York gangs (excluding those that are Irish) tend to offer both a percentage of the money obtained from the sale of goods and some portion of the goods themselves. These incentives are not used all the time, but only when certain members whose expertise is essential to the enterprise are reluctant to join because of other business ventures. In addition, as an incentive for those members who are not essential in themselves, but are needed for the venture to be successful, it is common for the leadership to propose that the organization purchase some items (such as video games or slot machines) to be used by the whole collective.

The leadership of the gang also encourages members to invest their time in collective economic projects by nurturing the social pressures to participate. Here, the leadership reinforces the ideology of group commitment, that every member must give of himself to the brothers of his gang. Those who give are honorable and should be admired and respected by the entire membership, while those who do not are an abomination and should be penalized.[13] This strategy on the part of leadership (and often the rank and file as well) was utilized by all the gangs in my study, regardless of their ethnicity. Here are two examples:

Joker was a nineteen-year-old member of a Irish gang in Boston:

> You see, there have been times that I really honestly did not want to do what the guys [gang] were about to do. You see, a couple of times I had some things going myself—some personal business dealings, you understand?—and did not want to commit the time to the ones the guys [gang] was into. But you know that if you don't help out in these things, you ain't worth a fuck with the rest of the members and they look at you like you are some kind of turd; and they shun you. That would be hard to take, man! So you do your part to help out.

Tokyo was an eighteen-year-old Dominican gang member in New York:

> Sure, there are plenty of times that I don't want to do what the gang has decided to do to get money. Sometimes I don't want to do it because I have something going myself and sometimes I don't want to because it seems too risky for me, but I always do it because you got to do your part for the organization. You see, people respect commitment to the organization, and they tell you they appreciate it . . . if I didn't do it, the others would say he doesn't have character and kind of exclude me from things.

There were two areas in which gang members were asked by their organizations to invest their time—the planning stage and the implementation stage. Most members are not given the opportunity to be involved in the planning stage. If they are, they do not participate in all aspects of the planning process. Those chosen to be part of the whole planning process are usually individuals whom the leadership considers to have expertise in whatever specific activity the gang is contemplating. On the other hand, those asked to be part of only a segment of the planning are those the leadership considers to have little expertise, but who are necessary in order to execute the plan. Interestingly, being asked to participate in the planning process often carries with it elements of prestige. Frequently, one will hear in street talk that so-and-so was in on the planning of a certain operation. To the nonleadership member, especially the young and ambitious, there is the mystique that those who are chosen to be part of the planning will be given a larger share of the spoils. This is not always the case, but rarely is this divulged to the larger membership (unless there is discontent that certain members are getting more than others) because the mystique is useful in creating prestige as a means of persuading individuals to invest their time in business ventures that benefit the entire organization.

It is at the business planning stage that we see a significant difference between the gangs of different cities and ethnic groups. Nearly all the gangs in New York (except the Irish gangs) devote considerable effort to organizational planning and investment, and they find they must do so because their legitimacy is based on their ability to provide entertainment for their members. The Chicano gangs of Los Angeles and Irish gangs in both New York and Boston tend to plan a great deal less, and they have much less in their collective treasuries than the non-Irish gangs of New York. For these Chicano and Irish gangs, viability as an organization is not totally dependent on generating large sums of money for collective use, and the result is that their business activities are on a smaller scale. Chicano gangs will continue to exist regardless of whether they have large treasuries, because most have been around for generations and a significant amount of their legitimacy as organizations derives from the fact that they represent a cultural tradition within the community. Likewise, the Irish gangs, which act as feeder groups for the adult Irish social clubs, represent a part of the cultural traditions of their community.[14]

Once a plan is set, gangs ask members to invest time in the execution phases. Contrary to popular myths, gang members do not automatically volunteer their time for every action that the organization deems to be necessary. Individual gang members must often be convinced, and some have to be coaxed. Much of the time, members are wary of participating because they do not want to jeopardize their ongoing business dealings by spending time on a new project, or because they do not like the level of risk associated with the venture. In particular, risk of being arrested and incarcerated is an issue for the older gang members, though less so for many of the younger ones. Take the example of Black Jack, a twenty-one-year-old African-American gang member from New York. His gang had decided to participate in a scheme whereby they would offer protection to stores in an area not directly under the gang's control. In order to get the business off the ground, those involved would have to demonstrate that they had the necessary guns to protect prospective clients and the will to use them in establishing control over the new territory. Black Jack had served time in jail for possession of a firearm with intent to commit a crime, and he knew that if he got caught again, a conviction for a crime involving a firearm would bring a relatively long prison term. Also, he was already associated in a lucrative venture with a gambling club. So after calculating the personal costs and benefits, he opted to decline participation in the protection scheme. When he informed the leadership, he made sure to explain that he did not want to jeopardize his gambling gig, and he also offered to do other tasks for the collective as compensation. The gang granted him an exemption from the new project, understanding (as do most gangs) that the organization must balance its interests against those of the individual members or else the organization will dissolve.

Here again there are differences between Chicano gangs in Los Angeles and Irish and multi-ethnic gangs in New York. The Chicano gangs in Los Angeles are less likely to be dissuaded from a venture by the risk of incarceration, because part of their status is associated with being imprisoned. So many Chicano gang members have gone to jail that imprisonment has ceased to be something feared and become something expected. Nearly every Chicano gang member anticipates that he will be incarcerated at some point in his gang career, and incarceration has been elevated to a position of high status. A gang member who has not been arrested, convicted, and incarcerated has not been an active and honorable member. Under this value system, Chicano gang members simultaneously abhor incarceration and look forward to it, as Shade, a sixteen-year-old member of a Chicano gang, explains:

> Sure, I expect to get into trouble with the law. They [the police] and we just got different interests. I don't worry about going to the pen 'cause it's no big deal, and if you don't go, you know you haven't been doing something right [a wry smile]. It's like when you're a bullfighter, you expect to get gored, and if you don't you weren't taking enough risks to merit any honor. . . . There were a couple of dudes who didn't go up [go to prison] and nobody did anything with them until they showed some courage. They're both serving time, but finally now they're well thought of.

In addition to having individual members invest their time, gangs as organizations must also invest other resources, the most important of which is the gang's contacts with other individuals and organizations. These contacts take two forms: contacts that the gang as a whole has established and contacts that individual members have established. In all gangs, there is a concerted effort on everyone's part to build a group of contacts with people who will be in a position to help at some future time. This effort stems from a worldview among low-income and working-class people in general, and gang members in particular, that it is who you know, not what you know, that gets you what you want. When challenged on this belief, gang members almost always defend their views by citing examples of the dealings between big business (primarily the defense industry) and government. The statement of Caballo, a seventeen-year-old Puerto Rican gang member, is representative:

> Yes, you got to make contacts otherwise you won't get nowhere. Just take the government of the U.S. and you see that—it's who you know, not what you know, that makes the difference. . . . All you have to do is look at the companies who sell the government arms. They don't get those contracts because they got a good product or they have the lowest bid, they get it because they got some contact in the government or the military. In fact, those companies are able to up the price of the goods because they don't have to compete, they just got to call in their chips with their contacts. That's what we doing too, it's just we get a lot less money!

Gangs have a much easier time utilizing contacts that they, as organizations, have established with other individuals and organizations than those established by individual members. One reason is that the leadership knows that such contacts really exist and can be figured into their planning framework, whereas some members' contacts are imaginary, created for the sole purpose of image-building and personal status. As gang leaders say, "It is difficult to make plans with myths"; or "It is difficult to plan on solid ground when you're working with loose sand." Contacts established by the gang do not, however, always produce the most benefits. Three factors limit their value. First, the number of contacts that organizations have been able to assemble are often considerably fewer than those of the general membership as individuals. Second, because these contacts are often with either influential organizations or powerful individuals, each time they are used, it marks a rather large investment of the gang's organizational resources. Therefore, in order to conserve its resources, a gang usually tries to get individual members to call on their personal contacts first. If that can be done, the gang may be able to generate a return with a relatively small amount of organizational investment.[15] Third, because they usually entail some type of procedure to seek approval from either the rank and file or the associating organization, organizational contacts are clumsy and time-consuming. Since time is nearly always a concern for gangs in making business deals, there is a tendency to avoid using organizational contacts whenever possible.

For these reasons, most gangs encourage members wishing to participate in organizational business enterprises to call on their personal contacts. Some gang members refuse to use their contacts in organizational business ventures because they want to keep them for themselves. Knowing this, the leaders sometimes refrain even from asking these individuals, thereby avoiding rejection, divisions within the organization, and challenges to their leadership. But other members are enthusiastic about using their personal contacts in gang business. For these individuals, offering their contacts is a sign of status, a way to show the general membership how many influential people they know.

Gangs must also make decisions about capital investment. The amount of money accumulated and banked through their other business ventures varies among gangs. Some gangs are not very successful in generating a surplus, while others are successful but quickly consume most of the profits. The gangs most successful at accumulating both profits and relatively large bank accounts, I observed, are also those most cautious about investing that capital in other business endeavors. By contrast, those gangs unable to accumulate large sums were usually plagued by the desire to consume rather than save, which facilitated their eagerness to invest whatever capital the organization had.

Gangs also have nonmonetary capital resources at their disposal: firearms, gasoline, cars, machinery, and property. The gangs that have accumulated a relatively large cache of such assets tend to regulate the investment of these items more carefully. Both the leadership and the rank and file understand that these assets are limited in quantity and that their replacement costs deplete the treasury of the organization. The following example of a gang's cost-benefit investment analysis occurred in an ethnically mixed New York gang. At one of its meetings, it was reported that a particular bar owner had refused to pay for protection. The person in charge of the operation said that force would be required and that he needed the use of the gang's van and a number of automatic weapons from the gang's arsenal. There was much discussion about the commitment of the van and weapons to this endeavor because the bar was in an area into which the gang had just begun to expand, and the leadership was not certain that it would be able to incorporate the area and make it into a steady market. The gang finally decided not to commit the van: the risks of it being confiscated by the police or being damaged by return fire were too high. As Goo, one of the leaders, said at the meeting:

> We don't know if we can get this fuzz head [the owner of the bar] to give up the money, even if we can keep him and the area from the Drakes [a rival gang]. This is just too chancy to invest our new van in. It took too much to get it, to mess it up on something we ain't sure of.

Finally, the type of leadership structure a gang has exerts an important effect on investment decisions. The better the planning and the decisions regarding goals, priorities, and timetables, the more easily projects are operationalized. The leadership model least effective in planning is the horizontal/commission type, a structure that poses consistent problems associated with the lack of a single source of authority. In practice, gangs based on this model tend to prolong the debating stage in the planning process, which greatly slows efforts to move toward implementation.

The vertical/hierarchical leadership structure is only somewhat more effective in planning. Because these gangs are usually large, with a relatively large number of people who are involved in the planning process, one finds a great deal of time being expended in either convincing people about certain projects or in developing coalitions with other factions to get certain plans to the implementation stage. This has the tendency to slow everything down and compromise the effectiveness of potentially beneficial projects.

The influential leadership model has the least problems in the planning stage. Because power is so centralized, few people have to be convinced and there is little debate. The quality of the projects, however, is often compromised by the lack of greater input at this stage.

Economic Activity: Accumulating

With a few exceptions, nearly all the literature on gangs focuses on their economic delinquency.[16] This is a very misleading picture, however, for although gangs operate primarily in illegal markets, they also are involved in legal markets. Of the thirty-seven gangs observed in the present study, twenty-seven generated some percentage of their revenues through legitimate business activity. It is true that gangs do more of their business activity in the illegal markets, but none of them wants to be exclusively active in these markets.[17]

In the illegal market, gangs concentrate their economic activities primarily in goods, services, and recreation. In the area of goods, gangs have been heavily involved in accumulating and selling drugs, liquor, and various stolen products such as guns, auto parts, and assorted electronic equipment. These goods are sometimes bought and sold with the gang acting as the wholesaler and/or retailer. At other times, the gang actually produces the goods it sells. For example, while most gangs buy drugs or alcohol and retail them, a few gangs manufacture and market homemade drugs and moonshine liquor. Two gangs (one African-American and one Irish) in this study had purchased stills and sold their moonshine to people on the street, most of whom were derelicts, and to high school kids too young to buy liquor legally.[18] Three other gangs (two Puerto Rican and one Dominican) made a moonshine liquor from fermented fruit and sold it almost exclusively to teenagers. Both types of moonshine were very high in alcohol, always above one hundred proof. While sales of this liquor were not of the magnitude to create fortunes, these projects were quite surprisingly capable of generating substantial amounts of revenue.

The biggest money-maker and the one product nearly every gang tries to market is illegal drugs.[19] The position of the gang within the illegal drug market varies among gangs and between cities. In New York, the size of the gang and how long it has been in existence have a great deal to do with whether it will have access to drug suppliers. The older and larger gangs are able to buy drugs from suppliers and act as wholesalers to pushers. They shun acting as pushers (the lowest level of drug sales) themselves because there are greater risks and little, if any, commensurate increase in profit. In addition, because heroin use is forbidden within most gangs, the gang leaders prefer to establish attitudes oriented to the sale rather than the consumption of drugs within the organization. In the past, when the supply was controlled by the Italian Mafia, it was difficult for gangs to gain access to the quantity of drug supplies necessary to make a profit marketing them. In the past ten years, though, the Mafia has given way (in terms of drug supply) to African-American, Puerto Rican, and Mexican syndicates.[20] In addition, with the increased popularity of cocaine in New York, the African-American, Puerto Rican, and Dominican syndicates' connections to Latin American sources of cocaine supply rival, and in many cases surpass, those of Mafia figures.[21] With better access to supplies, gangs in New York have been able to establish a business attitude toward drugs and to capitalize on the opportunities that drugs now afford them.

Some gangs have developed alternative sources of supply. They do so in two ways. Some, particularly the Chicano gangs, have sought out pharmacies where an employee can be paid off to steal pills for the gang to sell on the street.[22] Other gangs, particularly in New York, but also some in Los Angeles, have established "drug mills" to produce synthetic drugs such as LSD (or more recently crack cocaine) for sale on the street. The more sophisiticated drug mills, which are controlled by various organized crime families, manufacture a whole line of drugs for sale, including cut heroin, but gangs are almost never involved in them. Those gangs that have established a production facility for generating drugs, no matter how crude it may be, generate sizeable sums of money. Whether a gang is able to establish a sophisticated production and distribution system for drug sales depends on the sophistication of the gang organization and the amount of capital available for start-up purposes.

Stolen guns are another popular and profitable product. Gangs sometimes steal guns and then redistribute them, but most often they buy them from wholesale gun peddlers and then resell them. Sometimes the gangs will buy up a small number of shotguns and then cut the barrel and stock down to about 13 to 15 inches in length and then sell them as "easily concealable." A prospective buyer can get whatever gun he wants if he is willing to pay the going price. In the present study, the Irish gangs have been, commercially speaking, the most involved with guns, often moving relatively large shipments, ranging from sawed-off shotguns to fully automatic rifles and pistols of the most sophisticated types.[23] It was reported that these guns were being moved, with the help of the Irish social clubs, to the Catholics of Northern Ireland for their struggle with the Protestants there. No matter what the destination, rather large sums of money were paid to the Irish gangs for their efforts in acquiring the weapons or in helping move them. Although all the gangs studied were involved in the sale of illegal guns, illegal gun sales constituted a larger proportion of the economic activities of Irish gangs than they did for the others.

Gangs in all three cities were also involved in the selling of car parts.

All the parts sold were stolen, some stolen to fill special orders from customers and others stolen and reworked in members' home garages into customized parts for resale. Business was briskest in Los Angeles, where there is a large market, especially among the low-rider clientele, for customized auto parts.[24] The amount of money made from stolen auto parts varies according to the area, whether or not the gang has an agent to whom to sell the parts, and the types of parts sold. On the whole, revenues from stolen auto parts are not nearly as high as those from selling illegal drugs, guns, or liquor, and so less time is devoted by gangs to this activity.

Gangs' business activities also include a number of services, the three most common being protection, demolition (usually arson), and indirect participation in prostitution. Protection is the most common service, both because there is a demand for it in the low-income areas in which gangs operate and because the gangs find it the easiest service to deliver, since it requires little in the way of resources or training. Gangs offer both personal and business protection. Nearly all the gangs had developed a fee schedule according to the type of protection desired. Most, but certainly not all, of the protection services offered by the gangs in this study involved extortion. Usually the gang would go into a store and ask the owner if he felt he needed protection from being robbed. Since it was clear what was being suggested, the owner usually said yes and asked how much it would cost him. When dealing with naive owners, those who did not speak English very well or did not know American ghetto customs, or with owners who flatly resisted their services, the gang would take time to educate or persuade them to retain its services. In the case of the immigrants (most of whom were Asian or Near Eastern), the gang members would begin by explaining the situation, but usually such owners did not understand, and so the gang would demonstrate its point by sending members into the store to steal. Another tactic was to pay a dope addict to go in and rob the store. After such an incident occurred, the gang would return and ask the owner if he now needed protection. If he refused, the tactics were repeated, and almost all the owners were finally convinced. However, for those owners who understood and resisted from the start, more aggressive tactics were used, such as destruction of their premises or harassment of patrons. More often than not, continued pressure brought the desired result. However, it should be noted that in the vast majority of cases, no coercion was needed, because store owners in high-crime areas were, more often than not, happy to receive protection.

As one owner said to me: "I would need to hire a protection company anyway, and frankly the gang provides much more protection than they could ever do."

Gangs also offer their services as enforcers to clients who need punishment administered to a third party. Small-time hustlers or loan sharks, for example, hired some gangs to administer physical coercion to borrowers delinquent in their repayments. More recently one gang offered and apparently was hired by a foreign government to undertake terrorist acts against the government and people of the United States.[25] Although that was an extreme case, nearly all gangs seek enforcement contracts because the fee is usually high, few resources have to be committed, and relatively little in the way of planning (compared to other projects) is needed.

The permanent elimination of or damage to property is another service gangs offer. This more often than not involves arson, and the buildings hit are commonly dilapidated. The gangs' clients are either landlords who want to torch the building to get the insurance money or residents who are so frustrated by the landlord's unwillingness to provide the most basic services that they ask the gang to retaliate. In both cases, there is usually much preliminary discussion of the project within the gang. These service jobs require a good deal of discussion and planning because there is the potential to hurt someone living in the building or to create enormous hardship if people have no alternative place to live, and the gang will do almost anything to avoid injuring people in its community. The gangs of New York have had the most business along these lines, particularly in the South Bronx, but arson is a service offered in Detroit, Chicago, and Philadelphia as well. As one gang leader from the Bronx said:

> You just don't bomb or torch any building that someone wants
> down. You got to find out who lives there, if they got another
> place to go, if they would be for takin' out the building and if
> they'd be OK with the folks [law enforcement authorities]. Then
> you got to get organized to get everybody out and sometimes that
> ain't many people and sometimes it is. If there is lots of people in
> the building, we'd just pass [refuse] on the job . . . now if we can
> work all these things out, we take the job and we deliver either a
> skeleton [outer walls are standing, but nothing else] or a crema-
> tion [just ashes].

Many potential clients know that a gang will refuse to burn down a building in its neighborhood if some type of harm will come to residents of its community, and so they contract with a gang from another area to do the job. Such incidents always ignite a war not only between the affected gangs but also between the communities. Take the example of the Hornets, a gang from one borough in New York that had contracted to set on fire a building in another borough. Although no one was killed in the fire, a few people were slightly burned, and of course everyone who lived in the building became homeless. At the request of a number of residents, the Vandals, a gang from the affected area, began to investigate and found out who had contracted to torch the building and which gang had been responsible. Then, at the request of an overwhelming majority of the community, the Vandals retaliated by burning down a building in the culprit gang's community. Hipper, a twenty-year-old member of the Vandals, said:

> We got to protect our community, they depend on us and they want us to do something so this [the burning of an apartment building in the neighborhood] don't happen again . . . we be torchin' one of their buildings. I hope this don't hurt anybody, but if we don't do this, they be back hurting the people in our community and we definitely don't be letting that happen!

This is an excellent example of the bond that exists between the community and the gang. There is the understanding, then, among the community that the gang is a resource that can be counted on, particularly in situations where some form of force is necessary. Likewise, the gang knows that its legitimacy and existence are tied to being integrated in and responsible to community needs.

Prostitution is one illegal service in which gangs do not, for the most part, become directly involved. Gangs will accept the job of protecting pimps and their women for a fee (fifteen, or 40 percent, of the gangs in this study had), and in this way they become indirectly associated with the prostitution business. Yet they generally avoid direct involvement because they feel protective of the females in their communities, and their organizations are wary of being accused by neighborhood residents of exposing female members of the community to the dangers associated with prostitution.

The last type of illegal economic activity in which all of the gangs in the present study were involved has to do with providing recreation. Some gangs establish numbers games in their neighborhoods. One New York gang had rented what had been a small Chinese food take-out place and was running numbers from the back where the kitchen had once been.

(When I first observed the place, I thought it was a Chinese take-out and even proposed we get some quick food from it, which met with much laughter from the members of the gang I was with.) This gang became so successful that it opened up two other numbers establishments. One had been a pizza place (and was made to look as though it still served pizza slices); the other was a small variety store, which still functioned in that capacity, but also housed the numbers game in the back rooms.

Setting up gambling rooms is another aspect of the recreation business. Eleven of the gangs (or 30 percent) rented small storefronts, bought tables and chairs, and ran poker and/or domino games. The gang would assume the role of the "house," receiving a commission for each game played. Some of the gangs bought slot machines and placed them in their gambling rooms. Five (or 14 percent) of the gangs had as many as fifteen machines available for use.

Finally, ten gangs (27 percent), primarily those wth Latino members, rented old buildings and converted them to accommodate cockfights. The gang would charge each cock owner a fee for entering his bird and an entrance fee for each patron. All of these ventures could, at various times, generate significant amounts of capital. The exact amount would depend on how often they were closed by the police and how well the gang managed the competition in its marketplace.

Turning to the legal economic activities undertaken by gangs, I observed that two ran "mom and pop" stores that sold groceries, candy, and soft drinks. Three gangs had taken over abandoned apartment buildings, renovated them, and rented them very cheaply—not simply because the accommodations were rather stark, but also because the gang wanted to help the less fortunate members of its community. The gangs also used these buildings to house members who had nowhere else to live. Undertaken and governed by social as much as economic concerns, these apartment ventures did not generate much income.

Interestingly, the finances of these legal activities were quite tenuous. The gangs that operated small grocery stores experienced periodic failures during which the stores had to be closed until enough money could be acquired (from other sources) to either pay the increased rent, rebuild shelf stock, or make necessary repairs. For those gangs who operated apartment buildings, in every case observed, the absence of a deed to the building or the land forced the gang to relinquish its holdings to either the city or a new landlord who wanted to build some new structure. Though there was a plentiful supply of abandoned buildings, most gangs lost interest in the renovation-and-rental business because such projects always created a crisis in their capital flow, which in turn precipitated internal bickering and conflict.

Other legal economic activities undertaken by the gangs I studied were automobile and motorcycle repair shops, car parts (quasi junk yards), fruit stands, and hair shops (both barber and styling). However, most of these ventures contributed only very modest revenues to the gangs' treasuries. Furthermore, the gang leadership had difficulty keeping most of the legal economic activities functioning because the rank and file were, by and large, not terribly enthusiastic about such activities. Rank-and-file resistance to most of these activities was of three sorts: members did not want to commmit regularly scheduled time to any specific ongoing operation; members felt that the legal activities involved considerable overhead costs that lowered the profit rate; and members calculated that the time required to realize a large profit was far too long when compared to illegal economic activity. Thus, when such projects were promoted by the gang leadership and undertaken by the rank and file, they were done under the rubric of community service aid projects. The comments of Pin, a nineteen-year-old African-American gang member from New York, are representative of this general position on legal economic activity:

> No, I don't go for those deals where we [the gang] run some kind of hotel out of an old building or run some repair shop or something like that. When you do that you can't make no money, or if you do make something it so small and takes so long to get it that it's just a waste of our [the gang's] money. But when the leadership brings it up as a possibility, well, sometimes I vote for it because I figure you got to help the community, many of them [people in the community] say they sort of depend on our help in one way or another, so I always say this is one way to help the community and me and the brothers go along with it. But everybody knows you can't make no money on shit like this.

Success and Failure in Economic Activity

Four factors greatly influence how successful gangs are in their organizational economic activities: control of competition, type of organizational structure, the stability of the division of labor, and avoidance of antagonizing the community. Regarding competition, gangs are no different from other economic organizations in their effort to control the marketplace. They desire what Weber calls closed relationships, in which monopoly is the goal.[26] Like other small businesses, gangs have a critical need to control economic competition if they are to conserve their scarce resources and succeed in a constricted market. Indeed, the attitudes among gang members to market competition are analogous to those of the small entrepreneurs depicted by C. Wright Mills: "Whenever there is consciousness of scarcity, of a limited, contracting world, then competition becomes a sin against one's fellows."[27] Thus one often hears gang members describing their economic competitors as if they were the lowest form of human life. To survive in highly competitive illegal markets, gang members adopt the view that their competitors (who are actually co-participants) are immoral individuals who must be eliminated for moral as well as economic reasons. This line of thinking serves several mutually reinforcing purposes. First, it controls the individual entrepreneurial urges inherent in most gang members and keeps them from preying on each other. In this way, those in the gang who might attempt to move in on another gang member's economic activities can expect to be labeled by other members as immoral individuals who must be dealt with harshly. Second, this line of thinking is used to rationalize losses to competitors in the market—competitors who beat us were unethical and therefore won unfairly—without implicating either one's own personal or collective self-esteem in the failure. Lastly, if a rival gang is attempting to take a portion of one's market, the targeted gang can be more easily mobilized for collective action against the economic threat if members believe their rivals to be unethical or immoral.

Given these attitudes, it is not surprising to see extreme force used by gangs to control their market and ward off competitors. Two examples are instructive. The first involves a numbers game that began operating in a New York neighborhood controlled by the Diamond Pack gang. The numbers business was started by two men who had been residents of the community, but who had moved to an adjoining neighborhood two years earlier. The rumor was that the business had been financed by a much larger numbers syndicate and that these two men received a percentage of the business as managers. After about two weeks of operation, the gang leaders paid a visit to the business, informed the two men that the gang had its own numbers game going, and told them that they should have asked permission from the gang before they started. The two men agreed, apologized, and said that the gang should not worry about competition because most of the people who came into their game wanted to make large wagers, not the low and moderate ones that the gang's game handled. The gang leaders expressed some doubts but said they would be willing to see how things went. While they were evaluating the situation, though, they wanted a specific amount of cash as a fee. The two men said that they could not make the decision themselves and would have to check with their people. Two weeks passed and no decision was forthcoming. The gang then decided that, regardless of the decision, its own game would inevitably be affected, and that the competing business had to go. Members used tubing to pump an inflammable liquid through the mailbox and torched the building. The business never returned and the gang was able to maintain modest, but steady, profits.

Another example involved two Latino gangs in Los Angeles. The T-Men had ninety-seven members, most between eighteen and thirty-one years of age. The RRs had a membership of about twenty-eight, most of them from thirteen to seventeen years of age. The territories of these gangs were separated by one street, but historically, the proximity of their "turf" had resulted in relatively few fights. However, during a recent summer, the T-Men had begun to sell cocaine and heroin from both sides of the street that had been considered the demarcation zone. The RRs were also dealing drugs, but their much smaller business was primarily in barbiturates (reds) and marijuana. The RRs attempted to counter the larger gang's intrusion into their area by reaching the streetcorner they wanted to sell from before members of the older gang or, if that was not possible, by continuing to sell right next to them. Finding it impossible to carry on business with so many people on the corner, the T-Men told the RRs to leave the corner alone. The RRs protested that it was their corner in the first place and said that they were not about to leave their corner. The two gangs were competing for location, not in products, but the profits of both were affected by location. On the next business day, the T-Men came and beat up those members of the RRs who were selling marijuana on the corner. The RRs, both fewer in number and younger, decided that to retain their market they had to retaliate. That night they went to the T-Men's area and put an X through all the T-Men's graffiti insignias. The following day the RRs came with guns and shot at, but did not hit, the T-Men who were on their corner selling heroin.

Two nights later, when about six members of the RRs were standing in front of one of their member's homes (some distance from the demarcation street), a van drove up and three T-Men got out and started shooting; two RRs were seriously hurt. Three days later, in another attack by the T-men, one more member of the RRs was shot. Finally, three weeks later, two more RRs were shot. In about a month's time, the T-Men had removed the RRs as a competitive problem. During the war, both gangs spoke of the other as having neither morals nor honor, not because they were shooting at each other, but because they were trying to move in on the other's business interests. Here are two representative comments:

Jugo, a sixteen-year-old member of the RRs:

> The whole war between us and the T-Men shows what they are really about. They got no honor doing the shit they did, trying to move in on our area and mess up our business. So they can shoot if they want, but we will continue to resist them. And everybody knows that their whole gig is without any honor. So nobody cares if they win, lose, or get killed 'cause they got no honor.

Trini, a nineteen-year-old member of the T-Men gang:

> Hey, we're just trying to make some money. We didn't want to take over their area, we just were doing some business on one of their corners. Man, we need to do business and they tried to ruin our business. They got no morals, man. People who got some morals wouldn't try to ruin your business.

The second factor that influences the success of a gang's economic activity has to do with how effective members are at implementing the plans they have formulated. Because gangs do not have bureaucracies, they do not encounter the same implementation problems as other organizations. Nonetheless, the type of leadership structure plays a role in the gang's ability to implement plans. Here, the vertical/hierarchical leadership structure works best, because the lines of authority are clearly delineated and this facilitates the assignment of tasks to specific people. There is some bickering over who does which task, and some individual resistance to undertaking certain tasks, but this rarely inhibits implementation. Thus once a plan has been developed and accepted by the majority of the general membership, the vertical organizational structure is able to coordinate both the personnel and resources specified in the plan more efficiently than are the other two types of leadership structures. If the plan proves unsuccessful, as often happens, it is more often than not because of factors other than the gang's inability to organize itself in the implementation stage.

In contrast, the influential structure of leadership has difficulty in achieving the coordination needed to implement its economic plans. Leaders in this type of structure operate, as Pressman and Wildavsky have stated, under the premise that "achieving coordination means getting one's way," and this ultimately makes it difficult for these gangs to get the members with the necessary skills to participate consistently.[28] It should be recalled that this leadership model was able to be more efficient in the planning stage because the leaders had so much power that they did not have to sell their plans to the general membership. However, the exclusion of the rank and file from the decision-making process often made members reluctant to invest their time in collective projects. Members of these gangs tended to make themselves scarce when they knew that the leadership wanted to undertake a particular activity. The two observed outcomes of this situation both resulted in the organizations suffering economic losses. Those gangs that went ahead with their plans using inappropriate personnel often saw the implementation of this phase botched; those gangs that put their projects on hold until they persuaded members with the necessary skills to participate suffered the cost of lost opportunities.

The leadership structure with the most difficulty in implementing its plan is the horizontal/commission model. Power here is so decentralized that the organization finds it difficult to assign tasks to the appropriate members, and there is always a great deal of bickering and some level of resistance among the various factions. The resulting delays tend to undermine the coordinating aspect of the gang's economic plan.[29] This in turn has a negative impact on the overall economic activity of the gang by limiting both the number and scope of its ventures.

A problem that affects the economic activity of all gangs, regardless of their leadership structures, is the difficulty of establishing a consistent division of labor. Gangs find it hard to persuade the same people to participate in all their ventures. The main obstacle, though not the sole one, is that members engaged in their own personal ventures do not have the time to be consistently involved in the organization's economic ventures. Thus gangs have to use members who are not as competent or who must be consistently retrained. These personnel problems produce delays, lost opportunities, and failures.

A last constraint on economic success is the caution that must be exercised to avoid antagonizing the community. The gang must avoid economic activities that large numbers in its community will view as detrimental. This limits the number and kinds of activities gangs engage in.

For example, some of the easier ways to make money would involve taking advantage of members of their communities. To avoid this, gangs must often resort to ventures that are more risky, which increases the number of failures.

Gangs and Modern Organized Crime

From the earliest studies of gangs through many more contemporary ones, youth gangs have been depicted as the trade schools for organized crime (the mob, Mafia, Cosa Nostra, etc.).[30] The vast majority of these studies either state or imply that gang members graduate to the mob as a result both of learning the necessary skills to be a professional criminal and of having few opportunities in the legitimate, noncriminal sphere for achieving employment, advancement, and wealth.[31] These studies assume that gangs provide the necessary organizational and experiential environments for their members to gravitate into the established syndicates of their respective communities. While this does occur, it happens so infrequently that it cannot be identified as a significant pattern. Part of the explanation is historical. According to the interviews that I conducted with older men who had been in gangs from the 1930s through the 1960s,[32] in that era few gang members became participants in the local syndicates, and for two reasons: because Italians had an ethnic monopoly in the large crime syndicates, and because the syndicates wanted to limit their membership in order to maximize profits.[33] Thus most gang members who were not Italian stood little chance of being asked to become members of the syndicate. In recent years, however, the gang's relationship with the syndicate has changed, because the Italian Mafia no longer has a monopoly on all the profitable sectors of crime. For example, while the Mafia still controls a large portion of the supply side of illegal narcotics, it has relinquished much of its monopoly of the distribution phase of the business. African-American, Puerto Rican, and Mexican syndicates have emerged to challenge the Italian syndicate, for example, and have established themselves as the latest crime organizations in the African-American, Puerto Rican, and Mexican communities.[34] The gangs I studied all attempted to secure a relationship with the syndicate in their areas. This usually meant that they undertook either to act as the syndicate's retailers, for which they received a fee, or to buy drugs wholesale from the syndicate and do the retailing on their own behalf. While the syndicates preferred that the gangs act as their agents, enabling the syndicates to make more money, the gangs typically demanded the right to retail the drugs themselves, which would give them a larger profit. This conflict of interest usually precipitated a violent struggle. Interestingly, in more than half of the cases where this type of conflict occurred, the gang was able to persevere long enough to negatively affect the syndicate's business in the area; and this in turn was sufficient to induce the syndicate to accept the gang's demand for the establishment of a retail relationship.

In sum, contrary to previous studies' conclusions that gangs serve as preparatory schools for the syndicate, it would be more accurate to view today's gangs as independent components of the broad structure by which contemporary crime has been organized.

Crude Economic Activity

By *crude* economic activity, I refer to those acts of delinquency that most people associate with gangs: muggings, purse snatchings, holdups of various sorts, and small burglaries. I call these activities crude because little planning or skill are necessary, there is a high risk of being apprehended by the police, and relatively small amounts of money are involved. Two key disadvantages of crude activities are that they produce "bad press," which gangs are sensitive to (see chapter 10), and more important, they provide no foundation for steady revenues for the gang.

A common example of a crude activity was the robbery of people in their cars. A few members of a gang would get together on a street that was regularly used but not a major thoroughfare. They would pick a car whose driver and passengers were not from the community (and preferably someone who appeared to be wealthy) and just stand in front of it. The driver would then be forced to run into them or stop. As soon as the driver stopped, the gang members would surround the car, pull a gun, and rob the occupants.

It should be understood that when crude economic activity is pursued, it is sometimes done by individual members acting on their own and sometimes by individuals acting under the auspices of the organization. However, such activity is mostly undertaken by individual members of the gang acting in their own interest. Because individual members constantly seek their own interest and usually have few resources to undertake large projects, they are motivated to undertake this type of activity. Most of the crude economic activity recorded by the authorities as gang-related crime is thus in actuality done by individual gang members acting on their own, and this is a direct outgrowth of the defiant individualist character.[35]

When crude economic activity has been engaged in by the gang as a whole, it is generally the result of several factors, all of which are related to some type of organizational breakdown. Before identifying these factors, it ought to be noted that each of them may, for any particular incident, be the primary stimulus, or they may interact with each other (or additional factors) to produce the activity in question.

The first factor influencing gangs to pursue crude economic activity has to do with mismanagement during times of economic crisis. For example, when gangs lose money as a result of having taken too many risks, they have a tendency to panic and engage in crude economic activity as part of a "quick-fix" strategy. Second, when the leadership of a gang is syphoning off much of the profits, it may encourage the gang to undertake crude economic activities to replenish the treasury and disguise the embezzlement. Third, when gangs have been unable to convince a sufficient number of members to work for the collective, they may be forced, in order to pay the bills and keep the organization functioning, to engage in crude ventures that need only a small number of people. Finally, for those gangs whose primary source of revenues are dues or "income taxes," crude activities may be undertaken to cover the organization's costs until dues or taxes pick up.

Economic Activity: Consuming

Nearly all the economic activity that gangs undertake is for the purpose of financing consumption, which takes three forms: goods/commodities, recreation, and basic resources (material and psychological). In the first category, drugs and alcohol are the items most often purchased by gangs, and they try to provide quantities that will satisfy their membership. Some gangs, like Chicano gangs, purchase and use heroin, cocaine, marijuana, and various chemical drugs like barbiturates, amphetamines, and angel dust. Other gangs, like those in New York, forbid the use of heroin, but buy pure cocaine and crack cocaine. Alcohol is used by nearly all the gangs, but I found that the Irish used it most, not so much because they have a tradition of drinking as because the supply of drugs was controlled by nonwhites and they did not want to do business with nonwhites. However, most gangs do not dispense drugs or alcohol free of charge to their members. Rather they sell the drugs or alcohol at cost or provide a limited free supply to members at gang-organized parties. For example, in New York some of the gangs had rather sophisticated clubhouses whose bars sold drinks and small sandwiches (warmed in the microwave) at cost. In addition, at their parties they would have a limited amount of cocaine available to "help people get in the party mood." Furthermore, some of the gangs in all three cities purchased equipment for the members' use: pinball machines, table soccer machines, table tennis, pool tables, and slot machines. They also purchased some athletic equipment: baseball gloves, bats, balls, bases, some basketballs, and handballs. One gang went so far as to purchase a motorcycle for recreational use.

Parties and group recreational activities are an important aspect of gang life, just as they are for other social organizations like the Elks and Moose lodges. A good deal of money is spent on items that will be consumed at their parties, picnics, and outings (barbecues); at times some gangs will rent a hall for a party.

Lastly, gangs allocate money or resources on hand to assist those members or their families who are having difficulty procuring food, clothing, and shelter. A gang's emergency fund serves to reassure members that temporary relief will be available if times are bad for themselves or their families.[36]

Rates of Consumption

Gangs' rates of consumption, I found, vary by ethnicity and type of organizational structure. First, along ethnic lines, Chicano and Irish gangs were the most consumption-oriented. They tended to devote more of their time to deciding how to spend their money and to indulging themselves in consuming than they did on the planning and accumulating aspects of organizational economics. They were very "present-oriented" and wanted their rewards immediately, whereas other gangs were able to strike a better balance between enjoying rewards and deferring gratification through planning, accumulating, and saving.[37] Thus members of both the Chicano and Irish gangs were little inclined to devote time to complex and long-range economic planning or accumulating material possessions. This applied to both individual members and the gangs as collectives. This is not to say that such gangs did not plan or undertake complex economic projects, for they did, but they devoted a smaller proportion of their time to such projects and much less time than the other gangs. As a consequence, such gangs are more active in those ventures I have called "crude economic activity."

The primary reason for this pattern has to do with the historical development of these ethnic gang organizations. Many of the Chicano gangs in Los Angeles arose, not primarily as economic organizations, but as part of an effort to resist Anglo-American cultural prejudices and to defy Anglo ethnocentrism. They sought to maintain a cultural separateness and physically to protect their barrio from harmful elements. Similarly, Irish gangs (along with the Irish social clubs) were founded as part of an effort to defy Anglo-British ethnocentrism and to promote Irish nationalism.[38] In addition, both Chicano and Irish gangs also developed as part of adolescents' attempts to resist the perceived mundaneness that accompanied the working-class jobs that would eventually await them. It is important to emphasize, then, that many Chicano and Irish gangs were not developed primarily as economic organizations and thus do not behave like them. One will find Chicano and Irish gangs that do behave as purely economic organizations, but these gangs are relative newcomers, influenced by a new set of economic conditions that have seen certain ethnic groups caught in perpetual poverty. It is therefore necessary to pay close attention to the conditions under which a particular ethnic gang develops in order to understand the pattern of its economic behavior.

Patterns of consumption are also influenced by leadership structure. Gangs with horizontal/commission and influential models of leadership tended to devote more of their time to consuming than those with the vertical/hierarchical form. Hampered by internal political conflict and a looser authority structure than the vertical/heirarchical model, these gangs lacked the capacity and/or desire to devote significant amounts of time to planning the complex ventures most likely to produce long-term revenues. In the absence of long-term plans, they invariably became more active in crude economic ventures that led members to question the organization's prospects for longevity. That in turn influenced members to press their organizations to get whatever they could in the present and not become involved in activities with relatively long-term returns. The upshot was that consuming became both the foundation and integrating agent for these gangs' economic activities.

Conclusion

The economic activities of gangs involve a rather complicated relationship between the individual members and the organizations. Part of this relationship originates in a component of the defiant individualist character, whereby the gang member views his self-interest as split between identifying with the gang and acting on his own. The self-interest of individual gang members nurtures entrepreneurial attitudes that help the gang with its business ventures, but the gang must handle the difficult task of coordinating the organization's interests with those of its individual members.

Another aspect of the complicated relationship between gang members and their organizations concerns the organization's need to have individuals working for the benefit of the collective. The economic desires and creative abilities of its members are resources for the organization, but these same entrepreneurial attitudes also prompt members to work on their own projects. Optimally, the organization would like its members to devote all their time to projects that would benefit the organization, but any sustained effort to prevent individual projects would ultimately result in the dissolution of the gang. Hence, the organization must continuously mediate its own interests with those of the individual and coordinate those internal tasks necessary for the success of its business projects. Such delicate balancing acts have often been misinterpreted by outside observers, however, as disorganization and the inability to carry out anything other than petty economic projects.

Finally, the ambivalent relationship between the organization and its members, along with other factors such as organizational breakdown, incompetence, and economic panic, is responsible for producing sophisticated as well as crude economic activity by both gangs and their members. Here again, outside observers who fail to disaggregate the participants and causes of specific economic activity have generally misunderstood gang economic behavior.

Chapter Five

The Anatomy
of Gang Violence

*Violence . . . is distinguished by its instrumental character.
Phenomenologically, it is close to strength, since the imple-
ments of violence, like all other tools, are designed and used
for the purpose of multiplying natural strength until, in the
last stage of their development, they can substitute for it.*
                                 Hannah Arendt, *On Violence* (1969)

"The Great Equalizer"
                           Inscription on the barrel of a Colt .45 pistol

Of all the topics associated with gangs, it is likely that none is more important to the general public in the United States than violence. Gang violence has received the most attention from the police, community and political leaders, and the media. Despite all this attention, however, gang violence is also the least understood of gang activities. Recently on national television, interviewer Geraldo Rivera asked a teenage member of one of Los Angeles's African-American gangs (the Bloods) whether he felt badly that innocent people were killed as a result of his gang's drive-by shootings. With little expression and no apparent remorse, he answered, "No." [1] Most people are baffled, frustrated, and angered by such a response, and this reaction usually calls for harsher penalties for gang violence. However, putting aside the question of whether harsher penalties are appropriate or not, an understanding of the phenomenon of gang violence is essential. The general public's persistent questions about why young people become involved in violence and frustration at gang members' seeming lack of remorse for their participation in violence, indicate how widespread the public's failure to understand the gang violence phenomenon is. I am not suggesting that an understanding of violence will lead society to withdraw or temper its calls for harsher penalties, but I do want to suggest that we lack a full sociological understanding of this aspect of gang activity. Part of the problem is that it is difficult to obtain all the information necessary for developing such an understanding. Sociologists have been studying gang violence for more than one hundred years; but because it is both difficult and dangerous to be on the scene when violence is occurring, for the most part society has had to depend on ex post facto data. While often extremely valuable, this kind of information has limitations.[2] The data from the present study offer some advantage over much of the previously available information on gang violence, inasmuch as I report patterns I observed while present before, during, and after members of various gangs were involved in different aspects of violence. This study thus provides important data that have been generally difficult for sociologists to obtain. Unable to observe gang violence directly, researchers have treated it as a dependent variable, something to be explained using structural and individual-oriented independent variables. This study, providing important data that have been generally difficult for sociologists to obtain, seeks to understand the anatomy of violence as well as to explain it. In so doing, it furnishes information that supports, rejects, and adds to assertions made in past research. The result is a better understanding of the nature of contemporary gang violence in all its complexities.

Toward an Understanding of Gang Violence

Past research on the causes of gang violence has tended, with certain variations, to emphasize two factors. One body of research argues that gangs become involved in violence as a result of group leadership that is composed of psychologically disturbed individuals who are socially maladjusted. Within this framework, the sources of the individual's pathology may have been either socially or chemically (drug) induced; but whatever the source, the gang member's use of violence is a means to satisfy psychological needs that are pathologically sadistic. The early work of Lewis Yablonsky is an example of this line of argument.[3] A significant number of the contemporary observers who think this way attribute this pathology to drugs. Comments made by contemporary observers, particularly law enforcement officials, are frequently along the lines of, "When gang members are on angel dust or crack, they just become crazy and will do anything, including brutal murders of innocent people."

The second body of research most often cites status deprivation/achievement as the chief factor causing the violence of gang members. Such researchers argue that most gang members feel they have been deprived, either by the broader society or by their own community, of the status that is their due and that their use of violence is an effort to establish a reputation that, they hope, will translate into high social status within their own communities.[4]

Interestingly, both the social-status-deprivation and the psychosocial-pathology models have a similar logic. Both models assume that there are people deprived of adequate social status in American society, based on both class and race criteria, and that this obstacle to attaining goals is what increases frustration, which in turn is channeled into violence. However, the two models diverge over the source of these blocked aspirations. The social-status-deprivation model emphasizes that social institutions actively block these aspirations, while the psychosocial-pathology model emphasizes that the individuals themselves block their own aspirations because they are psychologically disturbed. According to the psychosocial-pathology model, deprivation of social status is simply an excuse offered by gang members for their use of violence.[5]

The violence associated with members of gangs emerges from low-income communities where limited resources are aggressively sought by all, and where the residents view violence as a natural state of affairs. There, the defiant individualist gang member (see chapter 1), being a product of this environment, adopts a Hobbesian view of life in which violence is an integral part of the state of nature. As we shall see, for the gang member, violence is the currency of life and becomes the currency of the economy of the gang. However, we shall also see that while gang violence is often vicious and brutal, it is not unrestrained. Gang violence is limited (not eliminated) by restraining mechanisms, such as fear of reprisal and the pain associated with such reprisal (deterrence); internal organizational codes; and a code of conduct that condones the use of violence to neutralize all enemies with some general (and sometimes vague) understanding of the level of violence necessary to do that.

One might well wonder why, if fear of physical harm is such an important factor inhibiting violent action, so much gang violence continues. The answer is that fear of physical harm does act to inhibit violent action a significant portion of the time, but it cannot eliminate it. Gang members are not absolutely adverse to being injured; to them, injuries can be used as commendations. Scars are displayed like medals, and members who do not have them are always a little envious. Anxiety, when it exists, is only about death, and gang members mediate their fears of death through two psychological exercises that have so far gone unnoticed in other studies.

The first is used by young soldiers; they believe that they are invincible, warriors just too good to be killed. The second is to believe in their immortality, an idea that may be common to everyone but is nurtured by all gang members. Gang members constantly talk about their loyal, honorable members who have fallen in the name of the gang. No one forgets who was killed where and for what purpose.[6] Some Chicano gang members can tell you who was killed twenty years ago, before they were born, because this history has been passed down to them. These members have attained a degree of immortality and each gang member perpetuates this by keeping the gang member's memory alive; they know that by perpetuating the immortality of others, they ensure their own immortality if they are killed. The consequence of these two psychological manipulations is to mute the fear of death and much of its inhibiting power.

In addition, to understand the violence associated with contemporary gangs, an important point missed by past research must be noted: not all the violence now labeled "gang violence" is in fact gang violence. A very large portion of it is violence committed by people who are members of a gang, but not as part of the gang's effort to achieve its objectives. To understand the contemporary violence associated with gangs, we must distinguish the individual-based violence perpetrated by members of a gang from the collective-based violence undertaken by the gang organization. However, while this distinction enables us to conceptualize gang violence, it does not sufficiently enable us to understand the causes of violence.

In the present comparative study of gangs, I have found four factors that cause both individual and collective gang violence: fear, ambition, frustration, and personal/group testing of skills. Each of these four factors assumes a different rationale, depending on the object (target) of the violence and whether it involves individuals or the organization. Regardless of whether gang members are acting as individuals or as representatives of their gang, there are six general spheres in which gang violence occurs: (1) violence in which a fellow gang member is the target; (2) violence targeting a member or members of a rival gang; (3) violence in which residents of the gang's own neighborhood are the target; (4) violence between members of a gang and people outside its community, in which the latter are the target; (5) violence involving attacks on property in the gang's community; and (6) violence involving attacks on property that lies outside the gang's community. In the sections to follow, I examine how the four abovementioned causal factors are associated with the targets and degree of individual and collective gang violence.

Individual Violence

Much of the violence attributable to gangs is, in fact, committed by members of gangs acting as individuals rather than as agents of the organization. These acts of violence do not directly represent "gang violence," nor, as gang literature often suggests, are they committed because individuals are members of gangs.[7] While these acts are not specifically gang violence, they are related to the gang phenomenon in that the individuals involved possess certain characteristics that, when mixed with other factors, produce aggressive and violent incidents. These characteristics are not related to a psychopathological predisposition toward violence, as some researchers have also suggested.[8] Rather, they are attributes associated with the desire to survive and prosper within a certain socioeconomic climate—that is, they are aspects of what I have called the defiant individualist character. These particular people become involved in violence as the result of the interplay between their defiant individualist character; the emotions of fear, ambition, frustration, and testing self-preparedness; and certain encounters in which these emotions are made manifest.

The following sections detail how the four emotions (fear, ambition, frustration, testing) operate to precipitate violence within each of the six spheres previously mentioned.

Violence between Members of the Same Gang

We begin with the sphere in which violence is perpetrated by one gang member against another member of the same gang. Each of the four types of emotions (fear, ambition, testing self-preparedness, and frustration) can precipitate such violence. Fear is one of those emotions that instigates violence between members of the same gang. Such violence is usually pursued by individuals who find it essential to establish and protect their independence, a resource that is considered indispensable by those who possess defiant individualism. This is manifested through the notions of "respect" and "honor," which more often than not have been considered the same thing by both the public and many researchers. However, while "respect" and "honor" are pivotal values in the identity/ethical development of the individual gang members I studied throughout the United States, they do not hold the same meaning from one place to another, and they produce different behavior patterns. Except for Chicano gangs, all the gangs studied used the concept of "respect" as a fundamental code in their interpersonal relations. The Chicano gangs used the concept of "honor" as the fundamental code governing their interpersonal relations.[9]

Let's take a brief look at some fundamental differences between the two concepts. "Respect" is something that is active—that is, it is the act of achieving deference. A gang member has to earn respect; it is not something that everyone has. In addition, once a person has earned respect, he must be willing to protect it, because a person's reputation depends upon respect, and reputation is an essential resource for success. In contrast, "honor" is a passive trait that equates with dignity. Honor, for Chicano gang members, does not have to be earned. It is something that Chicano culture imparts to every person, but it is the recipient's obligation to preserve it. Thus, Chicanos enter the gang with honor, whereupon they must guard against it being taken away through the actions of others.[10] Honor carries with it far more responsibility than respect. The Chicano gang member's honor is integrally tied to that of his entire family; he must protect both his honor and that of other members of his family. However, despite the difference between honor and respect, gang members committing acts of violence to protect their honor versus those doing it to establish respect were not found to be different in the amount or intensity of violence.[11]

Returning to the interrelationship among the emotions of fear, respect or honor, and violence, gang members generally directed aggression at those individuals whom they perceived to show a lack of respect or to challenge their honor. Such aggression was generally undertaken to reduce the risk of physical or psychological harm to themselves and/or to enhance their success in personal business dealings. Thus the acquisition of respect, the holding of honor, and the development of reputations are means by which gang members attempt to reduce the number of confrontations that would otherwise occur between them and their competitors for the limited material assets that exist in their markets. As Cone, a nineteen-year-old member of a gang in New York, commented:

> Well, there are times that I have to blast one of my brothers
> [members of his gang] because they be messing around with me or
> they would be doing something that could in the future mess with

me. So I let them know that I don't dig that shit. You see, if I didn't do that, I'd be worried that I'd get no respect, and respect is what everybody wants, because without it you can't get a reputation, and if you ain't got a reputation, you ain't going to be shit. You see, if you ain't got respect and a reputation, then people be messing with you and taking your women and stuff like that, you know stuff you have to fight over. Plus if people don't respect you, they won't hang [hang out] with you either.

Mariposa, an eighteen-year-old member of a Chicano gang in Los Angeles, said:

Honor is important to me and every homey [gang member] because if you ain't got honor, you got nothing, man. I mean, no amount of money can buy you honor, so you do everything you can to protect it. I mean, without honor, nobody will respect you, not your friends or your family . . . yes, sometimes one of your homies will say something that offends your honor, and then I just have to whip his ass, 'cause if I didn't I'd be afraid that everybody who wanted to could make fun of me, and I'd just be a target for everything and everybody.

Other researchers on gangs have identified the gang member's desire to establish a reputation as a critical variable in explaining why they become involved in violence, and have explained that this desire to establish a reputation is related to the need to establish personal identity and status.[12] While a reputation does provide personal identity and status, an important finding of the present study is that gang members use their reputations primarily to deter those who would physically confront them—in essence, as an instrument of personal defense. The comments of Jinx, a sixteen-year-old Dominican gang member in New York, are instructive:

Take BiBi there. That man is got a reputation for being one tough dude. Nobody messes with him because the word's out that he's too much. You see he hardly ever gets into fights anywhere because of his rep. In fact, I ain't seen him ever fight. A lot of members don't get into fights 'cause they got reps, so that's what we all trying to do. You see, if you got yourself a rep, you don't have to worry as much as if you don't.

Ambition is another emotional factor that influences one member to attack another member of the same gang. An act of violence is under-

taken because the attacker believes it will help him move up in the organization. Take the case of Shoes, a sixteen-year-old member of a New
York gang. Shoes wanted to be one of the officers of the gang, but there
were two obstacles: his age—the gang's leadership were all in their twen-
ties, and it was not the custom for young (thirteen- to seventeen-year-
old) teenagers to be allowed leadership positions—and the fact that he
had not been with the gang for a long time and therefore had not established any noteworthy reputation. The absence of a noteworthy reputation meant that there was little chance that the general membership would
elect one to a leadership position. Conscious of these obstacles, Shoes set
out to establish a reputation. His gang was fighting a rival gang in an
attempt to expand its business territory. In one of the fights between the
two groups, Shoes noticed that two members of his gang had retreated
and were waiting for the others to join them after the fighting had stopped.
Often in these situations, the scene is so chaotic that one rarely notices
that another member did not, as they say, have "heart" (courage) and
has withdrawn to protect himself. In this case, however, Shoes did notice,
and at the very next opportunity he took advantage of it. At the next
general meeting of the gang, Shoes picked one of the two who had withdrawn from the fight and viciously attacked him. A number of the other
members restrained the pair, and the leadership asked Shoes to explain.
He told the group what had happened, which was corroborated by two
other members of the gang, and requested that the two gang members be
punished.

Shoes's behavior produced two results: it established a reputation for
him and it awarded him a promotion—he was appointed deputy to the
war councilor, a position with little authority, but one that gave him
entry into the leadership circle. The use of violence by one member against
another in the same gang for purposes of rising within the ranks of the
organization occurs on a regular basis, but it does not always produce
the positive effect that it did in the case of Shoes. Even when such actions
do not produce the intended result (an increase of status within the organization), this will generally not deter the individual gang member from
repeatedly trying until he is successful. The result of these repeated efforts
is recurring internal violence.

The third source of violence that pits one member of a gang against a
fellow member is what I have called "testing one's abilities and skills."
The normal pattern in all gangs is to have members constantly wrestling
or punching one another. Sometimes this takes on very playful forms,

but sometimes a person starts the play with every intention of transforming it into a fight. Members do this because they want to test their capabilities at fighting with somebody of equal stature. If the person the member is fighting happens to be bigger and has a reputation as a good fighter, then the individual attempts to determine his competence as a fighter. Fighting in this manner, both members can test their abilities yet retain the excuse that they were "carried away." Under these circumstances, it is no disgrace to lose—especially if the loser is younger and if both combatants realize that they will be involved in similar actions in the future. However, on occasion, fights related to "social testing" are not initiated under the guise of friendly acts of jousting that have gotten out of control. When this occurs, the leadership usually mediates and symbolically reprimands both. On the whole, these acts are not as violent as those involving members of different gangs, but they do generally result in physical injuries to the participants.

The fourth factor is frustration/anger. Violence associated with frustration/anger emerges from three sources: (1) as a consequence of verbal combat; (2) in connection with women; and (3) as a result of physiological reactions to, in particular, deprivation of food and rest and ingestion of drugs. Verbal combat between gang members takes place throughout low-income areas and is considered a legitimate means of communication and interpersonal relations, often referred to as "the dozens." [13] Like most interactions involving competition, the participants understand that there are winners and losers. In fact, that is what makes this form of verbal interaction attractive to those who participate. Nevertheless, there are times when the exchange becomes heated and participants say things that touch a sensitive issue for one of the combatants; or one person may get the better of the exchange and the other may be unable to accept defeat. In these situations, frustration/anger builds and physical confrontation and violence are the result. This type of violence is associated more with those gangs where "respect" is the predominant value, rather than among Chicano gangs where "honor" is what matters. This is because members of Chicano gangs are much more conscious, when in conversation, of the need to avoid threatening another member's honor. When such a threat does occur, it is rarely inadvertent. Rather, it is a conscious act of provocation, in which the perpetrator not only expects but wants a violent clash.

Issues related to women are also a cause of much frustration/anger and violence. Some of the New York gangs had a rule that as long as someone had declared that a specific woman was his, the other members of the gang were to refrain from making sexual advances to her. In every gang I studied, women were considered a form of property. Interestingly, the women I observed and interviewed told me they felt completely comfortable with certain aspects of this relationship and simply resigned themselves to accepting those aspects they disliked. The one aspect they felt most comfortable with was being treated like servants, charged with the duty of providing men with whatever they wanted. While the role of a servant only applied to the man with whom the woman was sexually involved, it nonetheless established the women as the property of men. Behavior that gang women had the most difficulty with, but resigned themselves to, were unfaithfulness and the failure of men to accept their responsibilities and help raise the children they had fathered.[14] Regardless of the plight of women in gangs, any break in the social norms regarding appropriate behavior would precipitate a violent response. Because gang members viewed women as property, any sexual advance made to a member's woman was viewed by that member as either an attempt to steal his property or an insult to his ability to protect his property.

The third aspect of frustration/anger that produces violence between members of the same gang is the poor diet and the rest deprivation experienced by many members. While the present research did not reveal poor diet to be a direct cause of violence, there was consistent evidence that poor diet left gang members sensitive to emotions that precipitated violence. Gang members often do not have the money to eat nutritious food consistently and usually are able to satisfy their hunger with either alcohol or food that is high in fats and carbohydrates and low in protein and vitamins. Over a period of time, these individual gang members become more tired, lethargic, and irritable, a condition that often causes them to instigate a violent confrontation with other members.

One example involved Junior, a twenty-three-year-old gang member from New York. He was one of the leaders of the gang and he lived with his parents in a housing project. His parents were quite poor and they did not have the money to feed their large family (six children) adequately. Often there would be a shortage of food near the end of the father's pay cycle. On these occasions, Junior and his family would eat canned beans or canned spaghetti as their main meal. I shared similar meals with Junior twenty-two times and noted that he would subsequently be consistently irritable and inevitably would fight with other members of the gang for no apparent reason.[15] These fights were brutal and had to be broken up by other members of the gang. Afterwards, Junior would justify his actions by falsely accusing the other member. The organizational response would be a warning to Junior, followed by the general comment, "He's just a crazy nigger sometimes."

Gang members also eat poorly because they are on the streets a great deal and not at home to eat those nutritious meals that their families do make. In New York small storefront Chinese take-out eateries are open twenty-four hours a day, and gang members often frequent them very late at night. These establishments, many of which serve through an opening in bulletproof glass, sell extremely greasy deep-fried food. Gang members who consumed this over a period of time complained of tiredness and "just not feeling right," and they were inevitably more irritable and instigated fights with other members of the gang. Although it should not be considered one of the primary causes of aggression and violence involving gang members, poor diet is an important contributing factor and cannot be neglected if we are to have a full understanding of the reasons gang violence occurs.

In addition to an inadequate diet, two other factors lead to irritability and physical altercations among members of gangs: sleep deprivation and/or insufficient amounts of rest, and reactions to chemical consumption (drugs or alcohol). All gang members keep late hours. When the weather is warm, members normally stay awake until three or four o'clock in the morning. In colder weather, it is more common to stay awake until one or two o'clock in the morning. Because gang members do stay up late at night, they try to sleep until late morning or early afternoon. However, this is often difficult because of noise from other family members, noise from the street, poor sleeping facilities, or poor climate control (either too hot or too cold) in the buildings where they reside or they have to go to school.[16] Whatever the cause, lack of sleep (or merely rest) will lead to general irritability and outbreaks of physical aggression against fellow members.

Reactions from drug consumption will also bring about irritability and aggression toward others in the gang. Most commonly those who have used drugs will complain that they do not feel completely well during the periods when they are not taking them. Often they are shaky and feel weak and jittery. This condition was often the reason one member got into a fight with another.

For whatever reason, fights between members of the same gang are quite serious. One might assume that a fight between members of the same gang would be less intense than fights between members of two opposing gangs, but this is not the case. In observing these fights, I was struck by the viciousness that members of the same gang can exhibit toward one another. This can be confusing, because most gang members will refer to themselves as brothers, and they will frequently do this after they fight as well. Regardless of what they say, over time it becomes apparent that members of gangs really do not think of their fellow members as brothers. Gang members are fundamentally loners who have chosen to participate not because the gang represents a family (with brothers) that they have been deprived of, but because they perceive it to be, at least in the short run, in their best interests. Therefore, they have no aversion to being as brutal as is necessary to win a fight with another member. In addition, gang members know how to fight in only one way— an all-out effort to destroy or immobilize the perceived enemy. No matter who they are fighting, the objective is always the same—to beat the enemy before he or she beats you, and to never let them up.

Although violence between members of the same gang is quite common, it is rarely reported under the category of "gang violence," either because the gangs themselves often keep such squabbles secret from observers/recorders or because those who record the data are less interested in this type of gang violence than in that directed against people and objects outside of any particular gang.

Attacks on Members of Other Gangs

This section examines why members of a particular gang, acting on their own, would attack members of rival gangs. Its focus should not be confused with the issue of why members of a gang, acting as agents of that organization, attack members of another gang—a question that will be addressed later in the chapter.

Fear, ambition, frustration, and testing are also responsible for violent behavior between members of different gangs, but for different reasons than those stated in the preceding section. Fear is greatly responsible for why individuals in one gang attack those in another. When individuals in one particular gang, acting on their own, attack members of another gang, it is usually in a geographic area and/or social situation neutral to both. Thus, it is common to find one or a few members of a particular gang going to an area of the city to shop and, while there, meeting one or a group of members from another gang. Or, in another common scenario, a few members of one gang may go to a party held in a neutral geographic area and meet a number of members from a rival gang. On these occasions, a fight between gang members often occurs. My data indicate that those gangs who had fewer members would attack the larger group (at a ratio of 3 to 1) first. I talked to the member(s) before and after they attacked, and it became clear that the reason they attacked first was fear. Dobby, a seventeen-year-old member of an Irish gang in New York, explains this rationale best:

> You see, there were three of us guys from the [gang's name] and we was at this market in Manhattan and along comes about ten or eleven of the [other gang's name]. We both saw each other and didn't do anything for awhile. Then we just attacked them spics . . . 'cause you figure that you might as well attack them because they're going to jump us and, shit, you might as well do it when the situation is best for us and it was best for us now because there were a lot of people around. . . . Yeah, one of us got knifed and me and Tim got a lot of bruises, but two of them got concussions from our steel rods and one got knifed, so we did OK. It could have been a lot worse for us if we hadn't attacked when we did.

Ringo was an eighteen-year-old member of a Chicano gang in Los Angeles:

> Well, me and three other of my homies decided to go to this party. We walked in and there was this group of fifteen or twenty [name of gang] there. We checked each other out and then my homies and I decided to attack the *putas* [whores] because if we would've got outside we would have been in some tightness [trouble], but if we attacked them there, then the police would be called . . . well, when the police got there, I had already been cut [he needed thirty stitches in his arm] and Rolf got his neck messed up from a kung-fu stick. I don't know how many of them got hurt, but I know two got hit with a high-powered dart gun so they are definitely messed up for some time.

Often, this fear is disguised by statements about being more courageous than members of other gangs, but the feelings expressed both before and after such violent confrontations consistently indicate fear as a cause.

Personal ambition is also a cause of violence between a member or members of one gang and another. In this case, certain members attack members of a rival gang in order to move up in the organization. Their ambition to be organizationally mobile is what promotes their violence. Individuals attack members of a rival gang in order to gain a reputation for courage and/or fighting ability—two qualities recognized by gangs and other military-type institutions as status-worthy. The greater the reputation, the greater the recognition; the greater the recognition, the greater the status and power the individual will have within the organization. Flue was a twenty-year-old member of a gang in New York:

> I got into a gangbang about two weeks ago. I saw these four members of the [name of a rival gang] walking down the street, and I said, hey, I'm going to let them know who I am. I just figured that once they'd dealt with me they'd know my reputation. I also knew that if I wanted to move up in the organization, I had to show I had more heart [courage] than most of the others. So I attacked them with everything I had and I laid some good blows on them. . . . The whole thing worked out and I got a good rep [reputation] from the whole thing, and once I got a good rep, my name was circulated around as someone who should be in the war council.[17] Shit, I wouldn't have got nowhere if I hadn't attacked those other gangs on my own. I'd still be unknown, but I took a few chances and now everybody knows me and I got myself up there helping to make decisions about things.

Individual gang members may also embark on a mission of violence against members of another gang in an effort to test how strong other gangs' members are and how strong they themselves are. Individuals from gangs will often look for members of another gang to fight to see if the members of the other gang are as tough as their reputations indicate. This is a way for individual gang members to test whether they can do business close to the rival gang's territory. If members of the rival gang turn out not to be so tough, the assailants know they have more scope for their personal business ventures.

In addition, many members of gangs use a violent fight with members of a rival gang to test how tough they have become. Such violence is a way for gang members to test their own competence. This is especially true of younger members of the gang who want to move up in the organization. Before challenging the older members of their own gang, they will test their fighting ability out on other gangs' members.

Frustration/anger is the fourth factor that induces the members of one gang to attack those of a rival gang. This emotion is nearly always related to an ongoing conflict with a rival gang. Most often, one gang attacks the members of another. Sometimes the gang that was attacked is unable to retaliate as an organization. Members of this gang sometimes release their frustration/anger when they spot members of the rival gang in a neutral area and proceed to attack them. These episodes are particularly violent because so much frustration/anger is involved. Actually, much of their frustration/anger is with their own organization, which they believe to be incompetent and/or impotent, and they release this controlled frustration/anger toward their own gang by attacking the members of the rival gang in full force. Take for example the comments of Niner, an eighteen-year-old African-American gang member in New York:

> I was walking along in the Grand Concourse [in the Bronx] when I spotted these two [rival gang's name]. I just saw red and took my walking stick and went behind them and proceeded to beat them as hard as I could. I really messed them up, blood all over the place. Then I ran away . . . I really don't know why I did it, I guess it was because the [name of the gang] attacked our clubhouse and then they had attacked a group of our members and we weren't able to do nothin' back to them. I mean I was pissed that we was not able to do nothin', I don't know maybe I just took it out on those two that I saw. I don't know.

Attacks on Residents in the Community

Gangs want to avoid attacking residents in their community because the community plays a vital role in the organization's ability to maintain itself. Yet violence against members of the community does occur, and it most often involves members of gangs acting on their own. There are two reasons why members of a gang would attack someone from their own community. One is fear of being turned in to the police. When individual gang members fear that a member of the community will inform on them to the police, they may attack that person or a relative of the person in order to intimidate him or her into silence. The gang member attempts to alleviate his own fear by creating fear in others.

The second reason is when a member of the community threatens the respect or honor of a gang member. Any member of the community who insults the honor or respect of a gang member is likely to be target of some form of retaliation. Since reputation and honor involve more than a sense of self-esteem, are instrumental in avoiding fights, and help an individual gain mobility within the gang, they are a resource to be carefully preserved. Honey was a twenty-one-year-old gang member in New York:

> Hey, I didn't want to grind up this guy, but I had no choice. You see, man, he messed with me. He insulted me in front of about thirty people, calling me a punk, a pussy, an asswipe. I can't let him get away with that, because if I do that, I got no respect, and if I got no respect, then I'm fair game for everybody. I know he was forty or something like that, but I had to bloody him. That's it.

Frustration/anger also leads some gang members to commit violence against residents of their own community. Usually this frustration/anger is associated with issues concerning women or with being restricted from doing something that they want to do. In the case of women, when violence occurs, it generally involves a gang member attacking someone in the community who propositions his lover, or someone who is competing for and winning the affections of a woman he desires.

Gang members also will attack residents of the community when such residents have restricted their activity by, most often, prohibiting members from doing something they want to do. In one case, a resident told a gang member in New York that he could not play basketball because he did not have a guest pass to play on the private court. The gang member later confronted this resident and severely hurt him. In another case, a resident told a gang member in Boston that he could not enter the theater he was managing because the last time the member was there he and a few members of his gang had made a big mess. An argument ensued and the gang member lashed out and attacked the manager, bruising his nose and cutting the corner of his eye.

Fear and frustration/anger are the only two emotions that consistently influence a member of a gang to attack a resident of his own community. Since gangs need the support of the community, they will often punish members who attack people in the community.

Violence against People outside the Community

Sometimes gang members, acting on their own, become involved in violence against people outside their community. All four dominant emotions are involved in instigating these actions.

Gang members are frequently involved in violence because they have been threatened in some manner—that is, fear is the motivating factor. In a significant number of these cases, gang members may not have been overtly threatened in an objective sense, but have perceived a gesture as threatening, and attacked the gesturer in response.

The case of Gore, a twenty-two-year-old gang member from Boston, illustrates this type of attack. Gore and two other gang members were in a small grocery store in the Jamaica Plain section of Boston. The owner of the store, who was Puerto Rican, accused Gore of taking an apple without paying for it. Gore said he did not take the apple, but the owner insisted it was Gore and threatened to call the police. Just as the argument was in full force, a middle-aged African-American man who had been delivering furniture to a neighboring house trotted into the store. He was ten feet inside the store when one of the other gang members attacked him, hitting him the testicles. Gore immediately turned and rushed the man and began to beat him about the head and back. The third member of the gang rushed over and kicked the man while he was down. By this time, the owner had called the police and, having heard him making the phone call, Gore and the other two members ran out of the store and successfully evaded the police.

The dynamics of this event were that Gore and his two companions were in an area where many Latinos (Puerto Ricans and Cubans) were living. Because they were Irish, this environment made Gore and his friends feel alien and uneasy, and when the owner of the store accused them of stealing, I observed them becoming more wary and anxious. When the African-American man ran into the store, they thought he was going to attack them, so they reacted by striking first. In actuality, the African-American man was running into the store to get a quick snack before his boss could tell he had left the truck and was no longer unloading furniture at the house two doors down. To the Irish gang members, however, the fact of his running into the store, coupled with the fact that they were in an ethnically alien territory and were being accused of wrongdoing by a local merchant who was a member of an adversarial ethnic group, was perceived as a threatening act that required them to respond.[18] Later they told me that they thought the black man was a black Puerto Rican running to help the merchant.

There is another way in which fear produces a violent response on the part of gang members toward people who live in areas outside their community. When outsiders commit acts that gang members perceive as threatening to their respect, honor, and reputations, they tend to retaliate with violent force. An incident involving Box Car, a sixteen-year-old Dominican member of a New York gang, is a case in point. He and three other people went to a theater to see a movie. One paid to enter and then went to a side exit door and let in the other three. Two of the attendants caught them and escorted them out of the building. As they were being escorted out of the building, the manager came from his office and began to berate them, saying they ought to be ashamed of themselves, that their parents ought to be ashamed of themselves for not having taught them right and wrong, and that they were disgusting "parasites." Box Car told him to "shove it up his ass." The manager continued to complain, saying that this was the ninth time that day that someone had tried to sneak in. Everyone in the theater was looking at Box Car and his friends being escorted out, so there was a degree of embarrassment as well. However, the final incident occurred as Box Car and the others were walking out of the theater. Just as the manager and the two attendants let go of the four (they had been holding their arms), and immediately before the four went past the front doors, the manager gave Box Car a push and warned him never to do it again. This was the final straw; Box Car turned, ran back at the manager, and stabbed him in the side.[19] Then he ran away. Later he said to me:

> I didn't want to get into it with the dude, but he pushed and pushed and then he showed no respect whatsoever. Nothing! He does all that shit and then pisses on my respect too. Nobody does that to me, especially in front of my brothers. . . . I got him on the side, he's lucky. If he or anybody does that shit to me, I'll give them a new asshole!

Ambition can also be a factor that causes gang members to become involved in violence with someone from the outside community. When any person (especially a person from outside the gang member's community) attempts to block the entrepreneurial efforts of a particular gang member, that gang member usually retaliates with some form of force. Mole, a twenty-five-year-old member of a New York gang, was engaged in entrepreneurial activity for his own personal gain, like most individuals who have been gang members for some time. Specifically, he would buy stolen contraband and sell it on the street for reduced prices. He worked about six streets, and he liked to do business near a number of pawn shops because he could offer people better prices than they could get in the pawn shops. Two pawn-shop owners were disturbed by Mole's presence outside their stores and tried to get him to leave, one going so far as to call the police on him. The policeman arrived undercover and bought a piece of jewelry, then arrested him, and Mole had to go to court. However, since he had a receipt indicating that he had purchased the jewelry himself, the police could not prove that he had been selling stolen goods, so Mole was released and soon back in front of the pawn shop again. Again the owner called the police. This time they sent a regular squad car. This proved to be no threat of arrest to Mole because he could always hide the contraband as soon as he saw the police coming. However, it did hurt his business. Mole decided this was enough provocation; after closing time, he got into a verbal fight with the owner in front of a number of people. As the fight went on, they bumped; and as soon as that happened, Mole attacked the owner. Later, Mole told me that he waited till the owner bumped him so that he could legitimately say he had been provoked. This violent interaction did effect a change because Mole was successful in frightening the owner, who then stopped trying to interfere with Mole's business.

Testing one's ability to fight, or one's strength, is also a cause of violence between individual members of gangs and people who live outside their community. Young men often want to know how strong they really are or how able they are to use their strength in a fighting situation. This is particularly true for the youngest members of the gang. One or two members of a particular gang will often start a fight with a complete stranger in an area considered neutral to all the gangs. When they are done with the fight, many times these gang members will say that they do not know why they attakced that person. Tree, a fourteen-year-old member of a gang in New York, attacked a man in Manhattan and hurt him severely. When asked why he had done this, he replied: "I really don't know what got into me, it just happen!" Later, when he was asked again, he said that he had thought about it and realized that he wanted to test how tough he was. He had nothing against the person he attacked, he said; he just chose someone he thought was well built and seemed tough. In a much later conversation, he said that picking someone outside the area was important because you could test how good a fighter you were without much chance of negative repercussions from the authorities or victim. If you were to do this in your own community, however, you would have to be prepared for retaliation. Thus, when he and other gang members want to test their strength, they prefer to select people from other communities because they consider these areas "safe areas," where they were free from retaliation.

Members of the gang also test their own sense of vulnerability. Frequently they will attack someone because that person is vulnerable and this reminds them of their own vulnerability. Their attacks on others are a way of displacing the self-contempt inspired by their own feeling of vulnerability. For example, take the case of Crumbs, a sixteen-year-old member of a New York gang. One day Crumbs watched a boy walking down the street for five minutes. Then he walked up to the boy, hit him two vicious blows to the face and head, and called him a "fucking pussy." The boy bent down holding his face, and Crumbs ran away. After the incident, I asked Crumbs what that was all about. He said:

> Shit, I don't know, the guy just pissed me off. Did you see how he was walking down the street scared as a motherfucker? He was just tiptoeing along worried somebody was going to mess with him. He showed no guts. Shit all sorts of people, including me, go to neighborhoods they don't know and where something might happen to them, but they walk with balls, not like this guy. This guy disgusted me, so I blasted him.

Frustration/anger also stimulates individuals in gangs to undertake violence against people who live outside their communities. There are many sources of this frustration/anger, but because the vast majority of these sources cannot be confronted directly (either because they are too powerful, because gang members have limited access to them, or because they involve personal and intimate relationships in the community or at home), much of the frustration/anger must be controlled through internalization. As a result, frustration is vented through violent attacks on people who live outside the community. This is like "kicking the dog" when you are really frustrated or angry with your spouse. As Kite, an eighteen-year-old Jamaican gang member in New York, said:

> Yes, I have on occasions attacked people who lived in other areas that I did not know. A few times I really did beat on people, bloodied them good. . . . When you be frustrated, the advantage of kicking ass in another locality is that you may relieve yourself from frustration without any fear of retaliation. After all, what good would it do to take your frustration out on somebody who would retaliate? Good God, man, you'd just be substituting frustration with anxiety!

Attacks on Property in the Community

Ambition is the cause of the vast majority of cases involving attacks on property in a gang member's community. When a gang member is attempting to succeed in one of his personal projects, violence against property is often used as a substitute for violence against people. In this way a message can be given to those whom the gang member suspects of having blocked him from achieving his objective without having to use violence against an individual. It also can be a means of achieving his objective. In New York and Boston, for example, property owners often wanted to have vacant buildings they owned burned down so that they could collect the insurance, which they considered more profitable than renovating the building in order to rent it. In such situations some gang members would contract to set fire to these buildings.

Attacks on Property outside the Community

Ambition and frustration/anger are two factors that influence gang members to engage in violence toward property outside their community.

As with attacks on property within a gang's community, money is a primary cause of violence against property located outside the individual's community. As noted, gang members are often hired to set fire to apartment buildings so that the owners can collect the insurance money. Or they contract to set fire to business premises for a third party—for example, burning down a numbers establishment that the competition wants eliminated or torching a business to satisfy a personal vendetta.

Individual gang members sometimes attack the property of people who they feel have prevented them from securing a profitable business opportunity. For example, Dome, a seventeen-year-old gang member from Los Angeles, was blocked by a certain individual from taking advantage of opportunities in the stolen-car business. He had a business in stolen auto parts that dealt in orders only—that is, customers would contact him for a particular part that was either hard to find or expensive, and he would find it for them. Business had been so good that Dome had hired two others to work for him, and had begun to compete with another business that also dealt in stolen cars and parts. The owner of the other operation decided to squeeze Dome out of business and put out the word to all retailers in this market that Dome was being watched by the police. This resulted in a radical decline in business over a period of a month.

Dome retaliated by setting fire to the garage that his competitor used to strip the stolen cars. Dome was able to bring about a work stoppage at his competitor's business, which eventually led to a settlement between the two.

People are also attacked to hurt a competitor. For example, many members of gangs have set up their own small prostitution businesses. If other pimps attempt to hinder them, gang members will often attack their prostitutes. In the majority of cases, the individual gang members see themselves as attacking the property of the competing pimps. This rationale makes them psychologically able to deny the guilt associated with attacking people, which they rationalize as being a natural part of business. Within this rationalization is the idea that female prostitutes are property and not individuals to be respected. This is another example of the fact that gang members are, by and large, similar to others in society who view and/or treat women as property.

Frustration/anger is the other emotional factor that induces individual gang members to attack property outside their communities. When gang members believe that their honor or respect has been offended, they will retaliate. Thus, when someone from outside their community offends them and they are reluctant to retaliate against the person, they will invariably attack that person's property. Their favorite targets are the offending person's car or house, principally because they are the most accessible.

While retaliations for offenses to a person's honor and respect are the most common, there are many occasions when frustration/anger causes an individual gang member to attack the property of someone he believes is wealthy. Interestingly, when most members who have made such an attack are asked why they did it, they usually answer, "I just felt like it." However, given time, most eventually answer that they did it because they were envious and resentful that these people had what they wished they had and/or believed they should have. Most violent attacks of this type are related to emotions discussed by Franz Fanon in *The Wretched of the Earth*.[20] Fanon notes that nonwhite colonials were forced by the white colonizer to limit their aspirations, and that in order to survive, the colonized natives internalized the frustrations and aggressions arising from their predicament. Fanon argues that the eventual violence perpetrated by the colonial against the colonizer was therapeutic in that it liberated the colonial from this accumulated internalized frustration/aggression. Lewis Coser's studies of social conflict found Fanon's concept of violence to be a myth that was both "an evil and destructive vision" and "profoundly mistaken,"[21] but in my experience members of gangs do attack the property of wealthy people (most, but not all, of whom are white) as a result of pent-up frustration/anger associated with their perception of their limited opportunities, and they feel better as a result. Here are the comments of Top Hat, an eighteen-year-old Puerto Rican gang member from New York:

> Yeah, I smashed the windshield of this white preppy's Jag [Jaguar automobile]. I dropped a brick on it. . . . I did it because I hate those assholes. They got everything 'cause they're white and their fathers were rich and bloodsuckers. And you know, after I do it, I feel a little better that I made them hassled just a little.

The frustration/resentment associated with these attacks on property are not only attributable to nonwhite gangs. The Irish gangs of Boston have also been involved in this type of violence. These gangs usually attack the property of those they identify as Yankees, blue bloods, or Brahmins—that is, wealthy WASPS (white Anglo-Saxon Protestants) who have historically discriminated against the Irish in Boston.[22] These Irish gangs have the same contemptuous attitude toward wealthy Protestants (blue bloods) as the nonwhites have toward whites in general, in part for similar reasons—because the wealthy Protestants did, historically, view the Irish as the lowest level of human civilization. It is not uncommon, even in the 1980s, to hear wealthy WASPS refer to the lower-class Irish in Boston as "animals."[23]

The comments of Cory, a nineteen-year-old member of an Irish gang in Boston, depict the frustration and anger of some gang members:

> I torched the inside of that blue's [blue blood's] car, so what? I hate them, just like I hate the niggers. They think we're scum. You know they keep us in these low-paying jobs and these row houses and go off to their fancy houses in the suburbs which they bought by ripping us off from good wages. Hell, I won't be getting a job to get me out of this because I won't get the opportunity, they'd rather give it the niggers. So I think they're scum, and when I get the chance to make it a little hard for them, I take it! And you know what? I feel better afterward.

Thus, some of the data in the present study suggest that Fanon's contention that violence can be therapeutic for those who have endured long periods of frustration and anger is as true for whites as for nonwhites.[24] This tends to occur when specific white populations view their plight as similar to that of nonwhites.[25] All these acts of violence against property must be committed outside a gang member's neighborhood (or community) because, if they were committed within the community, the gang would likely intervene and the individual would be subject to punishment.

Organizational Gang Violence

This section analyzes the violence committed by gang members acting as agents of the organization. This type of gang violence is undertaken as a result of an organizational directive, almost never as a result of an instinctive response.

The six general spheres in which violence is perpetrated by individual gang members also exist for violence committed by members acting as part of the collective. Therefore the analysis in this section will use the same ordering as in the previous one.

Collective Violence against Members

There are occasions when the gang, as an organization, decides to use violence against one of its members. Given the defiant individualist character of their members, gangs do not prefer to use violence against members because they have found it to undermine the organization. Violence against members is undertaken only in the most extreme situations, and only for one reason: fear. When a gang becomes fearful that the organization is disintegrating from internal causes, it will use violence against its own members. Violence against members attempts to accomplish two objectives. The first is to establish authority and the legitimacy of that authority. There are two levels at which authority and legitimacy are being forged and/or defended: (1) the abstract level, in which the collective attempts to justify the need for authority in general (i.e., should there be any authority at all?) and at the same time to justify whichever authority structure is presently operative (e.g., vertical, horizontal, influential); and (2) the more immediate level, in which those who presently occupy positions of authority attempt to justify their doing so. Violence is thus used to counter challenges made by members both to authority in the abstract and to specific gang leaders.

The second objective in the organization's use of violence against its own members is to punish violation of the gang's codes or incompetence in a gang operation. In either case, the leadership rarely executes an act of violence against one of its members unless it has either consulted with the collective and received formal permission (which happens in a large number of cases) or become convinced that there will be no challenges by the membership to such actions. Any miscalculation by the leaders involving collective violence against a member will nearly always cause a crisis, which in turn will threaten their authority.

Violence against Members of Other Gangs

Three factors are most prominent among the causes of inter-gang violence. The first has to do with organizational ambitions. Most gangs are involved in accumulating capital, and the pursuit of this objective often leads two or more gangs into conflict. On numerous occasions, I observed one gang attack another in an effort to take control over a particular geographic area for purposes of expanding its economic activity or increasing the size of its membership.[26] In nearly every case, the initial attack was effectively repulsed. However, in 60 percent of the cases observed (160), repeated attacks ultimately proved successful and the aggressor gang secured control over the new territory.[27] The case of the Rockers, a New York gang, illustrates this type of attack. The Rockers wanted to expand their drug business, which meant that they had to take control over an area of the city that was already under the control of another gang, the Kicks. Numerous meetings were held in which the gang members debated whether to attack the Kicks. Since the Kicks were not considered an archenemy, it was not an easy decision; but economics won out and the leadership was given the responsibility of developing a war plan and presenting it to the membership. The leadership met and decided how best to attack, and the plan was presented, debated, and accepted. All members were required to participate, but because of the constant presence of police in the area, only a small number would be responsible for executing each action.

The strategy was to first offer the Kicks the opportunity to incorporate themselves into the Rockers organization, an offer everyone knew would be rejected. The idea was to let the membership of the Kicks know they could join if they wanted to. The Rockers heralded their expansionist policy with systematic attacks on the Kicks' clubhouse, followed by persistent attacks on members. The attacks were quite brutal, involving lead pipes, knives, and chains, and severe injuries were inflicted. After two months, the strategy began to work. Members of the rival gang began to desert their organization, and many joined the expansionist gang. Within four months, the expansionist gang was in control and operating a profitable cocaine business.

Testing the loyalty of members to the organization is also a cause of inter-gang violence. On some occasions, the gang leadership will devise a plan to attack the members of another gang for no reason other than to see whether a specified group of their own members is serious about its commitment to the organization. For example, the leadership of an Irish gang from New York decided to check whether eight of its members could be trusted. Six of these members were new to the gang, and two had been members for about two months. The leadership wanted to know if they could be trusted to carry out orders from the organization, so they developed a story that an African-American gang operating six blocks away had attacked one of their members in their own area. After telling the story to the members they wanted to test, they insisted that a retaliatory act be initiated. The leadership then devised a plan in which these eight members were to go to the rival gang's territory and attack a small number of that gang.[28] The plan was executed, and the gang found that the eight new members could be trusted. Of course, the incident was not without some costs: two people were stabbed, one from the Irish gang and one from the African-American gang, and both required hospitalization.

Fear is also an important factor in instigating inter-gang conflict. Fear can take various forms in precipitating inter-gang violence, but the present research found it expressed in four basic patterns.

The first appears when a leader of a particular gang feels that he has lost some of his status or authority and initiates a plan to attack another gang in order to regain it. Such individuals believe that by devising a creative, successful strategy and showing courage during the attack, they will regain the respect/status and authority that had been waning.[29] In this regard, gang leaders think like political leaders; they believe a successful military engagement can turn public opinion in their favor. The comments of Copter, a twenty-year-old leader in a predominantly Latino New York gang, are an example:

> Well, you [the author] could see that I was getting challenged
> every time I would suggest things at meetings. A lot of the dudes
> had issues with me. . . . I guess you could say they were losing
> their respect for me. So I decided that I would come up with this

plan for attacking the [rival gang's name]. Hell, we didn't get on with them anyway, and we would have had to attack them anyway, so I just decided to do it sooner. So I got this plan together, others in the leadership liked it and we went with it. We kicked ass, and I went in first and jellied a number of the [rival gang's name]. Shit, after that I was back at the top, just like nothing happened. Man, I was like President Thatcher of England after the Falklands shit, check it out!

On the other hand, one had better be successful, or there would be costs to such a strategy. Consider the case of Turtle, a nineteen-year-old member of a Los Angeles gang:

There was this time when I was the dude in charge of security. I was doing alright when a couple of my homeboys started talking shit about me and some of the other homies believed them. Then there was talk of putting some other dude in to be in charge of security. So I decided I had to prove myself and I got this plan together to attack the [rival gang's name]. Everybody went along with it and we did it, but it didn't work as good as it was suppose to. It worked, but not as good as everybody wanted, and then those guys who were against me and our *klika* won and somebody else got to be in charge of war and security.

The second way that fear induces one gang to attack another relates to the leadership's fear that their own organization is in decline. The perceived cause of the gang's decline varies. Sometimes leaders believe the decline is owing to a poor business climate in which little capital has accrued. Sometimes it is because the leadership has not been able to get the membership to act collectively in various business ventures for the benefit of the entire organization. Sometimes it is because there is a great deal of internal conflict within the membership that the leadership has not been able to mediate. Whatever the reason, the fear of organizational decline is crucial in the leadership's decision to launch an attack on a rival gang. They believe that such conflict will deter internal conflict, encourage group cohesion, and create more control over members.[30] Here are the comments of Lizard, a twenty-six-year-old leader of a New York gang:

You know, we was having some difficulty with the members. They be fighting with each other and all. We couldn't get anything going, you know we couldn't get any business going. We was really getting stretched, the whole thing could've fallen in [the gang could have dissolved as an organization]. So the leadership got together, made up a story that the [rival gang's name] were selling dope in our area. . . . We got a number of the members together and we hit a number of the [rival gang's name]. They turned around and attack us and we had a war for about six months. But you know what, the organization got stronger 'cause we was at war. . . . That war was necessary to save the organization.[31]

Fear of being attacked by a rival gang stimulates a "first strike" mentality. This fear is often not based on any hard evidence that another gang is planning an attack, but rather emerges from a worldview that sees people (and groups) as predatory by nature. This paranoia is an element of the gang member's defiant individualist character and can be seen in the comments of Jules, a twenty-two-year-old Jamaican who is a leader of a New York gang:

That's it man, we attacked the [rival gang's name] and leveled some impressive destruction. . . . No, I don't know if they were planning to attack us or not. If they weren't thinking of it now, they would have had to think of it in the future, so it was best we got them now.

Violence against Residents of the Community

The main reason why gangs attack members of their own community is fear of organizational decline. Because gangs need the support of their communities, they almost always avoid antagonizing neighborhood residents. Therefore, an organizational decision to attack a resident signals that something extraordinary is occurring in the neighborhood. Such events might include people from the neighborhood robbing their fellow residents; someone in the neighborhood acting as an informant to the police; or someone in the neighborhood not cooperating with the gang. In each of these cases, physical intimidation is used to reestablish control of the neighborhood. However, any time physical force is viewed as necessary to maintain control of the neighborhood, this indicates that the gang as an organization is experiencing a crisis. Funnel, an eighteen-year-old African-American member of a New York gang, tells what occurred with his organization:

When the [name of the gang] were still going, there were these times when we messed some people in the community up. . . . One time was when there was this group of niggers from the community who formed this crew [a name given to a group formed principally to steal]. They was taking money from kids in the neighborhood. All of us in the gang decided to stop it, so we waited for them and we really punished them. They was really hurting when we was done; and they was finished too! . . . Then there was this time when we wasn't getting help from the community. Two times the police came and there were people who didn't tell us when they saw them and two of our brothers got arrested. So we had to stop that shit, so we went over to their houses and roughed them up some. You know just to give them a message. But the whole thing backfired because after that the whole community stopped helping us and that was when we started to go under.[32]

Attacks against People Who Live outside the Community

Violent attacks against people who are not in a rival gang and who live outside the attacking gang's community are not numerous. When they do happen, they occur for three reasons. The first is ambition. A gang may contract to do bodily harm, ranging from beating to murder. In 1987, for example, it was reported that a Chicago gang had been hired by the Libyan government to assassinate a number of prominent politicians in the United States.[33] Most such contracts that gangs undertake are, however, directed against people involved in some form of illegal business.

The second reason involves a combination of two emotions—ambition and frustration. There are times when a gang enters into a business arrangement and finds that the other party has failed to honor the agreement. The gang's ambition to accumulate capital, and its frustration at having been prevented from doing so, leads to a violent confrontation. In addition, sometimes individuals who live outside the neighborhood observe the gang attempting to do business and call the police. If this continues and the gang's business suffers, then the person calling the police is sometimes attacked.

The third reason for attacks on people who live outside the community also involves two emotions—fear of organizational decline and frustration. If the police are harassing a particular gang enough to affect its operations negatively, then the organization will perceive this as a threat to its survival and will use violence to get the police to cease and desist. In these cases, the gangs will shoot at the police to send them a message to relax their pressure. These acts have proven overwhelmingly successful—that is, the message is received and the pressure is relieved.[34]

Finally, there are times when gangs violently attack a person who does not live in their community for no reason other than a case of mistaken identity or because the person was in the wrong place at the wrong time. There are times when the organization has given a directive to either beat up or shoot an individual or group, and those responsible for the assignment misidentify the targets. The Spears, a New York gang mostly composed of Latinos, illustrate this. For months they had been in an ongoing war with two gangs that were predominantly Irish, one of which was called the Pipes. During one particular period of this conflict, their members had been physically attacked while selling drugs in their own area. After two weeks of this, the word among the junkies who were their largest customers was to buy from some other group rather than risk being hurt buying from them. The leadership of the Spears decided that the Pipes were responsible for the attacks, and ordered retaliation against a number of the Pipes' leadership. The next day a group of fifteen Spears went out to attack two of the Pipes' leaders. However, it was difficult to find the Pipes because they never wore colors (some symbol identifying themselves as members of that gang). The Spears finally spotted two of the leaders going into a grocery store to shop for some food and they waited behind some parked cars for them to come out. Two young men came out carrying food, and the group attacked with long pipes, repeatedly striking the two indiscriminately. Blood was everywhere, all over the two being beaten, on the sidewalk, and on a number of the Spears. Women passing by began to scream, and the Spears ran to their car. Getting into the car, they saw the store owner and two young men running after them with baseball bats. As the Spears drove away, Dr. Zero, one of the members, said, "Oh, shit, that's the two we was after!" They had, in fact, attacked and severely hurt two young men who were not only not in the Pipes but did not even live in that neighborhood. The two victims had simply stopped to get some sandwiches from the store's deli. Later, when the Spears received information about who the victims were, the leadership pressed those in charge of the operation about what had happened. Hop, who was in charge, said: "Shit, we saw the two Pipes go into the store and we waited. Then these two Paddy-looking [Irish-looking] dudes come out and we just jumped them. Fuck, we didn't have time to wait and check everything out, we was in the middle of the Pipes' territory and we'd been waiting for ten minutes so there could of been some of the Pipes' people who had already seen us and told. We just saw these guys and they looked like the two Pipes we saw go in. You know, those Paddies look a lot the same, man, so [it's] fucking hard to tell quick!" Some of the members laughed at the insinuation that white people look alike, but the leadership of the Spears did not smile. Finally, the leader said, "Don't fuck up this time," and started to plan another attack on the Pipes.[35]

However, there are other instances when those in charge of an attack have accurately identified the targets but have lacked the necessary control to confine the violence to those identified. As a result, innocent people have been hurt or killed. One example involved the Dukes in Los Angeles, who were at war with another Chicano gang, the Dusters. One night a group of the Dukes were sitting in the living room of a member's home, drinking beer, when a car drove by and shots were fired at the house. Some shot (pellets from the shotgun blast) hit the window where the Dukes were sitting; but the house was a duplex, and a number of pellets from several blasts went through the living room window of the people who lived next door, injuring two people. No one was killed, but two people who were not gang members were critically injured. Most gangs make concerted efforts to avoid such incidents because they jeopardize their legitimacy in the community and usually precipitate calls for police crackdowns on gang activities. Nonetheless, they continue to occur all too often.[36]

Attacks against Property in the Community

Just as gangs try to avoid attacking people in their community, they also try to avoid attacking property in their community. This is because the destruction of property usually affects some community resident in a negative manner, which in turn generally elicits an antagonistic response from the community. When gangs as organizations do violently attack property in their community, it is for reasons related to organizational ambition. Sometimes gangs will attack property, such as a house, in order to rid the community of an undesirable element. These cases usually involve the destruction of prostitution houses, drug (crack) houses, or numbers establishments, which occurs primarily as a result of a request from the community (or a segment of the community).

At other times, gangs try to assert their dominance by attacking the property of people who live in the community. Such attacks occur when someone in the community declines to pay the gang for protection or when individuals have cooperated with the police against the organization. In both these cases, the organization's ambition to maintain its business interests is at the core of its actions.

Attacks against Property outside the Community

Gangs make violent attacks against property outside their territory for two reasons. One has to do with ambition. Gangs will often attack property in an effort to assert control in a particular market. When the gang engages in such activities, it is generally part of a strategy to expand its zone of business operation. Attacking property is intended either to disrupt the operations of other competing organizations, effectively rendering such organizations nonoperational, or to let these competing organizations know that they must now relinquish some of their market.

A second reason for such attacks has to do with frustration. Sometimes gangs decide to destroy the property of someone who lives outside their neighborhood in order to vent their frustration and regain a positive image. Usually these violent attacks are a retaliation against an adversary, such as another gang, the police, or some other law enforcement agent who has undertaken some action that has negatively affected the organization.

Situations and Violence

One of the most important findings concerning violence among the gangs studied is that the root cause of violence is not the precarious situations in which individual gang members (acting on their own behalf) and the organization (acting as a collective) often find themselves. However, these situations do determine the intensity and extent of the violence used. Thus, in order to understand how members determine the level and scope of violence to be used at any particular time, it is necessary to explain the interaction of four factors: fear, the organization, technology, and the specific situation. Although the interaction of these four factors is complex, there are four general patterns. First, the level (i.e., the degree of intensity and scope) of violence increases as the level of fear (and anxiety) in specific situations increases. For example, for about six months the Black Widows of New York had been in a war with the Monsters over territory. During one three-day period, four of the Black Widows had been beaten up by the Monsters. Deciding to retaliate, the leadership of the Black Widows planned an attack and selected those who would be involved in the operation.

On the night of the attack, those selected got into their cars and drove to the Monsters' area. It was a hot summer night, which made the attack more difficult, because there were more people out on the street who might recognize them, warn the Monsters, and help the Monsters counterattack. Tension was high, and the Black Widows parked their cars in a place that was easily accessible to facilitate their escape. They then went to a spot where the Monsters congregated. Finding no Monsters there, they decided to start back to the car and to attack if they saw anybody on his way back. Just as they turned the first corner, one of the Monsters saw them and started to run. Two of the Black Widows ran after him to catch him before he told the others, but he got away. They informed the leader of the unit that he had gotten away and began to run toward their car (which was eight blocks away) because they knew that it was merely a matter of time before the Monsters would be mobilized to hunt them down. The tension/fear was incredibly high as they made their way through the streets and alleys toward the car. Just as they emerged from one alley, three of the Monsters—or so it appeared—who had not been told that the Black Widows were in their area literally ran into them. All fifteen Black Widows immediately attacked them viciously with pipes, knives, and chains. The intensity of the attack was extremely high. The Black Widows continued to beat the three savagely, and there was an enormous amount of blood all over the pavement. They stopped when the leader said they should go to their cars. They went to their cars and left the area.

As for the victims of their attack, only one of the three was a member of the Monsters; the other two had just been walking with him. One was knocked unconscious and all three had fractures and multiple lacerations over their entire bodies. The violence used by the Black Widows was excessively brutal, but the Black Widows involved in this operation had such a high level of fear and anxiety about the situation that, when confronted by what they believed was the enemy, they were unable to use proper restraint. This is almost identical to situations encountered in military combat. In fact, in recording the events and listening to the members of the Black Widows describe their feelings at the time, I recognized their similarity to accounts given by combat veterans of the Vietnam War.[37]

High levels of fear among gang members in certain situations can also be responsible for increasing the scope of the violence used. Two examples of this involve situations in which a gang wants to kill a member of another gang. The police report, and other gang members confirm, that when a Chinese gang retaliates against another gang, it does not necessarily confine its assault to a specific person or persons, but—in what frequently appears to be a panicked response—indiscriminately fires weapons in the general area of its intended target. Often gang members express little concern over the fact that they may have gravely injured innocent people. In 1987–88 two African-American gangs in Los Angeles, the Crips and the Bloods, behaved in a similar manner. When I was discussing this matter with a number of African-American gang members in Los Angeles, they said that, because they felt vulnerable, they needed to warn the rival gang that if they attempted aggressive action, there would be a bloodbath. They acknowledged that more people than necessary occasionally become victims, including innocent people, but stated that they must continue to operate this way or else remain a vulnerable target. They argued that the threat to undertake extensive violence deters other gangs from attacking them. This argument is remarkably similar to the nuclear deterrent argument espoused by proponents of nuclear weaponry.

In sum, even when fear and anxiety are primarily responsible for the intensity and extent of violence, gang members never use them as justifications. No gang member ever wants to acknowledge that he is afraid; to do so would leave the person vulnerable to attack. The best defense against attack is to represent oneself as fearless. Therefore, gang members justify their use of violence on the grounds that if the victim of their violence had had the chance, that person would have done the same to them—that is, they see their actions as being fair because they believe the world operates under a Social Darwinist code.

The second pattern indicates that the intensity and scope of violence increases as the organizational hierarchy increasingly takes command and orders individuals to undertake action. Some of the most violent actions involving gangs occur when gang members are acting as agents of the collective and/or as part of a collective. The organizational leadership often simply directs a member or group of members to take violent action against a particular person or group of people. This increases the intensity of the violence because those effecting the violence feel that there are few restrictions on them. A good example is the drive-by shooting behavior of the Crips and Bloods in Los Angeles. Their belief that they are acting with the approval of the entire organization generally frees them from any misgivings about using unrestrained violence to achieve their objectives. The organization's directive creates an anxious situation for the gang member, and the more forceful that directive is, the more intensely violent its execution will be. Take the comments of J.B., an eighteen-year-old member of a New York gang:

> See, I and a lot of other guys have inflicted a lot of hurt on people over the years, but we was commanded at various times by the gang to inflict some hurt on people. We did it and did it mercilessly. . . . Nobody felt guilty about it because since the whole gang thought it was the right thing, it was the right thing. Plus it was an order and you had to follow orders.

In addition, when brutal violence was used, one would always hear such rationalizations as: "I only followed orders," or "They told me to do it," or "If I didn't do it, I would have been punished." All these rationalizations functioned to neutralize feelings of guilt and remorse, and ultimately restraint.[38]

Another way in which the organization can affect the level of violence perpetrated by gang members is when a directive to action is given to a number of members. When members act as part of a collective, they frequently go too far, becoming caught up in the dynamics of group action rather than considering the consequences of that action. Sometimes individual members and the group find it difficult to determine when enough force has been used—that is, when to quit. An incident involving the Snow Tigers, an Irish gang in Boston, illustrates this situation. An old Puerto Rican woman lived alone within the neighborhood that the Snow Tigers controlled. She had lived there for fifteen years, and every two weeks, her grandson would come and visit her. One day her grandson came to visit her accompanied by six other Puerto Rican boys. The Snow Tigers agreed that they would have to send a message to the Puerto Rican community that they were not to come into their neighborhood, so they decided to beat up the grandson. At the meeting the leaders told those who were to administer the beating, "Now we ain't got nothing against this guy so just give him a beating and send him home. We just want to send a message to the other spics." A week later they cornered the grandson when he was alone and attacked him with clubs. Once they started beating him, they were not able to determine when to stop, and they left him much more seriously injured than they had intended.

The third pattern indicates that the level of violence increases as access to and use of lethal technologies increases. As gangs have been able to secure more sophisticated and powerful weaponry, the intensity and extent of violence has increased dramatically. At the time of this writing, almost every sophisticated weapon is accessible to gang members. They can legally purchase many sophisticated weapons (particularly semi-automatic guns that can easily be made fully automatic) at any gun store. Those weapons that are not available through retail outlets can be purchased on the lucrative black market in guns. Violence increases geometrically when such weaponry is used, as the 1987–88 gang wars in Los Angeles proved. The intensity (loss of life as opposed to being severely injured) and the extent (number of people who may be killed) of violence is thus at its highest when gangs have these weapons at their disposal and are willing to use them. Technology makes it psychologically easy for the individuals to indulge in such violence. Take the comment of Biggy, a sixteen-year-old member of a Chicano gang in Los Angeles:

> Check it out, I got me a lot of shooting in and I hit a lot of people. . . . Yeah, I can remember when I first was told [by the gang] to shoot somebody. I was nervous, but I had this automatic rifle, and when I started to shoot, man, it was easy. That's what makes it easy, it's fast and there's nothing personal in it like when you use a knife. . . . Hey, you know what I like about carrying this pistol, you get respect no matter who you are or how big you are [Biggy is 5′5″] 'cause it evens everything up.

The fourth pattern indicates that the overall level of violence increases when it is used in a way that one of the antagonists thinks is inappropriate to the situation. For example, in Los Angeles some very young members of a particular gang (twelve and thirteen years old) were riding their bikes in another gang's territory, believing that a peace treaty had been signed between their gang and the gang controlling the area. In fact, no peace treaty had been signed, and both of the young boys riding their bikes were shot with a shotgun and severely injured. After the incident, the level of violence (both the intensity and extent) increased dramatically because the boys' gang thought that the shooting was an inappropriate response and that retaliation was necessary to let rival gangs know that such incidents would not be tolerated. Interestingly, the gang whose members had fired on the young boys also thought it was an inappropriate response. They knew what would occur next, so they armed themselves heavily and made ready to brave the storm. Such situations inevitably increase the level of violence because violence is justified on retaliatory grounds, which sets in motion a nefarious spiraling dynamic that increases the number of people involved (which usually includes the police).[39]

Type of Organization and Type of Violence

This section examines the possible relationship between the types of gang organization described earlier and the patterns of violence in which they are involved. Many of the previous studies of gangs have found that there were different types of gangs (some organized to fight and others organized for other activities) and that the level of violence associated with each gang was dependent on its type.[40] The present study does not focus on different types of gangs based on purpose (primarily because nearly all of the gangs now operating use force to some degree), but rather on gangs with different types of organizational structures. This section addresses the issue of whether organizational structure has an effect on the amount and type of violence in which gangs participate.

The data in Figures 1 and 2 indicate patterns that are strong enough to be considered indicators of specific relationships between organizational structure and type of violence, even though the data are not as complete as one would like. They indicate that gangs with a vertical/hierarchical organizational structure are likely to indulge in more organizational violence than individual violence, but that they are less likely to be involved in either type of violence than gangs having one of the other two organizational structures. This is because vertical/hierarchical gangs tend to have more discipline within the organization than other types of gangs. The result is that they have more control over their membership, which tends to lessen internal strife (because of the threat of disciplinary action), and partake in more projects that the organization directs to further its own interests. Thus, the more a gang is able to structure itself as an ideal type of vertical/hierarchical organization, the more overall control it is able to command; and the more control it has, the fewer cases of individual gang violence it will experience.

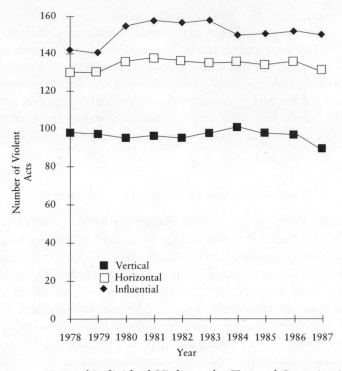

Figure 1.   Acts of Individual Violence, by Type of Organization

NOTE: The data for this table are derived from the author's fieldnotes. When an individual gang member acting on his own engaged in an act of physical aggression toward another person or object, it was recorded as "Individual Violence." Because the author could not be with every gang member or gang at all times, the number of events presented in the table is not the total number of violent acts committed by the individuals involved in the gangs studied.

Gangs structured along both influential and horizontal/commission lines have higher levels of violence by individual members and lower levels of collective violence than gangs using the vertical/hierarchical structure. However, this general pattern occurs for different reasons. Gangs with a horizontal/commission structure find it difficult to coordinate all the factions of the organization, each of which has its own power base. Because there is little centralized power, it is difficult to control all the factions. Thus, while some factions control their cliques quite rigidly, others are looser. The result is a higher aggregate level of individual violence than

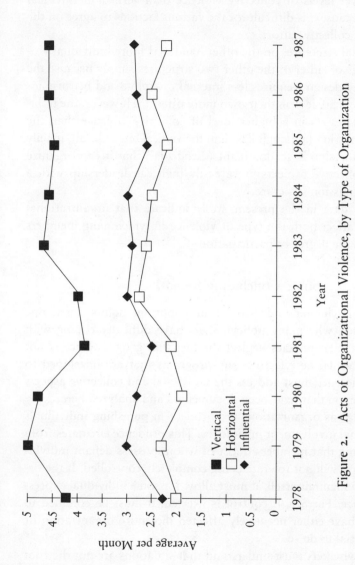

Figure 2. Acts of Organizational Violence, by Type of Organization

NOTE: The data for this table are derived from the author's fieldnotes. When an individual or group of individual members of a gang acting on the direction of the organization engaged in an act of physical aggression toward another person or object, it was recorded as "Organizational Violence." Because the author could not be with every gang member or gang at all times, the number of events presented in the table is not the total number of violent acts committed by the gangs studied.

in the vertical/hierarchical structure. In addition, horizontal/commission gangs have lower levels of collective violence than vertical/hierarchical gangs simply because it is difficult for the various factions to agree on the particulars of a collective effort.

The influential structure, on the other hand, has more individual violence than gangs of either of the other two structures simply because the organization, by design, requires less internal discipline and because individual members are left on their own more often.[41] However, the influential structure results in a higher level of collective violence than the horizontal/commission (although less than the vertical/hierarchical), mainly because the leadership is so dominant (dictatorial) that it can organize and execute collective projects more easily than can leadership with a horizontal/commission structure.

In sum, the data in the present study indicate that organizational structure does affect both the type of violence in which gang members participate and the degree of participation.

Some Concluding Remarks

The data in this chapter underscore four important points. First, one significant reason why many policymakers have difficulty coping with violence is that their policies neglect the fact that gang violence is not one-dimensional. To be effective, any programs that are developed to control gang violence must address the individual and collective aspects of the phenomenon that have been documented and analyzed here.

Second, gangs as organizations are prudent in punishing individuals for their personal involvement in violence. This prudence emanates from an understanding that members (most of whom possess defiant individualist characters) will not tolerate being completely controlled. If the organization is to maintain itself, it must allow for some individual expressions of violence. Further, if control is exerted, it must be confined to incidents that have either negatively affected the entire organization or have the potential to do so.

Third, policymakers must understand that situations are not the root cause of violence. The actual root causes are such factors as fear, ambition, testing, and frustration. Nonetheless, situations do affect the level (intensity and extent) of gang violence.

Fourth, people have commonly explained gang violence in terms of the personal attributes of gang members. "They like to fight," we are told about gang members (as opposed to non-gang members). This notion has taken on a mythological quality. However, only a small number of gang members enjoy fighting, and they are not concentrated in the leadership, as Yablonsky has argued. Most do not enjoy fighting at all and try to avoid it because the risks to personal safety are high. While this may run counter to many of the contemporary perceptions of gang violence, it must be understood in order to comprehend the phenomenon.

Fear of physical harm, however, is not sufficient to completely deter gang violence, because most gang members (and the organization) believe that if you do not attack, you will be attacked. In other words, even if you do not attack anyone, it does not mean that you will be able to avoid violence, because others will prey upon you. Such a worldview implies only one course of action: attack while the competitor is most vulnerable. Interestingly, the injuries incurred as a result of organizational violence become the social cement that creates group bonds in a defiant individualist setting.

In summary, what most gang members find attractive about violence is the things it sometimes can secure for them. In substance, violence is understood to be the instrument used to achieve objectives that are not achievable in other ways.[42]

Chapter Six

The Gang and the Community

The people are like water and the army is like fish.
Mao Tse-tung, *Aspects of China's Anti-Japanese Struggle* (1948)

Anyone who wants to understand gangs must examine the question of how low-income communities interrelate with the gangs that operate in their midst. Past research has described this relationship as either antagonistic or apathetic. Those who argue that the relationship is antagonistic believe that the gang usually assumes a parasitic role vis-à-vis the community, preying on the vulnerable and forcing "good young boys" to join its ranks, thereby ruining their lives.[1] According to these studies, this causes communities to assume a hostile demeanor toward gangs active in their areas.

On the other hand, other studies describe the relationship between community and gang as one of apathy. Most of these studies argue either that this apathy is simply a part of the general malaise associated with the social disorganization present in most low-income areas, or that gangs merely reflect the low-income adult world, which may or may not be disorganized. In the former case, the community and gang simply ignore each other as much as possible;[2] in the latter case, the gang becomes an integral part of the low-income community's social order, assuming a human/developmental position within the life-course of low-income community existence (i.e., lower-class boys—and, in some cases, lower-class girls—join gangs during adolescence before they move on to ordinary adult relationships).[3] In both cases, the gang is portrayed as being marginal within or isolated from the community either because of open hostility or because members of gangs are often young and have done little to achieve high social status.

However, my own findings show that this is not an accurate assessment of the contemporary relationship between gangs and the communities they operate in. In general, gangs are not isolated from their communities. They are not ignored or viewed with contempt, and neither (as the "social order" studies have argued) are they simply a rung of the social order of low-income, working-class neighborhoods. Rather, they are a formal element in low-income neighborhoods; they operate on an independent and equal basis with all the other organizations active in the low-income community. Within this context, the gang and community strike up a working relationship, which lasts as long as the two mutually aid and respect each other. If either breaks the code, the pact is terminated and both lose to some degree. However, the gang will experience the greatest loss because it is in more consistent need of the community rather than vice versa. For this reason, gangs make a concerted and aggressive effort to aid the community. If a gang violates the code and is not successful in reestablishing a reciprocal relationship with the community, it will become isolated, which will seriously weaken its ability to operate effectively. This more often than not marks the beginning of the end for such a gang.

As is evident from the data presented in chapter 5, gangs have been associated with much violence. Because of this, one might expect communities where gangs operate to be generally antagonistic toward them.[4] I found that some communities had been antagonistic toward gangs at different times, but most of the communities studied had either a working or a very close relationship with the gangs in their areas.[5] In 84 percent of the cases that I studied (31 of 37 gangs), the gang and the community in which it was active had established some type of working relationship. (This figure does not include cases where the community had assumed an apathetic relationship, which rarely happened.) In each of these cases, the gang and the community had reached a close or at least a working relationship. One should understand that whatever accord the gang and the community had attained was at times quite fluid. On some occasions, one could observe a close working relationship between the gang and the community; at other times, a difficult, if not antagonistic, relationship was observable.

Probably what is most crucial to understanding the relationship that gangs have with their communities is recognition that this rapprochement is very delicate and capricious. This chapter focuses on the two most fundamental aspects of the community-gang affiliation. First, an analysis of the data (field notes) indicates that the basis for a positive relationship lies in the social bonding that occurs as a result of two processes, one rooted in psychological factors, the other rooted in the process by which both parties strive to meet the other's needs and interests. Second, once a positive association has been established and bonding has occurred, the gangs assume a "militia type" behavior pattern: they conspicuously respond to the direction given them by the community rather than the community responding to them.

Social and Psychological Bases
for Community-Gang Ties

One of the important elements in community-gang ties is the bonding that occurs when both parties attempt to accommodate the interests of the other. The bases for this bonding can be separated into those interests that originate in the community and those that originate in the gang.

The Community's Interest in Close Ties
with the Gang

On the side of the community, bonding begins with certain psychosocial dispositions that I have found present among parents and adults in low-income areas with a history of gang activity. In interviewing countless numbers of parents in these areas, some who had children in gangs and some who did not, I found that the bonding between community and gang partly originated in the adults' identification with the gangs and their encouragement of young people from these areas to become involved with gangs. In many of these areas, parents have encouraged their own children to be active in gangs, and some have even encouraged other people's children to do so. Tradition plays a crucial role in parents encouraging gang involvement, especially among Chicano gangs in Los Angeles, many of which have existed for several decades. Many of the parents I interviewed were in the same gang that their children are now in, so there is a sense of tradition in which gang and family are intertwined. I found that 32 percent (24) of the fathers whom I interviewed in the Los Angeles area had been in the same gang as their children. In fact, 11 percent said that four generations of men in their family had been in the same gang. A representative comment was that of Pancho D., a forty-seven-year-old carpenter and parent of four living in Los Angeles:

> I don't like the shooting that goes on with gangs today. There is much more than when I was in the gang, but I am proud of my sons being members of the [gang name] because it keeps a family tradition alive; you know my father was in the same gang. It also keeps a community tradition going that is not as bad as the media want to portray it. The gang has helped our community . . . and as far as the violence, well, I just don't worry because, just like if they [his sons] were in the army, there is a chance that they could be killed, but that is up to God because life has chances that go with it.

I also found that tradition played a role in the neighborhoods of both New York and Boston, although not the way it did in Los Angeles. In the Irish neighborhoods in New York and Boston, the adult social clubs, which a vast majority of the parents belonged to, endeavored to encourage gang involvement because the gangs had traditionally been feeder organizations for them. Participation in the gang was thus seen as contributing to the tradition and culture of the neighborhood (or to the larger Irish community). Take the comment of Joe O'C., a forty-nine-year-old dock worker and father of five in New York:

> Well, I was in a gang, not the same gang that now is here, but a gang. And you see most of us moved on to become members of the [name of the Irish social club]. You see that's the way it's done here, you join a local gang or youth association of some kind and keep up your friendships and then when you get older you get asked and join a social club. Now that I am in the social club, I know how important it is to establish friendships, and that starts in the gang . . . so you see, through these gang friendships, members of the social clubs continue to keep close to each other. . . . I think that the gangs help keep tradition in the neighborhood alive because they feed the social clubs and keep the community going; and so I think it's a good thing my kids have been in the gangs here.

There are two other psychosocial reasons why gangs get adult support in the community. First, a significant number of adults from low-income areas identify with the "resistance component" of gangs. These people empathize with the desires, frustrations, and resentments that the youth of low-income neighborhoods experience because they have experienced them too. Thus they identify with the gang because they are sympathetic to the members' attempts to resist their poor socioeconomic position. Take the comments of Wayne, a fifty-seven-year-old African-American machinist who was the father of two girls:

> I know people think gangs are terrible and that the kids are just disgusting individuals, but that just ain't what's going down with these kids. Hell, they ain't bad kids, sure you gots some, but most ain't bad, they just not willing to quietly sit back and let the society take everything and give them nothing. . . . Sometimes I think some of the gangs go too far, but I understand where they're coming from, and I say, they ain't bad, they just made a bad decision that time, that's all.

Orlando, a thirty-three-year-old Dominican who worked as an apartment doorman and had five children (two of whom are boys, ages four and two), said:

> Those who are in gangs do a lot of things that a lot of people think is terrible, but I am not against them because I know how they feel. You see they are just not going to sit around and accept what society says is your place. They going to resist that stuff all the time. . . . So I don't get down on them because I know how frustrating it can be to think that all you going to have in life is poverty.

The second psychosocial reason relates more directly to the frustrations that the adults/parents have experienced. While I found a large number of parents/adults who were extremely frustrated with their lives, a small fraction of these people felt that they had failed in life. Most of these people did not make this point explicit, but in numerous conversations they implied that they found some comfort that their children were having the same difficulty and facing the same prospects as they had, because it confirmed that they were not the only losers and relieved them of personal feelings of failure. Thus, they responded to their children's involvement in gangs with an absence of discouragement (which acted as a form of encouragement). They knew that gang involvement would eventually result in difficulty with the law, but their "encouragement" was based on an ambivalence about wanting a better life for their children. It should be pointed out, however, that there were only a small number who identified with gangs for this reason. Nonetheless, when this group is combined with those who were sympathetic toward gangs for other psychosocial reasons, a basis for social bonding emerges.

Another reason for bonding from the community's perspective is functional: the community needs certain services that the gang provides. Probably the most important service that gangs can provide is protection. Yet, as we shall see, protection for low-income areas can take on a number of forms. Let us begin with the most common form of protection, that associated with physical violence. Most of the residents who live in poor and low-income areas are concerned with the threat of physical attack. In fact, as I have argued earlier, fear of being physically accosted plays a central role in the dynamics of life in low-income neighborhoods. This fear seems to be intensified when people live in or near public housing complexes, or in areas where there are multiple apartment buildings, because such housing conditions accentuate population density, enhance social contact, and increase conflict.[6] What gangs usually provide to residents of their neighborhoods is some relief from this fear. In most cases, they can protect the community better than the police, and the community typically recognizes this. This does not mean that the community is antagonistic toward the police (although this often is the case); rather, members of the community realize that the gang has some advantages over the police. Despite the fact that the police employed more personnel in the low-income areas under study, the gangs had more of a presence in these communities than did the police.[7] In all the neighborhoods in this study, gang members were extremely aware of any strangers who might be present in the neighborhood.[8] Since they usually occupied a wide range of street corners in the neighborhood, they were strategically located to quickly identify strangers or suspicious people. The comments of Tape and Jorge highlight this point. Tape, a fifteen-year-old gang member from New York, remarked:

> There ain't nobody who's a stranger that comes to our community
> that we don't spot right off. Our peoples is everywhere in this
> community. We on every corner, so we got it covered pretty well,
> so if you came to this community without our escort, you'd be in
> big trouble.

Jorge, a fifty-nine-year-old carpenter in Los Angeles, explained:

> People from outside the community are always down on the
> gangs, but they don't see the good they can do for us in the com-

munity. . . . For one they give us good protection from people outside our community who would rob and hurt our kids. You see
there ain't very many people who come into the neighborhood
that the gangs don't pick up right away. For most of us in the
community, we feel more safe with them than the police because
they can watch anybody suspicious because they know who the
people are that aren't from the community where the police don't
know.

Many adults have consistently emphasized that gangs are more able
to deter crime in their community than the police because gang members
are distributed throughout the community and are able to identify
strangers—or, as they put it, "who belongs and who doesn't"—more
accurately and quickly than the police.

Gangs also possess another resource that the community finds an asset: unlike the police, they are not restrained from taking immediate action against anyone considered a community threat. For example, once a
stranger or a suspicious individual was identified by the gang, he would
be tailed until he left the area. A few of the gangs had policies that directed members to confront anyone thought to pose an immediate or
eventual threat to the community. Those who attempted to rob or physically harm individuals in the neighborhood/community constituted a
"direct" threat. Anyone who simply appeared as though they were sur-
veying the area for a future robbery, or anyone from another gang who
had not been authorized to be in the area, constituted an "eventual"
threat. In both cases, some form of physical confrontation would be used
as a deterrent—that is, the gangs would administer some form of physical
punishment as a message to others who might be thinking of preying on
residents of their neighborhoods. Unlike the police, the gang can administer physical injury without regard to laws designed to restrain such action. The vast majority of the residents in many of the gang communities
that I studied saw this procedure as effective in controlling crime. The
comment of Wilma Y., a forty-eight-year-old Puerto Rican from New
York, is typical:

Well, the gangs have protected me and my family a couple of
times when we were getting attacked by some dope addicts. They
just came over and boy did they beat those guys. They beat them
with clubs and chains and they didn't show any mercy. . . . You
know that isn't nice, but it works and works better than the police, because with the police, they have to be concerned with the

criminal's rights and all that. And even if they do catch them, nothing ever happens to them because the courts let them back on the street to do it all over again. But the gangs don't have to worry about rights and that stuff and they let criminals know that if they come back they can expect exactly the same or worse. . . . People can think what they want, but this has worked here.

The fear of becoming a victim is felt most by older residents and parents of the very young, although parents with female children will continue to worry until they are married or move from the area.[9] Thus, there is a great deal of community support for the work that gangs do to protect those who are most vulnerable in the community. In one of the neighborhoods in New York, one gang both provided escort service for an eighty-four-year-old woman who lived alone and consistently went to the store for her and delivered her groceries each week. This particular gang provided other people in the neighborhood with this service as well. In 84 percent (31) of the cases that I studied, gangs provided at least escort service for anyone in the community who asked for it. The statement of Dorothy O'Hare, a fifty-two-year-old housewife and mother of three in New York, is typical of what is so often heard throughout the areas in which gangs operate:

I feel much safer when I see our boys around on the street corners. I know that I and my daughters will be able to walk around the neighborhood without being attacked by some drug addict or sexual pervert. Most of the time anybody who comes to the neighborhood is confronted by the gangs and chased from here so we don't generally have to worry about being attacked. . . . Though if anyone were to attack me or my family, the gang would be there so quick that we probably wouldn't be hurt too much. I know the police don't care for the gangs very much but the community appreciates what they do for us. Actually, I think the police don't like them because they are jealous that the gangs do a better job of protecting us than they do, even though they say they don't like them because they are taking the law into their own hands.

In protecting the neighborhood's residents from social predators, many gangs have come to resemble what Gerald Suttles has called "vigilante peer groups."[10] However, most of the gangs in the present study went farther than merely being vigilant; they assumed the more active role of a posse (in the old western sense of the word) as well.

In addition to trying to assume responsibility for protecting residents from being accosted and/or robbed, all but three of the gangs that I studied also tried to protect them from other social predators, like loan sharks, unethical landlords, and/or store owners who overcharged for their products. At various times, gangs took action against those thought to be exploiting people in their communities, but they would do so, for the most part, only after members of the community had indicated that something needed to be done. Two examples reveal this aspect of the gang's protective role vis-à-vis the community. The first occurred in New York, where a particular loan shark was not only lending money at a much higher rate than in other parts of the city, but was also lending to people who he knew would have difficulty meeting the payment schedule. When the customers missed a payment (or even made a payment, but less than required), he would raise the repayment rate; if they balked at this, he would send people to force them to accept and pay the added amount. This went on for four months. Finally, when a number of people in the community couldn't keep making the payments, they asked the Savage Profits to talk to the loan shark and warn him to stop doing business in that manner. The gang met, discussed the situation, and then went to talk to the loan shark. He told them, "This ain't your business, so blow off before you get hurt." In observing this exchange between the gang president and the loan shark, I was struck by the lack of effort to compromise. After the gang left, they decided to eliminate the loan shark from the community and proceeded to develop a plan to do so. They physically attacked him and his two companions, even though it was known that they all carried guns. In this particular case, the plan was exceptionally well conceived and the attack was extremely brutal, maiming two of the three. The loan shark never came back to the community, even to collect what was legitimately owed him. In addition, although the police became involved and had to make a report, no one in the community provided them with any information about the attack, because they wanted to protect the gang. So the police were left with another unsolved crime. As Liticia, a forty-six-year-old laundry worker who was married with two children (and had never had any dealings with this particular loan shark), said:

> That man got what was coming to him. He took advantage of the people here and he paid for it. . . . No, nobody would tell the police anything, 'cause it was the community who wanted that guy out. We're just lucky the [Savage Profits] were here to rid the com-

munity of this scum that's all. I don't know who exactly told the [Savage Profits] to get rid these guys, but once the [Savage Profits] was asked, they did what was wanted . . . and the community's happy about that.

The other example involved a small store owner in a New York neighborhood who for five years had contracted with the Dancing Devils to protect his store. The store owner kept a fuel dispenser in his store from which he sold oil for small heaters. In the winter, this was the store's most profitable item because so many people lived in apartment buildings where little or no heat was provided by the landlord. Of course, it was illegal as well as unethical not to provide heat, but efforts to rectify this situation in the courts can require a good deal of time, leaving the residents without heat for long periods.[11] The corner store had a virtual monopoly on heating oil, and the residents were always in a poor bargaining position. In one particular winter, the weather was extremely cold for about a month. People were going to the store for oil on the average of two to three times a week (the average for a normal winter would be about once every two to four weeks, depending on the type of stove and how warm the weather was), and the store owner was raising the price every five or six days. This put a great deal of financial pressure on those who needed the oil. When residents protested, the store owner argued that the increased demand had caused his supplier to raise the wholesale price, which in turn forced him to raise the retail price. People then complained to the gang that it was protecting a business that was taking advantage of them. The gang leaders accordingly investigated the store owner's allegations that the price increases were owing not to his greed but to that of the wholesaler, and they discovered that although the wholesale price had increased, these increases were small. The truth was that the small store owner had seen and used the opportunity to substantially increase his profit. So the gang went to speak to him, informing him that they knew he had been gouging the community and that they wanted him to drastically reduce his oil prices to a modest profit level and to return the overcharge to customers. The store owner refused, so the gang solicited a number of children to enter the store and steal as much as they wanted. When the owner saw that the gang, which was supposed to be guarding the store, just let it happen, he saw his business faltering. Consequently, he lowered his price for the oil and put up a sign offering to pay back to all those with receipts (or those who owed money to him)[12]

the excess amount he had charged them for the oil. As soon as that occurred, the harassment stopped and the gang resumed its job of protecting the store. It is important to emphasize that the gang undertook this
action against the store owner at the request of members of the community. As Boxcar, the twenty-six-year-old leader of the Dancing Devils,
said:

> We wouldn't do this to the store owner if the community hadn't
> told us that they wanted this done. You see, man, two years ago
> we decided that this other store owner was running a bad number
> down on the community, so we torched the place, and check this
> out, the community came down hard on us. First they said that
> the owner wasn't that bad, and then they went on to be pissed off
> because they said that we took away the only store in the area for
> the residents; and they had to go a farther distance to get grocer-
> ies. Hell, man, we learned from that one, I can tell you that; we
> don't do any shit that we thinks is helping the community unless
> we check to see if they think it helps them! It just ain't worth it to
> us in the long run 'cause we need the community.

As I mentioned earlier, community protection can assume different
forms. One area of community protection that has not been documented
much in the literature on gangs, but one that is extremely important, is
that associated with threats from outside the community. Two examples
of this type of protection are instructive. In Brooklyn, Boston, and Los
Angeles, gangs have provided their neighborhoods with occasional protection from outside commercial developers who have wanted to transform their area into high-value commercial property. In Boston, a developer had secured the rezoning necessary to construct a condominium in
a working-class Irish area. The development project was an attempt to
bring middle-class professionals to this section of Boston. Before construction began, it was necessary to demolish half a block of row houses.
The community looked on with trepidation, thinking, as one resident put
it, "If they keep this up, we working people will be forced out of our
homes. We'll just become wards of the state!" Of course, the new construction was the prevailing topic of conversation at the social clubs. As
the project proceeded, there was increased interest n doing something to
stop it. Some members of the community were trying to get city hall to
intercede; others were pursuing legal channels to halt the project. Within
the gang, however, talk was that community leaders were prepared to
pressure the developer to discontinue the project. Most of the talk in the

gang was like rumors circulating in the military. Some of the members said that they would be called upon shortly to sabotage the place. These rumors continued for some time, and one night after the apartment complex was more than 90 percent completed, the structure was attacked with stones and small explosives. The damage was not severe, but it proved expensive for the developer. Extra security was then provided, but the gang was able to inflict more damage on the windows and doors. Eventually the structure was completed, but the attacks and publicity continued and the developer found it difficult to interest people in purchasing the condos. As Packy, a nineteen-year-old gang member, said:

> We sure gave them the message. I knew it would take time, but we kept it up until they had had enough. They was smart getting rid of the building, because we would of been willing to keep at it an awfully long time.

Eventually the developer's project was abandoned. The gangs had followed the direction of the community, and they were praised in the social clubs for their efforts. Thomas, a sixty-eight-year-old lifelong resident of the community, said:

> We sent out a call to the [name of the gang] and they answered the call in splendid fashion. The boys at the club have been toasting their help.

A similar situation occurred in Los Angeles when a developer wanted to redevelop an area inhabited by low-income Latinos. The preliminary plan was for a large segment of the present population to be relocated to other areas of the city and their homes razed. A large shopping area and office buildings were scheduled to be built in the space where the people who had been forced to vacate had once lived. In an attempt to stop the project, a number of people contacted their local politicians, but they met with little success. Many asked the local gang to help. The gang decided that the best way to stop the project was to increase the number of crimes in the area, making it appear that it was a high-crime, unsafe neighborhood. They even used the insignia of two other gangs in a number of crimes to give the false impression that the gangs in the adjoining neighborhoods also operated in this neighborhood and that no one should expect that crime would go down even if the developer relocated the project to an adjoining neighborhood. For four months, the number of crimes continued to rise steadily and the developer decided to withdraw his plans. Ultimately, the residents of the entire community were extremely happy with the developer's decision and grateful for the gang's help. Raquel, a forty-seven-year-old resident and mother of five children, said:

> I know that a lot of people think the gangs are bad, but they don't
> see some of the good things they do for the community either.
> They helped me and my family keep the small house that we have
> because they got the developer to quit his plans.

Developers who operate legally are not the only type of speculator from whom low-income residents need protection. For example, an underworld syndicate opened a new numbers establishment in a New York neighborhood. The neighborhood had already had two numbers establishments and did not want another one, especially not one associated with this particular syndicate, which was vying for power within the organized crime network and always had a great deal of violence directed at its establishments. In addition, rumors were circulating that this particular syndicate wanted to open either a drug (dispensing) house or a brothel within the same block.[13] The community opposed the syndicate's desire to expand in their area because they thought it would generally be more dangerous for themselves and their children. So members of the community contacted the gang in the area to find out whether the gang would represent them and stop the syndicate from expanding into their area. The gang members made no commitment, but said they would discuss it. However, before the gang had the opportunity to meet and discuss the community's request, the syndicate contacted two of the gang's leaders and offered to hire the gang to protect its property for a considerable amount of monthly revenue. This offer complicated the situation for a short time, but after discussion, the gang members agreed that supporting the community was their main priority. As Cape Man, a nineteen-year-old member of the governing council, said:

> This ain't even a choice for us to debate. We gots to help the community because the community is us. It's our lifeblood, if we don't help them now we lose our body, and you can't go on living with no body! . . . Everybody has to know it's in our longer interests to help the community.

The gang leaders told the community leaders that they would help, and then went to see the syndicate representatives. They told them that the community did not want them to expand into the area because it was too dangerous for the children in the neighborhood. The representatives said they were sorry that they could not make a deal with the gang and they would pass on the information to their superiors. That night the gang leaders told everybody not to stay overnight in the clubhouse, as they were sure the syndicate would attack the building. Four days later, the building was sprayed with bullets from automatic weapons. Since no one was in the building, there were no injuries. However, the gang made plans to retaliate against the numbers establishment and to continue the attacks until no one would patronize the place. This went on for about five weeks, and finally the numbers establishment closed down. Here again, the gang had answered a call from the community to help protect it from those developers who represented a threat, and the community was grateful. The statement by Bertha, a forty-seven-year-old maid in a hotel and mother of four, was typical of those heard throughout the community:

> You [the interviewer] was here when they wanted to start that numbers joint and that drug house. We didn't want it in the community because all that stuff would bring in people from outside the community and the whole place would have got more dangerous than it already is. I was so glad the boys in the gang listened to some of the men in the community and helped us. I know the gangs can be bad, but they're good boys for the most part and the community appreciates a lot of things they do, like getting rid of that numbers place.

Gangs also fight off threatened changes in the social structure of the community. It is important to point out that this is undertaken more by white gangs than by nonwhite ones. In Boston, for example, I observed a case where young professionals were moving into an Irish working-class neighborhood. This process of gentrification was threatening to many of the residents, especially those on fixed incomes, for whom increases in property values would have meant higher property taxes. Gentrification also threatened the existing social structure of the community, which the working-class residents viewed as particularly ominous. Accordingly the gangs, again at the request of the patrons of local social clubs, began to harass the new inhabitants in an effort to persuade them to leave the area. As Rory, an eighteen-year-old gang member, said:

> Yeah, the community wants us to take care of the pointy heads [term used for young professionals or intellectuals]. You know,

get them to leave. So we will accommodate them and in a little while these pointy heads will be packing it in and moving.

The constant harassment did not force out all those who had moved to the area (although some left), but it did have the effect of slowing gentrification there.

Irish gangs also supported the efforts of low-income Irish communities to stop nonwhites from buying homes there and moving into the neighborhood. In both Boston and New York, Irish gangs made concerted efforts to pressure nonwhite residents to move from their areas. In all but three of the thirty-four cases observed, the harassment strategy worked and the minority family moved from the area. Each time this occurred, the gangs were given more deference in the community.[14]

The gang also helps the community in two other ways. First, it is called upon to accompany members of the community when they advocate some type of community need. In most of these cases, gang members have been involved with other people from the community in protests against government or the police and have assumed the task of carrying posters and/ or protecting the protesters from either counter-protesters or the police. In addition, gangs have also been involved in helping residents after some type of disaster. I have observed gangs in Los Angeles helping residents in their communities after a large earthquake had occurred.

In all three cities, gangs have been very helpful when fires have destroyed apartment buildings or row houses. Herlinda, a thirty-two-year-old textile worker in New York, commented:

> When a couple of big fires happened, and there was all these people being out on the street with no clothes and everything, the gang helped people get some clothes and they also helped people find other members of their families. Oh, I almost forgot that they let people stay in their clubhouse and gave them food. . . . When they didn't have more room in their clubhouse, they went out and found people places to stay. . . . They even got people over to the social agencies that help people get longer relief.

In summary, on the community side, the incentives to establish ties with the gang are linked to the bonding that occurs as a result of psychological factors that cause adults in low-income communities to identify with members of gangs, as well as with functional services that gangs provide the community. Not all these psychological and functional factors are present in gang communities on a continuous basis, but they occur often enough that some level of bonding takes place between the gang and its community.

The Gang's Interest in a Close Relationship with the Community

Four factors motivate gangs to make concerted efforts to establish ties with the community. The first, and most important, is the fact that a gang needs to have the community provide it with a "safe haven" from which to operate—a place where it is protected from the police or other hostile gangs. The importance of such a safe haven has been all but overlooked in most gang-related research, but gangs themselves acknowledge it. Without a safe haven, gangs could not undertake much of their illegal economic activity, and neither could a gang hope to survive constant harassment by the police, which would slowly reduce its numbers and ultimately impair its ability to operate. Furthermore, a gang needs a safe haven from other competitive organizations so that it has the time to plan, mobilize all the available resources, and assert itself in its desired social arena. If it found itself unable to do this, it would always be on the defensive—and defensive postures for gangs, as for other organizations, eventually result in general group demoralization.[15] What the gang requires from the community is total noncooperation with law enforcement officials. The community has to observe the code of *omertà* (silence), or the gang will spend too much time worrying about who might inform the police. If a gang has established ties with the community and someone breaks the code of *omertà* and informs on members, the gang is likely to use physical retaliation, and the community will generally show support for such retaliation by remaining conspicuously silent. For the most part, this show of support is undertaken not because residents are fearful that the gang will retaliate against them, but because a social compact has been established between them. Of course, sometimes members of the community observe *omertà* out of fear, but in each case, this goes on only for a short while before the community begins to cooperate with the police. If gangs were not able to establish a mutually beneficial social contract with their communities, ultimately they would cease to operate.

The second factor motivating gangs to maintain ties with the community is recruitment. The prudent gang among those I studied was the one that was able, to some degree, to project what would be required in the future for its continued existence. Gangs unable to do this eventually faded away. A population of potential recruits is essential for the organization's ultimate survival, and ensuring such a population requires close ties with the local community, because a community that is antagonistic toward the gang will undermine recruitment.

Gang recruitment can be negatively affected in basically two ways. First, parents can collectively affect the total number available for recruitment by simply telling their children (with the support of other members of the community) that they do not want them joining a gang, while threatening them with ostracism by the family if they do. Where parents took an active role in dissuading their children from joining a gang, one of two things occurred: either the total number of recruits dropped to levels that significantly affected the gang's ability to reproduce itself or the number of recruits who had the types of skills that the gang desired (or needed) was reduced to the point where the quality of the gang's operations was seriously/adversely affected. The comments of Match, a twenty-four-year-old member of a New York gang, represent the first situation:

> Oh, man, let me tell you, we been having difficulty with the community and they just fucking us up when it comes to getting more homies to join. We can't get hardly anybody to join, I mean most of the parents have said that they weren't going to put up with their kids in our gang so they [the youth] been cowardly shying away. . . . I tell you one thing man, if we don't get more people who will join, the [gang's name] is all dried up, that's it!

The comments of Comet, a sixteen-year-old member of a Los Angeles gang, represent the second situation:

> Two years ago we did some things that the community was very angry about. We had definitely messed up, and we paid for it. In fact, we almost died as an organization because we couldn't get people to join us. I mean, we could get people, but you see we needed people who could do certain things good, not just anybody. I mean we need dudes who could bop [fight] well and we needed people who could get around certain kinds of security systems, but shit, the community was so down on us and they told people not to join. So there we was needing certain people, but there were so few available we had no chance of picking up who we needed. Those who was available were just dead weights! It

wasn't easy, but we definitely corrected our position with the community and now we got more quality.

The third incentive for gangs to establish good relations with the community is that the community provides gangs with important information and constitutes a vital component in a gang's communications network. Gangs, like other organizations, need to have a capable communications system to coordinate their actions and gather information. Here is where the community plays a consequential role. The gang needs the community to assume two types of information-gathering roles. First, the community must act as a quasi-surveillance system for the gang. In this capacity, I found that the residents provided the gang with information concerning the intrusion of threatening individuals into the community. Sometimes this was provided immediately; at other times, it is provided after an event has already occurred. An example of the former was when the police, a rival gang, or some other group or person potentially threatening to the gang or community entered the area and someone immediately notified a gang member of the event. One summer, while I was with an Irish gang in New York and staying with a gang member named Macky, I was awakened early on a Tuesday morning by a phone call to Macky. Afterwards, he told me that a person in the community had seen what appeared to be agents of some sort looking around the community. Twenty minutes later, another call came, this one from a gang member, who told Macky that a neighbor had called to say that agents from the Treasury Department's Bureau of Alcohol, Firearms and Tobacco, or some similar agency, had been asking questions about an arms cache. Macky told me he had to take care of this situation and started to call up other members of his gang.

Gangs, like other organizations (such as the police), are often in need of ex post facto information and are thus dependent on the community's cooperation. One example of this involved a neighborhood in New York where there had been a series of robberies of stores a gang called the Bangers had contracted to protect. This put a great deal of pressure on the Bangers, since it was their responsibility to prevent this, and complaints by community residents were beginning to be heard in public. The victims reported that members of a rival gang had been responsible for the robberies (which were accompanied by beatings), but before the Bangers planned a retaliatory action, they decided to obtain more information from the general community concerning what had happened. As a result of their investigations, they found that it had not been the rival gang at all, but rather a group of young drug addicts from their own community who had formed a "crew." [16] Having finally established who the perpetrators of these assaults were, they proceeded to take action against them. As Sword, the nineteen-year-old president of the Bangers, said:

> You see, if we'd just gone out and done it to the [rival gang's name], we probably would've still been in a gang war. So we did what we had to do. We asked around the community for information, found out who did it, and then took care of business. . . . We counted on the community to give us good information, otherwise we would be stuck like the police are sometimes. And if we get stuck and don't do something to stop the robberies, we're in trouble with the folks around here.

This particular case illustrates a gang using restraint rather than acting on unsubstantiated rumors. Gangs often succumb to the desire to do something quickly and proceed to take direct action against another gang simply on the basis of rumor. This usually proves to be more disadvantageous than beneficial for the gang. [17]

Another reason why gangs need communities is because gang members often do not have the freedom to visit other parts of the city. Since most parts of the city are controlled by rival gangs, members of each gang find themselves limited in where they can go without threat of being attacked. [18] This creates a problem for all gangs because they need information about what is occurring in other sections of the city in order to remain competitive. Thus, most gangs find themselves in the position of having information about what is occurring in border areas (contested areas that lie between gang jurisdictions and control) but knowing little about areas under the control of rival gangs. In order to correct this informational imbalance, many gangs use members of their community as information sources. Usually, this includes older members of the community, who may have relatives living in another section of the city. After these people have visited other areas, they are often interviewed, or in some cases even questioned, about what they saw happening in the various neighborhoods, especially if they have seen activity involving a rival gang. As Cucumber, a twenty-six-year-old gang vice president in Los Angeles, said:

> Yeah, we use a lot of the people in this neighborhood to find out what's happening in a lot of the other areas of town. Since we

can't go there, we check on what's happening by asking those people who been there about what's going on. It's kind of interesting—they're kind of like our satellites to other parts of the world, they tell us what they seen just like a real satellite taking pictures for scientists. . . . We try to talk to a lot of people who visit the other neighborhoods, 'cause we got to know what's going on if we want to protect what we got and expand. . . . You got to understand though, you got to take everything these people say with some salt. I mean they don't always see things the way they are, so you got to see where there are a lot of people who be saying the same thing. Then you know there's something there.

The comments of Sheath, a seventeen-year-old member of a New York gang's ruling council, also highlight this community function:

We talk to as many of the community that we can about what's going on in other parts of the city cause it's useful to know and we can't go to a lot of areas. You see, we can't go to the Dago [Italian] or Paddy [Irish] neighborhoods or we'd be in a heap of trouble so we ask some of the people in the community who go there to make deliveries and such, what they'd see. Sometimes we don't learn nothing, but sometimes we do, so we got to keep asking. . . . This ain't perfect information, but for some areas it's the best we got!

Interestingly, what the evidence here suggests is that gangs, to varying degrees, depend on members of the community to connect them socially with other parts of the city.

Finally, the gangs I studied desired close ties with the community for psychological reasons. In every gang I observed, nearly all members wanted the residents of the community to view them as being helpful and responsive. I found four sources for this need to be helpful and responsive. First, all the gang members identified with their communities. They were proud that they were from the neighborhood or barrio where they lived, and they wanted to do something to help the people in it. This sentiment is based on a political understanding of their community's place within the society and, by extension, of their own place within the social structure. All the gang members with whom I associated understood the world in dichotomous class terms: there are rich people and there are poor people. Rich people obtained wealth either by being born to it or by taking advantage of poor people. In addition, they believed that rich people aided their own; therefore, poor people should also try to help their own.

The comments of Cupcake, Manos, and Jimmy represent these beliefs. Cupcake, a nineteen-year-old member of a New York gang, stated:

> Yeah, we help the community, because if we don't help, who's going to? You see even though you got a middle class, there is basically just two kinds of people in America, rich people and poor people, and this here is a community of poor people who is poor because the rich, with help of the middle class, keep ripping them off. All of us in this club [the gang] is products of this rip-off and are part of this community. We proud of this community and want to help it 'cause we know where we come from and we know that if we want to help them we got to do the way the rich people do. They help their community so it can maintain itself being rich. Well, we help our community to protect it from everybody who be trying to prey on us, including those who are rich.

Manos, a nineteen-year-old member of a Chicano gang in Los Angeles:

> Sometimes I sit and think about how the planet works or at least L.A. and then I take a ride out of the barrio and everything I sort of knew just gets clearer and clearer. What there is, is people who have money, and those who don't. That's the way it's always been in this country, so you are either one of those who's got money or somebody who don't. . . . There are people who are in the middle, but the fight is really between the rich people who get their money by cheating the poor and the poor who trying to get their money any way they can, but it's best to take it away from the rich . . . and the middle class, they're a joke, 'cause they just go with whoever is winning! We in the community got to act like the rich folks act, we got to help each other if we want to get a better life. That's why we [members in the gang] help the community when they want us to.

Jimmy, a twenty-year-old member of an Irish gang in Boston:

> The fucking world got those who live in the plush houses, you know Weston, Newton, Beacon Hill, and that shit, and those like us who live here. You don't have to be clubbed in the head to know that if you ain't got nothin', the only way you going to get anything permanent, is to take some away from those who got it. . . . I used to feel guilty about feeling that way, you can't feel guilty about taking from those who got money, 'cause they got it by taking it from a whole lot of poor people. . . . Me and the guys in our group we try to help the community because that's the only

way that all of us can protect ourselves from those rich bastards! That's the way rich people do it, they protect their own community, so we just got to do what they do, but with a little more effort.

At first, I thought that the remarks to the effect that people in their community should help each other contradicted one of the fundamental beliefs underlying gang members' defiant individualist characters—that the world works in a Social Darwinist way. However, I found that they have actually incorporated both beliefs—Social Darwinism and aid to the community—in their behavior. In terms of their Social Darwinist logic, the only way to help oneself is to try to help one's group and, in so doing, different groups attempt to take from each other (i.e., they struggle in a Social Darwinist way) to see which group is the most able. Thus gang members are willing to help others in the community, but they are cautious and constantly alert to those who might attempt to take advantage of them. Recorder, a sixteen-year-old gang member from New York, represents the comments consistently offered by most gang members:

> Sure, we help out the community and this helps the gang, and what's good for the gang is good for me personally. But you have to understand, everybody is trying to help their own community, both the rich and poor, so there is going to be conflict and whoever wins is the best. You see that constant conflict lets you know who is the best. . . . Yeah, we help the community whenever they ask, but you got to watch who you're helping because some people in the community ain't mentally ready to let you help them. You know what I mean? They let you help them and then they try to double-cross you. So until the community has got it all together, you got to keep your eyes out for Judases even when you be helping people.

Thus, although gang members are always suspicious, underlying all their caution one finds a strong social and political identification with the community. In his study of patriotism and nationalism, Leonard Doob has defined patriotism as "the more or less conscious conviction of a person that his own welfare and that of the significant groups to which he belongs are dependent upon the preservation or expansion (or both) of the power and culture of his society."[19] The gang member's strong identification with his community is therefore an expression of his patriotism toward his neighborhood and the lower-class ethnic groups who live there. In essence, the gang member usually displays two types of patriotism: a strong one for the community/neighborhood in which he lives and a rather weak one towards the United States. Psychologically, for the gang member, the patriotism associated with the community/neighborhood supersedes all others.[20]

The second psychological reason why gangs support the community is that most of the young men and women in gangs, like most young men and women in general, want to please adults. They are happy when people in the community ask them for help. Basically, they want to be "wanted," and they also wish to be recognized by the adult world as significant. These feelings are sometimes disguised by a hard exterior, but they are nonetheless a factor in their desire to help the community when asked.

The third psychological factor is that gang members are always eager to show the world that they are not antisocial individuals, which some popular newspaper accounts depict them as being. Ricardo, a twenty-one-year-old member of a Los Angeles gang, said:

> Sure we help the community and are close to the people who are in it. All the newspapers and television show people is the crime in the area, so everybody thinks that we're like animals or something. But that's just bullshit! You just ask around here and you'll see we're solid with the community, and that's because we help when they want us to.

The fourth and final psychological reason that gang members want to help the community has to do with the fact that they understand that their social status in life comes from criteria established in their community, not from the criteria of the larger society, and that the best way to attain this status is to be helpful to the community.[21] Take the comments of Dome, an eighteen-year-old gang member in New York:

> I know, we all know, that people outside our neighborhood wouldn't think much of us. You know, we would be just nobodies to them, but here we are given respect by the people in the community, and that is because we do things for them. So if we want to keep some respect, we need [to] continue to help the people here.

Shucker, a fifteen-year-old gang member from New York, said:

> We get status from this community and not from anywhere else. So if we want to keep it, we got to keep helping the community.

To conclude this section on the social and psychological bases of gang and community ties, it is important to highlight the three main findings. First, both the community and the gang have concrete interests that can be realized through mutual ties. Second, there are some psychological reasons why residents of the community and members of the gang find it important to have a close relationship. Third, in the process of realizing both functional and psychological interests, a bonding occurs between the gang and the community that builds a social adhesive that often takes a significant amount of time to completely dissolve.

The Decline of Community and Gang Ties

As was described in the preceding section, the gang and the community usually form either a close or a working relationship with each other. However, there are times when the relationship between the two is either strained or hostile. In order to explain why some communities have an antagonistic relationship with gangs and others a close association, it is necessary to understand that the mutual benefits resulting from the various tasks that each does for each other form the basis of this relationship. The reciprocal nature of these tasks has established a type of social bonding that has assumed the character of a recognized social contract between community and gang. When this contract is violated by one of the two parties, or at least is perceived to have been broken, the relationship is dissolved. What is unique about this social contract is that, while it is based on reciprocal benefits, it is only when the gang violates the contract that the entire relationship is undermined. Even when the community violates the contract first, the gang almost never breaks off the relationship. This pattern occurs because the gang is in need of the community more than the community is in need of the gang, and the gang is quite sensitive to this fact. I have observed violations of this social contract between community and gang countless times, and where members of the community were responsible for the violation, the gang never broke off relations with the community. On the other hand, in each instance where the gang had seriously violated the contract, the community broke off relations and became antagonistic toward the gang.

In cases when the community perceived that the social contract was violated by the gang, there was a consistent pattern of reaction. First, members of the community would stop assisting the gang by withdrawing their protection of members, by not supplying information, and by discouraging membership. At the outset of these actions, many of the residents seemed apathetic or indifferent. Yet they usually did not feel that way at all. Rather, they were in the beginning stages of a passive-aggressive posture. This stage may last a considerable length of time, depending on police action or inaction; but regardless of how long it lasts, it will mark a difficult period for the gang's operations. In this phase of community rebellion, if the gang members can make changes and convince the majority of the disenchanted that they are now willing and able to either establish new roles or resume their old ones as helpful resources, then they can ameliorate the hostilities and reestablish ties. However, if the gang is either unwilling or unable (because of organizational difficulties) to take steps to do what the community wishes, then relations will continue to deteriorate, leading to two subsequent phases of community reaction. Phase two occurs when members of the community begin to help the police by providing information; and phase three occurs when the community becomes openly (to both the immediate community and wider society) vocal in its opposition to the gang. If either of these latter two phases comes to pass, typically it marks the beginning of the end for the gang as a viable organization.

An obvious and important question is, What action on the part of the gang would cause a break in the social contract with the community? There are two types of situations that may cause a break to occur. One is when the gang no longer performs the established tasks that the community has come to expect of it and in some cases depend on. In this case, the community will withdraw its support. Withdrawal of support always relates to the gang's inability to provide the community with the various forms of protection and aid that it has provided or promised to provide in the past. For example, a gang called the Pink Eagles had been providing protection to the community in a New York neighborhood for about three years. During that time, it had managed to expand its area of control to some fifteen square blocks. As its drug business expanded, it became more involved in the business's day-to-day operations. Most of the gang members worked the streets selling drugs as agents of the organization. This consumed a good deal of each individual's time. After they had sold their quota for the gang, members devoted any additional time to their personal entrepreneurial projects. This left little or no time to patrol the area for the community or to help those in the community who had special needs. The crime rate in the community steadily increased, particularly robberies and assaults on individuals. There were complaints from the community, and the gang was aware that people were dissatisfied with its performance, but its response was simply to promise that things would get done. The problem was that these promises were at most only partially fulfilled.

Through discussions, the community incrementally became united in withdrawing its support for the gang. Thus when the police came requesting information about gang members, they were given it. In addition, people in the community did not bother to notify the gang when they sighted the start of a police operation and failed to provide information to the gang about other gangs. Instead, community residents almost always told gang members that they had no information to give them. The code of *omertà* had been turned on its head and was now working as a cancer on the gang's organizational life. Eventually the police were able to arrest and convict a number of the gang members for drug trafficking. Further, through harassment, the police were also able to deprive the gang of its dispensing locations, which created a surplus in its supply of drugs and eventually a cash-flow problem with the drug-syndicate wholesaler. With members going off to prison and the organization in financial difficulty, other gangs came into the area in attempts to take it over. Little by little, the gang became weaker and weaker. Before the difficulty with the community occurred, the gang had never been stronger. It had had a large and growing membership, a number of clubhouses, and a strong business; but once it lost the support of the community, it dissolved as an organization.

The second situation that may cause a break to occur with the community is when members of the gang act out of control—that is, when the organization is unable to control its membership. I previously discussed the fact that all the individuals in gangs possess a defiant individualist character, and that this character is both why members become independently entrepreneurial while they are in a gang and why they choose to leave and rejoin the gang at different intervals. It is also responsible for creating difficulty in organizational control. Control is always somewhat difficult, but when members continue to act without restraint and the community is negatively affected, the community believes that the social contract has been broken, and the gang as an organization loses the community's support.

The case of the Birdville gang of Los Angeles illustrates this situation. This gang expanded its business dealings, primarily its interests in drugs and stolen contraband. The process of expanding included not only volume of goods sold but also membership and territory. In the short run, the gang was at its strongest, and few rival gangs were able to compete. However, the expansion reached a point when control became problematic. Expansion had occurred too fast, without the establishment of a sufficient infrastructure to coordinate and control all the new subgroups of members. Thus, in the long run, the short-run successes involving expansion established the preconditions for the organization's demise.

In summary, the Birdville gang expanded its operations; business was brisk, particularly in the drug trade. The gang was adding members who were becoming drug traders at a very fast rate. Then, without the approval of the leadership or the general membership, a number of the new members began to expand into new geographic areas, which resulted in a battle with two other gangs. Individually, the two rival gangs were no match for the Birdville gang; therefore, they decided to join forces and repel what they perceived as the Birdville gang's takeover attempts. They decided to ambush Birdville's members by shooting at them when they were making their drug deals. After two Birdvilles had been killed, the gang decided to counterattack. They went to the rival gangs' areas and randomly shot at groups of young men who they thought were members. The shooting was so indiscriminate that community members were hurt in the process. In turn, the two rival gangs retaliated; consequently, a number of community people in the Birdvilles area were injured and a young boy was killed.

This action and counteraction continued unrestrained and the community complained bitterly. The gang leadership attempted to stop the shooting, but divergent factions within the gang were unwilling to give up their lucrative drug business and refused to desist from daily confrontations with the rival gangs. The outcome was that the shootings persisted and innocent people continued to be victimized. The members were simply out of control, and the gang was unable to do anything about it. The community then began to withdraw its support of the gang and called upon the neighborhood leadership for help. These leaders in turn contacted the Los Angeles Police Department. The police increased their presence in the area and members of the community, for the first time in many years, cooperated with them. They told the police where drug deals were being made and who was making them. In addition, if there was violence and they saw who had committed it, they told the police. As a result of the community's cooperation with the police, many of the gang members were arrested and imprisoned. The gang's leadership, understanding the significance of the community's behavior, made efforts to regain control over the membership. However, these efforts proved only partially successful. Ultimately, it did not matter whether the gang leadership was successful or not in regaining control over its rank and file, because the community decided that the gang had gone too far, and that as far as they were concerned, the gang had proved itself to no longer be a benefit to the community and thus to no longer have legitimacy. In fact, it had become such a threat to the safety of the community that the community decided that it must go. As one resident said to me:

> Some of the gang leaders tried to talk the community into not helping the police so much. They said that they could now guarantee that the violence would stop. The violence really never did stop, but it didn't matter because we in the community were fed up with them and wanted them out!

The community continued its cooperation with the police and eventually the gang dissolved as an organization.[22] It had broken its social contract with the community and, in the process, lost its base for operations.

The events surrounding the Los Angeles Police Department's anti-gang sweeps[23] in the spring of 1988 offer yet another example. The background is as follows: from 1985 to 1988, the south-central area of Los Angeles, which is predominantly African-American, experienced rapid growth in gang activity, much of which centered around the selling of drugs. At the time, the drug with the largest growth in sales in these low-income neighborhoods was crack, a processed derivative of cocaine.[24] The gangs organized themselves to take advantage of this boom in the drug market by establishing hierarchical organizations with centralized leadership and a large number of subgroupings. There were just two gangs in the entire area, the Crips and the Bloods (although each had many semi-autonomous branches), and they fought over drug-marketing territories. These fights to establish monopolies in certain geographic areas produced a large amount of violence. In fact, during this period of time, gang-related homicide rates were very high.[25]

To the community, the most feared gang act of violence was the drive-by shooting, which was usually so random that many of the victims would not even be in the targeted gang.[26] Of course, the fact that people who were not gang members were injured and/or killed was not an unintended consequence of the action. In a number of the cases, the gangs doing the shooting were attempting to send a message to that community that their local gang branch was not able to protect them.[27] However, as the Bloods and the Crips continued to enact these drive-by shootings, the communities where they lived became intolerant of the violence, and residents pressed their government representatives and leaders to do something to stop it.[28] In essence, the police sweeps were the result of these communities' reactions to being terrorized by both gangs' continual use of indiscriminate violence. They supported the police effort to break the two gangs' activities, and in the first wave of police sweeps, which involved 1,000 police officers and led to 1,300 arrests, there was little negative response from the community.[29] In fact, while the sweeps were occurring, civil rights violations were perpetrated by the police in a significant number of cases. Still, the community remained silent because it wanted these particular gangs' violent behavior to cease.[30]

The unusual fact of the community's complicity in these police actions must be emphasized, because it is usually the community that guards against police violations of its residents' civil rights by speaking out. When communities do speak out against police action, accusing them of violating civil rights, it generally acts as a type of social control over police activity. Thus, the absence of a community voice is significant. In the case of Los Angeles, it was not until two weeks later that community leaders decided to begin the process of regaining control of their community.[31] They staged a rally at city hall, to which they brought two caskets to dramatize the deaths that had occurred as a result of gang violence, and pressed local authorities to make more money available to community-based organizations for anti-gang programs. This can be best understood as the logical extension of the previous events. Basically the community had lost control of its area to the gangs and had then asked the police to step in and wrest control away from the gangs. Now that the police had begun their efforts to neutralize the gangs, community leaders wanted to make sure that the police did not try to fill the power vacuum that would be left when the gangs were neutralized, so they began efforts to reestablish their own authority over the area.

Organizational Type and Community Relations

Although each organizational type of gang has had some variation in its relations with the community, I also observed generalized patterns that cut across the different cities. The vertical/hierarchical organization is, for the most part, able to honor its obligations and cultivate a close relationship with the communities in which it operates. This type of organization has the most success in establishing and maintaining close ties to the community because it can pay more attention to the details that affect community relations. Because it has a defined division of authority and labor within the leadership, which the general membership has agreed on, it can exercise more precision in implementing its plans. This gives it the advantage of monitoring its members' activities. It also has the capacity to punish members who have committed acts that alienate the community. It is, in a Weberian sense, more rational in its orientation, and this facilitates its ability to coordinate everyday operations better than the other two types of gang organizations. As Sidekick, a seventeen-year-old African-American gang member from New York, said:

> I don't know about other clubs [gangs] but this here club is got the organization where they're able to follow your every moves when you on a job or off. You see if you on a job and you mess up everybody knows, 'cause each person gots a specific thing to do. And when you in the community, there is so many people who be watching you, like members of the community and other gang members, that if you be messing up the word gets back to the leaders. Then you better get ready to be punished 'cause that's sure as hell is what is going to happen!

Punishment is very stern because everyone understands how important the community's support is to the organization's ability to operate, and there is little tolerance or sympathy for those who would jeopardize close ties with the community. The comments of Hack Man, a twenty-one-year-old African-American gang member from New York, are instructive on this point:

> You see that guy over there? The one with the red shoes? The order's been given to lay some muscle on him to let him know not to mess with the community. You see he really jacked up [beat up] an old guy from the community. You see the old guy has a little store and sells vegetables and this dude goes and tries to take an apple. Well, the old man don't like that, so he gets his whip and starts in on the guy. The guy then turns around and takes the whip from him, beats him up, and takes another dozen apples. This is the second time he did something like this and the community is getting pissed at us! Well, tonight he is really going to be set

straight—don't fuck with the community or you going to get
fucked up real bad!

That night, just as Hack Man had predicted, the boy in the red shoes
who had been pointed out earlier was in fact severely beaten. The comments of Duck, a twenty-five-year-old Chicano gang member from Los
Angeles, are also illuminating on this point:

> When I was younger, I was selling pills to young kids at school.
> You know, kids in grade school. Well, the parents found out
> about it and complained to some of the leaders [gang leaders].
> Hey, at the time, I was young and thought I could do anything I
> wanted, I also thought that the gang would let you do what you
> wanted, so a couple days later I peddled some more pills to these
> kids. Then at the next meeting they [the gang] really beat me up, I
> mean they really took me apart. I couldn't do anything for two
> weeks. I even had blood in my piss from getting kicked in the kid-
> neys . . . but I got the message, and I stopped. . . . I didn't like get-
> ting it at the time, but now I understand that if you [the gang]
> ain't got the community with you it's just a matter of time before
> you got to close up shop. It's crazy, but I just voted the other day
> to punish some homey for screwing up with the community.

The vertical/hierarchical structure has certain organizational advantages in maintaining good community relations, but there are some dangers in this organizational type as well. For one, if the organization becomes too large, there is usually a deterioration in community relations
(this happened in six cases). Thus, success for the organization in one
area (such as growth) can lead to a setback in another. For example, as
vertical/hierarchical types of gang organizations become larger, they find
it increasingly difficult to control all their members in the different satellite clubs/branches. As a result, the organization is unable to perform
those duties associated with their part of the social contract that they
have had with the community. The community relations of gangs using
this type of organizational structure are therefore particularly vulnerable
to the problems of control associated with rapid growth. Interestingly,
three of the gangs, recognizing the dangers inherent in too much growth,
took steps toward limiting the growth of their organizations.

The horizontal/commission type of organization demonstrated two
trends. Those gangs that have adopted this organizational structure have
done so in an effort to reduce the strains and breakdowns present when

they operated under one of the other two organizational forms. As a result of these strains and organizational breakdowns, many of the leaders in these gangs felt that their groups were vulnerable to a variety of organizational predators such as the police, other gangs, social service agencies, church groups, and so on. In other words, they felt vulnerable to all those organizations that had ever attempted to recruit their own members from gangs. Because the leadership (as well as many of the rank and file) felt that their organizations were held together tenuously, they did not want to antagonize a resource as important as the community. To do so would undoubtedly tip the scales against them and they would be in a crisis situation. Gangs that use a horizontal/commission type of structure are therefore particularly conscientious about avoiding harm to anyone in the community. However, while most community members in those areas that contain this type of gang structure report that the gangs are outwardly friendly and desirous of being helpful, they also complain that they are inconsistent in their efforts to provide this help. There is no doubt that the horizontal/commission type of structure has difficulty coordinating each of its units. There is a great deal of inefficiency, which the gang members have usually tolerated in exchange for more intraorganizational equality.[32] However, the price has been inconsistency in all its operations, including those associated with the community. Thus, residents of those communities that had a gang operating with this type structure usually became frustrated with the inconsistency and eventually perceived the social contract between themselves and the gang to have been broken. Once this occurred, the community began to withdraw its support.

The third type of gang organization is the influential model, which has two tendencies. The first is that because gangs adopting it typically have fewer members, they sometimes seem able to blend into the community better than the other two organizational types. That is, because these gangs tend to be smaller in size and to have fewer formalized roles, they are able to project the image of a collective of people indistinguishable from other residents of the community. Thus, the residents in their communities have often viewed members of the gang as merely local boys who can be counted on for help when needed; but more often than not they are disappointed with their performance. Gangs with the influential type of organization simply do not have the infrastructure necessary to consistently execute all the duties the community desires, or expects. Gangs with this type of structure can act quickly, because they have fewer members to contact and because the leadership has total power to decide what action will be taken; however, these gangs lack both adequate numbers of people and the self-discipline to meet their obligations to the community with consistent success. When such failure occurs, the community becomes frustrated over the inefficiency and the destructive episodes of the undisciplined members and withdraws its support. As a forty-nine-year-old resident of Los Angeles said:

> We needed to have the [gang's name] go with us to protest for some street improvements. You know, carry some posters and things. They came, but a number of them was drunk or on drugs and they was acting like fools. So instead of focusing on what we needed for the community, the media focused in on how foolish they were acting and nothing came of our effort. . . . So we not only didn't get any help from them, we had to put up with their shooting back and forth with another gang. Well, I tell you, we basically liked the boys in the gang, but all us got together and decided we would cooperate with the police to rid ourselves from the shootings and we didn't care if that meant hardship for the boys in the gang or not, 'cause they weren't any help anyway. . . . We were fed up with them. And after we did that, they started to clean up their act and tried to help us more.

Since the community tends to identify with the members of the gang, what is most often observed is a pattern in which the community withdraws its support, the gang makes amends, the community renews its support, the gang becomes incompetent again, and the community again withdraws its support. This can go on for months; but when this pattern emerges, eventually the gang and the community sever their relationship and the gang becomes an ineffectual organization.

Concluding Remarks

In those neighborhoods where gangs operate, the gang and the community have established a working relationship. This relationship is predicated on a number of exchange relationships in which both the gang and the community provide each other with certain services. Although both parties benefit from this social arrangement, the gang has much more need of the benefits provided by the community than the community has of those provided by the gang. Consequently, the gang assumes a position of responding to the community's lead. It will almost never take the lead in anything that would commit the residents of the community to take some type of action, since this would risk a negative response from the community, which could result in the withdrawal of support—and this is precisely what gangs are trying to avoid. Thus, the role that gangs have found most comfortable assuming vis-à-vis the community is that of a neighborhood militia. This allows them to be both a part of the community and a protective agent of it. If successful at establishing such a role (and many are not), the gang need only be ready to respond to the community's call.

In the process of acquiring such a role, the gang establishes an understood social contract with the community. If it is successful in meeting its obligations under this contract, the community provides it with certain services that ensure its ability to exist and carry out its own business operations. However, if it is unsuccessful in meeting its obligations under this contract, the community will withdraw its support. Withdrawal of community support ultimately serves as a fatal blow to the gang's existence. However, generally there is an interval between the time the community withdraws its support and the time the gang ceases to function as an organization. During this time period, residents may appear to be apathetic, but they are more often simply passive-aggressive toward the gang. The simple fact is that gangs, like Hobsbawm's "social bandits" or various guerrilla organizations, need a sanctuary, a safe place to operate and regroup in, and their communities provide this sanctuary for them.[33] Since the gang needs the community more than the community needs the gang, without community support the gang will wither away.

Part Two

The Gang
and the Outside World

Chapter Seven

Gangs and Governments

I seen my opportunities and I took 'em.
George Washington Plunkitt, *Plunkitt of Tammany Hall: A Series of Very Plain Talks on Very Practical Politics* (1905)

Few studies have dealt with the relationship between the political structure of cities and the gangs that operate within them. The studies that have treated this relationship have tended to describe two quite different associations. The early study by Thrasher described the relationship of gangs to the political structure as consisting of the gang being incorporated into the local political machine and performing a number of small campaign tasks. In this scenario, the gang is simply a local organization that is manipulated by the local political boss.[1] Later studies, however, either have described the relationship of gangs to politics as quite distant or have tended to completely ignore the relationship, leaving the impression that there was no meaningful association at all. There were two reasons for this. First, because political machines had become less prevalent and the Mafia had changed its mode of operation in most of America's large urban areas, it was assumed that any political association that gangs might have had with politicians had also vanished.[2] Second, politics was perceived as an activity associated with the adult world and not that of youth; and since gangs were considered totally adolescent organizations, politics was something gangs had little relationship to.[3]

Interestingly, what both the old and more recent studies present us with are two rather different pictures concerning the gang's relationship to politics. Yet they have something in common. They both take a rather limited view of politics by identifying political behavior as behavior that to some extent involves elected public officials. However, this conception is much too limiting for gangs of today, as it probably was for the gangs of the past. As we shall see, for present-day gangs, political involvement would include involvement with: (1) elected officials, (2) non-elected politicians within the community (community leaders), (3) government bureaucrats charged with officially administering gang programs, and (4) nongovernment bureaucrats who work in nonprofit community organizations. This chapter adopts this broader definition of politics and analyzes how gangs have related to each of the abovementioned governmental elements.

In general, the gang's relation to each of these elements in the political structure can be described as an "exchange relationship." However, the character of this exchange relationship assumes a different form, depending on which element the gangs interact with. Exchange relationships among gangs, politicians, and government officials take two basic forms, *expedient* and *prudential*. *Expedient* means a relationship that is temporary and occasional, whereas *prudential* means a relationship that is more ongoing and institutionalized. This chapter identifies and analyzes the bases of these different exchange relationships, and thereby describes the linkages between the gang and some of the primary institutions of the wider society.

Relations with Politicians

All thirty-seven gangs observed throughout the ten years of this study established some type of *expedient-exchange relationship* with the politicians in their city.[4] Although not all thirty-seven maintained a consistent relationship with the same politician, twenty-seven developed a consistent pattern of periodic contact. The nature of the relationship depended on the type of political culture operating in the city and whether the relationship involved an elected official.

Only the New York and Boston gangs had consistent and direct contact with the offices of elected mayoral and council politicians. None of the gangs of Los Angeles established any direct contact with the elected politicians of the their city. This trend is related to the influence of political culture in the three cities. In cities like New York and Boston, where partisan elections still occur and where a political-machine culture once existed, gangs and elected officials (or their organizations) usually have established a more direct and instrumental relationship. However, in Los

Angeles, which has no history of a political machine, a direct working relationship was not established.

The main reason why politicians and gangs established a relationship in Boston and New York was that both viewed such a relationship as beneficial. The politicians of these cities view the gang as a potential political resource. As the staffs of these politicians recognized, gangs represent an integral part of the community and, as such, a resource. After all, gangs are organized; they know the people in their community and the community knows them. The political machine in its classic form has withered away in these two cities, and gangs offer politicians a collective resource to partially fill the organizational vacuum left by its demise.[5] Here are two representative comments from the aides of politicians in New York and Boston.

H.O. is a political organizer for a New York politician:

> We definitely get in touch with some of the local gangs to help us organize an effective campaign in certain areas. This is not necessarily public knowledge, but of course it makes perfect sense. Gangs know the people in their community and they can act more efficiently and effectively than anything we could develop ourselves in getting our message out to the residents. It's simple. They are useful. If they weren't, I wouldn't be here.

P.K. is a political organizer for a politician in Boston:

> I've been at this [organizing] for a long time and as the old organization broke up, we need[ed] to rebuild. It was difficult organizing because conditions had changed in the neighborhoods. But the gangs help us out because they are organized and can work as an organization to get votes for the party. After all, they know most of the people in their neighborhood and can communicate with them. They are really quite useful to us at times.

Every gang in this study recognized the importance of political connections for the maintenance of their organization. They believed that being connected to those in power gave them the opportunity to request certain benefits at various times. None of the gangs had a specific "graft list" for the politicians they wanted to establish linkages with. However, they were politically astute enough to know that when there was something they wanted, not only was it appropriate to ask for it but there was a high probability that they would get it. Here are two of the comments of different gang members. One is a leader in an Irish gang and the other is a rank-and-file member of an African-American/Puerto Rican gang.

Hammer is an eighteen-year-old leader of an Irish gang in Boston:

> We don't have any specifics that we want from various politicians that we help. We just know that when the time comes and you need some help here and there, you ask and you get. There has only been three times that we asked for something and we didn't get anything. And then in two of those times, they made it up to us in another way. So you see, we help and just wait till we need something.

Disk is a sixteen-year-old rank-and-file member of an African-American/Puerto Rican gang:

> I been in this gang for two years and I know when we try to get tight with one of the big elected politicians, we never go to them and say this is what we want. That would be dumb! First, 'cause they would tell you to shove it. And second, you never know what you're going to want in the future. So it's better to just wait and then ask. . . . When we have asked in the past, we got what we asked most of the time. There were a few times we didn't and the guys were pissed, but most of the time we get what we ask for as long as we ain't asking all the time.

One of the important questions associated with the relationship between gangs and politicians has to do with how contact is made between the two parties. Here, one generally finds two trends. Among the Irish gangs, contact between the two parties occurs through members of the social clubs, regardless of who initiates it. Usually, members of the social clubs have close ties to a particular political party or to a particular politician's organization. They also have close ties to many of the gangs. When either party wants to initiate contact with the other, this is done through various members of the social clubs. What actually occurs is a member of the social club is given the details from the political organization of an elected official (or would-be elected official) of what they would like the gang to assist in. The member then takes the message to the leaders of the local gang, discusses the details, and orchestrates the activity for the political organization. When the activity has been completed, it is usually that member's responsibility to distribute the favors requested by the gang as return payment. In most cases, the member chosen to be the conduit between the gang and the political organization is not always the same person. In the case of all the Irish gangs in this study, a small group of social club members trade responsibility for arranging this political interaction.

Among non-Irish gangs in New York, contact between gangs and politicians was facilitated through representatives of the various politicians. Thus when a politician decided to use a gang in a particular area, a staff member within the politician's organization was given the responsibility of arranging the gang's participation. In 42 percent (fifty-seven) of the cases recorded during the ten years of this study, the individual making the contact with the gang was a person of color who had originally been from a similar neighborhood. However, in 58 percent (seventy-eight) of the cases, the individual making contact was either middle- or upper-middle-class. On first observing this interaction, I found it odd to see someone dressed so nicely (in a conservative suit) interacting with gang members in their poverty-stricken areas. Despite the fact that contact was nearly always in the gang's territory, neither party seemed particularly self-conscious or intimidated by the other. As one representative told me, "Why should I be afraid? They [the gang] know why I'm here. They are not going to hurt me, they understand business is business."[6]

When the gangs want to make contact with the representatives of a particular politician's organization, they usually call a telephone number that has been provided to them during past discussions, or they contact a "street-level politician" who has ties to the political organization.[7] However, no matter how contact is initiated, the gang's requests are passed along a chain of people. Despite these rather clumsy logistics, gangs receive relatively quick replies to their queries.

As one can imagine, politicians always avoid any direct contact between themselves and the gang. In fact, politicians always deny having anything to do with gangs, because they understand that the public image of gangs is one of a social disease.[8] Indirect contact is politically prudent. That way, the politician can deny any type of knowledge of gang involvement in his or her organization. In essence, indirect contact acts as a means to politically launder the political currency gained through such transactions.

Three principal questions remain concerning the relationship between gangs and politicians. The first is, What do gangs do for the politicians? Gangs provide politicians with six types of services. First, they often disseminate campaign literature for candidates, not only at the polling booths on election day but also to the homes of residents in their neighborhood.

Second, they place signs at various public places throughout the neighborhood and carry signs at the polling booths. Third, they are active in getting people to the polls on election day. Sometimes they are assigned the task of going to people's houses to remind them that they have not voted; or they are given the task of physically helping people who are having difficulty to get to the polls. The latter task usually entails going to people's homes and driving them to the polls. Fourth, they are sometimes used to pressure people to vote for a particular candidate by continually harassing individuals during the campaign and by being physically present at the polls on election day. Fifth, some gangs are rather large and relatively prosperous, and two of these have actually made financial donations to a specific politician's campaign. (This is, of course, the exception rather than the rule.) Sixth, some of the gangs undertake a crude form of fund-raising for certain politicians by coercing various individuals and businesses to donate to the campaign. (This, however, occurred less than the other activities.)

Of course, most of these activities occur during an electoral campaign. However, one service was sometimes provided before the campaign: different incumbent politicians solicited seven gangs (one apiece) to undermine the campaigns of other politicians contesting their positions. First, six of the gangs talked to neighborhood residents in an effort to discourage them from supporting the challenger. Three (including the one gang that decided not to try to persuade the residents by talking to them) attempted physically to intimidate the staffs and supporters of the politicians challenging their client. In two of the three cases, physical intimidation produced the intended effect, and the politician withdrew his candidacy. However, the gangs did not undertake any activity that involved physical intimidation without discussing the potential effects on relations with the community. If any act was thought potentially to compromise its relations with the community, the gang refused to participate. This occurred fourteen times throughout the more than ten years of the study and involved all the six different gangs.

The second principal question concerning gangs and politicians is, What do gangs receive for their efforts? The answer to the question depends on the ethnic composition of the gang. For Irish gangs, participation in elections is done in close connection with the social clubs, so their participation is expected—that is, they are part of a political tradition. Yet this political tradition is not without its rewards. The reward for political involvement is the understanding that later on gang members will be

aided in securing employment. This does not necessarily mean that the
politician they are working for will give them a patronage job in local
government. The promise is more general than that. The assumption is
that a patronage job is possible, but so is the opportunity to work for
some other business that has contacts with the politician being supported. In addition, even if the politician they worked for is unsuccessful
in his or her political bid for office, they believe that the contacts they
make within the social clubs will reward them for their work for the
politicians, since the social club made this request in the first place. The
comments of two members of Irish gangs from different cities illustrate
these beliefs. Pen is a seventeen-year-old member of a Boston gang:

> Look, we [the gang] work for the politicians that the social club
> thinks would be the best. If they win, some of the older guys will
> get some jobs if they want. You know, we did some work and we
> get some reward. . . . Most of these jobs are working for the city,
> but a lot of times they get us some jobs with other people they
> know, like contractors . . . well, those of us, like me, who are
> young will get jobs later because we did our part for whoever they
> wanted in the social club and they remember.

Bridge is a sixteen-year old member of an Irish gang in New York:

> The people in the [social club] take care of us. You see it's all con-
> tacts; you know, it's who you know that gets you a job. So when
> we help somebody in politics, everybody knows that they got to
> remember and take care of us at some time. They got to get us a
> job if we want it at sometime. . . . It don't have to be the guy we
> helped, it could be, but it don't have to be him; 'cause if he ain't in
> office, the guys in the club will talk to someone to get whichever
> one of us wants a job a job. You see politics is like an investment.

What is interesting is that these youths worked with politicians in nearly
the same manner as in past generations, when the political machine was
at its full maturity. Thus, although the political machine has in fact dis-
appeared, certain remnants still remain, at least among the Irish.

For the non-Irish gangs, the reward most often obtained for political
help comes in the form of favors. Of the seventeen gangs in New York
that were politically involved, fifteen received money for services rendered. As the representative of a politician said, "There is nothing wrong
with paying a gang for campaign work done. We would have had to hire
some group of people to do this work anyway, so we might as well hire

a group that knows the community. It's just with this group, I'm not going to tell [the candidate] and we're not going to publicize it."[9] Of course, all the gangs saw the opportunity for financial gain, so they attempted to negotiate as large an amount as they could. The exact amounts obtained depended on such circumstances as whether it was an important public office that was being contested, whether the election was close, whether the gang's district was critical to winning the election, whether the gang was able to deliver the votes, and the amount of experience the gang had in negotiating with political organizations. There were times when inexperience produced rather small amounts of money, but with more experience the amounts negotiated increased.

On some occasions, a gang would negotiate for a supply of drugs. Sometimes these drugs would be used for a few parties; or they would be resold. Only six of the gangs received this kind of reward, and it was not a consistent form of payment. In every case where drugs were a form of payment, the party negotiating with the gang was not directly connected to a particular political candidate. Rather, they were members of various quasi-political action groups that had a political agenda in which they believed the gangs could help.

One of the most prevalent rewards that gangs get from their involvement with politicians is the assurance (from certain political camps) that they will receive some type of protection from continued police harassment. The gangs find this form of payment to be quite appealing and often are willing to accept it in place of money. The problem for gangs is that they sometimes find they are not receiving all the aid they believe they are entitled to. When this occurred, they found that they had little or no power to force the other party to honor their agreement. In cases where the gang felt it had been defrauded by a particular political organization, it ceased to accept any form of payment other than money for a very long time afterwards. As Bookman, a twenty-four-year old leader of a gang in New York, said:

> Check this out, we enter into this agreement with a slime who says
> he is working for the election of [candidate's name]. He says to us
> "What do you want?" and we says, "To see to it that the police
> lay off us for a while." He says "OK, you got it. There won't be
> any heat on you for a while." We seen that the police relaxed a
> little. So we say to ourselves, that's great, and we go out and work
> the community for the jive's candidate. The guy wins, the police
> seem to be cool for a little while and then they start hitting on us.

I call the slime, and all he says is that there really isn't anything he can do. Well, we was reamed, so now we only negotiate for money. It'd be better to get relief from the police than money, but you can't trust them to deliver it consistently. . . . You know, they may get it to you for a little while, but then out of nowhere their help ends and some of your people get busted or something. So we just go for the money now.

Lastly, nine of the gangs received space in small buildings as a reward for their work. In many of these instances, the rent for the space had been paid for a specified period of time, while in other cases the gang received the use of the space indefinitely.[10] Seven of the gangs used the space for recreation; the other two used it to store stolen equipment.

Relations with Politicians in the Non-Machine City

The relationship between gangs and politicians was significantly different in Los Angeles, a city that had not experienced a political-machine culture. In Los Angeles, the pattern of relationship is indirect. In this regard, there was rarely an attempt made by either the gangs or the elected officials (or would-be elected officials) to establish any type of direct contact. Yet when communication was necessary, both used established community leaders to communicate with each other. More will be said about the nature of these community leaders in the section that follows. All that is necessary to understand about them at this point is the messenger role they assume between the gangs and the politicians.

Over the years, non-machine cities like Los Angeles have developed or cultivated a civic culture in which politics is seen as part of a citizen's duty to the state.[11] In this type of political culture, politics is viewed as being undertaken by people who are honorable and not corrupt. Politicians are not to be involved in graft and citizens are not to participate in politics because they want to obtain something; rather, both are to be involved for purely civic-minded reasons.[12] Within such a political culture, there is a concerted effort to nurture the symbols associated with high morality in the political arena. Thus, both politicians and citizens try to avoid anything that might be construed as being politically corrupt. Yet politics sometimes forces people to deal with individuals they do not consider politically honorable or civic-minded, and this is the case with both gangs and politicians in Los Angeles. Each group believes that the other is politically corrupt and lacks "civic-mindedness." The gangs think that the politicians are racist and do not care about nonwhite communities like theirs. Thus, they attempt to avoid contact with them for fear that their community will believe that they are associating with an unconcerned—and therefore corrupt and "undesirable"—element.

Ironically, the same dynamic occurs with the politicians. They believe that the gangs are just a bunch of criminals, and that they must limit contact with such an element lest they be characterized by members of the larger, mostly white, community as associating with morally suspect individuals who are threatening to undermine the values of American society.[13]

For the most part, any direct communication between gangs and politicians in Los Angeles is through the agency of community leaders. However, both parties realize that each will use the other to establish some advantages. For the politician, the gang is used as a negative political symbol, a catch-all for crime in general (i.e., stopping gangs is synonymous with stopping crime). Thus, politicians who want to indicate that they are hard on crime will talk of controlling or eradicating gangs.

Politicians also use the gangs to indicate to constituents that they care about the community and are actively trying to be constructive in addressing important issues. They do this in two ways. First, some politicians use the gangs in an attempt to indicate their own intention to protect the community from crime, and to protect non-gang children from gang violence. Second, they use the gangs to convey their intention to protect those boys who are already in the gangs by encouraging them to leave and become involved in educational programs instead. Therefore, they adopt the strategy of creating an image of being against gangs and making an effort to get the children in the area to become well-educated professional people who will be looked upon as productive citizens. As one politician remarked, "I wanted to indicate to all the residents that I wanted to help everyone in the community to better themselves; and I am going to do so by telling them that I will try to protect their children through eradicating gangs in their area."

For politicians, gangs are a valuable political resource, providing a social object on which to focus the public's attention. Because of the youth of many gang members, politicians can pretend to be sympathetic to the community by appearing to be concerned with saving young people's lives. In addition, because gangs are associated with crime, politicians can present a public image of being responsive to the larger community as well. Thus, despite the obvious fact that politicians can at best make only a marginal difference in the material conditions that affect gang development—and that often they make little effort to do even that— they can take on the appearance of being responsible.

Gangs have attempted to use politicians as a political resource as well. Nineteen leaders representing seven gangs were aware that they could not elicit any direct material benefits from elected officials in Los Angeles, but they knew that they could benefit from politicians. These gangs continued to be involved in crime in an effort to influence politicians to initiate social programs that would help some members of the community. The comments of Pato, an eighteen-year-old leader of a Chicano gang, represent this line of thinking:

> Check it, man, we know you don't deal with the politicians in this city and expect to get anything. Hey, we know this ain't Mexico, but we also know that you don't need to do that to help yourself out. . . . We know that if we keep the pressure on them, we can get them to do something for the community; you know, try to get some program for the community. Even if it [the social program] is trying to get rid of us, it may help some other people in the community. And if that happens, the community will know we helped and they will give us credit and that shit helps us within the community.

When programs were initiated, most of the community residents knew that it was owing to the gangs, because the politicians themselves would say they hoped that such a program would help alleviate the conditions that encouraged gangs. The result was that such efforts increased the gang's status within the community. Ironically, both the politician and the gang used each other to strengthen their positions among their constituents.

Non-Elected Politicians and Gangs

While gangs and politicians neither trust nor respect each other, they both realize that they sometimes need or can use the other. Therefore, they nurture an agency—the community leader—to facilitate periodic cooperation. The community leader is a person who either runs a community organization or is active in local affairs. Whatever they represent, community leaders are, in essence, "street-level politicians." Their legitimacy in the community is predicated on their ability to provide the residents with services; and because they are more fluid in their social and political relationships than elected politicians, they are present in both machine- and non-machine-oriented cities. However, they take on more importance and power in cities with non-machine political cultures because they assume a critical position in the communication between political elites, gangs, and community residents. Here are two comments that show how gangs and politicians view each other and the role that the community leaders play. Gordo was a nineteen-year-old leader in a Chicano gang:

> Shit, I wouldn't deal with those slimy *culos* [literally, "asses," but referring to politicians here]. They are all just down on Chicanos, they don't give two shits if we die, starve, or get shipped back to Mexico. They are slimy, and I don't deal with them unless we got to. . . . Sometimes you got to deal with people you don't like for the greater good. When that happens, we get in touch with our barrio *jefe* [community leader] and he makes the contact. Then if we got to cut a deal, we do it through him.

The politician's perspective can be seen in the comments of T.H., a forty-three-year-old politician representing an area in which a large number of gangs operate:

> We never want to give the impression that we are in contact with any gangs because the public would not believe that is proper. But there are times, you know, that it is important to have some contact. So when that is the case we establish some contact through a local community leader and do all our talking through him. . . .
> Of course, we would deny we had any contact with a gang; we are not interested in committing political suicide.

Gangs seek the assistance of street-level politicians for four main purposes. First, they often ask the street-level politician to communicate something they desire to the various political elites of the city. This was particularly true in Los Angeles, which has no history of machine-type politics. Here, the street-level politician was solicited to act as a broker for the gangs. He would have to communicate with the appropriate political elite and negotiate some type of deal for the gangs. Of course, on numerous occasions many political elites got in touch with street-level politicians in order to communicate something to the gangs. The street-level politician was therefore required to initiate contact in both directions, something that required prudence, and he had to be careful not to negotiate in bad faith with either party. To maintain his own political position, he had to be considered trustworthy by the political elites, the gang, and the community. However, while it is true that the street-level politicians tried to establish their trustworthiness with all the parties, they emphasized the interests of the gang and the community because their primary source of power was associated with these two groups. The comments of two street-level politicians underscore this point. G.N. was a thirty-nine-year-old African-American man who had been a political leader in a section of New York for about five years:

> Sure, I am often called on by members of the gangs and politicians to communicate something to one or the other of them. And sometimes I act as the middleman in a deal between the two . . . and while I need to be trusted by both or nobody will use me any-more, I try to represent the interests of the community and the gang more. Because, let's face it, that's where my power origi-nated. I mean, who in the outside community would use me if I didn't have the respect and support of the community?

A.T. was a forty-seven-year-old Chicano and had been a political leader in a section of greater Los Angeles for nine years:

> Well, I try to work with the community, the gang and various po-litical people in Los Angeles. When any of them asks me, I try to work out deals like a stockbroker. And I try to do the best for everyone involved, 'cause if I don't, nobody will use me. But as everybody knows, I try to make the best deal for the community and the gang because that's where my constituency is. If I don't help them the most, someone else from the community will take my place.

Street-level politicians make it their business to gather as much infor-mation as possible because they need it to operate effectively within and between each sociopolitical segment of the city. The second way in which street-level politicians are used by gangs is thus as a source of informa-tion. The exact type of information sought by gangs varies, depending on their political needs and agenda. They may request information about the community itself or want to know what politicians or government agencies, like the police, are planning or doing. Whatever type of infor-mation they need, the street-level politician is the person they approach to ascertain it. The comments of Rico, a twenty-two-year-old leader of a

gang from New York, are an example. Rico is addressing all the members
at one of the gang's general meetings:

> Look, before we start this project with the vacant building, we
> need to find out if the city is going to let us do it [they wanted to
> renovate the building]. Then we got to know if we go and do it,
> whether they are going to send in the police and take it away from
> us. So we need to get in touch with [their street-level politician]
> and see what he knows. If he don't know nothing, then we got to
> tell him to find out. So I say we do nothing until we find out from
> him what's happening.

The comments of Candle, a nineteen-year-old member of a Chicano
gang in Los Angeles, are another example. Candle is also addressing all
the members of his gang at their weekly meeting:

> We need to talk to [the street-level politician] and see what he
> knows about whether the police are going to let us have that
> picnic in the park. Hey, we want to make money, and if they are
> going to harass us, then the people who would come and buy food
> and beer from us are going to leave. And if that happens, we're
> going to be out some money! So have P.Y. [the street-level politi-
> cian] check it out.

The third way in which gangs use street-level politicians is as media-
tors or ombudsmen. When rival gangs are warring with each other, they
often seek the aid of a street-level politician to act as a mediator in the
dispute. The street-level politician's role is critical, because gangs cannot
talk directly to each other for fear of losing face and eroding their legitimacy in the area they already control. Sometimes the situation is so complicated that a street-level politician from one area has to make contact
with a street-level politician in another area and negotiate a peace treaty
between the two (or more) rival gangs. Take the comments of Blacky, an
eighteen-year-old leader of a Puerto Rican/African-American gang in New
York. Blacky is addressing the general membership at a regular meeting:

> We need to discuss the war we are in with the [rival gang] and the
> [another rival gang]. Besides the fact that one of our brothers is
> dead and four have been hurt, business is down and so is our trea-
> sury. We got to see if we can get a peace treaty with them. So I
> think we should get [the street-level politician] and have him talk
> to who he knows in the [rival gang's] area and have him [the

street-level politician in that area] see if we can cut a deal with them . . . I don't like it either [trying to make a peace pact with the rival gangs], but if we don't pretty soon, we will run out of money. So I say we get [the street-level politician] on this now.

In sum, since the community usually looks favorably on the local street-level politician (otherwise he or she would not be effective), gangs attempt to establish and maintain a close working relationship. If they do not, they weaken their position within the community and compromise the overall health of their organizations.

I now turn to the question of why the street-level politician is receptive to doing business with gangs. The most fundamental reason has to do with the fact that gangs are an important institution within the low-income community. They simply cannot be ignored if a street-level politician has any hope of becoming and/or maintaining his or her position as a "community leader."

There are five reasons why street-level politicians maintain a close relationship with gangs, four of which are directly related to the interests of the politicians. First, some street-level politicians want to provide a better environment for the youth of the community. They are legitimately concerned both with protecting the youth of their community from the violence associated with gang conflict and with creating an environment that offers the youth of their community economic mobility. Second, street-level politicians have small businesses in the community and know that it is beneficial for business if they have a close working relationship with the gangs. Third, some have aspirations to run for public office and understand that in order for them to switch from being street-level politicians to being elected officials, the cooperation of the community and the gang are needed.[14] Fourth, many of the street-level politicians are afraid that if they do not negotiate a working relationship, they will be physically attacked by the gangs in their community.

Thus, the development and maintenance of a working relationship between the street-level politician and the local gang is predicated on: (1) the street-level politician's desire for a better life for the community's residents and their children, (2) the residents' own interest in the community, (3) the interests of politicians outside the community, (4) the political ambitions of the street-level politicians themselves, and (5) the interests of the gangs.

Some Reasons for Intermittent Patterns
of Cooperation between Gangs and Politicians

Gangs limit their relationship with either elected or street-level politicians for four reasons. The first has to do with the gang's perception of the politician's ability to deliver rewards. When gangs believe that a particular politician does not have the power to deliver rewards at the present or some reasonable time in the future, they will not attempt to either develop or maintain a relationship with that politician. As Glue, a twenty-three-year-old leader of a New York gang, commented:

> Shit, this dude [the politician] can't give us fuck-all [anything] and he ain't never going to be able to do it. He's just smoke, that's all. There ain't no way we going to help this dude. There ain't no way we're even going to talk to him about it, 'cause we don't got the time for his shit. The only time we talk to these shit-head politicians is if they can really do something for us; if they can't, we wave them off, 'cause we ain't in the business of philanthropy here.

The second reason for intermittent contact between politicians and gangs has to do with the fact that many of the gangs have difficulty making contact with the politicians who they believe can help them the most. Sometimes making contact with a particular politician was perceived to be so difficult that the gang simply discontinued the effort. This was either because the gang lacked the necessary skills to get access to the politician or the result of barriers established by the politician's organization. In a certain number of cases, such barriers were simply indications of an over-structured organization, while at other times the advisors to the politicians in question saw no advantage to establishing any type of contact with a local gang and created barriers to obstruct any such contact.

The third reason involves the level of difficulty that gangs and politicians encounter in their efforts to communicate efficiently with each other. In this type of situation, the gang and the politician are capable of making contact with each other, but not in the time frame that each expected. This invariably leads to frustration and periodically to a severance of ties. For example, the Black Rose gang in Boston had a working relationship with a local politician, who in one instance needed the gang to mobilize the residents of the area to attend a meeting at which the zoning commission was to consider a petition by a large developer to rezone a section of the politician's district for the purpose of building a hotel and shopping area. The politician believed that if the zoning commission allowed the developer to undertake the proposed project, it would be detrimental for both the community and himself.[15] As it turned out, the politician had difficulty contacting the gang's leaders in a quick and efficient manner, and the gang's leaders had difficulty getting the gang organized quickly enough to mobilize the community. The result was a low turnout of residents at the zoning meeting, and the zoning commission allowed a portion of the project to go forward. The ramification for the politician was that he had to prepare himself for changes in his constituency and more difficulty in the next election. He blamed the gang and temporarily severed his relationship with it. Five months later, he needed the gang's help and reestablished the connection.

The fourth reason for there being an inconsistent relationship between gangs and politicians has to do with the gang's evaluation of the quality of the compensation for the work or favors they undertake or bestow. Of the gangs studied, 81 percent (thirty) made some attempt to evaluate the compensation they were receiving for the services they rendered, asking first about the quality of the compensation—that is, how good was it? For example, some gangs received drugs as compensation for their services. For these gangs, the salient questions were whether the supply of drugs was sufficient and what the quality of the supply was. If there was a problem with either supply or quality, then there would be some type of renegotiation between the leadership of the gang and the politician.[16] However, if there was a problem with both the supply and the quality, the gang would give the politician or his representative warning; and if the situation continued, the gang would break with the politician and his organization.

There were other gangs for whom payment for services involved a politician's help in controlling police activity with respect to them. Sometimes the gang would enter into an agreement with a politician in which the politician agreed to intercede with the police in its behalf. Agreements of this nature were, for strategic purposes, left rather vague by the politician. There were times when the politicians either could not influence police policy or did not want to. Such vague agreements allowed the politician elasticity in what would be delivered. The gangs, on the other hand, countered this strategy by assessing the degree, quality, and consistency of a politician's ability to influence law enforcement officials. If the leadership or the rank and file believed that they were not receiving what they had bargained for, they would break off their agreement with the politician. Nearly all the gangs empathized to some degree with the fact that it was a delicate situation for politicians attempting to influence law enforcement officials. However, if they found that there was a consistent pattern in which they had solicited the politician's aid and he had been unable to deliver, then they would call off their agreement. An example of this involves a gang from New York. At the gang's general meeting, they discussed the fact that the police had continued to harass their numbers business. Pupet, an eighteen-year-old member, said:

> OK, it is difficult for [the politician] to make deals with the police, but he's done it before and everything was alright. Now all we been hearing is how difficult it is. We been putting up with nothing being done for two months now. Fuck, we did work for him, so now he's got to get the police off of us or we will be losing some money. So I say the next time he gives us this story, we tell him to shove it. We need results and if he can't deliver, we got to break it off with him and find somebody else. Hell, if he wants to get sympathy, let him tell his story to Barbara Walters.

This ability on the part of gangs to discontinue their association with politicians was one of the main factors that prevented politicians from establishing undue leverage with them.

Before leaving this section on the interrelationship between gangs and politicians in machine-oriented cities, it must be emphasized that not all of the gangs in a city are represented in politics. In fact, there was one time when three gangs had no contact with politicians at all. There are two main reasons for a gang not having any direct relations with politicians. The first has to do with the amount of power of any one gang in a particular political district. Whichever gang had established itself as the dominant force within a certain community was most likely to have established some direct contact with some politicians. Thus, gangs that were unable to establish contacts with politicians were those that lacked a significant level of influence in their area. Politicians were only willing to deal with those that had the potential to influence votes in their areas. As it turned out, sometimes one particular gang was influential enough to develop political contacts, but would then lose control of its area to a rival gang, and then reclaim it again. Therefore, there was a good deal of fluidity in the development and maintenance of political ties among gangs and politicians.

The second reason why a gang may have no political connections is that the politician (or his or her political organization) does not believe that a relationship with the local gang is necessary in order to get elected or remain in office. In such situations, the politician has been able to obtain the necessary support from other sources, such as political brokers in the community.

Politicians and Gangs: Some Concluding Notes

Whether a direct relationship between politicians and gangs is established has to do with the willingness of both parties—but primarily the politicians—to enter into such a relationship. This relationship can best be characterized as an "expedient exchange relationship," in that each party receives benefits as a result of each undertaking tasks that will provide the other with benefits. This exchange relationship is expedient and differs from the prudential form of exchange relationship in that: (1) it is established for a specific end—primarily, the benefit of both parties involved—and is not concerned with fairness or rightness; (2) it is for a shorter period of time; and (3) there is a pattern to these relationships that involves intermittent contact.

Finally, it must be pointed out that city councilors and street-level politicians have much more involved interactions with gangs than do mayors, mayoral staffs, or mayoral candidates because their power and influence is more grounded in the local community and they therefore need to establish a working relationship (or at least a rapprochement) with the gangs in their area. Mayors and mayoral candidates are more removed from politics at the neighborhood level, and so they can and must be more cautious in their formal ties with gangs. Yet the bottom line is that gangs do have relationships with politicians.

Government Agents and Gangs

Gangs have ties to government that involve people other than politicians. One major group that gangs have ties to are those people who work for the government bureaucracies that manage social services. The ties between the two involve the general interaction associated with patron-client relations. A large portion of the encounters between the gang and the government bureaucrat involve the gang attempting to secure something for either its members, its members' families, or other families in the community. However, this relationship is not a one-way street. Many of the bureaucrats whom gangs have contact with see value in establishing good relations with them. This is because, for many of these bureaucrats, it is essential that they receive cooperation from gangs in order to realize their personal and organizational goals. There are three broad social areas in which contact has been established between the gang and the bureaucracy of the local government: recreation, vocational training, and social services. Within the social service category, contact is mostly, but not exclusively, associated with various agencies responsible for housing; AFDC and welfare support services for single-parent women; food/health programs; and programs related to drug and alcohol abuse.

In each of these areas, the gang interacts with local government through one of its bureaucratic agencies. More specifically, the gang will interact with agents of these bureaucracies—people whose position and authority have been described as those of "street-level bureaucrats." [17] The formal nature of this interaction, for both the government agents and the gang, is what I have called a *prudent-exchange relationship*. Within this relationship there are two overriding concerns. The first is the preoccupation of the agency (i.e., the authorities within the agency) with its mandate to service a particular segment of the community. The senior authorities within the agency are aware of and concerned with the agency's ability to manage the responsibilities designated to it competently, and they communicate this concern to those agents authorized to provide the mandated services to the specified clients. The second is the gang's preoccupation with establishing a mode of interaction with the "street-level bureaucrat" that is both smooth and provides for the maximum amount of service for its members, their families, and its neighborhood. Therefore, gangs are generally concerned not only with establishing a relationship in which they can receive the available services, but also with establishing a relationship whereby they receive these services relatively quickly. Thus, regardless of the specific concerns of each party, both the gang and the bureaucracy establish a prudent posture toward the other.

The Prudent-Exchange Relationship: The Gang's Perspective

While both the gang and the government bureaucrat proceed with a prudent-exchange relationship, the meaning and therefore behavior of this prudent relationship is different for both. For gangs, prudence is the act of creatively extracting as many services as possible from the various government bureaucracies. Some might call this "shrewdness in the acquisition of services." The comments of Sack, Teak, and Angler are representative of this concept of prudence. Sack was a seventeen-year-old member of a Los Angeles gang:

> Well, yeah, we deal with a lot of people that are part of the city government, you know, people that work for housing or recreation, things like that. And sometimes they have job programs. We try to have a good relationship with them because we can get things, but when you deal with them, you got to be creative. 'Cause if you plan to put something over, you got to be clever.[18]

Teak was a sixteen-year-old member of an Irish gang in Boston:

> The fellas in our gang try to be on good terms with the people who run the programs in our area. . . . . There are a lot of programs that the government has for poor areas and if you want to get a lot of what they have to give, you have to be crafty. You see we want to get a lot from these programs if we can, so we are on good terms with the government guys who run it and we're foxy in how we go about it.

Angler was a nineteen-year-old member of a New York gang:

> The guys in the gang always try to have a working relationship with the government peoples who be running the rec and other programs; because if you ain't good with them, it makes it difficult to get things. But being on good relations ain't good enough, if you wants to get the most, you gots to be savvy!

Gangs are consistently involved in this prudent-exchange relationship in three social areas. The first, and most prevalent, has to do with recreation. Most policymakers have long thought that one of the main reasons why young men (and boys) become involved in gangs is because they have too much idle time on their hands and few resources with which to spend this time in a creative way. Since the policy most often pursued to affect change has been the development of recreational services, this is the area where gangs attempt to capture as many services as they can. While gang members devote a large amount of time to making money, they also spend a significant amount of time relaxing and trying to have fun. There were times when the topic of increasing recreational activities was the main issue at the various gangs' general meetings. In fact, there were many times when the leadership decided that increased recreation, funded by a government agency, was a project worth pursuing for purposes of internal gang politics.[19] In both cases, the gang decided on a strategy to secure this from the appropriate government agency and then pursued the strategy.

Gangs generally use three strategies to obtain greater recreational services. First, sometimes all the gang needs is to have greater participation in the existing programs, so that the agents of the appropriate bureaucracy can justify maintaining and/or increasing the program. In these situations, the gang simply orders a specified number of members to increase their participation and involvement in the program. As Dooby, a nineteen-year-old leader of an Irish gang in Boston, said at one of the general meetings:

> Me and the other heads [leaders of the gang] want about twenty-five of you to use the facilities at the playground more. These are the guys we chose. [He reads the names.] We want you guys to show everyday and stay the day, until we tell you stop. It should be about a week and half. And make sure you show interest in the stuff they are doing, otherwise the city won't invest in the equipment we want.[20]

On other occasions, the gang decides that the best strategy is to have some of the leadership talk directly to the bureaucratic agent in charge to request increased activities. Rust was a twenty-one-year-old leader of a Puerto Rican gang in New York. Addressing the gang at their weekly meeting, he said:

> Lamb, Duper, and I are going to go to the field and talk to the dude who is in charge there. We're just going to tell him if he orders some new stuff and keeps the field open later, we'll be there in force every day. I know that if we do that we'll get what we want, 'cause he is just praying to get us involved.[21]

Finally, sometimes the gang decides that it is best to start some limited amount of trouble in order to convince upper-level bureaucrats and policymakers that certain programs need to continue. An example involved Tippy, a sixteen-year-old leader of a Chicano gang in Los Angeles. Addressing the gang at their weekly meeting, he said:

> Look, we asked for some ping-pong tables to be set up in the park and for some new basketball courts and nothing has happened for

five months. So let's send a message. We will hit a couple stores tonight. This'll get their attention. They will know that they can either pay for us now with recreation or later with insurance.

All three strategies generally result in the gang gaining some (and, a few times, all) of the desired policy outcomes because they provide the various bureaucratic agents with the necessary information to justify continued social involvement in this area.

In all three cities, the gangs used one of these three strategies to influence the recreational department agents to provide three types of services. First, they attempted to get more athletic equipment and to persuade the various agents to schedule more events in which they could use the equipment. The comments of three gang members represent this pattern. Copper was a seventeen-year-old member of a gang in Los Angeles. Talking at a gang meeting, he said:

> Hey, now that we got them to buy us that new softball equipment, we need to pressure them to set up more games for us to use it. Shit, right now they don't have enough time available for us to use the stuff enough. If we don't get them to set up more time, it was useless getting them to buy the new stuff because we won't be able to have fun with it anyway![22]

Dred, a nineteen-year-old member of a gang in Boston, said:

> I am telling you guys that we gotta go down and talk to the guy who's in charge of the swimming pool and tennis courts about keeping the places open more, 'cause a lot of us are busy during the day and we don't get a chance to use it enough. . . . Everybody knows that if we ask him he'll do it, 'cause he's so afraid of getting blamed for more crime if he doesn't.[23]

Sting was a twenty-year-old member of a New York gang. While talking to a group of members around a park bench, he said:

> We gots to get the brothers together and go sees the dude who's running the rec. program at the community center. 'Cause we needs to get him to keep the courts open more or we won't get to play much. There is just too many trying to get the courts, so we need to see if he would keep it open longer and give us more time to use them.[24]

Second, the vast majority of gangs in all three cities (twenty-six of the thirty-seven studied) made an attempt to influence the person in charge of recreation to take more field trips to rural areas. Camping trips were the most sought after, although horseback riding, canoeing, and fishing trips were also desired. The comments of Eel and Coco are representative. Eel, a sixteen-year-old member of a gang in New York, said:

> Yeah, we got to get the parks people [recreation department] to take us to the country more 'cause it's a lot of fun. One time we went to Maine and went canoeing and fishing. It was a trip. We had a great time. I really liked it. Don't get me wrong, I wouldn't want to live there, but I would like to spend periodic time there.

Coco, a seventeen-year-old member of a Chicano gang in Los Angeles, observed:

> We're trying to get this here agency to take us to the mountains. About six months ago, we all went to the Sierras and we all really had a good time. I even went fishing and caught some. I don't know what they were, some kind of trout or something, but they were good! I hope we can pressure them into taking us regularly 'cause its good to get away sometimes.[25]

Third, thirty-three of the thirty-seven gangs sought to have those responsible for recreation plan more field trips to amusement parks, picnics, and the beach. In both areas, the recreation department was usually able to provide for increased services. The gang's efforts proved successful.[26]

Providing jobs and job-training is the second area in which policymakers believe they can make an impact on reducing gang activity, and thus the second realm in which gangs and government bureaucracies establish a prudent-exchange relationship. Throughout the more than ten years of this study, there have been innumerable programs related to job-training. These programs have been managed by a variety of agencies, ranging from departments concerned with community development to those in charge of issues affecting youth. However, regardless of the agency involved in managing these programs, the same behavioral patterns emerged between the personnel of the various agencies and the gangs, producing relatively the same results.[27] First, there is a pattern of gang cooperation with the various agencies' efforts to administer the job-training program. The gangs cooperated for three reasons. First, many of the members used the stipends paid for the training period to pay gang dues or for small miscellaneous expenses. Second, some of the gangs' members hoped that one of the job-training programs was linked to a large corporation, and that they would have the opportunity to jump from the training program to a well-paying job. The comments of Tape, a seventeen-year-old member of an African-American gang in New York, indicate this view:

> Hey, man you never know, I hear that some of these programs is tied to some big corporations, and after you done with the training they [the corporations] just suck you up to one of their good paying jobs. . . . You see these job programs is like the lottery, man, you never know when you hooked into the right one. So you gotta check it out.

The third reason why gangs cooperated with the programs had to do with their efforts to indicate solidarity with residents of their low-income neighborhoods, who believed that having more youth employed was better for their community. Local residents (and the gangs) generally assumed that government would not provide many job-training programs (or social programs in general) if it were not for the fact that there were gangs in the area.[28] Many of the residents who felt that the community needed more job-training and placement programs encouraged the gangs to participate in these programs for purposes of legitimizing the programs. It should be remembered that not all poor young males (or females) are in gangs, and many of these other youths badly want to have a job, so residents have a strong desire for increased opportunities for employment. Jim was a fifty-two-year-old father of two living in New York:

> Let me tell you that if it weren't for the gangs, this community wouldn't see any social program and especially any job-type programs. You see, we got a high unemployment rate among people in this area and especially young people. But none of the government leaders cares about that. If nothing happened, they'd continue to let 'em be unemployed. They only care when the gangs get active in illegal stuff, then they start a job program. So you see, we need the gangs to help us out. It's their behavior that the policymakers are concerned about, not some regular kid who's unemployed.

The gangs realize this as well and cooperate with the programs in order to solidify their relations with the community. The comments of Horn, a sixteen-year-old leader of an African-American gang in New York, are indicative:

Sure, we know that nobody in government really cares if you be unemployed. They care about gang activity so they start this job-training program and it helps some people. And the community likes it so we know that if the program is going to continue it gots to show some results, you know, like getting us gang-bangers to be involved. So we get involved some, even if we don't like the jobs they be training us for because we gots to keep close to the community.

Although there is a pattern among the gangs of cooperation with the agencies managing job-training programs, this cooperation is limited. Most of the gang members did one of three things: dropped out of the job program before they had completed the training; completed the program, took a job for a short period of time, and then quit; or completed the program and refused to take a job at all. There are several reasons for this pattern. The first is that from the beginning, many of the youths never intended to stay in the program or to take a job associated with the training. They had participated in the program for other reasons, such as wanting to obtain a little spending money during financially difficult times, or as part of the gang's effort to help the community. However, for those gang members who did intend to finish the program and possibly assume a job afterwards, the primary reason why they did not take a job was because most of the jobs they were being trained for were the type most gang members had been trying to avoid. In fact, most of the gang members were trying to secure the type of job that would catapult them from poor or working-class conditions into the upper middle class. When a job was a skilled manual job or one that paid only a modest amount of money, they would quit and revert to efforts to accumulate large amounts of capital through one of their illegal business ventures. While these ventures have more risk involved, they remain attractive because they have the potential for accumulating large amounts of money in short periods of time. However, despite the fact that cooperation is limited and therefore, in a majority of cases, did not produce the policy's intended results, most of the thirty-seven gangs studied cooperated at a level sufficient to both legitimize the various programs and, in the process, create an important bond with those individuals (and agencies) responsible for implementing social policies.

Finally, gangs initiate a prudent-exchange relationship with those government bureaucrats who have the authority to provide general socioeconomic assistance to either their members, their members' families, or families in the community.[29] In their effort to obtain these services, they attempt to establish and nurture a relationship with one or two street-level bureaucrats. Interestingly, these bureaucrats are usually not directly responsible for administering the service the gangs desire. Generally, although not always, the person they establish their relationship with is a street-level bureaucrat working in the area of recreation or substance abuse. It is not by chance that the gangs choose such street-level bureaucrats for this type of relationship. First, the gang has more access to them than to many other bureaucrats. Second, the gangs believe that they have more leverage over these bureaucrats because they need them to participate in their programs if the programs are to continue. Basically, what the gangs want from this relationship is for the street-level bureaucrat to help them secure the desired services from other agencies. The gangs are able to negotiate with a significant number of these bureaucrats the necessary information as to who is eligible for certain services and the logistics and procedures for obtaining them. In addition, gangs successfully get many of these bureaucrats to intervene in their behalf. Sometimes the intervention is simply a phone call to ascertain who would be the best person to contact. At other times, the street-level bureaucrat contacts the appropriate person and makes the necessary logistical arrangements for the gang to successfully fulfill the requirements to be eligible for the services. Ultimately, the gang seeks these social services either because gang members or their families need them or because the community in general desperately needs such services and the gang attempts to help as part of its efforts to be responsive to community needs. The gang's ability to secure services for the community usually contributes to its broad efforts to get the community to view it in a positive light and to help it when needed.

Before moving to the street-level bureaucracy's perspective of its relationship with gangs, it is important to reemphasize that in order to establish and maintain this prudent-exchange relationship, all the gangs studied developed the strategy of being both cooperative and uncooperative with the various government bureaucracies they wanted services from. This strategy of interrupting cooperation created uncertainty in the bureaucracy, which in turn encouraged the bureaucracy to make a maximum effort toward providing the services. For example, at times when the bureaucracies were moving slowly in providing the requested services (dragging their feet), some gangs would undertake a number of destructive acts in the community. This functioned as a type of message to policymakers that something was needed to control the situation, and was usually followed by increased assurances from the appropriate bureaucracy that the desired services would be forthcoming.[30]

The Prudent-Exchange Relationship:
The Bureaucrat's Perspective

Whereas for gangs, prudence assumes the form of being cunning in the effort to secure services, for the street-level bureaucrat prudence assumes the character of being cautious and wary of the risks associated with interacting with gangs (gang members) and with weighing these risks against the calculated benefits of such an association.[31] Therefore, this section analyzes the reasons for the street-level bureaucrat's involvement in this prudent-exchange relationship with gangs.[32]

In order to understand the nature of the relationship between gangs and street-level bureaucracies, it is necessary to focus on both the individuals responsible for administering those bureaucracies whose policies are directed at gangs and those street-level bureaucrats responsible for implementing these policies. I begin with the upper-level bureaucrats who administer bureaucracies that, at some level, deal with gangs. All those interviewed encouraged a prudent-exchange relationship with gangs for reasons of self-interest. Every one of these individuals realized that their agencies' mandate required them to do something that would contribute to the control of gang activity. Fifteen (44 percent) said they really did not care about or for gangs.[33] Nearly every one of these individuals said that they actually despised them. Nonetheless, all tried to establish or maintain a functional relationship with the various gangs within their jurisdiction. The comments of D. B., a forty-eight-year old administrator of an agency that provides services to gang members in Los Angeles, illustrate these views:

> Gang members are not my favorite group of people. As a matter
> of fact, I really have contempt for most of what they stand for, but
> my agency is responsible for helping to control the gang problem
> and this involves providing various services to gang members. I at-
> tempt to provide the best services that I am responsible for, and
> ironically this means that members of my staff must develop a
> somewhat close relationship with the gangs themselves in order to
> maximize their cooperation.[34]

Among the reasons why such a relationship is nurtured, probably the one most often cited has to do with these administrators' desires to run a bureaucratically efficient and effective program. In some cases, such programs provide an expansion of the agencies' official roles, which increases the agencies' power and prestige. In addition, these administrators believe that the ability to demonstrate competence in managing an efficient and effective program means that they will gain more attention within city government and position themselves to move up to other agencies that have greater authority, responsibilities, salary, and status. The comments of R.K., a thirty-eight-year-old administrator of a government agency in New York that provided services to gang members, are representative:

> It is true that we, I should say I am, concerned about running an effective program that meets the needs of those individuals who are members of gangs, and that we do that with efficiency. For that reason we make every attempt to work as closely with the gangs as possible. We take special precautions to consult them and to get feedback in an effort to solicit the greatest amount of participation from them. The result of this effort has been the fact that our agency has been given increased responsibilities concerning other areas that involve gangs. I know that other administrators in other agencies are probably envious. . . . Yes, of course, this has benefits for me personally. It has been rumored, and I expect to be offered, a position to head another agency that is much larger and that has more responsibilities and status.[35]

Of course, the administrators of these agencies were not directly responsible for implementing policy. The people in their agencies who were responsible for implementation were those I have called street-level bureaucrats. For these individuals, the need to develop a relationship with gangs was imperative if the policies were to have any chance of obtaining their desired impact. Thus, the street-level bureaucrats developed and operated under a strategy of providing the services they had been mandated to provide to members of the gang or those residents who were identified by the gang as needing them, and doing so as efficiently as possible. Street-level bureaucrats who were consistently successful were given a promotion as a reward, providing them with greater income, more prestige and power in the bureaucracy, and a work environment with less physical and emotional stress. As J.Q., a thirty-one-year-old street-level bureaucrat who dealt with gangs in New York, said:

I worked hard with the gangs, trying to meet their needs and the
objectives of the agency. But I can tell you, I was so happy when I
got my promotion to head another division of the agency. Now I
could get more money, and I had more responsibility, but mostly I
now could relax more. I didn't have to go home mentally and
physically exhausted as I used to do when I was working with the
gangs. It wasn't so much that they threatened or harassed me, although that did happen, it was more the combination of the harassment and the problem of trying to service the gangs and getting their cooperation in order to meet the policy goals of the
agency. Trying to get all that to work out I found exhausting, and
so did my co-workers.

The comments of P.L., a twenty-eight-year-old street-level bureaucrat in
Los Angeles, also indicate this feeling:

I was greatly relieved when I got my promotion. I worked really
hard for it and I tell you, I was relieved! It's kind of strange, but
it's not working with the gangs that's so stressful. It's trying to
follow the guidelines, you know the mandate of the agency and in
the process trying to satisfy both your bosses and the gangs so
they will cooperate. It's just tedious to do, and I'm glad I don't
have to do it anymore.

All the bureaucrats responsible for managing programs connected with
gangs were concerned about the risks associated with such clients. The
risks that most concerned them were all related to protecting the agency
from being used by the gangs. They did not want the gangs to enter and
leave the program whenever they chose—that is, they did not want the
gangs to simply consume the services offered with little compliance with
the program's rules or goals. Therefore, they all adopted a similar strategy of policy implementation to encourage more cooperation and compliance from the gangs. This strategy consisted of making it a little difficult for gang members, their families, or members of the community for
whom they functioned as advocates to get the services they sought. The
street-level bureaucrats initiated a strategy of sometimes providing services quickly and sometimes slowly. This unevenness of delivery created
a degree of uncertainty for the gang; it told each gang that it did not have
leverage over the street-level bureaucrat or the agency she or he represented, and that if it wanted the bureaucracies to cooperate, it needed to
cooperate itself. The street-level bureaucrats were attempting to avoid
delivering too much or too little—that is, trying to establish a strategic

level of equilibrium in the delivery system. Here one can see a clear difference between the goals of an administrator of an agency and those of the street-level bureaucrat in charge of delivering the service. The administrator is concerned with delivering services as efficiently as possible, in an effort to minimize risk to him- or herself and the agency, whereas the street-level bureaucrat is concerned with client cooperation and compliance (not necessarily efficiency) in an effort to minimize the risks to him- or herself.[36]

In sum, the prudent-exchange relationship finds each partner (gang and bureaucrat) with a somewhat different perception of the nature of the relationship. Yet in terms of intergroup behavior, it is a relationship that both have become comfortable with.

The Nongovernment Bureaucrat and Gangs

What is a nongovernment bureaucrat, and what role does he or she assume in the arena of social policy? Among the large cities of the United States, nearly every low-income area has "nonprofit" social agencies that provide services to the community. I shall call these bureaucracies grassroots agencies and the people who work in them grassroots bureaucrats. For nearly all these agencies, the largest portion of their operating costs are funded from government sources.[37] In a sense, these agencies are subcontracted by local governments to provide services directly to the low-income community and, as a result, are extensions of government. In addition, grassroots bureaucracies are considered an extension of government (and included in this chapter) because they are so dependent on government money that they are preoccupied with meeting the various policy guidelines and objectives, or at least with not violating them.

The various governments are willing to provide funding to these agencies for two basic reasons. The first has to do with money. Generally, the various governments have found it less expensive to give grassroots agencies funding than to expand the already-existing bureaucracies of the various levels of government. Take the comments of L.B., a forty-eight-year-old administrator of a governmental bureaucracy responsible for certain social services in low-income areas in New York:

I can tell you quite simply why we find funding for a number of community social agencies to provide services to low-income residents. It is because this agency and any other in the local government could not provide these services for the same amount. We could not even come close to that figure. The difference is in the cost of wages and benefits that we would have to pay as opposed to them. We not only pay higher wages to start, but we have to pay medical, retirement, workman's compensation, and things like that. The plain truth is that a lot of these services are not going to keep kids from joining gangs and causing havoc, so we at least save money.

Second, government bureaucrats believe that because these grassroots organizations were born out of the community, they are in a better position than their own street-level bureaucrats to garner the cooperation of the community and the gangs. In short, they believe they have the chance to be more effective. Take the comments of N.T., a fifty-two-year-old street-level bureaucrat in Los Angeles:

Let's be honest here, it does not matter how much I or other people in my agency try, we will not have the chance to have the impact that the people who work for [the grassroots organization's name] could have. They have the advantage of knowing the people who they are attempting to work with because they live and work in the same community. That in a nutshell is why we gave them the money to work with the gangs.[38]

Grassroots bureaucrats are like street-level bureaucrats and politicians in that their relationship with the gangs is predicated on the principles of a social exchange relationship. Yet the nature of this exchange relationship is quite different from that involving the other two governmental agents. In essence, the gang and the grassroots bureaucrat have formed an exchange relationship based on interdependence, which I have labeled a *dependent-exchange relationship*. Within this type of exchange relationship, the gang and the grassroots bureaucrat become advocates for each other to those agencies that distribute services and money.[39]

There are two reasons why gangs act as advocates for these grassroots bureaucracies. The first is that these organizations are a part of the community. Physically, they are located in the community, and the people who founded them are usually from the same low-income neighborhoods. In fact, many are former gang members.[40] Since these grassroots organizations are so much a part of the community, gangs believe that if they help these organizations receive funding to run their social programs, they will get credit from the residents for helping the community. Take the comments of Piper, a fifteen-year-old member of an Irish gang in Boston:

> You see, if we help [name of the organization] get some of their funding, then we will get more community backing because we helped to bring money into the community and we helped out some folks in the community [the grassroots bureaucrats] make their rent. So we let people in the government know, actually we let anybody who can give money to stop gangs know, that we would prefer to deal with the people at [name of the organization] because we can trust them.[41]

The second reason why gangs act as advocates for grassroots agencies is that they can control the grassroots bureaucrats better than the street-level bureaucrats of the government. It has been most gangs' experience that grassroots bureaucrats are generally much less suspicious of them than are the street-level bureaucrats of the government. This is because both are from the same community and each understands what the other wants from the relationship. In addition, gangs realize that grassroots agencies are more dependent on them for their funding than are other governmental agencies. Therefore, gangs believe that they can exert more control over these agencies and ultimately receive more services. However, the reality of the situation is more complicated. While gangs usually receive a higher proportion of services from grassroots organizations than other governmental agencies, because grassroots organizations receive small amounts of funding, the gangs actually receive less than from the other agencies. To alter this situation, gangs will advocate greater funding for their local grassroots agency. The usual strategy is to publicize to policymakers that they feel more comfortable working with these grassroots agencies, and combine this with prudent noncooperation with one or more of the various governmental agencies that are administering programs. The comments of Sale, a nineteen-year-old member of a gang in New York, illustrate this strategy:

> We try to help out the brothers at the [name of the organization] and try to get them more money to run these programs. . . . Well, what we try to do is to talk to everybody and anybody who has money to give and tell them that we like to deal with that agency. You know, we trying to pass on the message that we trust them and can work with them better. And if the message don't get

through that way, we mess with the other programs so it looks
like they ain't as effective. . . . You got to understand that we
know that agencies like [name of the grassroots organization] will
never get that much money, but we try to get as much as we can,
'cause we get a better deal from them than those other agencies
that the government runs. Hey, the reality is that we try to help
them and they do the same thing to try to help us.

The grassroots bureaucrats advocate for the gang in an indirect and
subtle manner. They begin their rhetoric by warning about the dangers
that gangs create and their potential to be destructive if the problem is
left untended to. They also advocate the rehabilitation of gang members
into productive members of society, decrying the waste of talent occurring at present. Finally, they state their case for increased funding by
arguing that because they can relate better to gangs, they can work better
with the gangs and thus ultimately have a greater possibility of modifying
their behavior (effecting change). Their appeal for increased funding argues that they have been doing this type of work for a long time, that
they have a track record of success without the benefit of adequate funding, and that if they were to receive adequate funding, they could be
increasingly effective. In addition, much of their appeal is couched in the
vocabulary of community development—that is, their efforts with gang
members are one aspect of their efforts to help create economic development in the area. The comments of H. P., a thirty-eight-year-old worker
in a Los Angeles grassroots agency, are typical:

> The gang problem is very bad in this community and the present
> programs are only partly effective. We here at [name of the orga-
> nization] have been doing work with the gangs for five years and
> have been able to do a pretty effective job. The reason is that we
> are a part of the community and we can develop a closer relation-
> ship with the gangs than, say, some other agencies. It's a shame
> that so many kids that have such potential are being lost because
> there are not enough programs to reach them. The real problem is
> that there is not enough funding around. We have had effective
> programs and we would expand these programs, but our biggest
> problem is getting funding to operate. Instead of setting up new
> programs, we got to continually worry about whether we are
> going to have enough money to survive as an agency.

In general, grassroots bureaucrats were able to relate to gangs better
than the agents of the other government bureaucracies. There also were

situations in which they were better able to get the gangs to temporarily modify their behavior; but in general, they were not significantly more effective than the other agencies in controlling gang behavior or in inhibiting the growth of gangs.[42] What sets these grassroots agencies apart from other social agencies is their dependency on gangs for their own survival; without the presence of gangs, their utility and therefore their legitimacy would be seriously diminished. This is why grassroots bureaucrats become advocates for the gangs in their area. Gangs know this and build on it, as the comments of Fat Mack, a seventeen-year-old member of a Los Angeles gang, highlight:

> You see [name of the grassroots agency] do not get much money to run their organization, so they are in a position where they got to depend on us. If we didn't exist then there would not be as much of a need for them, so sometimes you read where they say we are running wild in the streets, doing this and doing that. I mean it's like when college dudes talk about the CIA, you would think they were everywhere doing everything. That's the way they describe us sometimes. We just laugh. We know they need to do that so they get some of their funding; and if they don't get it, we act out a little, and then they make their pitch. And there are a lot of times they get their money. . . . So we do help out, but then we cash in later when we deal with them, because they know we can mess up their gig.

Some Concluding Remarks

This chapter has focused on how gangs have related to the institutions of government in the cities where they live. It presents data identifying politicians, government bureaucrats, and grassroots bureaucrats as the three main agents in which gangs and governments interrelate. It also presents evidence indicating that all of the parties had established a type of social exchange relationship. Furthermore, it indicates that the gang and each agent of government worked out a specific type of exchange relationship. For example, the gang and the politician worked out what I call an expedient-exchange relationship; gangs and government bureaucrats developed a prudent-exchange relationship; and gangs and grassroots bureaucrats developed a dependent-exchange relationship.

This evidence indicates that the basis for each of these exchange relationships is socioeconomic and political self-interest. Thus for the expedient-exchange relationship, politicians are prepared to use gangs to maintain political power, and gangs are prepared to use politicians to gain material and political advantages. Both are prepared to have contact only during those times when the potential for political and material gain exists. One of the fundamental characteristics of this type of exchange relationship is that contact between the parties is more intermittent than with the other two types. However, because there is such a consistent pattern of intermittent contact, which both parties acknowledge and plan for, an exchange relationship has emerged that has incorporated periodic contact into the composition of its structure.

The chapter also presents data indicating that the various government bureaucrats and gangs were involved in what I labeled a prudent-exchange relationship. What is important about this relationship is that both the government bureaucrats and the gang members had a different understanding of the concept of prudence. For the gang, prudence meant the task of shrewdly acquiring services from these street-level bureaucrats. For the street-level bureaucrats, prudence meant providing services efficiently to those who qualified, but proceeding cautiously so as to minimize any potential threat to their ability to be mobile within the bureaucracy. Thus it is quite common to find street-level bureaucrats arguing for their bureaucracy's right to have jurisdiction over the distribution of certain services to gangs, while at the same time avoiding being advocates for the gangs because they want to avoid the risk of a public outcry that tax dollars help gangs (which would jeopardize the agency's legitimacy and threaten the bureaucrats' professional aspirations). The nature of this relationship differs from that of the expedient-exchange relationship in that it is less surreptitious and there is more consistent contact between the two parties.

Lastly, there are data that indicate an exchange relationship existed between gangs and local nonprofit community organizations I call grassroots bureaucracies. I label the relationship forged by the gangs and these organizations a dependent-exchange relationship. The basis of this relationship lies in the gang's belief that they could trust the grassroots bureaucrats more because they were from their community, and that they could receive more services from them because, being from the same community, they had a certain amount of leverage over them. Since they were able to get more services from them, the gangs depended more on them than on the other agencies, and often advocated for them to receive more funding. For the grassroots bureaucrats, the gang represented the most important resource in their efforts to secure funding for their organization. They were fundamentally dependent on them and thus they became advocates for the gang because this was a means to secure legitimacy with the government and ultimately the funding essential for employment stability. Given the dependency of the association, there was more contact and closeness between these two parties than in the other two types of exchange relationships.

In closing, there is an important point to emphasize: all the political groups (politicians, street-level bureaucrats, and grassroots bureaucrats) have in common the fact that they either operated or supported a policy that was designed to either eliminate gangs or at least significantly control their activities. Yet because of the desire to expand or protect their own interests, they constructed a working relationship with gangs. This had the effect of establishing some quasi-formal linkages, which in turn resulted in the greater interpenetration of the gang and the general society.

Chapter Eight

Gangs, Criminal Justice, and Public Order

*Punishment then, as applied to delinquency, may be unprof-
itable in both or either of two ways: 1. By the expense it
would amount to, even supposing the application of it to be
confined altogether to delinquency: 2. By the danger there
may be of its involving the innocent in the fate designed only
for the guilty.*

Jeremy Bentham, *The Principles of Morals and Legislation* (1789)

*Man, us dealing with the people in the courts is like a dance
contest. If you and your partner is in step, you may get your
toes stepped on, but you be still in it; but if one of you really
goes out of step, you both lose the contest, man. That's the
way they be thinking too, so everybody adapts.*

Buck, a member of the Dukes gang in Los Angeles

When most people in society think of gangs, they think of crime and
crime control. For example, at a public forum on crime in the United
States, a man got up and asked the panel of law enforcement officials:
"How come the authorities cannot wipe out gangs?" The members of the
panel each took a turn answering the question, most describing what
they had done to combat crime and what they intended to do in the
future. Only one answered the question directly. He said that the answer
was simple: there was a general lack of resources for police departments
to do an adequate job. Yet, as the data in this chapter will indicate, the
answer is much more complicated. If one were to interview most criminal
justice officials, one would come away with the impression that their
policy is to eliminate gangs.[1] However, if one observes the relationship
between officials of the criminal justice system and members of gangs
over a sustained period of time, one finds that the various officials of the
criminal justice system may say they want to eliminate gangs, but this is
not how they ultimately behave.

Previous chapters have shown that gangs are an integrated element within the social fabric of low-income areas. This chapter indicates that the various law enforcement institutions have, in pursuit of their goals, bonded with the very entity they are attempting to combat.

Police Action, Gang Action

A number of factors influence police-gang relations and make it difficult for the police to eliminate gangs. The first has to do with city politics. The police in the three cities of this study used two general approaches to counteract gangs: physical force, in the form of quasi-military action; and "social worker" indoctrination, where the police officer attempted to win the hearts and minds of gang members in an effort to persuade them to quit participating in gang-associated activities. Of course, there were efforts made by the various police departments to incorporate both approaches, but the approach that took priority was determined first by what the politicians of the city were willing to allow.[2] In turn, what the politicians of the city were willing to permit was influenced by their perception of constituent approval. In a city such as Los Angeles, there is among the general white population a general endorsement of the police's use of physical force to provide public safety.[3] This reinforced both the police's use of, and the politicians' consent to, a military-operations approach to combat gangs.[4]

However, New York and Boston had the opposite political situation. In those two cities there was less consensus among the various politicians concerning the police's use of physical force. This was partly owing to the fact that there were more politicians who represented low-income areas and they were particularly sensitive to the possibility that residents would find the police's actions a form of harassment. Thus, these politicians were more vigilant toward any police action that consistently used force. As an aide for a politician in New York said:

> The people in my boss's district [the politician he worked for] would be distressed if the police went in there with a lot of force and tried to stomp out the gangs. There are just too many people who would view this as police harassment, so my boss has to keep an eye on this so that his constituents aren't ready to complain to him that he's not doing anything to protect them from police harassment.[5]

Another example involved a politician in Boston, who said:

I support the police and I commend the effort they are doing to keep order for my constituents. However, I try to keep an eye on their efforts in order to act as a check in case they try to go too far in using force in the community. My constituents don't want the police to be using too much force in their community unless it is absolutely necessary. Most times it would not be completely necessary because the kids in our neighborhood are not that bad to have the police come in there and use a lot of force. If that happened, the residents would justifiably think the police had gone too far and were harassing them rather than helping.

The major difference between the three cities was that the majority of politicians on the city council in Los Angeles were from middle-class areas and their political support was from these areas as well. Because they were not dependent on the support of lower-class nonwhite areas, where most of the gangs operate, they were freer to support the use of intense police power in those areas. New York and Boston, by contrast, had more politicians who were dependent on the residents of poor working-class neighborhoods for their support, so they were more sensitive to community backlash caused by the residents' perception of excesses in police action. As a result, there was less consensus in New York and Boston and more consensus in Los Angeles in support of the police's consistent use of force to combat gangs.

The nature of the police chief's position in each of the cities also affects the approach of the police. In Los Angeles, the office of police chief is a political position that differs qualitatively from the same position in New York and Boston. Many of the people who become police chief view the position as a stepping-stone to other political offices, such as those of mayor or governor. The result is that rather than being part of the mayor's administration and executing the mayor's policy on public safety, the police chief tends to be politically autonomous and is, indeed, often in opposition to the mayor. A more independent policy is therefore often pursued. The massive use of force that has often occurred in Los Angeles, as compared to New York and Boston, has been influenced by the fact that the police chief has fewer political constraints than the police chiefs in the other two cities. In addition, if the police chief has political ambitions that involve gaining support from areas other than Los Angeles, the opportunity to appear tough on crime—without the pressure of having people complain of being abused by the police—presents potential advantages.

Although the post is also a political one in New York and Boston, the police chief there has a more direct link to the mayor. In New York and Boston the police chief is more like a cabinet member in the president's administration—that is, the police chief attempts to execute policy laid down by the mayor's office and is likely to be reluctant to establish and implement policies that might create political problems for the mayor, because if the mayor has political problems arising from police action, the chief of police will also have employment problems.

This distinction has not gone unnoticed by the cities' gangs, which have in each case attempted to develop the most effective strategies for action given the local situation. Take the comments of Blacktop, a twenty-year-old leader of a New York gang, addressing a meeting:

> Look, if we goes down to peddle our wares in [section of the city], we can make some money and not have the police on us. Check it out, remember two weeks ago when that police guy shot that young dude he thought was dealing crack? Well, now, this here area is perfect to do business, and I say we do it, 'cause the police won't chance making another mistake or the mayor will be gettin' some heavy heat, man. And you know, like everybody knows, if the mayor is gettin' heat, the police chief is catching some intense shit, man! And that dude [police chief] be letting those grunts [police patrolling the areas] know that they better relax for awhile.

Stinger was a nineteen-year-old member of a Los Angeles gang, also talking at a gang meeting:

> I tell you we got to cool it for awhile, a few weeks at least, because you know the other day there was that drive-by [drive-by killing] and the peacock [police chief] he's going to send his boys to be mean . . . you know the peacock's going to tell his people to get down, 'cause he wants to be some hot shit like governor or something like that. Man, he does that all the time, you know that, so we need to lay low for awhile until he blows his wad for the public.

The second factor affecting police-gang relations has to do with the relationship of the police to the low-income community in which gang members live. As discussed in chapter 6, the community plays an important part in determining what the character of police-gang relations will be. If the community wants help and perceives that the police are, in fact, being sincere in their efforts to curb crime, then there is a greater degree of community cooperation with the police. When there has been community cooperation, the police have interpreted this as a signal from the community that it will support the police in doing everything possible to reduce the amount of crime in the area. This is followed by a period in which the police not only make a maximum effort to curb illegal gang activity, but also act in a particularly aggressive fashion toward suspected gang members who have committed a crime as well. As R.G., a policeman who had been in the LAPD for eleven years, said:

> When the community cooperates and tells you who has been doing things, why they have been doing them, and how long they been doing them, you jump at the chance to get the sons-of-bitches. The community don't help that much, so you got to take what you can get while you can get it! Because the community may change its mind, so you got to act quickly and decisively or else you'll lose the opportunity. That's why when we know the community is behind us, we're going to be aggressive, break their asses and put their butts in jail.

C.M. had been a police officer in the NYPD for fourteen years:

> When we get the community support, we go with it. It is so frustrating because there are some times when gang members commit a crime in the neighborhood, then we come by, but nobody is willing to help. They say they know nothing. Sometimes I don't feel like doing my job, because I know that the community is not going to cooperate in helping us get any of those who have broken the law. I say to myself, if they don't want to help me, then they can kiss my ass—I am not looking for the bastards who have been terrorizing the community, let the community live with them! But if the community is willing to help, well then me and the other members of the force give a 100 percent effort.

However, when communities did not cooperate with the police, three things tended to occur. First, the police were more cautious in their use of indiscriminate force, for fear that the community would produce a political reaction detrimental to the employment status of those involved. Second, the police tended to be enormously frustrated and resentful toward the community. Seeking to make their jobs easier and/or being spiteful toward the community produced a less aggressive police response. W.R., who had been a member of the Boston police department for fifteen years, commented:

There are times when I have so much resentment toward the community. I mean this here gang has been operating in their area, but they won't cooperate. When this happens I just feel like telling them that if they don't want to cooperate, then let the gangs act like animals in their area. But I also let them know that no matter how they're acting in their own community, the gangs won't be allowed to operate outside their community.

Finally, sometimes the built-up frustrations and resentments of police officers over the community's resistance to helping them solve crimes caused the police to engage in a violent response toward gang members that was inappropriate for that particular incident. The comments of J.F. and T.O. are good examples. J.F. was a thirty-eight-year-old member of the NYPD:

Yeah, there was this one time when I really whipped this gang kid with a nightstick. I don't think that I really had to use as much force as I did, but quite honestly, it had been so frustrating trying to find him. He had been the gang's hold-up architect and had been responsible for a number of older women having been hurt as a result of being robbed. Well, my partner and I kept going to the community and asking questions, but nobody would give us any information. This went on and on as old ladies were being beaten. It was so frustrating dealing with the community, they knew nothing even though you knew that they knew. Well, when we got this guy, every bit of frustration came out.

T.O. was a forty-year-old member of the LAPD:

I have a lot of resentment toward the communities that I work. The gangs are like animals and nobody in the community knows anything. Something happens right in broad daylight and nobody seen anything. . . . So we go and pick up a number of gang members for questioning. Then I go and ask questions in the community and still nobody knows anything. It's a weird feeling when you ask questions in these areas, there is a look on the residents' faces that is pure contempt toward us. I haven't seen anything like it; well, not since Vietnam anyway. The fact is that most of the gang members are a bunch of creeps and you got to treat them like that. It's the only thing they understand.

The use of force because of frustration and resentment generally further alienated residents from the police, in turn producing even more hostility and uncooperativeness. Probably the most significant result of the community's unwillingness to assist is that it forces the police to deal more directly with the gangs themselves.

Police-Gang Relations

All things being equal, the police generally prefer the military to the so-cial-worker approach. It is not simply that most police officers think that gang members are the lowest form of vermin on earth (although there are a large number of officers who do think this way); it is rather that their training tends to be military. They are simply not trained as social workers. Most of the police officers I talked to would have preferred an unrestricted military policy toward the gangs, including the necessary financial, material, and logistical support, as well as the moral support of their superiors and the community. Yet the political leaders of the city, their superiors in the police force, and the society itself could not (be-cause of self-interest) provide this. This left the police officers in the field to deal with an often nebulous and changing strategy. Faced with not getting the support they felt they needed successfully to combat the "gang problem," the police officers in each of the three cities generally pursued a strategy of accommodation and regulation. This strategy basically as-sumed a "balance of power" perspective, a strategy that many officers believed could act as a deterrent and thereby regulate the situation.

In conjunction with the fact that police officers often feel that they are not given the necessary support to successfully complete their job, there are three other factors that influence officers in the field to adopt an accommodation-regulation strategy. The first has to do with the officer's concern for his and his partner's safety. Police officers believe that unless everyone else is going to make an all-out effort, there is no reason to put oneself or one's partner in unnecessary danger either. This has especially become the case now that more gang members have access to very so-phisticated weaponry. Take the statement of P.K., a twenty-seven-year-old police officer in New York:

> If we got the support that was needed to wipe out the gangs that would be one thing, but that will never happen. There are just too many people who are protecting their interests. So, hey, there is no way that I am going to go gung-ho and put myself and my partner at risk of getting killed unnecessarily. That would be really stupid!

The best thing to do under the circumstances is to try and moderate some of what they're [the gangs are] doing.

This belief varies a good deal among police forces. It is probably more prevalent in Boston and New York than in Los Angeles, but it is present there as well. This does not mean that the police do not do their job, because they do. However, they also attempt to establish some relationship between the gangs and themselves, regulating what is appropriate behavior. When behavior by either of the two falls within the agreed-upon definition of appropriate behavior, then relations between the two remain friendly, albeit uneasy. However, if one of the parties violates the accepted understanding of appropriate behavior, there is tension, uncooperativeness, and sometimes violence. Two examples illustrate this point. The first involves a gang from New York, where the police had beaten up one of the gang's members. The comments of Staple, a twenty-three-year-old vice president of the gang, during a general meeting highlight the use of social agreements among gangs and the police concerning appropriate behavior:

> Yeah, we all know that Dutch got fucked-up by those police nightsticks, but look, Dutch messed up with the police, man. He was out there trying to do a hit on that store, and when they caught up with him, he turned and fired that shot at them. . . . So, hey, what can we say to the police about the incident? The dude knew he shouldn't be shooting like that. He fucked up and got fucked-up! That's it!

The second example involved gangs and police in all three cities. There were times when gangs decided that specific police officers were too aggressive when apprehending suspects who were gang members. They sent messages to the police officers through one of their intermediaries (a community person who was friendly with both) to stop behaving that way. When the warning was not heeded, then a number of actions were taken against the police, including destruction of police property (usually police cars); refusing to help the police with information on other criminals; and physical intimidation by shooting at them.[6]

The second reason why the police adopt an accommodation-oriented relationship with many of the gangs is that the gangs can make their jobs easier. For example, crime committed by gangs is only part of the total crime committed in cities. Since the police effort to solve a whole range of crimes depends heavily on information, the gang represents an important resource. Gangs are perfect sources of information because so much of their activity involves street life. For example, members are physically on the streets, where they can see the things that go on, and talk to so many people that they are a reservoir of intelligence on crime. Many police officers nurture a close working relationship with gangs in order to have access to their intelligence. The nature of the relationship is usually the relaxation of surveillance and apprehension of gang members for low-level crimes.[7]

The third reason why police are accommodating toward gangs has to do with police corruption. Corruption does not involve a great number of police, but even a few can have an impact on enforcement behavior. In such cases, the police are usually involved in illegal activities with the gangs, or at least know that the gangs have information about their activities. In either case, the police are prepared to moderate their enforcement practices to protect themselves and their interests. These relaxed enforcement practices have the result of regulating gangs rather than seeking to wipe them out.

In sum, although the police's public policy is one of destroying gangs, their operational policy is one of accommodation and regulation. This is because gangs can be a strategic asset for gaining additional resources for the police department, as well as for providing officers with information on other criminal cases considered much more important to society than those associated with the gangs. In addition to these reasons, police officers operating on the beat are often put in a position similar to soldiers in a guerrilla war. They are asked to contain the identified enemy, but are given conflicting messages concerning the commitment of the politicians and their superiors to such a policy. This encourages them to look out for their own safety and interests, to socially negotiate (through verbal and physical interaction) what Erving Goffman has called an "interaction ritual"—that is, a behavior pattern where both parties express, verbally and with body language, dislike, sometimes even contempt, for each other simply as a ritual, but where both also strategically accommodate each other.[8]

Para-Police and Gang Control

In Los Angeles and one other city, local officials have experimented with a somewhat unusual crime-intervention program that uses non-police personnel to monitor gang activity.[9] Such monitoring has traditionally been carried out by the intelligence units of police departments, but with the Crisis Intervention Units, men and women from the community (many of whom have themselves been in gangs, or have had some association with them) have been trained both to monitor and to help control gang violence.

At the most general level, there are a number of Crisis Intervention Units, each composed of two unarmed people in a car. These units patrol to see which gangs are fighting or planning to fight each other; they then attempt to negotiate a truce between the warring groups. The units also respond to calls from the community informing them that a fight is about to begin; in response, a Crisis Intervention Unit is dispatched to the scene to try to arbitrate peacefully before the police are called in to intervene with force. Policymakers assume that if the intervention team can get to the scene quickly enough, it can prevent the deaths that would likely occur as a result of fighting between the gangs and the police.

When this plan was first proposed in Los Angeles, it was vigorously opposed by the police department for two reasons. First, the police believed that the intervention teams would get in the way of police operations. They contended that in addition to having to worry about the safety of their own officers and of innocent people in the vicinity of a gang fight, they would now have to worry about two more people in the middle of the violence. The second reason was more fundamental: the police were concerned that such units would undermine the traditional authority of the police department by competing with it.[10] Despite police opposition to the plan, the Gang-Crisis Intervention Program was passed by the Los Angeles City Council and monies were allocated for its operation.

Since the Crisis Intervention Units have become operational, the police have reached a rapprochement with them. They no longer consider them to be competitors or a burden. In fact, they are more willing to pay them guarded compliments, because they have found them useful in a number of ways. First, for the most part, the units have not interfered with police operations. Second, they have been able to intervene and defuse some potentially violent confrontations between gangs. Third, they have provided information concerning gangs that has been useful to the police. Finally, they have provided a buffer between the police and the community that has reduced some conflict between the two. For example, the police can now use the fact that the intervention team was unable to stabilize a particular situation as a justification for their actions.[11] Since most members of the unit were from the community (or similar types of communities), the unit did have an impact.

On the other side, the gangs have cooperated with the Crisis Intervention Units. It is not that they completely trust the people in the units, because it is clear to them what side the people in the units are on. However, the gangs find them useful in selective situations—namely, when a gang (or gangs) does not want to fight out of a concern that they may lose. In such situations, the gang that feels vulnerable has the option of using the Crisis Intervention Unit to defuse the situation. This option has been used by a number of gangs in order to protect members and maintain organizational integrity. The comments of Rocky and Tito are representative of gang opinion concerning the Crisis Intervention Units. Rocky was a sixteen-year-old member of a Los Angeles gang:

> We don't really trust these people [in the Crisis Intervention Units]. I mean, we know what side they're really on. They're on the side of the police and the people who are trying to get rid of gangs. They got to be or they won't be in business. But we use them sometimes, because it has been a help to us. One time we [his gang] was going to be in a fight, but we were shot up pretty bad so we used them to call off the fight. We needed them then, or we would have been done as a gang, but now we are strong again and so we won't be calling on them.

Tito was an eighteen-year-old member of a Los Angeles gang:

> Yes, they [the Crisis Intervention Unit] have helped my homies [gang members] when there was going to be a lot of shooting and killing. We used them this one time when the [gang's name] and [gang's name] had entered into an agreement to attack us. We would have been in big trouble, but they helped the situation get worked out. . . . Nobody is going to be close to them [the unit] because they're on the side of the police. I don't really resent them or anything because if they don't side with the police, they're out of work. I mean, if the police think they are helping us, they just go to the city council and take their [the unit's] money away. Then that's it for them.

Nearly all the gang members I talked to understood the political position of those who worked for the Crisis Intervention Units. Their interaction took on certain predictable and repetitive forms. The Crisis Intervention Unit would come by, talk, and be friendly to the gang members, and the gang members would talk and be friendly in return. Nonetheless, both understood that they were involved in a ritual of interactive pleasantries intended to facilitate their interests. Neither assumed that their interaction would radically alter the gang's activities. The comments of Nova, an eighteen-year-old member of a Los Angeles gang, explain:

> They [the Crisis Intervention Unit] come by and they talk and talk. It's really kind of weird. I mean we're both friendly, respectful and stuff, but when they talk to us about not fighting and killing, we just listen and shake out heads. You know, we just kind of go along. It's really strange, 'cause we don't plan to do things different and they know that, but we both just go through the motions. And what's a trip is, we both just keep doing it no matter if somebody got killed the day before or not.

D.K. was a member of one of the Crisis Intervention Units:

> Well, whenever I see the gang kids, I talk to them and they listen, and they talk a little and I listen. But I know that we're both just being polite to each other, not really anything much more. You see, I don't really believe that what I am doing will make gangs go away or stopping them from fighting and killing themselves. I just hope that I can keep a few kids from dying needlessly.[12]

In sum, the Crisis Intervention Units, which I have called para-police units, neither can nor try to eradicate gangs. Their position does not allow for anything so grand, because they are structurally in a vulnerable position and must walk a fine line between the police and the gang. In essence, their interaction with the gangs is more ritualistic than substantive. Ultimately, their impact on gangs is similar to that of the police; they control some of the gangs' behavior, but they do little to eliminate them.[13]

Criminal Justice System and Gangs: Procedural Rituals and Social Control

In order to explain the relationship between gangs and the criminal justice system, it is necessary to give some idea of the social geography in which they interact. The police are not the only organization with responsibility for maintaining public order. After the police have performed their duties, the responsibility switches to the court system. It is the courts that must decide on the proper action toward those who are accused of violating one of society's codes. This decision is thought, in principle, simply to be a matter of weighing the evidence in each case, but when it comes to gangs, it is a much more complicated sociological matter. Gangs present the criminal justice system with a difficult problem. For the most part, society has felt threatened by gangs, and this is the case today, especially when serious crime is associated with their activities. But the criminal justice system is constructed to deal with individuals rather than with organizations. When organizations commit crimes and society seeks a policy to manage the problem effectively, the criminal justice system thus finds itself in an awkward position. Its task is to administer justice, and there is the presumption that in so doing it is also maintaining public order. Yet, because of the way it is set up, it has no more control over maintaining public order than education does in producing socioeconomic mobility. That is to say, it has some influence, but does not have the power to produce public order. Since society expects the courts to administer justice and to rid it of public nuisances and/or threats such as gangs, the people who operate the court system, particularly judges and prosecuting attorneys, generally feel themselves to be in a quagmire. The combination of judicial restraint on the officers of the court and gang members' own awareness of these constraints has thus led both parties to assume behavior patterns that are centered more around procedural rituals than social control.[14] Ultimately, these behavior patterns produce social control through the regulation of gangs rather than by eliminating them.

Gangs have presented those who operate within the legal profession with a number of challenges. Throughout the more than ten years of this research, as crime associated with gangs increased, the public increased its demand that more be done to stop it. In addition, as court officials (parole officers, prosecuting attorneys, and judges) became more aware of the increasing amount of crime associated with gang involvement, they also became more sensitive to citizen complaints that the legal system was not doing enough to arrest the problem. Yet the gang presented the legal system with difficulties that other juvenile crimes did not. The comments of one court official are indicative of the concerns associated with gangs:

> There is absolutely no question that something has to be done
> about gang crime. We in the courts will have to consider more
> harsh penalties for those individuals convicted of gang-organized

crime. However, you have to understand that it will be difficult to completely solve the gang-related crime problem in the courts because there are a number of constraints that make the solution to this problem impossible in the present legal system.

The courts faced three primary problems in their effort to suppress or restrict the criminal activity associated with gangs. The first has to do with the structure of the problem. Most law enforcement officials, as well as those involved in the criminal justice system, continue to assess the crime problem as one involving a group (i.e., the gang); but the courts are structured to handle individuals, not groups. Therefore, no matter how harsh the court's penalty was on an individual gang member, it had little impact on his gang. In fact, there was not one case among any of the thirty-seven gangs in this study where the incarceration of a particular gang member for a substantial amount of time produced a collapse of the gang's organization and a cessation of the gang's operations.[15] Even in those cases where a number of a particular gang's leadership were incarcerated, the gang was able to continue. As Jumper, an eighteen-year-old member of an Irish gang in New York, said:

> There ain't no way those fuckers in the courthouse can do anything to stop us, unless they're going to shoot us. They think by putting some of our leaders in the pen [the penitentiary] for a long time, that we will just be dried up and the gang will die. What a joke, they're just living in dreamland!

Crow, a sixteen-year-old member of a Central American gang in Los Angeles, put it this way:

> I gone to the court about three times now to see some of the brothers get tried. And each time I went, the judge said he was going to get tough with gangs because they were a social threat to society. Then he said that he was going to give the brothers a long sentence because they were leaders and he wanted to take the lifeblood out of the gang. I didn't even know what he meant when he said the "lifeblood," but after another brother explained it to me, I just laughed, 'cause there is no way that sending anybody to prison can kill the gang. . . . They may wish it would happen that way, but that's just a hope.

The second problem that the courts face in their efforts to control gang-related crime has to do with the mismatch between the structure of the criminal justice system and the social composition of gangs. Gangs contain both juveniles and adults, while the criminal justice system consists of two jurisdictional structures, one that deals with juvenile offenders and one that deals with adults. The problem is that the juvenile and adult courts have competing, and at times conflicting, approaches to crime prevention. The juvenile court is oriented toward rehabilitation, and its procedures have been established in order to protect individuals who society felt might be too young to fully understand the ramifications of the acts they were committing, and/or who were young enough to be rehabilitated into productive, law-abiding citizens. The approach to adult offenders, by contrast, is dominated by the desire for retribution. These differing approaches prevent the courts from developing a consistent and concerted policy that would have an impact on all members of the organization. Gangs are thus able to make extensive use of juveniles, knowing that they will, providing that it is the juveniles' first offense, receive probation or a relatively short amount of time in jail.[16]

In recent years, as the gangs have become more active and violent, the juvenile courts have also sought to be more retribution-oriented, and a number of states have modified certain laws to permit juveniles who have been arrested for repeated violent offenses to be tried in adult courts.[17] In addition, a number of states have provided the district attorney's office with the responsibility of deciding how each particular case should proceed. While these changes were enacted in order to establish a legal context for harsher penalties for those juvenile offenders, such as gang members, who repeatedly engage in serious crimes, at the same time the courts have been concerned with a number of legal questions that have tended to dilute the full effects of these modifications. Probably the most important concern of court officials has been the protection of the juvenile offender's civil rights. Hence, the rights of juveniles to a lawyer and bail have been added to ensure that the individual's rights have been protected. These new procedures were helpful to gangs, because using legal council to represent them has successfully protected some gang members from being incarcerated. Of the thirty-seven gangs in this study, eleven had hired a lawyer to represent their members, and eight more had access to a lawyer if they needed one; twelve used the public defender's office when they needed it; and six were totally unrepresented by lawyers. Take the comments of Doodle, a fifteen-year-old member of a gang in New York:

Look, I get busted for this charge of attacking this guy who owns a store. I call the president of the club [the gang] and he sends our lawyer. They got no evidence and he gets me released quick like. . . . This guy [the lawyer] is great, one time he represented me in court on a charge, and he got me off.

Despite the desire on the part of those who work in the courts to control gang crime, they are also concerned with avoiding any action that would undermine the authority of the legal system in general. Therefore they believe that the courts must treat the gang member, if she or he is a juvenile, as a juvenile and not simply as a "juvenile gang member" with a set of governing legal principles that are different from those applied to other juveniles. As one of the court officials said:

All we would need to do is set up some new legislation or procedures that would treat juvenile gang members different, just so we could rid ourselves of gangs. Can't you just see it? A juvenile is arrested, the cops think the person is in a gang and the courts think the person is a gangbanger too and they use these new procedures that, if they were in an adult court, would be a violation of the individual's rights. But they do it anyway because they want to break the gangs. Then they find out that the person wasn't in a gang. Can you imagine the implication of that when it was multiplied a hundred times or more across the city? It would begin to undermine the whole system. You see it would be easy to get gang members and try to incarcerate them the first time they commit an offense. But the fact of the matter is that if they are juveniles, they got to be treated like other juveniles, or the whole system can run into trouble.

Another court official comments:

What if we were to prosecute juvenile gang members different from other juveniles? We would be setting up a legal Pandora's box. Because if we did not protect the rights of juveniles in general, then juveniles who commit offenses in other areas, and who are not gang members, or even know what a gang is, will have their rights abused and the system will begin to erode away.

The courts, therefore, have found it difficult to coordinate a consistent set of legal principles that would apply to both juvenile and adult gang members, and this in turn has impeded efforts to curb gang activity.[18]

The third factor to have an impact on the courts' effectiveness in dealing with gangs has to do with the general feeling of impotence that many court officials have about their ability to solve the "gang problem." For example, most of the officials that I talked to believed that poverty was the main cause of the rise in gang activity.[19] They also believed that the problem really involved the labor market, the family, and the schools—institutions over which the courts had little or no control. Take the comments of J.O., a court official in Los Angeles:

> The problem of gangs in this city has to do with jobs—the fact that there are not enough jobs to go around for everybody. After all, until we can provide employment for these kids, they will join gangs. . . . I suppose that is the most frustrating thing for me. Society wants the criminal justice system to do something about the gangs. I suppose that means me as an official of that system, but the fact of the matter is, the criminal justice system, and me as a person in it, do not have the power to stop gangs because we do not have the power to control poverty.

V.R. was a court official in New York:

> Well, I can tell you I get awfully frustrated when I deal with gangs. The people in the community want the courts to do something to eradicate the gangs in this city, but by the time they get to the court, it is usually too late to rehabilitate them. The real causes of the problem are the broken families, poor schooling, and poverty they come from. And all of these are outside the control of the legal system. It can be frustrating and demoralizing when you know that there is little that you can do to resolve the gang problem.

As a result of these feelings of powerlessness about eliminating or reducing gang activity, court officials tend to focus their attention on procedures. The comments of D.K., a court official in New York, are instructive:

> A number of us involved in this business [the courts] often talk about how frustrating it is to deal with the gangs. The general public wants us to do something, but a number of us realize that there is not much we can do to affect how gangs behave. We can lock them up, and there are a lot of gang members that do need to be locked up, but that really won't stop it. Creating jobs is the answer, but we don't have the jurisdiction over that. It gets so

frustrating that the best that you can do for these kids, and many of them are just kids, is to make sure that there is some degree of consistency in legal procedure. In other words, just see to it that they get a fair trial.

Another reason that court officials are concerned with procedure is that many worry that creating a special set of practices for gangs may potentially violate the individual rights not only of the guilty but also of the innocent, since such laws would be highly biased against persons (especially nonwhite males) in low-income areas.[20] To many of these officials, this situation is potentially counterproductive, because gangs are so integrated into their communities that a consistent violation of their rights will more than likely create an outcry from the greater low-income community. Thus, such a situation could create more tension and social unrest than their efforts to control the gangs would alleviate. Take the comments of K.E., an officer of the court in New York:

> The thing that we must protect against is abusing people's rights in order to protect them. We are always tempted to do that with gangs because they seem to be so difficult to get rid of. But I can tell you, if you start to abuse their rights, you usually abuse other people's rights, people who are innocent. And when you start doing that, then you got yourself in a big fix. Then people start to say the whole system is rotten and they start protesting. You get civil unrest when all you were trying to do was create public order. So like with everything, we got to realize that the gang problem won't be solved by us [people in the courts] and see to it that we follow the procedures of the law and not violate anybody's rights. Basically we got to calculate what is best for the most people.

Ultimately, the courts' behavior does little to impede the existence of gangs, because officers of the court do not simply focus on gangs. Rather, they tend to be involved in weighing and acting on a broad range of competing interests (i.e., calculating the greatest good from a list of competing interests), which attenuates the courts' impact.

The Gang's Reaction to Court Action

Through both individual and collective group experience, gang members learn the structural strengths and weaknesses of the criminal justice system. Having this knowledge, they construct strategies to minimize the courts' impact on their ability to operate. To begin, they attempt to use the separation of the juvenile and adult court systems to their own advantage. First, they use juveniles more in their illegal business activities because juveniles generally receive probation for the first offense and less harsh sentences than if they were adults tried in adult courts. Second, they use the fact that juveniles usually do receive lesser sentences as a recruiting ploy to secure more members for their organization. The comments of Sky, a nineteen-year-old member of a New York gang, represent this tendency:

> You see when you're creative, you don't fight the law, you understand it and use it to help you. Like you [the researcher] know how we do things in this club [gang]. We use what the law [legal system] gives us. We use [the] legal system to help us do business and to get new members. Like when I'm talking to the young brothers [juveniles] about joining our club [gang], I tell them about the advantage they have and how they can use it to their advantage. I tell them that if they want to join us, they can make some big spending money. They can work some of the streets for the older brothers and get paid good money. I tell them that. They can work some of the streets and make some big money and not worry about getting put in jail. I tell them that too. I tell them, hey, the courts is on your side. You're too young to get jail on your first bust, and even after that you so young you won't spend hardly no time in jail. Then I tell them [about] all the brothers who've been through it, and they be ready to come on board. You see, young brothers don't get in the older brothers' way, they help the whole club [gang].

Second, the gangs also realize that most people in the criminal justice system attempt to maximize a number of interests and, as a result, are maneuvered into emphasizing judicial procedures to such an extent that the behavior associated with these procedures takes on the character of ritual. The comments of Axe, a fifteen-year-old member of a gang in New York, are illustrative of this point:

> When you deal with people in the courts, you get to realize that they ain't just thinking about how they're going to convict you. No way, baby, they be thinking of all the ways that what they do might help or hurt everybody, including themselves. What I'm trying to say is, they're thinking about all kinds of shit, and so then they just go through their procedures and shit. You see, if

they go through the motions with that procedure shit, they think they can convict a few people. But most of all, since they know that they can't really stop all the gangs, following procedures is a good way to cover their asses!

This realization has also encouraged the gangs to cooperate in these procedural rituals in an attempt to minimize any negative effects on their organizations. The comments of Gabby and Buck are good illustrations of this tactic. Gabby was a sixteen-year-old member of an Irish gang in New York:

Hell, when you're in court they have it set up so certain things happen and so you know when something is supposed to happen. Then there are these times when they got it set up so that you say what they want you to say. I mean, well, I don't mean that they want you to confess, actually they want you to say you didn't do it or you did it, but there was these reasons. . . . We've [the members of his gang] talked a lot about how they set things up to get certain things. So even when one of the guys did do something [commit a crime], we give them what they want to hear, like I didn't do it or I did it, but I was forced to do it. Things like that. And if you do it that way, it works out better for us.

Buck, a sixteen-year-old member of a Los Angeles gang, said:

Sure, you go to court, and really they'd rather hear you say, "I didn't do it" or "I didn't mean to do it" or "Somebody made me do it" 'cause it's easier for them to handle that than to hear you say, "Yeah, I did it, and fuck you!" 'Cause if they hear that shit, then they get nervous that they be dealing with some psychopath or something. And then if they think that, they'd start singling the gang out, start putting some heavy shit down on us. But if you go through the motions with them, they don't fuck with you as much. . . . Man, us dealing with the people in the courts is like a dance contest. If you and your partner is in step, you may get your toes stepped on, but you be still in it; but if one of you really goes out of step, you both lose the contest, man. That's the way they be thinking too, so everybody adapts.

Gangs and Prisons

For the gang member and the gang, incarceration is a reality that must be managed on both a personal and an organizational level, and it is handled through a process of socialization. The first steps in this process are for the organization to establish a status hierarchy associated with incarceration. Those who go to prison are given high status, as are those who serve long terms, those who are active in the gang in prison, and those who have served a number of sentences and maintain their resolve to continue doing what they had been doing. The establishment of such status-achieving criteria helps individual gang members maintain a commitment to the group, which in turn provides the foundation for group cohesion.[21] Take the comments of Gernsey and Score. Gernsey was a twenty-one-year-old member of an Irish gang in New York:

> Before I went to the pen, I was just a regular in the gang. But while I was in, I stuck with my guys against a number of other gangs. Boy, we had some wars in there. When the prison authorities tried to screw with me, I stood my ground and they gave me more time. But after that, while I was still there and when I got out, all the gang members that I came around gave me respect and everywhere I went the guys looked up to me.

Score was a twenty-year-old member of a Los Angeles gang:

> I'll tell you the way it is. Those of us who have spent time locked up get the respect of everyone in the gang. We get more respect than those who haven't because we been to the wall and walked through it. You get my drift? So even though you get locked up for awhile, you know that if you stand for your homeboys in the pen, then you be given high respect in the pen, and when you get out your homeboys will be looking up to you too.

The second step in the process of socialization is for younger gang members to hear of the experiences of those who have been incarcerated. These stories help to prepare those who have not been to prison for what the experience will be like. The comments of Pat and Hood highlight the importance of these stories and are representative of the comments of others. Pat was a sixteen-year-old member of an Irish gang in Boston:

> There were a lot of times that I used to think what it would be like to get locked up in prison. It kind of scared me, but then there would be gang meetings and some of the guys who had been locked up would tell us what it was like. After listening to a whole lot of stories, I wasn't afraid anymore. I am still not. I know that I'll probably get locked up sometime, but I ain't afraid of it anymore.

Hood was a twenty-three-year-old member of a New York gang:

> Before I went to prison I had heard all the brothers talking about
> what it would be like. That helped, because when I got there, it
> wasn't new or anything. It was like they said, and that helped me
> a lot. So now I be telling the brothers my story, trying to help
> them know what it's like in case they get put there.

The third step in the process of socialization is the experiences that
many of the gang members will have in association with the juvenile
courts. Many will be detained, some will be put on probation, where they
will have to deal with being watched, while others may serve time in
juvenile facilities. Each of these experiences, combined with the procedures of the courts themselves, will act as steps in establishing coping
mechanisms for longer-term incarceration. Deadly, a nineteen-year-old
member of a Los Angeles gang, commented:

> I took their best shot and am still standing. They get scared of
> that, then they call you a "hard-core gang member," but I ain't
> any different than I was before I went into the pen when they
> would have called me somebody who was "reachable" and could
> be changed. The only thing that is different is that their best shot
> wasn't good enough to stop me. Except now they're all upset and
> so they put some mark [by calling him a hard-core gang member]
> on me to try to make it harder on me when I get out. . . . They
> want to do that so they get me back here and keep me for a long
> while . . . but you see, if I can keep them scared, then they can't
> try to pressure me to change.

What is important in this observation, and was true for all the gangs, is
that gang members have a sophisticated view of the tactics used against
them for purposes of social control. For example, in the remarks quoted
above, Deadly is aware that, having been unsuccessful at rehabilitating
him, the authorities have decided to label him a "hard-core gang member," which carries with it the stigma of a "program-resistant youth"
who should be locked up in order to protect the public. Yet he is also
aware that his resolve frightens them and that, if he plays his cards correctly, he can neutralize their efforts to change him by keeping them on
the defensive.[22]

According to gang members who have served time in prison, the authorities there often attempt to rehabilitate individuals in both a direct
and an indirect manner. Direct rehabilitation is where the individual is

conscious of his crime, is repentant for his acts, has been retrained for a job, and is eager to become a productive, law-abiding citizen. Indirect rehabilitation is where prison officials get gang members to cease and desist from their past activities in the gang through deterrence—that is, through fear of being or remaining in confinement. Yet despite these efforts, the vast majority of gang members have resisted such efforts. There are several reasons for the gang members' resistance. First, gang members believe that the efforts of the authorities to rehabilitate them—to accept the premise that they were wrong in what they did and that they need to learn a skill and become productive members of the society—are acts of indoctrination that must be resisted. They see rehabilitation as identical to government brainwashing or thought reform.[23] The comments of Evan and Boat are interesting on this point. Evan was a seventeen-year-old member of an Irish gang in Boston:

> Look, they want you to think that what you did is wrong. A lot of times they ask you if you're sorry for what you did and they keep asking you. It's just brainwashing that's all. Hell, they keep hollering about the Moonies [the followers of Reverend Moon and his Unification Church], but they're doing the same thing. . . . I wouldn't believe what they wanted me to, no way! They would have to do some heavy stuff to get me to believe that what I did was any different than what they do.

Boat was a fifteen-year-old member of a Chicano gang in Los Angeles:

> Hey, when those dudes locked me up, they tried to tell me that what I was doing was wrong and that I should clean up my act and make something out of myself. I mean they would be putting some heavy stuff out there to check out. I mean there was some pressure, like threatening to keep you there and stuff. Shit, I just acted like they were toads, and they knew that I wasn't digging their shit, but they kept going with it. That'll be the day I believe their shit, no matter how much they try to brainwash me.

Secondly, the fact that gang members are not isolated from other gang members is a critical factor in resisting the pressures that exist within prisons. It is now a prison reality that the gangs that exist outside of prison have simply reproduced themselves inside the institution. This has contributed to the strengthening of individual resolve, the maintenance of group discipline, and the continuity of the organization.[24] The comments of Lamp and Jersey are representative of the dominant pattern of responses from ex-inmates concerning this issue. Lamp was a twenty-six-year-old member of a New York gang who had served time for extortion:

> When you're in prison they try to get you to change the way you think. They try that because they want to get you to stop doing what got you in there in the first place. But it don't have no effect. You see, we got brothers from our club that's in here, so anything they say we can pass the word, that it's just a bunch of garbage and don't believe them. . . . Really, it's a losing fight for the law because even when they send us to prison, our club is able to stay together in there and we get stronger because of it.

Jersey is a twenty-four-year-old member of a Los Angeles gang:

> When you're in *la pinta* [the penitentiary], you got your homeboys in there too. You hook up with them as soon as you get there. So, there's nothing to worry about because it's the same as when you're out in your barrio.

Thus, despite the fact that prison officials attempt to punish inmates for being in gang-related activities, the gangs have penetrated prison life to the extent that they have a significant impact in organizing life in the prison.[25] Take the comments of Coaster, a twenty-five-year-old member of a New York gang:

> When you be in prison, the first thing you find out is your brothers in the club [the gang] got it all set up for you. They can set you up with certain jobs and then they can get you the goods you want. You name it, they can get it. . . . They got it organized real well.

In sum, prison officials have wanted rehabilitation to occur in the form of retraining, but having achieved little success, they have emphasized retribution. For gang members, this has meant that prison life has become a ritual revolving around procedural routines.[26] Take the comments of Goofy and Temp. Goofy was a twenty-six-year-old member of a New York gang who had served time in prison:

> The one thing that hits you as soon as you get in the pen [prison] is all the rules. They got rules and rules and rules. I mean they gots some crazy rules. What's really crazy is that they just want you to follow the rules, even if the rules ain't doing what they suppose to. . . . The prison officials know that it ain't doing any good, but [like] an ostrich who is scared they put their head below ground

and tell you to follow the rules. So all of us just follow the rules, but we and them just be going through the motions.

Temp was a twenty-four-year-old member of a Los Angeles gang who had served time in prison:

> Prison is like [a] huge pile of rules. All they want you to do is just follow the rules. Even though a lot of the rules are crazy and they make things worse, they make you follow them. This is even when they know the rules are crazy, they make you follow them. Man, it really can get to you sometimes, but then everybody just says, "Fuck it!" If they want us to do this, we just do it for them.

Thus, both the prison officials and the gang members adhere to the formal rules by going through the motions. Ultimately, both the goals of rehabilitation and retribution have given way to the rituals associated with the routines of everyday prison life. In this scenario, prison officials and gang members play out the ritual with no expectations other than the fact that each put in their time.

Parole Officer Syndrome

Having served some period of detention for a criminal act, the convicted gang member comes into contact with the parole officer.[27] The association between the parole officer and the gang member completes the series of relationships within the formal cycle of the criminal justice system. For both the officer and the gang member, the point of interaction is undertaken with two distinct sets of interests in mind, and both of their attempts to realize their interests are played out as ritual.

For the parole officer, interests are divided between two diametrically opposed roles. The state asks parole officers to assume the role of a social worker on the one hand and a surveillance agent on the other. Some parole officers attempt to assume both roles, but ultimately all must choose one or the other.

The role most often assumed by the parole officers in this study was that of the surveillance agent. Nonetheless, not all of them philosophically subscribed to that role or behaved in a surveillance manner. A small number did attempt to assume the social-worker role. These officers would constantly be on the road visiting their clients at their hangouts, counseling them, and trying to find them employment. They assumed a posture of being concerned about the client's future, just as family members would be concerned about the future of one of their own. These parole officers developed close relationships with the individuals assigned to their case loads. They attempted to establish a relationship based on cooperation and respect. Yet despite the effort of these officers, most of them eventually abandoned the role of social worker. The vast majority remained philosophically committed to that role; behaviorally, however, they became more oriented toward the role of surveillance agent.

This occurred for three reasons. First, there are time constraints. Given the case load of many of these parole officers, they have very little time to spend with any one individual. Generally, they will have only about forty-five minutes a month with an individual. This makes it extremely difficult to develop a close relationship in which the parole officer can counsel the parolee. In this situation, the officer can only ask questions about how the individual is doing. This comes across to the parolee as merely a check on his behavior and not an act of genuine concern. In fact, there may be honest concern, but time constraints never allow it fully to emerge. The comment of L.E. highlights this points:

> The problem is that I just don't have the time to adequately counsel the people on my case load. I do care about most of them, but there is not really a good way to communicate that. I tell them, but they really don't believe me. Hell, I'd have a hard time believing me too, given the amount of time I spend with them. All I can do is just check on what they've been doing.

Secondly, the constant noncompliance of the parolee influences many officers to be more surveillance-oriented. There are two reasons for this. The first is that many of the officers who do try to act as social workers to gang members find it very frustrating to have put in so much time only to have the parolee lie and/or break one of the conditions of parole. This frustration is often converted by the parole officer into feelings of being betrayed by the parolee, and then into feelings of resentment. The feelings of resentment are usually followed by acts designed for retribution, such as seeing to it (through surveillance) that the parolee follows the terms of parole to the letter, and revoking the parole when there has been a violation. The comments of R.D. are a good example of these feelings of resentment and revenge:

> Shit, I worked with this guy and worked with this guy. I even worked with him on my day off. I can't tell you how much I worked with him. I thought he was turned around, and then I get

this call that he was missing work and making trouble when he was there, and then he got into this big fight and hurt one of the foremen. I asked him about it, but he had stupid excuses, they all have excuses. It was so pathetic, it just made me so mad! I couldn't believe he would do this to me. I said to myself, if he wants to do that shit to me, fuck him! Then, I decided to give him no slack. The next violation he made, I revoke his parole and back in he went. What a waste of my time that was.

Thirdly, there are pressures from other criminal justice agencies to have the parole officer act more like a surveillance agent than a social worker. These pressures usually come from the police and the courts. The police believe parolees who violate the conditions of parole should be put back in prison. Policemen believe this makes their job easier, as the comments of S.O., a police officer in the Los Angeles area, indicate:

I believe that if a convict violates his parole in any way, they should lock them back up. Most officers believe the same thing and we tell people in parole all the time. . . . You see, we all feel that if somebody violates parole and gets locked back up, it makes our job one person easier.[28]

The wishes of the police do have an effect on parole officers. The comments of P.L., a parole officer in Los Angeles, are indicative:

I certainly know what most of the police think. They want you to be hard on them. If they do anything wrong, revoke their parole. . . . I have lots of friends in the police force. Guys I can go drinking with. So I do feel a little pressure to keep my eye on the gang kids in my case load. I sympathize with them [the police], I sure wouldn't want to see anyone of them if one of my guys shot one of them. That would be really tough.

The court—essentially the judge and the prosecuting attorney's office— wants to avoid the pressures associated with a parolee committing a violent crime while out on parole. To avoid both personal stress and pressures from the general public, the officers of the court (judges and district attorneys) want the parole officer to keep a careful watch on the individuals they believe are most likely to commit additional crimes. Members of gangs are prime candidates for special surveillance. The comments of I.R. and W.P. are representative of the feelings of many parole officers. I.R. was a parole officer in Los Angeles:

Yes, well there are a lot of times when I have felt pressure from a number of people in the courts to keep an eye on certain individuals, usually gang kids. More than anything they are worried about one of the parolees going out and committing some horrendous crime while they are out. You see a lot of them would feel awful guilty about it even though they really didn't have anything to do with it. But then you got the public to deal with too. You see, if something happens, the public is looking for anybody and everybody to blame; and everyone is trying to stay away from that kind of pressure. . . . So, yes, with a lot of these guys [gang members], I don't really work with them to rehabilitate them, I just keep an eye on what they're doing.

W.P. is a parole officer in New York:

Sure I like to work with the kids who are out on parole. You know, try to get them turned around. But a lot of times there are pressures to forsake all that stuff and just be a spy. Usually the pressures come from somebody in the courts to keep a close eye on so and so to see if he has violated his parole. You see most times they are afraid that if the parolee does commit a crime, all hell will break loose against them and their jobs will be in jeopardy, so they want to pass down a little of that concern to us. . . . Most of the people they are worried about were in gangs. You see gangs scare them because the public says, "You should have known they would do something like that, they were in gangs before." So us P.O.'s get the message, the hell with trying to save them [gang members], just keep the strings tight on them!

On special occasions, law enforcement authorities have coordinated their efforts to keep gang members off the streets. Before the 1984 Olympics, for example, it was decided that various techniques ought to be used to disrupt the capacity of the gangs of Los Angeles to interfere with the Olympics. One technique was to coordinate the actions of the police and the parole officers. Their coordinated effort included the police picking up gang members who were merely congregating in public areas (e.g., parks or street corners), seeing if any were on parole, and then getting the parole officers to revoke their parole and put them back in prison/ detention. This action required the sharing of information and the co-operation of the parole officers to revoke parole on some very technical matters. Of course, it also raised a number of constitutional rights issues, which most of the authorities attempted to camouflage within the rhetoric of procedures. This approach was tolerated by most of those concerned (authorities of the criminal justice system, and members of both the local and larger community) because it was understood that it would only be temporary until the Olympic games had finished. Such actions reinforced the idea that law enforcement officials should try to calculate the whole range of interests associated with the larger community and not simply those related to the immediate case. Over time, this has the tendency to reinforce the importance of procedure over goals.

The Gang's Response to the Condition of Parole

The rules associated with parole are quite strict, yet seem to have a limited effect on gang members' behavior. Most of the gang members I observed who had been out on parole remained involved in illegal acts.[29] A number of considerations influence the paroled gang member to remain involved with crime. The first is that many are committed to making their "fortune" through illegal means. These individuals believe that time is money, so they continue their efforts to accumulate capital. In addition, most of them think they can outsmart the authorities by disguising their activities through the operations of the gang.[30] They hold this belief even though their present condition (parole) is evidence to the contrary. One finds among all the gangs a belief structure similar to that found among most athletes when they lose a crucial game in a championship series. They simply believe, no matter what the odds are, that they can win the next game and win the whole championship. There is nothing that anyone can say to them to convince them that the odds are against them. They simply do not believe in probability, only in themselves—another indication of the strength of the defiant individualist character. The major difference between gang members who are out on parole and athletes is that the negative repercussions are greater for the gang members.[31] Take the comments of Cutty, a twenty-year-old Irish gang member in New York:

> I plan to do some business while I am out on parole. Hey, I got to do some business. If I don't, I lose all this time and the less chance I have of making it rich. . . . I ain't afraid of them finding out about me. They ain't good enough to get me, if I take care of my business. . . . Yeah, well when I got caught and sent up, they were just lucky that's all!

Fundy is a twenty-one-year-old member of a gang in Los Angeles:

> I can do what I want when I am out. The only thing I got to do is
> be more careful. I plan to try to help myself and my homes [home-
> boys] to get some big money. If we can do that, we're in the pink
> Cadillac riding low and slow. . . . No, I don't worry about the
> cops. If me and my homes do things the way we know we can,
> then the cops can't touch us, they just like the song says—purple
> haze. . . . Sure, I been busted twice, but each of those times the
> cops just fell into it. I mean they were really just lucky as shit. I
> ain't never worried, because it ain't like the cops did anything
> right, it's that me or some of the homes fucked it up. It won't be
> like that this time.

The second reason why many of the gang members indulge in illegal
behavior while still on parole is that they do not believe that the parole
officer can help them find good jobs or is sincere in trying. In essence,
they do not trust a parole officer who tries to act like a social worker.
They have two major complaints. First, they believe that the parole officer can only find them jobs that would keep them in the same socioeconomic position forever. Second, they realize that although parole officers
say they want to help, all they do is watch what the gang members do.
This strengthens the belief that the parole officer is insincere and should
not be trusted. The comments of Squeeze and Wicket are representative
of these beliefs. Squeeze was a twenty-year-old member of a New York
gang:

> Man, I don't pay no attention to my P.O. The dude be talking
> about getting me a job here, and getting me a job there. But if you
> look at the jobs, they ain't nothing I want to do. They're the same
> jobs as my pop has and there ain't no way that I want to go
> through life doing that kind of shit. I don't want to live that way. I
> been living that way.

Wicket, a twenty-five-year-old member of a Boston gang, said:

> Shit, I don't trust any P.O. They got their job to do and all it is is
> to be an agent of the government. They always tell you that they
> want to help you. That if you got problems, tell them about it. But
> they just keep this eye on you all the time. Especially if you're in a
> gang. . . . So they say they want to help you, but all they really do
> is spy on you.

As a result of the strength of these beliefs, gang members make every effort to follow the formal procedures established for parole. Most realize that the best way to maximize their interests is to pay attention to the rules the parole officer is governed by. In addition, most gang members reported that in their interviews with their parole officer, they said what they thought the parole officer wanted to hear. All believed that this made the parole officer's job easier and in turn was the best way to minimize trouble for themselves. The comments of Grady and Benito are representative. Grady who is a twenty-two-year-old member of a New York gang:

> Yeah, I go and talk to my P.O. and I do all the things I know he is looking for. I am on time, I got the information he wants if he wants something. I got it all. I follow all the procedures he sets up. You see he likes it that way because that's what's making his life easier. You see procedures let you and your P.O. go through it all without nothing changing. Just like prison, it [procedure] makes the whole deal easy on everybody.

Benito is a twenty-six-year-old member of a Los Angeles gang:

> I don't trust any P.O. They got their procedures and stuff, so you got to follow them. They try to talk to you once in awhile, but since they got their own people to answer to, they want things to go smooth. So there ain't nothing they're going to say to really change what I think is best for me; so I tell what I think they want to hear, and they're happy, and that helps me be happy.

The gang member who is out on parole generally has little respect for the parole officer. He is looked upon as a social parasite who does the government's dirty work. This contempt for the parole officer, along with the gang member's desire to maximize his interests, results in the gang member's complying with established procedures. Yet for the gang member this ritual behavior is, in reality, a masquerade for resistance.

Some Concluding Remarks

The judicial path of the gang member, seen in terms of who has responsibility for controlling his behavior, begins with the police, proceeds to the intake officer or the court (depending on the age of the defendant), then moves to the various prison officials, then to the parole officer, and finally, back to the policeman. In sum, it is a nefarious circle that has little impact on making gangs impotent organizations. In fact, the system often had the unintended consequence of strengthening both the defiant individualist character of gang members and group solidarity. Let us review why.

While it is true that the various authorities in the criminal justice system are concerned with immobilizing gangs in an effort to create public order, they also consider and juggle many interests related to public order. For the most part, their modus operandi as it relates to gangs is utilitarian in character. They attempt to manipulate a judicial equation that calculates the greatest amount of good for themselves and/or the society. Often, the attempt to realize their interests, as well as those of the greater society, influences them to emphasize judicial procedures. It is this emphasis on judicial procedures that will lead them into a policy quagmire, because when criminal justice officials and gangs interact at the procedural level, the interaction assumes the characteristics of a ritual. It removes the gang and the judicial system from a simple adversarial relationship. Instead, they become integrated strands in the web of social relations. That is to say, each is a structural support for the other. Thus, social order (which is the mandate and goal of the criminal justice system) as it relates to gangs is obtained more from the interactive behavior of procedural ritual than for the structural power relations of dominance-submission.

Chapter Nine

The Media and Gangs: Image Construction and Myth Management

Crime constantly monopolizes the headlines, but the criminal appears there only fugitively, to be replaced at once.
Albert Camus, *The Fall* (1956)

Throughout various periods in American history, gangs have received a great deal of attention from the media. This was especially true during the 1970s and 1980s, when there was not one branch of the media that did not devote a significant amount of time and resources to the topic of gangs. During this period, one could find stories of gangs in newspapers, magazines, radio news shows, television news shows, television documentaries, radio and television talk shows, docu-dramas, and, finally, the movies. In short, the media became the general public's primary source of information about gangs and, as a result, became an important actor in the gang phenomenon. Interestingly, despite the fact that there have been a number of sociological studies of gang behavior, none have actually analyzed the relationship between the media and gangs.[1] This chapter attempts to analyze this relationship and, in the process, to reveal the media's contribution to the maintenance of gangs in American urban society.

Before proceeding with the analysis, it would seem appropriate to mention briefly the three sources of data for this chapter. The first is the personal observations made as a result of being with the gangs when various media personnel were interviewing and/or filming them. The second involves my interviews with a number of media personnel. The third has to do with my review of (1) radio and television transcripts of programs concerning gangs; (2) the actual tapes from radio programs on gangs; and (3) videotapes of television news broadcasts, documentaries, talk shows, docu-dramas, serial episodes (such as "Hill Street Blues"), and movies (such as *Colors, The Warriors,* and *Fort Apache, The Bronx*) in which gangs play a significant role.

The Media on Gangs:
Reporting, Understanding, Entertaining

As mentioned above, there are a variety of news mediums that deliver the issue of gangs to the public. Each has assumed one of three formats: reporting, understanding, or entertaining.[2] Each of these formats represents the self-understanding of the media itself, and for each of these formats, the people involved in the media have a somewhat different orientation and relationship with gangs. I shall discuss the nature of these relationships beginning with the format of reporting, moving to the format of understanding, and ending with the format of entertaining. The order of the discussion is substantively relevant because the formats of understanding and entertaining emerge from the information presented in the format of reporting.

The Format of Reporting

In beginning this section on gangs and the media, it is important to emphasize that the news media are in business not only to disseminate information but also to make a profit. This being the case, newspaper editors and radio and television news show producers have both to gather information and to get people interested in reading, listening to and viewing their presentation of it. The news media report about gangs as part of the "routine of journalism."[3] In this endeavor, gangs are reported as events, and in the process they assume a certain image. This image (in the reporting mode) cannot be an accurate representation because limitations of time and space restrict this, but nonetheless the image of gangs provided by most of the news media does accomplish the desired economic goals of creating a general interest in buying a particular newspaper or listening to and viewing a news program.

Information concerning gangs is most often delivered to the public in newspapers and radio and television news shows under the format of reporting. Newspapers and radio and television news shows all report the current day's "news." Of course, rarely does a story about gangs become newsworthy unless it has something sensational to it. After all, it is the nature of the media that they cannot include *all* the news (even if the *New York Times* proclaims "All the News That's Fit to Print") because time and space are limited. This means that gangs must provide enough interest to merit a specific amount of space and time, which usually means that the story must involve violence and/or crime. The more violent the crime, the more likely it is that it will be included in the nightly news. Hence, it is the public's interest in violence that is being addressed, not simply the occurrence of a crime in the city. News shows (as well as newspapers) need a significant number of "interest-generating" events to hook listeners/readers into their respective mediums. The violence and crime associated with gangs are perfect topics for this because they accommodate the public's interest in violent acts, while avoiding many of the technical problems that reporters encounter with other stories related to violent crime. For example, all reporters recount what they consider to be the important events of the day, and they do so in a manner that presents these events as verified facts. Yet in most cases involving gangs, the suggestion that the events being reported are verified facts is somewhat deceptive. In all three cities studies (Los Angeles, New York, and Boston), an inordinate number of violent events were reported as "gang-related" crimes. In a significant number of these cases, the public was presented with an event as "truth" despite the fact that the nature of the event was not substantiated. When experts (usually the police) were asked to comment on an incident, they most often used guarded language, such as "we believe this to be a gang-related crime." In such cases, the news industry is able to report an interest-generating crime (event) without having to identify a specific person or group of persons who committed it. In addition, such stories about gang violence allow a reporter (and the news establishment) to identify a perpetrator (the gang) without having to worry that they may have impaired the criminal justice process. In essence a story about gangs is perfect. It creates reader-listener interest with few journalistic liabilities. The comments of D.X. and X.S. illustrate these points. D.X. was a reporter for a television station in Los Angeles:

> Gang stories are one type of story that is valued because it gets people's attention and creates enough interest so that people will continue to watch the rest of the news. It is also true that gang-related violence is easier than some other stories that we are as-

signed to cover. The main reason is that we have an incident that's occurred, some violent act, and if the police report that it is "gang-related" or some of the witnesses believe that it is "gang-related," then we report it as being "gang-related" and a lot of our investigative job is over. We don't have to run down a lead here, or a lead there, we have just been able to save time and get the same result—a story that the public will probably find interesting.[4]

X.S. was a television reporter from New York:

Reporting on gangs is optimal for any reporter, and the news station for that matter. . . . To begin with, since we would usually only cover a gang story if it had crime or violence associated with it, establishing who committed the criminal act or violence is made easier because it can be attributed to a group and not just one individual. It is easier identifying a group than trying to run down an individual, and that really helps everyone make their deadline! . . . This saves everybody time and the story is just as good. Basically the station gets the biggest bang for the least amount of bucks. Plus, by identifying the culprit as being a gang, there is the benefit of not having to worry whether you have identified a person as being the attacker and thereby jeopardized their ability of getting a fair trial.[5]

News stories related to gangs not only are attractive because of their interest-generating capabilities, they have the added benefit of being able to cover up potential errors in a reporter's investigation. For example, crimes are frequently misidentified as "gang-related." What most often happens is that a crime is committed by a number of individuals, and then the police and/or reporters inaccurately attribute it to a gang by calling it "gang-related." In some of the cases I observed, the mistake was made because the reporter was ignorant of other forms of group crime, such as crimes committed by "crews" (a "crew" being usually a small group of three to five individuals who band together to commit burglaries). Such "crews" often commit violent crimes that are then reported as "gang-related." Similarly, crimes committed by gang members on their own without the organizational authority of the gang may also be mislabeled "gang-related." Even when such errors are made, the reporter and the news agency are protected from harsh criticism because any group of people involved in a crime can be considered a gang even if they do not have a formal organization. In addition, the general public is concerned not with whether these individuals constitute a gang in the technical sense but only about their collective violent action. Thus, the news agency's administration is generally protected from public criticism for being involved in a deliberate attempt to report inaccurate information. The comments of T.X., a reporter for a newspaper in New York, illustrate this point:

> Well, there was this multiple robbery in which a number of people had been shot by their assailants. I was sent to cover the story. I got there, did some investigating, and found that there were about six who did the robberies. I reported that victims were robbed and assaulted by a gang. Well, a short time later I found out that the robbers were not members of a gang, but were what the community called a "crew." If this had been a different situation, I would have been upset that I had made a mistake in my reporting, but not with this, because nobody really cares. Do you think the general public cares whether the people assaulting these individuals [were] technically a gang or not? No way! All they care about is the fact that a gang of thugs attacked and robbed them, and in a sense that's what I reported. . . . And my bosses don't care about that mistake either because the story generated some interest and they have the excuse that it was a gang of some sort.

The personal relationship that exists between the news media (within the event-reporting mode) and gang members is extremely limited, to say the least. Most reporters rarely interview gang members about each event they are reporting because of time constraints. They are faced with deadlines, and this prohibits them from spending time seeking out the appropriate gang member(s) to interview or developing the trust necessary for them to cooperate.[6] Furthermore, most reporters find it unnecessary in their immediate tasks of reporting an event to make contact with the gangs themselves.[7] Therefore, the contact that reporters have with the gangs is mostly through the police. The comments of E.X. and X.O. highlight this point. E.X. was a reporter in New York:

> The fact is that I almost never have had contact with any of the gangs that I reported on. I really never needed to have contact with them because I was only reporting the occurrence of a homicide. It was just as good to get the police's comment on the crime. You have to understand that I was not doing a feature article, the editor didn't want that from me. The only thing they wanted was

for me to cover an interesting story and get it in before the deadline.

X.O. was a reporter in Los Angeles:

I have covered a lot of stories concerning gangs, but as a rule I
don't interview gang members when I'm asked to cover a crime or
homicide. For these stories, talking to gang members is not necessary because the station only wants me to cover the incident, not
analyze it like one would do if it were a documentary. Most of the
time, I just interview law enforcement officials, because it's just as
good for what we're going to do with the story and, hell, even if I
wanted to interview a gang member, I wouldn't have the time or
I'd miss my deadline. . . . I have interviewed gang members, but
only when helping with some in-depth story.

The Format of Providing Understanding

Given that reporters have limited contact with gang members, it is not
surprising that the news-reporting mode of the media offers the public
little in-depth information (and sometimes even inaccurate information)
on gangs. Nonetheless, the gang-related story serves a useful purpose in
that it provides a hook to secure readers and viewers.[8] After all, TV producers are aware of the impact of "audience flow," the phenomenon
where someone chooses to continue to watch a particular station because
of liking the previous show, and they try to take advantage of this by
producing an interesting and informative news program.[9] Editors of
newspapers and magazines attempt to provide a hook by producing interest-generating headlines, lead stories, and covers.[10]

These same editors and producers are aware of the limitations of the
news-reporting approach, but they know that if they do a good job with
the news, the audience's appetite for additional information will be stimulated. The reporting approach thus provides editors and producers with
an opportunity to generate an interest that can later be capitalized on by
developing presentations such as feature articles, segments in TV magazine shows, and documentaries to provide more understanding of an event
reported in limited fashion in the daily news.

The second format in which the topic of gangs is presented to the
public is that which I have labeled understanding. Within this format, the

goal is to provide a greater understanding of the nature of gangs. For television, Edward R. Murrow's CBS documentary "Who Killed Michael Farmer?" is the classic on gangs and is often used in college media courses as the prototype of how to do a documentary. In this documentary, Murrow takes an incident reported in the news (as an event) and provides a deeper analysis in an attempt to explain the events that led to the death of a crippled young man at the hands of a street gang in the Bronx. In so doing, he sought to provide the public with a general understanding of gangs in urban America.[11] The show aired in the 1950s, but its format has been, to a greater or lesser extent, utilized by subsequent reporters doing documentaries on gangs ever since.

If one were to compare Murrow's "Who Killed Michael Farmer?" with Dan Medina's "Our Children: The Next Generation," Dan Rather's "48 Hours: On Gang Street," or Tyne Daly's "Not My Kid" (all done in 1989), one would discover that they all used similar techniques to format their shows.[12] Each started with a recent event and then proceeded to weave information on related events into a general story about gangs. In the case of Murrow, the event was the death of Michael Farmer; for Dan Medina and Dan Rather, it was the multiple deaths that have resulted from gang conflict in Los Angeles. Each of these events was reported on the nightly news, and each was used as a core around which a story could be developed. Those who viewed each of these documentaries were presented with programs that alternated between focusing on the core event(s) and those related to specific gang members. All the programs tried to present an interesting and moving story. For Murrow, the task was somewhat different, in that he was focusing on one gang and one event, whereas for Medina and Rather the focus was on multiple acts committed by several gangs.

In Murrow's documentary, the story begins with the murder of Michael Farmer and then proceeds to weave in those events that occurred prior to Farmer's death in an effort to inform the audience more fully about its cause. The documentary is quite compelling because as it moves toward the actions that ultimately would kill Michael Farmer and badly injure his friend, it intersperses the personal histories of his assailants and the attitudes of Michael Farmer's parents. It thus includes both emotion and suspense in the telling of the story. Yet, although it is masterfully done, it has serious shortcomings where gangs are concerned. The show starts with the death of Michael Farmer at the hands of a number of gang members. It addresses the question of who killed Michael Farmer and proceeds to present information on the individuals involved in the murder. The information provides insights into some of the circumstances that influenced the perpetrators of the crime, but offers almost nothing about the nature of the gang itself. What is presented about the gang is that Michael Farmer was the innocent victim of a gang war. However, the program offers little information concerning gang organization and behavior. Even when Murrow answers the question "Who Killed Michael Farmer?" at the end of the program, his answer is that society killed him by neglecting the horrible socioeconomic conditions that lead boys to form groups that attack people. In a sense, the answer to the question reinforces the imagery of the gang as a group of individuals resembling a pack of hungry predatory animals, such as wolves or coyotes. Thus, because the viewer is not given any in-depth understanding of gangs, she or he has no way of comprehending the relationship between the gang and the crime. The result is that the documentary acts to reinforce another American myth—the gang.

As mentioned earlier, the programs by Rather and Medina differ somewhat from Murrow's in that they attempt to present programs based on multiple murders attributed to gangs. Each attempts to provide insight into the nature of gangs in an effort to understand the high number of gang-related murders in the Los Angeles area. Like Murrow's documentary, both promise to tell a story about gang members and their activities, and both utilize emotional scenes of death to maintain interest, continuity, and pace in their programs. Even though both shows have the benefit of thirty years of experience since Murrow's endeavor, they are remarkably similar in presentation. Far from being sociological analyses of gangs or gang murders, they provide only snapshots or glimpses of gang life. Their main concern is to seize the opportunity provided by recent gang-related events in Los Angeles (what in the media business is called the "peg") and produce a program whose time frame will allow deeper exploration of the Los Angeles gang phenomenon.[13] Their similarity with each other and with Murrow's film is owing to professional guidelines, certain technical difficulties associated with covering gangs, and professional and business interests influencing which stories get aired or run in the press; such factors need to be analyzed if one is to understand the effects of the media on the maintenance of gangs.

The Influence of Professional Guidelines

Certain professional considerations have had an important influence in producing television programs that look very much alike. Each of the

considerations that I shall discuss has been previously identified and discussed in more detail by Herbert J. Gans.[14] It is my intention to discuss
them as they relate to the stories on gangs done by Murrow, Rather,
Daly, and Medina. In so doing, I hope to provide an explanation of why
the stories, and news stories about gangs generally, are very similar to
each other and provide surprisingly little understanding of gangs themselves.

The first professional consideration has to do with what journalists
call "story suitability," the question of whether the story has an impact
on the nation. (Does it have national interest?) Since none of the stories
compares gangs in a variety of cities, national interest must be created,
and in order to address the question of national impact satisfactorily,
each of the shows employs a variety of techniques. One device used in all
the shows is the exploitation of the concept of violence. In each of the
shows, the reporter mentions the fact that gang violence occurs in every
large city in America, and then goes on to say something about there
being "none more than is occurring in city 'X'." The first part of this
statement indicates national relevance and the second justifies focusing
on the city about which the story is being done. The message is that
viewers can come to understand the violence in their own communities
by focusing on the extreme cases of New York and Los Angeles. Thus
violence becomes the concept that creates national interest. Other techniques used exploit the emotions experienced by people who have lost
relatives to gang violence and those associated with being a victim. Interestingly, at the end of "48 Hours" and "Not My Kid," both Dan Rather
and Tyne Daly make statements such as, "It is not just a problem for
people in Los Angeles, it is a problem for all of us." These ending statements are inserted to supply an affirmative answer to the question most
reporters ask themselves, "Does it have national interest?" Yet given the
content of these programs (lack of comparative data), it is difficult to
make the connection between the events of Los Angeles and the nation.

The second professional consideration that affects the content of
documentaries on gangs has to do with the novelty of the story. Most
reporters will ask themselves, or be asked by their superiors, whether
there is something new about the story. A story can be considered novel
if it is completely new or if it is a topic that has been done before, but the
reporter takes a new slant on it. This accounts for the many variations
on the same theme that characterize stories on gangs. Two examples would
be the story in "48 Hours" and that of "Not My Kid." Both deal with

gang violence in Los Angeles, but whereas "48 Hours" focuses on its impact on a broad range of people within the community, "Not My Kid" focuses on how it has affected the families directly involved.

The third consideration has to do with action. (Does the show have enough action?) By action, the profession generally means emotion. In every show on gangs, there is a concerted effort made to create emotion in the viewer by presenting people gripped by emotion. The two most important concepts used to develop action are violence and those emotions associated with death (particularly sorrow and anger). Therefore, scenes related to gang violence are included not simply because they depict life in poor, working-class communities but because they provide one of the ingredients for creating a "good" news story—action.

The fourth professional consideration is the pace of the show. It is generally believed in the news profession that a program must be paced so that the viewer does not lose interest. In the programs on gangs mentioned above (although this is true of others as well), pacing is evident from the limiting of people's comments in the interviews (comments generally being viewed as creating a slow pace) and the films' moving relatively quickly from one aspect involving gangs to another. The result is that almost no aspect of gang life is covered sufficiently to provide an understanding of the phenomenon.[15]

A fifth consideration involves the clarity of the story. Reporters believe that the story must be clear for all segments of the general public to understand. In order to facilitate this, the comments of informants and experts are restricted to their barest elements (sometimes to such a degree that their statements are simply undeveloped expressions with little meaning). It is quite common for reporters to ask gang members a question and then try to change their answer by forcing them to say things in simple terms. For example, a reporter was asking a particular gang member from New York about why his gang was fighting with another gang. The gang member, named Nimble, said it was related to a number of factors and then started to discuss each one. After he started on the third one, the reporter interrupted and said: "Well, what you're basically saying is that it's over turf." Nimble responded, "Well, sort of, but there is more to it. . . ." The reporter interrupted and said, "But basically that's really what you're saying." Nimble responded, "Yeah, if you want it to be basic, then, yes, I guess that's it." Later, after the reporter left, Nimble said: "I guess he wants people to understand, but there ain't no fucking way they're going to now! But if that's what he wants, fuck it!"

The sixth professional consideration is to have balance in the report. Among other things, this includes story mixture, subject balance, and political balance. As it relates to gangs, this most often manifests itself in the form of a story that attempts to present multiple aspects of gang life and then proceeds to offer various perspectives on each. While this may seem both professionally reasonable and honorable, it routinely results in an extremely short, or even one-line, commentary about many very important and complicated issues related to the gang phenomenon. Thus, like the other considerations, it, too, contributes to a lack of understanding.[16]

The Influence of Certain Technical Difficulties

In addition to the internal professional considerations that influence the content of gang stories, there are technical difficulties that also influence the content. First, deadlines that dictate when a story has to be completed and filed have a direct impact on the material. Deadlines affect the length of contact the reporter can have with the subjects. This makes it difficult to gather all the information desirable and limits what a reporter learns about gangs. Obviously, if a reporter has limited knowledge of important facts, the public's knowledge will also be limited. A common theme of reporters can be observed in the remarks of X.S., who had been a reporter for six years in Boston prior to this interview:

> I was doing this feature story on youth gangs and it really had the potential to be a blockbuster. But I needed to spend more time with them than I did. I mean I would have liked to have spent more time with the gangs, but my editor had this deadline and so I had this deadline. I was kind of frustrated because I knew I needed more time, but I really wasn't mad at my editor because he had a deadline himself; but then again, I really didn't write the story I could [have].

Another technical difficulty involves getting access to gang members. (This is a problem similar to one that social scientists have as well.) The problem is not one of making contact with gangs, because that can be arranged quite easily. The problem is one of becoming trusted enough to be allowed to observe all aspects of gang activity and to be confided in by gang members. In most cases, reporters are not accepted and are not allowed access to the inner world of the gang. Nor are they allowed access to the inner world of the gang member (what he thinks and feels). This does not create an insurmountable problem for the reporters. They will be able to produce their stories by substituting the observations of others (usually social scientists) for those areas in which they have no firsthand information. The problem created relates to the quality (depth and accuracy) of the information presented on the show. Usually, reporters faced with gaps in their information will rely on what has been said previously to fill these gaps.[17] The result of this tendency is to reinforce similar images of gangs.

The third technical problem concerns the reporter's training. Nearly all reporters doing in-depth stories on gangs attempt to do some type of sociological analysis. Yet all of them lack sufficient training for the purpose. Most are aware of this and are somewhat self-conscious. To compensate, they often ask so-called experts to comment on various aspects about which they feel particularly vulnerable. The problem is that sometimes the expert must comment on some aspect of gang life that the reporter may have seen or been told about but that the expert has not been able to observe personally; or the expert may be asked to comment on something he or she may either never have studied or have studied too long ago for these observations to be valid. This often occurs because the reporter has had difficulty getting the appropriate expert on the show and has substituted a less knowledgeable person. Consequently the so-called expert's analysis is often not based on current data but on images of gangs previously developed.

The fourth technical problem relates to the time/space constraints imposed on the show/article itself. Reporters may wish they had unlimited time and space, but this is not a professional reality. Limitations of time and space affect both the depth and quality of a story because the reporter (and editor) must make decisions as to what aspect(s) will be covered, as well as determining how much time will be devoted to each.[18] One particular problem here is how to use the comments of experts. Reporters often ask experts questions about gangs and then force them to answer the question quickly. On occasion I have observed reporters asking experts questions like: "What is your take on gang violence?" The expert, who may have spent years studying the topic, often begins a relatively long explanation, only to have the reporter interrupt and force a short answer. On one occasion, a reporter even suggested to an expert that there might be something wrong with his theory of gangs if it could not be stated in a few sentences. At other times, an expert may be allowed to make as long a statement as desired, which someone in production will later edit to fit the story. The final result is that time and space regulate substance and understanding.

The Influence of Professional and Business Interests

Finally, professional and business interests also influence why programs on gangs are so similar to each other. To begin with, gangs have consistently been identified with crime, sex, and violence. In addition, they are usually associated with something secretive, sinister, and mysterious. These images, which the media have helped build, are exactly the type that can be used to generate sizeable audiences. This makes gangs an attractive topic (commodity) for the media, and one that has the potential to produce increases in money, status, and power. Utilizing the traditional images of gangs as groups that are secretive, sinister and mysterious in their involvement with crime, sex, and violence, and then developing a new slant on these images, has therefore been a popular formula for achieving professional mobility.

Reporters believe that a good story on gangs can increase their prestige within the profession and correspondingly within their organization; and that this can lead to their being offered more opportunities to do other shows/articles, ultimately with a higher position (more responsibilities) and a higher salary. The comments of J.X. and V.X. illustrate this view. At the time of this interview, J.X. had been a reporter in Los Angeles for only a short time:

> Sure, I want to do a story on gangs. Quite honestly, gangs are a good topic to do a story on because they have violence and crime associated with them—things that the general public just crave to hear about. This makes an ideal story for a young reporter like me, because if I can get a new scoop on the gangs, then I know some good things will come my way. . . . Well, the things that I would hope a good story would get me would be greater respect from my colleagues, and some greater opportunities to do other shows, and I don't want to leave out more money. You see, a young reporter needs a couple of good stories like this to jump his career.

V.X. had been a reporter in New York for a number of years before this interview:

You ask why I want to do this story on gangs? It's really not complicated in my case. Gangs are an important issue in urban America. They always have been, because they represent groups that are violent and dangerous to the average person. By taking a subject that is on the news quite often these days, I can convince myself that I am still doing the job. Seriously, by taking on a story that is difficult and has general interest and importance, I can maintain the respect that I have gained over the years from my colleagues. I can, if I present a fresh look at the gangs, or any topic that is explosive like gangs are, even gain more respect and status in the profession and this would please me.

Interestingly, all of the reporters that I either formally interviewed or merely talked to while they were trying to interview the gangs I was with either believed that they could (once they got the necessary information) present a new slant on gangs or that they were in the process of presenting a new slant on gangs. In most cases, the new slant that they shared with me was not new at all; it was simply new to them. In some cases, reporters even would admit to me that in talking to other people who had done work on gangs, they had been told that their presentation was not novel, but during the conversation with me, they would completely disregard these comments and proceed as though they indeed had a novel approach that could be sold to their editor/producer. The comment of I.X. is an example of such a case:

E.X. and X.R. [two fellow reporters] told me that my take on the gangs had been done, but I really don't believe it's exactly the same. I spent a good deal of time on this story and I think I can convince Y.X. [the editor] that what I have is new.[19]

In other words, I.X. was aware that the slant on gangs in question was not novel or fresh, but driven by the goal to be professionally successful (and mobile), the reporter believed it could be sold to the editor or producer as such. Thus, what reporters often see (or want to see) as "new" works to reinforce the familiar take on gangs, which is mostly an inaccurate picture.

Thus, professional and business interests work to produce similar stories about gangs because they influence reporters, editors, and producers to focus on issues in which the general public has traditionally shown an interest—namely crime, sex, and violence.

In sum, the feature stories on gangs that appear in magazines, newspapers, television news magazines, or documentaries seize upon the interest generated in the daily news and sell themselves as in-depth looks at the topic. Yet rarely have they provided an understanding of the gang phenomenon. This is because they are not concerned with "understanding" gangs per se; rather, they use "understanding" as a format in pursuit of professional and business interests. The net result of this type of story has been to reinforce images of gangs that derive less from gang reality than from the myths surrounding gangs.

The Format of Entertainment

Television talk shows and the movies take the public's interest in gangs one step further. Rather than attempting to inform the public about gangs, these two mediums attempt to entertain the public with the topic of gangs. Although each differs in the manner in which it entertains, both produce similar consequences.

Television talk shows such as "Geraldo," "The Phil Donahue Show," and "The Oprah Winfrey Show" present/sell themselves as programs that not only inform people on various topics, but also depict the "human side" of stories because they emphasize people's feelings about issues. For such programs, it is imperative that they maintain high ratings or they will be discontinued. Therefore, all focus on those topics believed to be the most stimulating. They must use their topics to sell the event (show). Therefore, their particular format is constructed to produce this effect.

The topic of gangs is one that can stimulate viewer interest, especially if it is sensationalized. Talk shows begin with the host setting the focus for the topic and the tone of the show. In order to do this, the most popular images concerning the topic are used. In relation to gangs, each of the hosts begins with an introductory statement in which the inflection and tone sensationalizes the gang as an important problem facing America. This is done by describing the violent incidents associated with gangs, reporting the experts' estimates of the magnitude of the problem, and stressing the seriousness of the situation. Usually this means that incidents involving violent crime are reported along with the number of innocent people injured, especially the number of innocent people who reside outside gang neighborhoods.

Since these programs present a different topic each day (five days a week), there is little time to do a substantial amount of research on any one topic. To compensate for this, the program offers the audience in the studio and at home a panel of so-called "experts" in the field who are called upon to comment on various statements made in the program.[20] The guests are manipulated by the host for the most dramatic effect. The statements by the guests are severely limited by the host to only a few brief paragraphs and are ultimately used to establish the groundwork (substance) for what is the essence of the program: the various interactions of the host, the guests, the audience in the studio, and the audience at home. In the shows on gangs, a number of obvious questions were asked, such as, Why do young kids join gangs? Why do they act violently? What can be done about them? It is next to impossible to give an informed answer to these questions in a thirty-minute program in which there are a number of guests with varying degrees of expertise and opinions on each of the subjects.

The host interacts with the guests, drawing out different and opposing positions on the topic. The objective appears to be to initiate conflict among all the participants (apparently because it is believed that conflict is capable of arousing viewer interest) and to maintain the show's intensity by stimulating interaction among the guests, between the audiences in the studio and at home, and between the guests and the members of the audiences. The main function of the host is to act as provocateur and to incite verbal combat between the different groups involved in the show.[21] It is apparent that producers believe that if they can get the audience in the studio worked up, they can excite the audience at home. Although the general strategy of the shows I reviewed produced lively discussions on gangs, there was little understanding provided of the gang phenomenon. Of course, the format of the show, and its primary intent, was not to provide understanding, but to use the topic of gangs to sell the spectacle of the participants' interactions. Ultimately, these programs provide entertainment and in the process reinforce the public image of gangs and the gang problem.

Motion pictures are the other medium in which gangs are utilized to entertain people.[22] Although there are a number of pictures in which gangs are the focus, three of the more memorable are *West Side Story, The Warriors,* and *Colors.* Each of these movies depicts the gang in a different era, with *West Side Story* focusing on the 1950s, *The Warriors* on the 1970s, and *Colors* on the 1980s. Yet despite the fact that they are obviously bound by their respective time frames, they are also remarkably similar in the way they depict gangs and the people with whom gang members intimately interact.

Let us begin with Hollywood's depiction of gangs. Each movie mentioned above depicts gangs as composed of poor or working-class males who lack the skills and desire to be upwardly mobile and productive citizens.[23] Essentially, they are not only "losers" but "losers" who are also primitive and brutally violent. Their values are painted as both an anathema to the values held by the society as a whole and a threat to them (society's values).[24]

Those who are intimate associates of gangs are likewise characterized in a negative manner. The parents of gang members are presented as individuals who do not care and/or are negligent in their parental responsibilities. However, while most people closely associated with gang members are presented in a negative light, none are represented worse than the women with whom they interact. Gang movies, by requiring a love/sex angle, make gangs revolve around sex in a way that is both sexist and racist, and this distorts their picture of gang behavior. In each of the movies on gangs, the women whom gang members interact with (regardless of whether they are girlfriends, lovers, or acquaintances) are portrayed as having loose morals. They are willing either to engage in open, nonmarital sex or to sell sex (prostitution), or they are alcoholics and/or drug addicts. This imagery is particularly provocative because most of the movies focus on nonwhite gangs in nonwhite neighborhoods. One need only compare the portrayal of nonwhite women and white police officers in *Colors* with those in *Fort Apache, The Bronx*, an earlier film that focused on life in an extremely depressed community.[25] In each of these films, all the nonwhite women but one are portrayed as being immoral and/or irresponsible in some significant way. In both films, the one nonwhite woman introduced as being different from the rest is also portrayed as having escaped the corrupting influences of the others in her community. One is a Puerto Rican nurse (in *Fort Apache*) and the other is a Mexican who sells food from a take-out stand (in *Colors*). Of course, in each movie the white police officer (Paul Newman in *Fort Apache* and Sean Penn in *Colors*) falls in love with the "different" woman. Yet later in each film, we find out that neither woman is "good" at all; it has just been a masquerade. The Puerto Rican nurse is a heroin addict and the Mexican waitress is actually a slut who hangs out with her barrio gang. Both are not only portrayed as dishonest with their white boyfriends but betray them in ways the dominant society sees as morally reprehensible. Both women have been offered a way out of the slum and the immoral life that pervades it, yet both are depicted as incapable of seizing the opportunity. The Puerto Rican nurse refuses to give up heroin and dies from an overdose, and the Mexican waitress refuses to continue to date Sean Penn, who later finds her at a gang party having sex, not only with a gang member (his symbolic enemy), but with the only African-American member of a Mexican gang! The symbolic message is quite striking here. Having sex with a Mexican gang member would be immoral enough, but having it with the only African-American in the gang is the ultimate in betrayal.

Finally, I turn now to Hollywood's depiction of the gang's social environment—that is, the community. In all these movies, Hollywood has depicted the low-income community in which gangs operate as completely disorganized and out of control. These communities are characterized as being composed of individuals who are incapable of governing themselves. In each film there are a number of scenes showing how the community people find it impossible to create order and control. These people are portrayed as wanting civic control, but lacking the necessary skills to establish it.[26] The only way that control is reestablished in these movies is through the police. In essence, these movies tell the audience that if it were not for this outside force (the police force is an institution whose authority emanates from outside the community and that is composed of individuals mostly from outside the community), the community would remain in total chaos. Hollywood has in essence presented a contemporary urban situation in a traditionally colonial fashion: if it were not for the police (the colonial army), these low-income communities (the colonized country) would be in continuous chaos because the well-intentioned citizens of these neighborhoods (poor countries) lack the skills to control the various gangs (factions and tribes) from warring with each other. The colonial symbolism is even more striking given that the recent movies about gangs have focused on nonwhite gangs and nonwhite communities.

Thus the image of gangs and their intimates (and by extension nonwhites in general) is that they represent a world that is immoral compared to the general society.[27] They are the demonic element within society—that is, an immoral enemy that threatens society's basic moral codes.[28] In fact, Hollywood has been able to portray the gang, particularly the nonwhite gang and its nonwhite women, as the carriers of moral malignancy.

In sum, Hollywood's portrayal of gangs adds more vivid imagery to the gang myth. When dealing with gangs and their communities, Hollywood has created mythical kingdoms with mythical characters. When producers and directors have been criticized for this, as they have been in the case of *The Warriors, Fort Apache, The Bronx,* and *Colors,* they have defended themselves by saying that their productions were meant, not to be documentaries, but to entertain.[29] However, the sociological consequence is that images have a way of maintaining themselves in the public's mind and in the absence of quality information and analyses, these images have become the primary prisms through which people construct an understanding of social reality.

The Gang and the Media: Hamming It Up for Glory and Gain

Gangs are not so awestruck by the media and the prospects of being written or talked about that they unequivocally give reporters whatever information they want. They are willing to give information, but only on their own terms. They assume this position because they are suspicious of reporters (part of their defiant individualist characters) and conscious of the fact that information about them is in high demand and therefore has value. All the gangs studied realized that the media were consistently interested in doing stories about them, provided the information imparted was novel. Therefore, they all offered information, but they regulated its flow in terms of both depth (degree of intimacy) and quantity. The comments of Coal, Bird, and Jammer are examples of the media consciousness displayed by gang members. Coal was a nineteen-year-old member of a New York gang:

> You see, there was this reporter who wanted to get a story on us. She really needed one bad, you could tell. It was like her career depended on it or something. She sent a whole lot of messages through Mr. G. [a particular community worker]. We all talked about what to do with her at our regular meeting. We decided we could use a little publicity and so we mapped out what we'd give her. You know, like who she'd talk to and what we'd say. Stuff like that . . . she came out and talked to who we had set her up with and asked questions, but we gave her what we wanted to. She didn't even know what was happening, man, we're so good at this shit, they don't even dig what was going! She was happy, but before she left, we left some sugar to keep her fancy. You know, we dropped some lines that we knew would interest her, so she'll

be back sometime, or she'll tell another reporter and they'll be back.

Bird was an eighteen-year-old member of an Irish gang in Boston:

> Sure, there were a lot of times that reporters wanted to do stories about the community and us, but we wouldn't talk to them. Then we said to ourselves, "They're going to write the story anyway, so we might as well tell 'em what we want." So we started to do it and then more came. They would ask all kinds of questions, like whether we're running guns for the IRA and things like that, but we'd just string 'em along, giving them little tidbits. We kept them coming back for more and more, and we told 'em the story we wanted. They didn't know the difference and hell, the story was believable and exciting, so I don't think they cared.

Jammer was a twenty-year-old member of a gang in Los Angeles:

> Hey, reporters need good stories, and let's face it, gangs are good press. Peoples is interested in the dark side of the city, you dig? But being in the news can be useful to a lot of us individually and for the organization too, so we gets the information to the report-ers, it's just that it's our information. They get what we say they get and no more. We be feeding 'em a little bit to set their taste buds, but not enough so they get all they want. It be like a pool hustle, man, if it be good, everybody's happy 'cause nobody knows. . . . We just trying to take care of business.

As mentioned earlier, all the gangs in this study understood the advan-tages of media exposure, but not all of them were capable of developing and executing a strategy resembling that described above. Many times a gang that was having difficulty manipulating the media would blame it on the fact that a number of its members were resisting any contact with the media because they were either afraid that they would be identified by the authorities and arrested or were complaining that there was no reason to cooperate since the media always portrayed them negatively. However, both explanations disguise the real reason for their gang's in-ability to devise a manipulative plan to deal with the media, which was that their gang was experiencing organizational decline (as discussed in chapter 3). Consider the comments of B.B. and Dodger. B.B. was a sev-enteen-year-old member of a New York gang:

> We was approached by a lot of reporters, but we don't give inter-views anymore 'cause a number of brothers [gang members] didn't

want the gang to. They said that they didn't want to have their
faces on television because then the cops would be able to identify
them and arrest them. This was such shit, because they didn't even
need to be there when the interview was going on. Other gangs do
it that way. . . . You see, what it really was—you [the researcher]
know what it was 'cause you was there, it was the fact that they
didn't want the dude who is president now to get credit for some
good publicity because they wanted another guy to be president.
Doesn't matter now, 'cause they were still able to stop us from
doing anything with any reporters.

Dodger was a twenty-year-old member of a Los Angeles gang:

There were a number of us who wanted to take the reporters up
on their offer to give us some media coverage, but a lot of the
other homies from the other *klikas* [branches] wanted to have a
say in who got to be in the interview. . . . It ended up that we
couldn't get anything out of the media, because nobody could decide on what we should do. We just sat around and argued about
it. It was a real mess and we didn't have any strong leadership to
stop it. . . . Those of us who wanted to do interviews all told them
that gangs is in now, but they won't be in forever and that we
missed a good chance to help ourselves, but it didn't matter.

In the more than ten years of my research, I never observed gangs
receiving money from the media for their cooperation in giving information. At no point did I ever observe any member of the media even
offering money. The obvious questions are: (1) If gangs do not receive
any money, what do they get for their cooperation with the media? and
(2) Why do gangs believe it is important to have some policy guiding
their interaction with media?

To answer the first question, we can begin by stating that gangs are
able to secure a number of organizational and personal advantages (albeit modest) from media coverage. First, media coverage can help them
recruit new members. A gang that has been given media exposure will
often be able to start another branch of their organization in another
selection of the city because the publicity has created interest among enough
young males who live there. Take the comment of Jade, a twenty-one-
year-old member of a Los Angeles gang:

You know, if some of the television people do a story and we cooperate, it helps get us more members. The thing is that you got to

cooperate enough with them, you know, be cool, so that you get to send some messages out that is going to help. . . . Like they [the reporters] be asking us some questions and we be telling 'em in a way that it makes what we been doing look good to the dudes around here. You see, it's like this, we say some things that the rest of the world listens to and it sounds strange to them, even stupid; but to the dudes around here, it means something else. It sounds like there are some opportunities to them. It's the power of language, man, like when you hear that TV ad for the military, you know, something like "Some people start their careers green" [an ad for the U.S. Army], or some shit like that. Now that didn't sound too enticing for me. In fact, that sounded stupid to me, to join the military, learn some things, and then get a career. But some dudes go for that shit. The same with our pitch. Some dudes hear it and see opportunities. That's just the way it is.

Nody was an eighteen-year-old member of a New York gang:

I was just sitting watching television and the news was on when they did this segment on one of the gangs. Those brothers were bad [i.e., good], and they were saying some things [so] that I said, "Hey, they may have some good shit there." So I decided to check it out and I joined. . . . No, I wouldn't have joined this particular club, I might have joined another club, but I wouldn't have joined this one if it hadn't been for what they said on that TV program. They had it down, man!

The second advantage that gangs receive from media coverage is advertisement for business. They want the television coverage to depict them as being in control of a specified territory and willing to use physical coercion if necessary. This has helped them in their protection business. When they approach a new business with the proposition of providing protection, being in the news sometimes helps them secure the new client. Of fifty-three small business people I interviewed after they had agreed to have a gang protect their businesses, 30 percent (sixteen) said that they had been influenced (intimidated) by stories about that gang in the media. The comments of E.X., the owner of a small vegetable store in New York, are representative of the business people I talked to:

I saw this show on television about this gang called the [name of the gang] who was in this neighborhood. I heard what they were saying and then I saw some things the police said they did. Well, I was a little scared. And when they came and talked to me about them protecting me, I said, sure, you can do that. Well, I am only in this country a short time, so I don't want no trouble from anybody, and since I hired them, I get no trouble.

Media exposure also produced another form of advertising for the gangs. It occasionally acted as an illegal yellow pages. It provided people operating other illegal businesses with the name of an existing organization that could be helpful in producing or distributing their goods. For example, there were times when some group involved in an illegal business noticed a story about a gang controlling an area and then proceeded to establish contact with it in an effort either to expand its market or to subcontract some of its operations out to the gang. Those who operated illegal businesses and tried to make such an effort did so because they viewed the subcontracting to gangs as an opportunity to avoid or reduce the costs of having to organize and/or train a new group of people to do a particular job.

Media exposure is also viewed by gangs as a means to get a message out to other gangs (or other potential threats) that they had better stay away from their areas or face a serious physical challenge. Therefore, whenever a gang has a story done about it, members attempt to present an image that is particularly formidable. The members of every gang studied believed that if they acted appropriately, their interview would at a minimum produce this benefit. Take the comments of Coffee, an eighteen-year-old member of an Irish gang in New York:

> When we do an interview with a reporter, we act out as crazy as we can and as mean as we can because that way we get to send a message to everybody who might want to come into our neighborhood and try something that if we catch them they ain't going to be given any mercy. They will be butchered.

Finally, there are gang members who act more outlandishly during an interview than any of the others. They believe that this will enhance their reputation and that they will either get more respect (status) within the gang and/or make it safer for themselves on the street.[30] Take the comments of J.D., a seventeen-year-old member of a Los Angeles gang:

> When I was interviewed by this reporter, I kind of was outrageous. You know, I said some things that were sort of extreme, but I planned it that way because I wanted to sound crazy. You see, if people think you're crazy, they don't mess with you. So I try

to be as crazy as I can be when I get around a reporter because they will pass the word around not to fuck with me![31]

In order to better obtain their objectives, nine of the thirty-seven gangs studied developed a strategy to influence the content of media stories in a way they believed would benefit them. Although they did not always succeed, they were more successful than gangs that did not develop a strategy. As E-Man, a twenty-one-year-old leader of a Los Angeles gang, said:

> For years we would have reporters come here and ask us questions and do their thing and we would get nothing out of it. Then we decided to see if we could get some money from them and they said no. Then we decided to try to get some messages out to help us, you know things like recruiting and letting people know where our turf was. But it wasn't until we started to think of exactly what we wanted to get across and had a plan of what to say and do when the reporters were around that we got what we wanted. But I ain't going to tell you that it worked all the time, because sometimes it worked and sometimes the reporter, or whoever, did their thing and fucked us up. But then again we had more success than those dumb motherfuckers [other gangs] that just said whatever they wanted and didn't have a plan. And also we couldn't complain if it didn't always work the way we wanted it 'cause we were getting prime-time advertising for nothing, man! Right now we're having some problems with the organization, so it ain't possible to be thinking of media strategy 'cause we got more pressing problems. But when we get it straightened out then we can think about a media plan again.

Because the media provide potential benefits, gangs want the media to continue to cover them. Therefore, they have developed certain schemes for stimulating and/or maintaining media interest. The first tactic they use is to criticize what other reporters have done by saying that it is not accurate. Most of the time, the gang members do not criticize all of what any one reporter has done, because to do that would suggest that the gang lied to the reporter. Rather, they say that only parts of the story are true, trying to establish that it was not that the gang lied to the reporter, it was that the reporter just did not get it right. This acts as bait for another reporter or news agency to come looking to do another, more accurate story. When the news reporter comes for his or her story, the gangs nearly always offer to provide the "real story." This helps to reinforce the reporter's interest. Of course, in most cases the gang regulates what is said and what the reporter is allowed to see. This allows gangs to remain mysterious and establishes a situation in which they can again criticize the story as being partially inaccurate. The comment of Sonic, an eighteen-year-old leader of a New York gang, illustrates this point:

> You can't be telling them [reporters] everything. You gots to tell them just enough to keep their interest and hold a lot more back. Then when you say that the last story about us had a lot of things in it that were wrong, it's the truth. And if you do it that way, you can always get another reporter to do a story, because most of them think they'll be the ones to do a better story on gangs.

When it comes to the media, gangs do have one marketing advantage, and that is the fact that street culture changes so rapidly. This allows the gang to offer something new to the reporter, who in turn will be able to sell it to a producer, who in turn will sell it to a sponsor and the general public.

Some Concluding Remarks

Both today and in the past, gangs have received a good deal of media attention. Yet what is striking about the media's coverage of gangs is how similar it is. As discussed at length in this chapter, there are two sets of reasons why media stories on gangs are very similar. The first set involves certain professional and business interests among the various components of the media that, along with some technical problems, influence stories on gangs so that they assume a similar form and content. The second set pertains to the fact that the gang members themselves influence the form and content of the stories about them in order to maximize their own interests. Thus, the gangs and the media have established a relationship that ultimately helps both to maintain a status position within society. Together they have reinforced the folkloric myth of gangs within American culture. Of course, it is important to emphasize that this myth is one that carries a negative image. It is one that has demonic qualities. For gangs ultimately are depicted as not only physically threatening average, law-abiding citizens, but also as undermining the morals and values of the society as a whole. They are carriers of moral disease within the social body. It is this image, an image based on personal and group fear, that has excited the interest of the general public; and it is this image that has reinforced the status of gangs within American culture.

Although the media present gangs as demonic, the organs of public opinion actually participate with gangs in a mutually beneficial exchange relationship that does not contribute to the elimination of gangs. Gangs in the media constitute a sustaining cultural myth, a myth predicated on shared cultural images and distortions of actual social reality. The media distort gang operations in several ways. First, the media emphasize the violence associated with gangs and the violent nature of gang members; but while violence does occur involving gang members, it is less central to gangs (or their members) than the media would lead one to believe. Second, gangs are not exclusively a nonwhite phenomenon, as the media's portrayal would suggest. Although poor nonwhite communities have produced the largest number of gangs, poor white communities have had gangs in the past and continue to produce gangs. This study reports on Irish gangs, but there are, for example, Italian and Appalachian white gangs as well. Third, poor communities are no more socially disorganized than other communities and no less capable of establishing civic control. Finally, the depiction of promiscuous nonwhite women entrapping upright white men has a long history in the American imagination and speaks more to white racial and sexual fantasies than to anything that happens in gangs.[32] The findings in this study suggest that gangs are a commodity, whose depiction produces value for those who work in the media industry. Because the general public is interested in understanding gangs, a story that exploits that interest can produce revenues for the media business and money, mobility, status, and power for the reporters involved. This is why reporters want the so-called "experts on gangs" to tell the truth, but want them to do so within the context of images that create interest among the general public: sex, drugs, crime, and violence. As with the first gangs, the western outlaws, this folkloric myth of gangs is a distorted picture of them.

Conclusion

> *But that is the provoking thing about these people: they foist*
> *this barbarism on us, and then try to make us content with it*
> *by having us adopt their own mass-man inability to distin-*
> *guish between things. We are to end by no longer knowing*
> *that the whole of their "technical comfort" amounts to noth-*
> *ing more than one gigantic swindle, a shabby little ersatz-*
> *life, and that the mass-produced amenities they are providing*
> *us are about as much like the genuine article as aniline colors*
> *are like a rainbow.*
>
> Friedrich Reck-Malleczewen, *Diary of a Man in Despair*
> (February 1942)

There has been a continual interest on the part of the general public and social scientists alike in understanding the gang phenomenon in the United States. For the most part, this interest stems from a desire to control the crime associated with gangs. Yet despite all the research that has been done and all the programs that have been instituted to combat their growth and activity, gangs have vigorously persisted. As the evidence and analysis presented in this study show, gangs persist in part because the gangs themselves make concerted organizational efforts to ensure their own survival, and in part because public policymakers (including social scientists) either fail to understand gangs or find themselves in a policy quagmire. Let us review some of the issues related to this assessment.

The Individual

As I have shown throughout this book, we in the social science and public policy communities have not fully understood gangs. To begin with, we have failed adequately to understand the individuals who are in gangs. Much too often we have thought of gang members as the lowest of the lower class, individuals with low intelligence, psychological disorders (like sadism), and/or no initiative to work for a living. This view is simply not accurate. A great range of individuals are in gangs, but the vast majority are quite intelligent and are capable of developing and executing creative enterprises. We have failed to see these traits mainly because when agents of society meet gang members, it is usually in situations where the gang member, being cautious and untrusting, assumes a reserved or defensive posture that camouflages his capabilities. In addition, because gang members are often involved in activities that society has labeled illegal or illegitimate, the social and policy science community is reluctant to view them as being similar to the law-abiding "best and brightest" in our society. Maintaining the contrast between the "deviant" gang member and the "normal" young adult supports the existing social system and the ideology of inequality that justifies it.[1]

The idea that gang members are more likely to suffer from some psychiatric disorder (particularly sadistic behavior) than other members of the society is another fallacy.[2] Certainly some gang members display symptoms of personality disorders, but their number is usually lower than that found among the general population, because the gangs themselves, in effect, screen their membership. Simply put, most gangs want to eliminate or at least limit the number of individuals who display mental disorders, because they are unpredictable and create too many problems for the organization. What has occurred is that social observers have generally mistaken toughness (physical aggressive behavior), resolve (lack of remorse), and open defiance as indicators of sadistic behavioral tendencies. A more accurate interpretation rests on the understanding that gang members grew up and live in communities in which the socioeconomic environment has produced a great deal of aggressive and violent behavior; thus a given gang member's display of aggressive traits or his involvement in violent exchanges is not necessarily pathological; rather, it is appropriate behavior in an environment whose socioeconomic conditions are pathological.

A third misconception about gang members is that they have no initiative, are lazy, and do not want to work for a living. While some gang members do have some or all of these traits, the vast majority of gang members are quite energetic and are eager to acquire many of the same things that most members of American society want: money, material possessions, power, and prestige. Indeed, because they want the "good life," they energetically seek entrepreneurial opportunities that might lead them to it. Although their behavior is often described as "hustling" or preying, it is different only in scale, not in kind, from competitive behavior observable in the corporate world. Although gang members do not possess the traits of self-denial or worldly asceticism, they do share an important part of what Weber called the "spirit of capitalism,"[3] the drive to accumulate capital, and this drive reinforces their resolve to compete strenuously in various economic markets in order to improve their socio-economic condition and possibly even attain substantial wealth.

Another misconception is that gang members are resistant to social programs that would alter their association with gangs and criminal activities. In truth, gang members are not resistant to social programs in general, but only to those programs designed to control their behavior, provide them with no more than low-level vocational skills, and take them out of competition in the larger entrepreneurial market. In other words, they are resistant to programs that attempt to control their behavior and offer them little in return.

Finally, it is a gross oversimplification to attribute all gang members' reasons for joining a gang to any one motive, such as the lack of a father figure, the desire to have fun, or submission to intimidation. Gangs are composed of individuals who join for a wide variety of reasons. If there is one pattern in the evidence concerning gang involvement, it is that individuals make a rational choice when deciding to join a gang, stay in a gang, or rejoin a gang. Each individual's choice is based on many factors, but, by a substantial margin, the one that is foremost is the assessment of what is best for the individual at the time.

The United States, which often prides itself as the bastion of individualism, has produced a pure form of its own individualism:[4] a person of staunch self-reliance and self-confidence whose directed goals match those of the greater society and whose toughness and defiant stance challenge all who would threaten him. Ironically, in the defiant individualist gang member, American society has found it difficult to control its own creation.

Gangs as Organizations

Like *band, crowd,* and *mob,* the term *gang* labels collective behavior that frightens members of society. Although social scientists and public policy analysts employ the term *gang* (sometimes in a rather cavalier fashion) to designate organized behavior of some type, most have treated the gang as a loosely structured collection of individuals. As the data in this study indicate, however, gangs are more than loose temporary associations.

They are collectives in which the interaction of individuals, both leadership and rank and file, is organized and governed by a set of rules and roles. In short, they are organizations. Unlike other organizations, though, gangs function without a bureaucracy and this has tended to obscure their other organizational characteristics. In addition, most observers have failed to articulate the variations in both the kind of organization gangs employ and their level of sophistication. Some gangs appear not to be very well organized, but we should not conclude this disorganization is the nature of all gangs. Rather, like other organizations, gangs thrive and decline and their ability to plan and act is affected by the phase of the organizational life cycle in which they find themselves.

Ultimately, the fact that gangs have not been understood as organizations has crucially impaired our understanding of their behavior. As an organization, the gang sees its primary concern to be organizational survival. This goal influences the recruitment of members, with a gang being careful neither to admit individuals with questionable credentials nor to admit too large a number for the governance structure to control. Organizational survival also influences a gang to provide leadership, roles, and rules to govern the interactions of the membership, as well as incentives for continuing membership. The trickiest area for gangs to negotiate with their members is that of personal freedom. Gangs as organizations must establish group cohesion and discipline while at the same time allowing individuals the freedom to pursue their own goals. The navigation of these requirements is a delicate task, but all gangs realize that they are dealing with defiant individualist characters and that the organization cannot survive unless it allows individuals the freedom to come and go. Outside observers sometimes note that a relatively large number of members are leaving a gang and conclude that the gang is dissolving. In most cases, this conclusion is premature, because some members depart for a while and return at a later time. Allowing members to take a leave of absence does not signify the dissolution of the gang; not only will a significant proportion return, but the organization can cite its flexibility as one of its promos for recruiting new members.[5] In fact, gangs that must use physical intimidation to keep their members are in a state of organizational decline and it is only a matter of time before they will cease to exist.

What happens to gang members after they leave the gang? Some members have been extremely lucky at one of their business ventures and have saved enough money to live comfortably for a time. Some former members move on to other organizations that operate illegal businesses and make a reasonable income. Some wind up in jail, others die young from some type of accident, such as a drug overdose, a violent confrontation, or a medical problem. Most, however, lose some of the will to resist the pressure to assume the socioeconomic positions of their parents, and they finally take the jobs that they had dreaded taking all along. Ironically, they will have grown tired of dealing with the hardships, as well as the fear of death, that accompany gang life, and face the challenge of dealing with the fear of "social death" that accompanies the dead-end occupations that have trapped their parents and nearly all their neighbors in their low-income communities. Orlando Patterson uses the term "social death" in his penetrating analysis of slavery, but I believe it can also be used to describe those who work in the tertiary or secondary labor markets, whose lives are but routines of managing scarcity and the feelings associated with self-worth and dignity in the presentation of self in everyday life, but whose hope for improvements in each of these areas has been lost. As this relates to gang members who have gotten tired of gang life and taken one of these types of jobs, it will be seen that the air of defiant individualism that these members possessed has been maintained in the presentation of self, but that the fire inside the individual to act out defiant individualism has been reduced to mere embers.[6]

As members come and go, the fate of any particular gang depends on how well it is able to manage its internal affairs and outside pressures. Some gangs maintain themselves for generations, as have many of the Chicano and several of the Irish gangs in this study. Other gangs fall apart as a result of internal dissension or outside pressures from other gangs and/or the authorities. Still others are taken over by competitor gangs, just as small businesses are taken over by larger ones. What most people have not understood very well is that gangs as organizations have their own survival dynamic. As individuals move on, or the pressures from the outside mount, the gang as an organization will make every effort to revitalize itself through recruitment and/or structural reorganization. At one time a gang may be thriving. As conditions change and it encounters difficulties in fulfilling all its organizational responsibilities, it may stagnate or begin to decline. It may then regroup and thrive again, or continue to decline, or simply perish. In other words, a gang's effort to survive can produce different states of organizational development, and these states can be quite fluid. Ultimately, the fate of any one gang will depend on how well it is able to recruit individuals who can help the organization; effectively manage individuals inside the organization; establish authority and become a viable and efficient economic organization; maintain good relations with its local community; and establish linkages with social institutions outside the local community by constructing mutual exchange relationships with certain individuals in them.

Two remaining issues regarding organization need to be addressed. The first has to do with the impact of ethnicity on gang organization and behavior. I began this study with the intention of examining what differences exist between gangs of different ethnic groups, and for that reason studied gangs whose membership was composed of a number of different ethnic groups. As discussed at various points above, I found that in some cases involving Irish and Chicano gangs, ethnicity was a factor in influencing their behavior. More generally, however, I found that ethnic differences were less powerful in explaining why an individual gang member acted the way he did, or a gang acted the way it did, than were the dynamics associated with organizational matters. Ethnic differences were generally (but not exclusively) muted as a result of the various organizational concerns and operations that have been discussed.

As many readers familiar with the research literature on gangs may be aware, the gangs described in this study seem to be more sophisticated than those described in the past. Thus the second issue has to do with whether the gangs of today are becoming more sophisticated than they were in the past or whether my gangs are atypical of gangs in general. First, it is important to reemphasize that among the gangs I studied there were varying levels of sophistication within gang organizations over time; and that the level of sophistication within particular gangs at a particular time was dependent on a number of contingent factors that have been discussed throughout the book. In fact, as has been highlighted in this analysis, gangs unable to develop or maintain a sophisticated organization simply withered and died. However, I also believe that the gangs of today are more sophisticated than they were in the past. In my estimation this has occurred because structural conditions in the economy have encouraged it. First, because there have been fewer opportunities for males from poor and working-class backgrounds to enter the legal labor market and become socioeconomically mobile,[7] there has been a tendency for teenage males to continue their involvement in gangs well into adulthood.[8] Second, the gangs of today have had the experience of other gangs, particularly other organized crime units, to learn from and emulate. Third, a number of factors have caused the traditional (primarily Italian) Mafia to lose its total control over many of the illegal markets in large urban areas. This has opened up new economic markets and encouraged other groups (including the youth of these groups) to turn their creative energies toward capitalizing on these new opportunities in the illegal economy.

In sum, if we hope to understand gang behavior and persistence, we must attend to gangs' organizational ability to regenerate themselves, to their organizational capabilities and sophistication. Policies aimed principally at individuals will not have much impact on gangs. Only policies that affect both the individual and the organization's ability to operate can pose a serious challenge to gang persistence.

The Gang and Its Community

People who live in areas in which there are no gangs are sometimes baffled by the local residents' responses to gangs. When outsiders learn of residents' organizing to combat gang activity or pleading with local authorities to do something about gang violence, the outsiders are generally sympathetic. On other occasions, however, outsiders hear that local residents are complaining that the police are using unnecessary force in combating gang activity, and it is difficult for outsiders to grasp community sympathy for gangs. Unable to reconcile the two responses and confused by continual altercations, outsiders usually withdraw from any type of involvement with events in low-income communities. What these outsiders do not understand is that inhabitants of low-income neighborhoods will always be ambivalent about gangs. There are a variety of reasons for this ambivalence (see chapter 6), five of which bear mention here. First, many of the gang members are the children of residents, and while residents do not want to see their children killed in gang warfare, they do not want to see them incarcerated either. Second, gangs are often the residents' best protection against people who would prey on them. So while residents may not like the gang violence that occurs, the fears associated with urban dangers and the protection provided by the gangs have created a bond between residents and the gangs.[9] Third, some residents identify with the gangs because they themselves or relatives were gang members when they were younger. While these adults may disapprove of what the gang members are doing at times, they cannot wholeheartedly reject them because when they look at the gang members they see themselves. Fourth, residents are reluctant to support the eradication of gangs because gangs have existed for so long that they have become community social institutions. Thus, like the Little League, the gang is one of the institutional options (there are others) that a low-income boy can use to make the rite of passage to adulthood.[10] Fifth, residents often believe that if the authorities did not consider there to be a "gang problem," their communities would not receive any attention or resources at all.

Finally, residents of low-income communities are also ambivalent about gangs for reasons that have more to do with general perceptions of community control than with the gangs' behavior. When residents feel they are losing control of their neighborhood to the gangs, they will support the authorities' efforts to counteract gang activity. However, if the authorities' efforts make residents feel they are losing control of their community to the authorities, they will criticize the authorities' zealousness and appear to be siding with the gangs. In essence, the changing of their position is their effort to act in their own interest.

The Gang and Society

Throughout this book, I have indicated how gangs emerge from low-income communities to establish linkages with a number of important institutions that govern American society. For agents of the various institutions examined in this study, there are four incentives to establish links with gangs: money, political power, job mobility, and stress reduction.

Most obviously, an outsider can accrue personal gain by developing a relationship with gangs and participating in their illegal business activities. However, there are other financial incentives for developing a cooperative relationship with gangs. For example, street-level bureaucrats in community organizations know that their budgets depend on their program results, which are in turn dependent on eliciting the cooperation of the gangs. Similarly, branches of law enforcement know that their budgets for anti-gang programs hinge on obtaining the cooperation of gangs. For various branches of the media, gangs represent a commodity to be sold, an endeavor that also requires gang cooperation.

For other government officials and some politicians, the cooperation of gangs, while usually not pivotal, can be helpful in efforts to gain and maintain political power. Government bureaucrats whose official duties entail dealing with gangs find that establishing a working relationship with the gangs helps them do—or appear to be doing—an excellent job, which creates possible opportunities for them to move up the organizational ladder. Other agents who have to work with gangs find that developing a cooperative relationship with them has the advantages of making their work easier and reducing their on-the-job stress.

Of course, gangs also have incentives for developing close relationships with various social institutions. The two most important incentives here are money and political favors (broadly defined), both of which are understood to be pivotal to the gang's ability to function as an efficient and vibrant organization.

Although the incentives for developing a good relationship were there for both the gang and the agents of these institutions, the exact nature of these linkages was the result of the social negotiations that occurred between the gangs and these agents. There were two ways in which links were established. One was through direct negotiations. In these instances, a representative of one of the institutions initiated contact with the gangs concerning some type of cooperation. However, there were other times when the negotiations were more subtle and indirect. In these situations, a negotiated relationship was achieved through the natural interaction of both parties; that is, through the process of everyday interaction between the representative of a particular institution and the gangs he or she had contact with, a relationship was negotiated that met with the satisfaction of both.

In most of these instances of cooperation, the agents associated with the various institutions described in this study saw nothing wrong with their actions. They saw themselves, not as acting improperly, but merely as rationally realizing their broader interests. This interpretation, however, ignores two profound consequences of such actions. First, the agents' behavior only reinforces in gang members their defiant individualist belief that the world works along Social Darwinist principles, that individuals are out for their own interests, and that each individual is pitted against the other. Second, these cooperative relationships spread the Social Darwinist message to young kids who are not yet in a gang, but who are prospective members, and this aids the gang's recruiting process.

Finally, as the various agencies and institutions become more entangled with gangs, they cease to focus on eliminating them and become more focused on merely controlling them. Ultimately, this becomes instrumental in enhancing their persistence.

Gangs and Social Policy

As long as gangs have been around, public policies have sought to counteract their activity. Yet, as we know, these policies have had only a minimal impact. Among a host of reasons for the failure of public policy in this area, four seem most crucial.

First, the development and implementation of a comprehensive anti-gang policy has been stalled by the lack of a broad public demand for such a policy. Because gangs, for the most part, operate in geographic areas that do not affect middle- and upper-class people, the general public is usually apathetic. Only on those occasions when gang activity spills over into middle- or upper-class areas is there an outcry that something be done. Yet such events are infrequent, and the complaints of middle- and upper-class citizens are neither sufficiently prolonged nor intense enough to pressure government to begin the process of developing a comprehensive policy. As a result, policy is fragmented and unlikely to prove effective.

Second, while everyone seems to acknowledge that poverty and lack of job opportunities are instrumental in the formation and maintenance of gangs, no one has seriously addressed either of these two problems. Sporadic efforts at job-training programs have been largely cosmetic. These programs accommodate only a small number of those who live in low-income areas, and these programs have often provided training for jobs in which there are few openings, or jobs that resemble those working-class jobs held by the participants' parents—exactly the jobs they are trying to avoid.

Not knowing what to do, or unwilling to do what would be required to ameliorate urban poverty, public policymakers focus on tougher law enforcement procedures and longer prison sentences. This strategy, however, has had and will continue to have difficulty reducing gang activity for two reasons: improved law enforcement procedures will, over time, be compromised by the working relationships that are developed (for reasons mentioned in chapter 8) between gang members and the various government and law enforcement agents; and longer jail terms will not affect gang persistence because, as described in this and other studies, gang members simply reproduce their gangs in prison.

Third, many people in policy positions are concerned that in trying to solve the problem of gangs, they do not create larger problems for the society. This caution, though perhaps well-intentioned, has tended to inhibit the development of innovative, far-reaching policies and programs; to play it safe, policymakers shy away from proposals whose negative consequences are difficult to determine or are unpredictable. As one policy planner in New York said to me:

> You got to be prudent in how you approach gangs, because in instituting social control, you don't want to attack the right to public assembly. I mean, you don't want to wound the Bill of Rights, because then a lot of people would be hurt. Then there's the question of inequality. You don't want to end inequality because that's the reason the U.S. was able to get all that it has. As we often remind ourselves here, "You got to make sure that in controlling the pest, you don't develop a pesticide that poisons you."

Interestingly, this planner used the word *prudent* in the same way that Edmund Burke used it to warn against governments instituting rapid change. Burke was also concerned that rapid change had the potential to create consequences for which the whole society would suffer.[11]

Finally, policy analysts shy away from investigating why existing policies have failed to control gangs. The reason for this is generally that either the issues are potentially too sensitive, and people do not want to open a social and political Pandora's box, or the problem extends into so many areas of American life that it seems overwhelming. In one of the last interviews I conducted for this study, I was talking with a government official involved in developing policy to control crime. This was my third formal interview with him (although we had talked many times on the telephone), and over the years we had developed a friendly relationship. The interview had lasted twenty-five minutes, and I had just asked him what I thought was my last question. While I was checking my notes to see if there was anything else I wanted to ask, he leaned back, reflected for a moment, and said:

> You know, I've often thought about a lot of the questions you asked me today. There's very few that I really haven't thought about. To solve the gang problem in this country, there is just so much that would need to be changed. There are just so many areas of everyday life that would need to be changed; there's inequality, there's incompetence, there's corruption. All these years I've put in and I just don't know where to start.

The comments by this policy analyst not only depict the frustration and complexity of the situation, they also reflect a troublesome predicament—a predicament that has developed as gangs have been woven into the structural and cultural fabric of American urban society. Thus policymakers, in trying to keep the other parts of the fabric from unraveling, have had little success in solving the gang problem.

Appendix:
Summary of Gangs Studied

Name of Gang	Ethnicity	Leadership Structure	Group Age
Dukes	Latino	V/H	12–19
Steel Flowers	white	I/H/V	14–22
Terminators	black/Latino	V/H	12–31
4 Aces	white	I/V/H	15–24
Savage Hands	Latino/black	V	14–30
RRs	Latino	I/V/H	13–30
Green Street	white	I/V/H	15–26
Savage Profits	Latino/black	V/H	13–21
Spears	Latino	I/H	14–30
Silk Irons	black/Latino	V	14–35
Vandals	black	I/H/V	15–31
Pink Eagles	Latino	V	14–30
Drums	Latino	V/H	15–34
Lord Squares	Latino/black	V/H	13–28
Ivory Bats	black	V	15–26
Royces	black/Latino	V/H	13–29
Rockers	black	I/V/H	15–37
Diamond Pack	Latino/black	V	14–32
Scorpions	Latino	I/H/V	14–20
Black Rose	white	I	15–17
Black Widows	black	I/V	14–18
Dancing Devils	Latino/black	V/H	13–18
Black Bullets	black/Latino	V/H/V	12–41
Titans	Latino	I/H	11–23
Fire Ice	Latino	I/H	13–16
Deacons	black	I	14–21
Bangers	black	V/H	15–23
Royal Dons	Latino	I/H	12–20

Name of Gang	Ethnicity	Leadership Structure	Group Age
Pearls	Latino	I	14–16
Ravens	white	I/V	15–20
Birdville	Latino	I	13–17
Jones Park	Latino	I/V/H	14–42
Snow Tigers	white	I/H	14–18
T-Men	Latino	I/V	14–19
"O" Street	Latino	V	14–31
Fulton	Latino	V	14–27
Stone Tower	white	I/H	15–22

NOTE: All the gang names used in this table are fictitious. The ethnic identifier "black" includes African-Americans and Jamaicans. The identifier "Latino" includes Chicanos (Mexican-Americans and Mexicans), Puerto Ricans, Dominicans, Salvadorans, and Nicaraguans. The letters *I, V,* and *H* refer to the influential, vertical, and horizontal organizational structures described in chapter 3. The order in which the letters appear represents the sequence of organizational structures adopted by the identified gang. Additional demographic detail about gang membership is not presented in view of objections by informants who indicated that specific description of ethnic background and locale could compromise their identities with law enforcement agencies, violating my agreement of confidentiality with the informants.

Notes

Introduction

1. See *The Life and Tragic Death of Jesse James, the Western Desperado* (Cliffside Park, N.J.: Barclay & Co., 1886), by "(one who dare not now disclose his name)."

2. See Stephen Tatum, *Inventing Billy The Kid: Visions of the Outlaw in America, 1881–1981* (Albuquerque: University of New Mexico Press, 1982).

3. See Amy Bridges, "Becoming American: The Working Classes in the United States before the Civil War," in Ira Katznelson and Aristide R. Zolberg, eds., *Working Class Formation: Nineteenth Century Patterns in Western Europe and the United States* (Princeton: Princeton University Press, 1986), pp. 157–96.

4. Daniel Bell points this out in "Crime as an American Way of Life: A Queer Ladder of Social Mobility," in *The End of Ideology: On the Exhaustion of Political Ideas in the Fifties* (Cambridge, Mass.: Harvard University Press, 1988). Most people identify Sicilians and Italians as being the ethnic groups involved with organized crime; however, there were a variety of ethnic groups represented. See Frederic Thrasher, *The Gang: A Study of 1303 Gangs in Chicago* (Chicago: University of Chicago Press, 1928); Herbert Asbury, *The Gangs of New York: An Informal History of the Underworld* (Garden City, N.Y.: Garden City Publishing Co., 1927).

5. In the beginning, the term *gang* was mostly used to designate those organizations involved in crime, and the people who participated in them were called gangsters. Later the term *mob* was used interchangeably with *gang* to refer to formal groups involved in crime. Asbury uses the terms

gang and *gangsters,* whereas Thrasher begins to use the terms *gang* and *mob* interchangeably. This is because Thrasher was dealing with formal youth groups and their relationship to formal crime organizations and found it analytically useful to utilize both terms. Later still, the term *syndicate* was utilized to describe those groups that were involved in organized crime.

6. On the linkage between the end of the frontier and symbolizations of the city, see Richard Slotkin, *The Fatal Environment: The Myth of the Frontier in the Age of Industrialization, 1800–1890* (New York: Atheneum Press, 1985).

7. By saying "first set," I do not mean to imply chronology, but rather the nature of the researcher's focus. In each of the two sets that I discuss there have been major studies in various decades.

8. Richard A. Cloward and Lloyd B. Ohlin, *Delinquency and Opportunity: A Theory of Delinquent Gangs* (New York: Free Press, 1960).

9. Albert K. Cohen, *Delinquent Boys: The Culture of the Gang* (Glencoe, Ill.: Free Press, 1955).

10. Herbert A. Bloch and Arthur Niederhoffer, *The Gang: A Study in Adolescent Behavior* (New York: Philosophical Library, 1958).

11. Walter B. Miller, "Lower Class Culture as a Generating Milieu of Gang Delinquency," *Journal of Social Issues* 14 (Fall 1958): 519.

12. Yablonsky's study of violence and gangs in New York found a large number of gang leaders who were sociopathic, and based on these findings, he offered his "near group theory" of gang behavior. In this theory, Yablonsky argues that gangs are a "near group" in that they lack the cohesion, norms, consensus, and consistent membership to be considered a formal group. See Lewis Yablonsky, *The Violent Gang* (New York: Macmillan, 1966) and his "The Delinquent Gang as a Near-Group," *Social Problems* 7 (Fall 1959): 108–17. Short and Strodtbeck investigated many of Thrasher's propositions about various aspects of gang life and developed their theoretical statement concerning the impact of group processes in the development and persistence of gang delinquency. See James F. Short, Jr., and Fred L. Strodtbeck, *Group Process and Gang Delinquency* (Chicago: University of Chicago Press, 1965). See also Walter B. Miller's "White Gangs," *Trans-Action* 6 (September 1969): 11–26, and *Violence by Youth Gangs and Youth Groups as a Crime Problem in Major American Cities* (Washington, D.C.: Department of Justice, 1975). And see Irving A. Spergel, *Racketville, Slumtown and Haulberg* (Chicago: University of Chicago Press, 1964).

13. See Thrasher, *The Gang,* pp. 5–22. The quotations are taken from page 20.

14. The three most important studies of this type are William Foote

Whyte, *Street Corner Society* (Chicago: University of Chicago Press, 1943); Gerald D. Suttles, *The Social Order of the Slum: Ethnicity and Territory in the Inner City* (Chicago: University of Chicago Press, 1968); and Ruth Horowitz, *Honor and the American Dream: Culture and Identity in a Chicano Community* (New Brunswick: Rutgers University Press, 1983).

15. The first of these studies was the work of Joan W. Moore in her very important book *Homeboys: Gangs, Drugs, and Prisons in the Barrios of Los Angeles* (Philadelphia: Temple University Press, 1978). See also her "Isolation and Stigmatization in the Development of an Underclass: The Case of Chicano Gangs in East Los Angeles," *Social Problems* 33 (October 1985): 1–12. Three of the more recent studies are John M. Hagedorn, *People and Folks: Gangs, Crime and the Underclass in a Rustbelt City* (Chicago: Lakeview Press, 1988); James Diego Vigil, *Barrio Gangs: Street Life and Identity in Southern California* (Austin: University of Texas Press, 1988); and Mercer Sullivan, *Getting Paid: Youth Crime and Work in the Inner City* (Ithaca, N.Y.: Cornell University Press, 1989).

16. A number of new studies include discussions of gang organization, but they are not asking the question of what the nature of the organization is and what accounts for its successes and declines over time. Like many of the earlier studies, a large number of these studies have used gangs as an independent variable to explain crime and delinquency patterns and thus focused more on the consequences of gang actions rather than on the internal structure and the social dynamics of the organization itself. See, for example, G. David Curry and Irving A. Spergel, "Gang Homicide, Delinquency and Community," *Criminology* 26 (August 1988): 381–406; Jeffrey Fagan, "The Social Organization of Drug Use and Drug Dealing among Urban Gangs," *Criminology* 27 (November 1989): 633–70. Short and Strodtbeck's *Group Process and Gang Delinquency* is one of those pieces of research (there are a few others) that falls between neat categories. The authors provide data and analyses on the internal dynamics of the gang organization, which they use to explain crime and delinquency. However, for the most part they focus on those factors that explain the commission of violence and crime.

17. There are a number of studies that have argued that the gang has very few organizational qualities—that it has loose cohesion and a changing leadership and is held together by what Thrasher calls an *esprit de corps*. See Yablonsky, *The Violent Gang;* Malcolm W. Klein and L. Y. Crawford, "Groups, Gangs and Cohesiveness," in James F. Short, Jr., ed., *Gang Delinquency and Delinquency Subcultures* (New York: Harper & Row, 1968), pp. 256–72; and Malcolm W. Klein, *Street Gangs and Street Workers* (Englewood Cliffs, N.J.: Prentice-Hall, 1971). Some studies ac-

knowledge that some leadership exists, but find it less formal and variable. See Horowitz, *Honor and the American Dream,* pp. 97–101, which is quite an interesting study, and one that is not easy to categorize, because although Horowitz found gang organization related to friendship and kinship, she also found some formal structure as well. However, the argument of these studies is not entirely accurate today, and from the interviews that I did with gang members of past generations, it may well not have been true for a large number of gangs at the time the authors wrote.

18. See Hagedorn, *People and Folks,* pp. 110–14; Horowitz, *Honor and the American Dream,* pp. 177–97; and Irving Spergel, "Violent Gangs in Chicago: In Search of Social Policy," *Social Services Review* 58 (June 1984): 199–225.

19. See James F. Short, Jr., introduction to the abridged edition of Thrasher's *The Gang,* pp. xxi–xxii.

Chapter One

1. See Ruth Rosner Kornhauser, *Social Sources of Delinquency: An Appraisal of Analytic Models* (Chicago: University of Chicago Press, 1978).

2. Two of the more recent works on gangs are Vigil, *Barrio Gangs,* and Hagedorn, *People and Folks.*

3. In *The Gang,* Frederic Thrasher began with the theoretical premise that social disorganization causes a weakening of social institutions, which in turn creates the conditions for the development of gang crime and delinquency. Many of the contemporary researchers into gangs have accepted this premise as well. See Fagan, "Social Organization of Drug Use and Drug Dealing among Urban Gangs," pp. 661–62; Curry and Spergel, "Gang Homicide, Delinquency, and Community," passim.

4. See Kornhauser, *Social Sources of Delinquency,* pp. 51–61.

5. This argument is stated most clearly in Suttles, *Social Order of the Slum;* and Thrasher, *The Gang.* It is also advanced by Kornhauser, *Social Sources of Delinquency,* pp. 59–61.

6. Erich Fromm and Michael Maccoby, *Social Character in a Mexican Village* (Englewood Cliffs, N.J.: Prentice-Hall, 1970), p. 16.

7. Erich Fromm, *Escape from Freedom* (New York: Avon, 1965), pp. 304–5.

8. See Edward C. Banfield, *The Moral Basis of a Backward Society* (Glencoe, Ill.: Free Press, 1958).

9. Thomas Hobbes, *Leviathan,* ed. Michael Oakeshott (Oxford: Basil Blackwell, 1947; paperback ed., New York, 1962), pt. 1, ch. 13, p. 82.

The page numbers given in subsequent citations of *Leviathan* all refer to this edition.

10. Ibid., pp. 84–88. Cf. also Terrence Des Pres, *The Survivor: An Anatomy of Life in the Death Camps* (New York: Oxford University Press, 1976), pp. 76, 201–3. Of course, by mentioning that many of the traits of survivors of the Nazi concentration camps are similar to those found among gang members (or residents of low-income areas), I do not mean to imply that the latter face conditions similar to those faced by the inmates of concentration camps. Both have their own realities, but the will to survive these realities has produced similar traits.

11. See Paul E. Willis, *Learning to Labor* (New York: Columbia University Press, 1977). The young males in Willis's British study were all aware of the types of jobs awaiting them, but unlike the American youth in the present study, they lacked a strong belief that it was possible to avoid these jobs. This difference between the low-income youth of the two countries is a result of the differences in the degree of class stratification and in the dominant ideologies that govern each system.

12. I am drawing on Weber's classic description of bureaucracy (see Talcott Parsons, ed., *Max Weber: The Theory of Social and Economic Organization* [New York: Free Press, 1964], pp. 329–41). Weber stresses that an administrative staff is a central feature of bureaucracy. He also specifies the attributes of the administrative staff and its role in building authority. One of the important elements of my definition of a gang is the statement/premise that a gang pursues its goals irrespective of whether its actions are legal or not. The concepts of legal and illegal have no effect on the thought and behavior of its members. Thus my theory incorporates one of the elements in Klein's theory—involvement in illegal acts— and is at odds with Jeffrey Fagan's proposal to include groups that do not undertake illegal acts, such as the Guardian Angels and Chinese secret societies. Fagan's suggestion runs too high a risk of including simple youth groups that may contain gang members but lack the elements that would make them a gang. See Klein, *Street Gangs and Street Workers*, p. 13; Fagan, "Social Organization of Drug Use and Drug Dealing among Urban Gangs," p. 643.

13. See Walter B. Miller, "Gangs, Groups and Serious Youth Crime," in David Shichor and Delos Kelly, eds., *Critical Issues in Juvenile Delinquency* (Lexington, Mass.: Lexington Books, 1980). He also sees the need for a group to have a formal authority structure if it is to be called a gang.

14. This aspect of the theory has been influenced by and draws on the work of rational-choice theory. A work that has made a significant contribution to linking sociological concerns to rational-choice theory is Mi-

chael Hechter, *Principles of Group Solidarity* (Berkeley: University of California Press, 1987).

15. See Ralf Dahrendorf's discussion of the concept of "life chances" in his *Life Chances: Approaches to Social and Political Theory* (Chicago: University of Chicago Press, 1979), pp. 45–53, esp. pp. 49–50.

16. The New York City Youth Board uses the terms *vertical* and *horizontal* (but not *influential*) to describe the organization of certain gangs in New York. However, its use of these terms is different from the way I am using them. Where I employ these terms to describe the structure of authority in gangs, the Youth Board uses them primarily to describe age differentiation and territorial divisions in gang organizations. See *Reaching the Fighting Gang* (New York: New York City Youth Board, 1960), pp. 22–24.

17. This is similar to one of Weber's motives for obedience, what he calls material interests and calculations of advantage. See Max Weber, *Economy and Society: An Outline of Interpretive Sociology* (Berkeley: University of California Press, 1978), 1: 212–13.

18. Obedience achieved through negative sanctions, intimidation, and other forms of coercion has generally been regarded by organizational theorists as being effective in conjunction with some degree of socialization by people to accept the rules of the game. Through this socialization, people can rationalize their obedience without the shame or guilt associated with complying for fear of being punished. See Daniel Katz and Robert L. Kahn, *The Social Psychology of Organization,* 2d ed. (New York: Wiley, 1978), pp. 302–7. The Milgram experiments are examples of this rationalization, because in these experiments, the subjects rationalized their behavior by saying they were being deferential to the authority figure. See Stanley Milgram, *Obedience to Authority* (New York: Harper & Row, 1969).

19. I have purposely avoided the use of the term *controls,* because gangs are often integrated into the neighborhoods in which they operate but do not control these neighborhoods. In other words, there are many gangs that operate in a single neighborhood where no one gang has control, but all are integrated (or need to be integrated) with the residents in the area.

20. Hobsbawm goes on to say: "Admittedly almost anyone who joins issue with the oppressors and the State is likely to be regarded as a victim, a hero or both. Once a man is on the run, therefore, he is naturally protected by the peasants and by the weight of local conventions which stands for 'our' law—custom, blood-feud or whatever it might be—against 'theirs', and 'our' justice against that of the rich." See E. J. Hobsbawm, *Primitive*

Rebels: Studies in Archaic Forms of Social Movements in the 19th and 20th Centuries (New York: Norton, 1959), p. 16.

21. There are a large number of other differences between the social bandit and the gang. For example, Hobsbawm states: "The fundamental pattern of banditry, as I have tried to sketch it here, is almost universally found in certain conditions. It is rural, not urban. The peasant societies in which it occurs know rich and poor, powerful and weak, rulers and ruled, but remain profoundly and tenaciously traditional, and pre-capitalist in structure." See Hobsbawm, *Primitive Rebels*, p. 23.

Chapter Two

1. See Thrasher, *The Gang;* Suttles, *Social Order of the Slum;* Hagedorn, *People and Folks.*

2. Of course, some of the studies cited here overlap these categories, and I have therefore placed them according to the major emphasis of the study. See Cloward and Ohlin, *Delinquency and Opportunity;* Hagedorn, *People and Folks;* Moore, *Homeboys;* Short and Strodtbeck, *Group Process and Gang Delinquency.*

3. Here again it is important to restate that many of these studies overlap the categories I have created, but I have attempted to identify them by what seems to be their emphasis. See Block and Niederhoffer, *The Gang;* Yablonsky, *The Violent Gang.*

4. See the qualifying statement in nn. 2 and 3 above. See Horowitz, *Honor and the American Dream;* Cohen, *Delinquent Boys;* Miller, "Lower Class Culture as a Generating Milieu of Gang Delinquency"; Vigil, *Barrio Gangs.*

5. See Jack Katz, *The Seduction of Crime: Moral and Sensual Attractions in Doing Evil* (New York: Basic Books, 1988), p. 9.

6. Although the present study is not a quantitative study, the finding reported here and the ones to follow are based on observations of, and conversations and formal interviews with, hundreds of gang members.

7. For a discussion of the political machine's role in providing psychological and financial support for poor immigrant groups, see Robert K. Merton, *Social Theory and Social Structure* (New York: Free Press, 1968), pp. 126–36. Also see William L. Riordan, *Plunkitt of Tammany Hall* (New York: Dutton, 1963).

8. There are numerous examples throughout the society of social clubs using the lodge or clubhouse as one of the incentives for gaining members. There are athletic clubs for the wealthy (like the University Club and the Downtown Athletic Club in New York), social clubs in ethnic

neighborhoods, the Elks and Moose clubs, the clubs of various veterans' associations, and tennis, yacht, and racket ball clubs.

9. See Anne Campbell, *Girls in the Gang* (New York: Basil Blackwell, 1987).

10. For the use of drugs as recreational, see Vigil, *Barrio Gangs;* and Fagan, "Social Organization of Drug Use and Drug Dealing among Urban Gangs," who reports varying degrees of drug use among various types of gangs. For studies that report the monitoring and/or prohibition of certain drugs by gangs, see Vigil, *Barrio Gangs,* on the prohibition of heroin use in Chicano gangs; and Thomas Mieczkowski, "Geeking Up and Throwing Down: Heroin Street Life in Detroit," *Criminology* 24 (November 1986): 645–66.

11. See Thrasher, *The Gang,* pp. 84–96. He also discusses the gang as a source of recreation.

12. See Moore, *Homeboys,* ch. 2; Horowitz, *Honor and the American Dream,* ch. 8; and Vigil, *Barrio Gangs;* Hagedorn, *People and Folks.*

13. For a discussion of these types of jobs, see Michael J. Piore, *Notes for a Theory of Labor Market Stratification,* Working Paper no. 95 (Cambridge, Mass.: Massachusetts Institute of Technology, 1972).

14. See Horowitz, *Honor and the American Dream;* and Ruth Horowitz and Gary Schwartz, "Honor, Normative Ambiguity and Gang Violence," *American Sociological Review* 39 (April 1974): 238–51. There are many other studies that could have been cited here. These two are given merely as examples.

15. The testing of potential gang members as to their fighting ability was also observed by Vigil. See his *Barrio Gangs,* pp. 54–55.

16. This quotation was recorded longhand, not tape-recorded.

17. I first met M.R. when he was in one of the gangs that I was hanging around with. He subsequently left the gang, and I stayed in touch with him by talking to him when our paths crossed on the street. This quotation is from a long conversation that I had with him during one of our occasional encounters.

18. See Frederic Thrasher, *The Gang,* pp. 66–67. A great number of studies take a similar position. I shall mention but a few. See Suttles, *Social Order of the Slum,* and Whyte, *Street Corner Society.* The work of Ruth Horowitz represents a modified exception to the other findings. While she does imply that gang members grow old and abandon their street lives, she also reports that involvement in gangs may last well into the thirties for individuals. See her *Honor and the American Dream,* pp. 177–97.

19. Some of these people have died from illnesses, food poisoning, and various accidents.

Chapter Three

1. Yablonsky, *The Violent Gang;* Klein, *Street Gangs and Street Workers.*

2. See New York City Youth Board, *Reaching the Fighting Gang;* Bloch and Niederhoffer, *The Gang;* R. Lincoln Keiser, *The Vice Lords: Warriors of the Streets* (New York: Holt, Rinehart & Winston, 1969), p. 16.

3. Although all but a few of the gangs changed leadership structures while I was observing them, nineteen of the thirty-seven gangs I studied (51 percent) had a "vertical/hierarchical" structure as their *primary* mode of organization during this time. More gangs are recorded as using the vertical/hierarchical type of structure in the Appendix, which reports the total number that employed it *at some time* during the period of study regardless of whether it was for a long or a short timespan.

4. Over the course of time, certain titles associated with positions of authority changed. Gangs are part of the street culture in urban areas, and street customs and language change rapidly. Some gangs used military titles like *"commandante"* or "colonel," for example; others used titles like "skywalker" for the president and "earthwalker" for the vice president. Irrespective of the title used by a gang at any particular time, however, the lines of authority and the duties associated with them are as described in the text.

5. Of the gangs studied, eight out of thirty-seven (22 percent) had a "horizontal/commission" type of leadership structure for most of the time I observed them. As pointed out in n. 3 above in connection with the figure for the vertical/hierarchical model, however, the number recorded here as possessing the horizontal/commission type of structure (eight) is lower than indicated in the Appendix (twenty-three), which reports the total number that employed it at some time during the study.

6. The commission form of government that some cities use is quite similar to what I have called the "horizontal" type of structure. For a discussion, see Demetrius Carley, *Urban Government* (Englewood Cliffs, N.J.: Prentice-Hall, 1976).

7. Ten out of the thirty-seven gangs (27 percent) had this type as their primary mode of operation during the time I studied them. As with the other two modes of organization (see nn. 3 and 5 above), the number of gangs identified as possessing this form (ten) does not equal the number given in the Appendix (twenty) because although many of the gangs employed other models of leadership too, they did not adopt them as their primary mode of operation during this time.

8. Weber, *Economy and Society,* pp. 246–47.

9. Ibid., p. 241.

10. Ibid.

11. Ibid., pp. 246–47.

12. Stability in the lines of authority is one of the elements that Philip Selznick has identified as necessary for the maintenance of an organizational system (see Selznick, "Foundations of the Theory of Organization," *American Sociological Review* 13 [February 1948]: 25–35).

13. See Keiser, *Vice Lords,* pp. 12–14. Although Keiser's description is of a Chicago gang, what he describes also applies to the gangs of New York. Also see Fagan, "Social Organization of Drug Use and Drug Dealing among Urban Gangs," which reports some gangs using a very hierarchical structured organization.

14. For a discussion of the Mafia as a means of economic mobility, see Bell's chapter, "Crime as an American Way of Life," in *End of Ideology,* pp. 127–50.

15. See Cloward and Ohlin, *Delinquency and Opportunity,* pp. 202, 206–7.

16. One reason why Chicano gangs had a considerable number of members who were related to each other was that relatives (and their families) tended to seek housing around each other. Part of this pattern was owing to the cultural trait of emphasizing family cohesion and part was owing to the fact that many immigrants from Mexico came to the United States with the help of relatives already living here, or sought out relatives living in the United States to help them find work and housing.

17. See Horowitz, *Honor and the American Dream,* p. 111, and chs. 4 and 5.

18. See Hagedorn, *People and Folks,* pp. 87–89, and Vigil, *Barrio Gangs,* pp. 87, 92, 102.

19. See Joan Moore, Diego Vigil, and Robert Garcia, "Residence and Territoriality in Chicano Gangs," *Social Problems* 31 (December 1983): 183–84. For supporting evidence of age segmentation in non-Chicano gangs, see Keiser, *Vice Lords,* pp. 15–16; and Suttles, *Social Order of the Slum,* pp. 183–84.

20. See Thrasher, *The Gang,* p. 32.

21. See ibid., pp. 200–202.

22. See, for example, Klein, *Street Gangs and Street Workers.*

23. Horowitz, *Honor and the American Dream,* p. 99.

24. Sometimes these formal codes would be written on a special tablet kept by a specific member, who had the responsibility of protecting it. At other times the codes were written into the minutes of the gang's general meeting as part of the business of that meeting (which made it difficult to retrieve the codes because to do so it was necessary to go through all

of the notes). Finally, there were times when the codes would be passed along verbally, in a form of cultural/oral tradition closely resembling those of the traditional societies reported on by anthropologists.

25. It is important to draw attention to the fact that women are rarely what is wanted. This is an indication of how women are considered property and not full participants in the organization.

26. Any physical evidence that included bruises, cuts, and so on was considered sufficient for guilt to be established.

27. In fact, where the New York gangs sell drugs (even heroin) in order to make money for other recreational activities, Chicano gangs often sell drugs in order to provide their members with drugs to consume. Interestingly, the African-American gangs of Los Angeles tended to adopt the eastern model, because they were attempting to build organizations that could accumulate large sums of money.

28. It is important to point out that nearly all individuals in gangs understand society as predatory and racially/ethnically discriminatory. The gang acts as an agent to reinforce this understanding on a collective level.

29. Keiser, *Vice Lords,* pp. 49–55.

30. Many of the gang studies have posited that gang members find that the gang can provide the close ties that the broken family cannot provide. See Thrasher, *The Gang,* p. 340; New York City Youth Board, *Reaching the Fighting Gang,* p. 17; Vigil, *Barrio Gangs,* pp. 90–91.

31. Georg Simmel, *Conflict,* trans. Kurt H. Wolff (Glencoe, Ill.: Free Press, 1955).

32. See Lewis A. Coser, *The Functions of Social Conflict* (New York: Free Press, 1956), pp. 39–48.

33. This type of effect is similar to Hobbes's rationale for government—that without it individuals would simply be in constant conflict with each other. See *Leviathan,* pt. 2, ch. 17, pp. 109–13.

34. See Coser, *Functions of Social Conflict,* pp. 42–47.

35. Seymour Martin Lipset, *Political Man: The Social Bases of Politics,* expanded ed. (Baltimore: Johns Hopkins University Press, 1981).

36. Ibid., p. 387.

37. In a sense, Lipset is concerned with the social conditions that affect democracy and is forced to address Robert Michels's theory concerning the relationship between large bureaucracy and oligarchical power structures (see Robert Michels, *Political Parties* [Glencoe, Ill.: Free Press, 1949]). See Lipset's two studies of the internal operations of unions: *Political Man,* pp. 387–436; and Seymour Martin Lipset, Martin A. Trow, and James S. Coleman, *Union Democracy: The Internal Politics of the International Typographical Union* (New York: Anchor Books, 1956).

In addition, some of the work of Daniel Bell also touches on the internal operations of unions and the question of whether oligarchic private governments undermine the values of liberal democracy. See his "The Racket-Ridden Longshoremen: The Web of Economics and Politics," in *End of Ideology*, pp. 175–210.

38. The notion of gangs as monolithic organizations was influenced by the stories about the structure of the Mafia, with its dictatorial leaders who came to power through the use of force and who maintained their power the same way. Studies of gangs that found physical attributes to be the basis of leadership power include Horowitz, *Honor and the American Dream*, p. 98; Whyte, *Street Corner Society*, pp. 3–5.

39. Some of the gangs only ceased operations for a matter of a few weeks until the remaining leadership could work out a new arrangement. However, in fifteen cases the gangs ceased operations for as long as five months.

40. See James Madison's Federalist Paper #10 in Alexander Hamilton, John Jay, and James Madison, *The Federalist Papers* (New York: Modern Library, 1937), pp. 53–62; and Robert A. Dahl, *A Preface to Democratic Theory* (Chicago: University of Chicago Press, 1956).

41. See Weber, *Economy and Society*, pp. 289–90. Also see Lewis Anthony Dexter, *Representation vs. Direct Democracy in Fighting about Taxes: Conflicting Notions of Sovereignty, Legitimacy, and Civility in Relation to a Tax Fight, Watertown, Massachusetts, 1953–59* (Cambridge, Mass.: Schenkman, 1981), pp. 9–11.

42. See Niccolò Machiavelli, *The Prince and the Discourses* (New York: Modern Library, 1950). For empirical work on the success of people who possess (or use) Machiavelli's principles for attaining and maintaining political power, see Richard Christie and Florence L. Geis, *Studies in Machiavellianism* (New York: Academic Press, 1970).

43. Over the more than ten years of this study, there were countless individuals who attempted to move up in the organization using this same process. I systematically observed seventeen (from their beginnings on) who were successful.

44. Interestingly, political maneuvering between factions was salient only in large gangs, where anonymity could be preserved. In the smaller gangs, everyone knew what everyone else was doing, which tended to inhibit this type of political style.

45. See Thrasher, *The Gang*, pp. 242–43. See also Short and Strodtbeck, *Group Process and Gang Delinquency*.

46. See Lewis A. Dexter, "Court Politics: Presidential Staff Relations as a Special Case of a General Phenomenon," *Administration and Society* 9, no. 3 (November 1977): 267–304.

47. Ibid., p. 271.

48. See Weber, *Economy and Society*, pp. 266–67.

49. Those who have argued that gangs do not have cohesive leadership are Yablonsky, *The Violent Gang;* Klein, *Street Gangs and Street Workers;* and, to a certain degree, Horowitz, *Honor and the American Dream,* pp. 98–99.

50. The evidence in this chapter supports the claims made by a number of other studies that gangs are cohesive organizations with structured leadership. See Whyte, *Street Corner Society;* Bloch and Niederhoffer, *The Gang;* New York City Youth Board, *Reaching the Fighting Gang.* The data in the present chapter provide more in-depth information than the previous studies as to how gangs are organized and what impact they have on individual behavior.

Chapter Four

1. Nearly all studies of gangs incorporate this theme into their analysis. One of the exceptions is Cloward and Ohlin, *Delinquency and Opportunity,* which argues that many delinquents have the same values as other members of American society. However, even Cloward and Ohlin incorporate some of the conventional argument by accepting the premise that gang members' skills to compete in the larger society have been retarded by a lack of opportunity.

2. See Charles Sabel, *Work and Politics* (Cambridge: Cambridge University Press, 1987), pp. 1–30, on the importance of worldviews in affecting the behavior of individuals in industrial organizations and politics.

3. David Matza mentions a comparable tendency among delinquents to deny guilt associated with wrongdoing when he discusses the delinquent's belief that he is nearly always the victim of a "bum rap" (see Matza, *Delinquency and Drift* [New Brunswick, N.J.: Transaction Books], pp. 108–10).

4. I use the term *economic oriented action* the way Weber does: "Action will be said to be 'economical oriented' so far as, according to its subjective meaning, it is concerned with the satisfaction of a desire for 'utilities' *(Nutzleistung)*" (Weber, *Economy and Society,* 1:63).

5. See Karl Marx, *The Economic and Philosophical Manuscripts of 1844,* 4th rev. ed., (Moscow: Progress Publishers, 1974), p. 38.

6. See David C. McClelland, *The Achieving Society* (New York: Free Press, 1961), pp. 233–37.

7. See Lee Rainwater, *What Money Buys: Inequality and the Social Meanings of Income* (New York: Basic Books, 1974). Also see Richard

P. Coleman and Lee Rainwater, *Social Standing in America: New Dimensions of Class* (New York: Basic Books, 1978), pp. 29–45.

8. See the accounts of successful entrepreneurs from poor families who dreamed of grandeur and became America's most renowned business tycoons in Matthew Josephson, *The Robber Barons: The Great American Capitalists 1861–1901* (New York: Harcourt, Brace & World, 1962), especially the chapter entitled "What Young Men Dream," pp. 32–49.

9. Being respectful maintains the social etiquette established in the gang and acts to deter physical confrontations between members. For an example similar to that reported here, see Kaiser, *Vice Lords,* pp. 41–42.

10. See Thrasher, *The Gang,* pp. 198–200.

11. Ibid., p. 86.

12. In comparing the interviews of older men who had been in gangs during the 1930s, 1940s, 1950s, and 1960s with those who are in gangs today, I found a clear and significant difference in the role that money plays in the everyday lives of these individuals from different generations. Simply stated, the interviews indicate that the importance of money for "normal everyday activity" increases from the 1930s generation to that of today.

13. In many ways this is similar to the pressures that formal religions, at least Christian ones, attempt to place on members to create group participation.

14. Not all the Irish communities have strong social or athletic clubs, but a large number do, especially in working-class areas. In those areas where there are social clubs and gangs, like those I studied, both become aspects of cultural tradition.

15. If the organization does utilize one of the contacts of an individual member, it usually promises to give that individual something in return. Thus the organization usually makes some limited amount of investment.

16. Both the theoretical and empirical literature focus on the gang's criminal activity. For theoretical discussions, see Kornhauser, *Social Sources of Delinquency,* pp. 51–61. For empirical studies, see nearly all of the classic and contemporary work on gangs. A sample of this literature would include Thrasher, *The Gang;* Herman Schwendinger and Julia Schwendinger, *Adolescent Subcultures and Delinquency* (New York: Praeger, 1985); Cloward and Ohlin, *Delinquency and Opportunity;* Cohen, *Delinquent Boys.* Two exceptions are Horowitz, *Honor and the American Dream,* and Vigil, *Barrio Gangs.*

17. There are two factors that have encouraged gangs to be more active in illegal markets. First, gangs, like organized crime syndicates, attempt to become active in many economic activities that are legal. However, because so much of the legal market is controlled by groups

that have established themselves in strategic positions (because they entered that market a considerable time in the past), gangs have found it difficult at best to successfully penetrate many legal markets. Further, there are financial incentives that have encouraged gangs to operate in the illegal market. These include the fact that costs are relatively low, and while personal risk (in terms of being incarcerated and/or physically hurt) is rather high, high demand along with high risk can produce greater profit margins. Despite the fact that these two factors have encouraged gangs to be more active in the illegal market, it is important to emphasize that nearly all the gangs studied attempted to, and many did, conduct business in the legal market as well.

18. The Schwendingers indicate that "youthful tastes regulate the flow of goods and services in the [adolescent] market" and gangs do take advantage of these tastes. See Schwendinger and Schwendinger, *Adolescent Subcultures and Delinquency*, p. 286.

19. See Fagan, "Social Organization of Drug Use and Drug Dealing among Urban Gangs," pp. 633–67; and Jerome H. Skolnick, *Forum: The Social Structure of Street Drug Dealing* (Sacramento: Bureau of Criminal Statistics / Office of the Attorney General, 1989).

20. See Francis A. J. Ianni, *Black Mafia: Ethnic Succession in Organized Crime* (New York: Simon & Schuster, 1974). Also see Moore, *Homeboys*, pp. 86–92, 114–16.

21. See Peter Lupsha and K. Schlegel, "The Political Economy of Drug Trafficking: The Herrera Organization (Mexico and the United States)" (Paper Presented at the Latin American Studies Association, Philadelphia, 1979).

22. This paying off of employees for drug supplies began, according to Joan Moore, in Los Angeles in the 1940s and 1950s (see Moore, *Homeboys*, pp. 78–82).

23. These gangs can procure fully automatic M-16s, Ingrams, and Uzzis.

24. Low riders are people, nearly all of whom are of Mexican descent, who drive customized older automobiles (1950s and 1960s models are preferred), one of the characteristics being that the springs for each wheel are cut away so that the car rides very low to the ground. Some of these cars have hydraulic systems that can be inflated at the flip of a switch so that the car can ride low to the ground at one moment and at the normal level the next. For a discussion of the importance of customized automobiles in Los Angeles, especially among Chicano youth, see Schwendinger and Schwendinger, *Adolescent Subcultures and Delinquency*, pp. 234–45.

25. The El Rukn gang in Chicago was recently indicted and convicted

of contracting with the Libyan government to carry out terrorist acts within the United States. See *Chicago Tribune,* 3, 4, 6, 7 November 1987.

26. See Weber, *Economy and Society,* pp. 341–48.

27. C. Wright Mills, *White Collar: The American Middle Class* (New York: Oxford University Press, 1951), p. 38.

28. See Jeffrey L. Pressman and Aaron Wildavsky, *Implementation: How Great Expectations in Washington Are Dashed in Oakland; or, Why It's Amazing that Federal Programs Work At All, This Being a Saga of the Economic Development Administration as Told by Two Sympathetic Observers Who Seek to Build Morals on a Foundation of Ruined Hopes* (Berkeley: University of California Press, 1973), p. 135.

29. For a discussion of the anatomy of delays as they relate to implementation, see ibid., pp. 113–21.

30. For early studies, see Asbury, *Gangs of New York,* pp. 238–46; Thrasher, *The Gang,* pp. 281–92; Whyte, *Street Corner Society,* pp. 121–22.

31. See especially Cloward and Ohlin, *Delinquency and Opportunity,* for discussions concerning the lack of legal opportunity for gang members and their resultant efforts to become a part of organized crime. Also see Bell, "Crime as an American Way of Life," in *End of Ideology,* pp. 127–50, where Bell argues that the Mafia is simply an alternative organization for upward socioeconomic mobility.

32. In the course of this research project, I interviewed 184 men who were members of gangs dating from the 1930s through the 1960s.

33. This tendency to limit the number of people in the syndicate regardless of whether they are Italian or not is brought out in Gerald Suttles's examination of an Italian slum with a long history of Mafia presence (see Suttles, *Social Order of the Slum*).

34. For the African-American and Puerto Rican syndicates, see Ianni, *Black Mafia;* for the Mexicans, see Moore, *Homeboys,* pp. 75–92, 114–16.

35. Law enforcement authorities often, however, designate crime committed by gang members acting on their own as "gang-related crime," which has tended to lead to inaccurate analyses and conclusions.

36. The gangs give many of their members, and sometimes the community as a whole, the same psychological comfort that the political machine provided urban ethnic groups in the late nineteenth and early twentieth centuries. See Raymond Wolfinger, "Why Political Machines Have Not Withered Away and Other Revisionist Thoughts," *Journal of Politics* 34 (May 1972): 365–98.

37. There is much literature on individual and group differences in value-time orientations. Most of it relates to differences between people

with different social class and ethnic backgrounds. The general conclusion is that culture (whether it is social class or ethnic) forms the foundation for such orientations. Some of the better-known statements of the value-time orientation thesis as it relates to culture and class are to be found in Florence Kluckholn and Fred Strodtbeck, *Variations in Value Orientation* (Evanston, Ill.: Row & Petersen, 1961); Edward Banfield, *The Unheavenly City Revisited* (Boston: Little, Brown, 1974).

38. In this case, the word *Anglo* has a more accurate meaning than when Chicanos use it, for the English are ethnically Anglo-Saxon whereas the Irish are ethnically Celtic. The English have been extremely ethnocentric toward the Irish and have tended to reinforce these attitudes through economic and political domination. See Michael Hechter, *Internal Colonialism: The Celtic Fringe in British National Development, 1536–1966* (Berkeley: University of California Press, 1975). The continuation of British rule in Northern Ireland has tended to reinforce Irish nationalism not only in Northern Ireland and the Irish Republic, but in the United States as well; and the Irish social clubs and gangs have been integrated into this nationalist movement.

Chapter Five

1. "Geraldo," ABC, 17 May 1988.

2. Research based on the observations of individuals making the analysis other than the researcher also creates a problem in that the phenomena observed have been filtered before the primary researcher has undertaken her or his own analysis.

3. Yablonsky, *The Violent Gang;* and the prevailing attitudes of many police departments.

4. A number of studies have found the achievement of status to be of critical importance in explaining why gang members participate in violence. Ruth Horowitz's use of Han Toch's identity types is in essence an attempt to link gang violence to the attainment (and maintenance) of social status (see Horowitz, *Honor and the American Dream,* pp. 88–97; and Horowitz and Schwartz, "Honor, Normative Ambiguity, and Gang Violence"). Others who have stressed status attainment are James F. Short and Fred Strodtbeck, "Why Gangs Fight," in James F. Short, ed., *Gang Delinquency and Delinquent Subcultures* (New York: Harper & Row, 1968), pp. 246–56; and Miller, "Lower Class Culture as a Generating Milieu of Gang Delinquency."

5. For an example of the social deprivation models using this assumption, see Cloward and Ohlin, *Delinquency and Opportunity;* and Miller, "Lower Class Culture as a Generating Milieu of Gang Delinquency." For

an example of the psychosocial pathology model, see Yablonsky, *The Violent Gang.*

6. See Kaiser, *Vice Lords,* p. 54, which describes how gang members pour a small amount of liquor on the ground in memory of those members who have been killed before anyone takes a drink from the bottle.

7. See Kornhauser, *Social Sources of Delinquency,* pp. 51–61.

8. See Yablonsky, *The Violent Gang.* In *Honor and the American Dream,* Ruth Horowitz combines ethnic culture (i.e., idiosyncrasies of Chicano culture) with the issue of frustration. My own analysis argues that violence is a function of low-income conditions, a particular characterological response (defiant individualism) adopted to overcome such conditions, and certain occurrences that activate emotions associated with defiant individualism into aggressive action.

9. The work of Ruth Horowitz has made a significant contribution in documenting the importance that honor plays among the Chicago gangs she studied in Chicago. See Horowitz, *Honor and the American Dream,* pp. 77–113; and Horowitz and Schwartz, "Honor, Normative Ambiguity, and Gang Violence."

10. Although much of the evidence on Chicano gangs in Los Angeles in the present study supports the findings of Horowitz's study of Chicano gangs in Chicago, there is one fundamental difference. Horowitz postulates that violence emerges from situations in which individuals with different identity types (she uses Toch's typology) attempt to maintain their honor, and relates the incidence of violence to how well the different identity types build reputations that augment honor and self-esteem. My own study of Chicano gangs in Los Angeles did not find this relationship between the identity types she employs and violence. Rather, I found that violence was a response that occurred when the emotions of fear, ambition, and frustration, and personal tests of preparedness, are powerfully activated. In my analysis, respect, honor, and reputation are resources by which gang members manage these emotions and reduce the use of violence. All of which is related to the gang member's quest for prosperity and/or survival.

11. Horowitz, *Honor and the American Dream.*

12. Most of those who have emphasized that gang violence is a vehicle for reputation-building are within the status-deprivation theoretical tradition. See ibid., pp. 77–113.

13. For a discussion of this aspect of ghetto life, see Ulf Hannerz, *Soul Side: Inquiries into Ghetto Culture and Community* (New York: Columbia University Press, 1969); also see Thomas Kochman, *Black and White Styles of Conflict* (Chicago: University of Chicago Press, 1981).

14. See Campbell, *Girls in the Gang.*

15. I also was with Junior when he ate better meals and did not fight.

16. In places like New York and Boston, most of the individuals who were in the gang lived in apartments where they did not have control over the temperature. Some of the apartments in the winter actually had no heat coming from the radiators, so the families had to keep the oven on to heat at least the kitchen.

17. The war council in Flue's gang made the decisions as to when, where, and how the gang would use force to obtain a stated objective.

18. This perception of threatening gestures is described by Kochman, *Black and White Styles of Conflict,* p. 47.

19. The manager required a number of stitches to close the wound, but recovered. However, the attack had shaken him, and he resigned his position.

20. See Franz Fanon, *The Wretched of the Earth* (New York: Grove Press, 1965).

21. See Lewis A. Coser, *Continuities in the Study of Social Conflict* (New York: Free Press, 1967), p. 221.

22. Historically, there were signs that read: "No Dogs or Irish Allowed" and "Irish need not apply."

23. For contemporary evidence of bias against lower-class Irish-Americans, one only has to recall the resistance of wealthy white suburbanites to a plan to bus their children to schools attended by inner-city Irish children. In Boston there was as much resistance on the part of affluent white suburbanites to busing involving white Irish children as to busing of black children, and some observers said even more. One should also consult the work of Edward Banfield and James Q. Wilson, who view the Yankees of Boston as having an ethos that is more "holist," community-serving, and good government-minded than other groups, including the Irish. See Edward Banfield and James Q. Wilson, "Political Ethos Revisited," *American Political Science Review* 65 (December 1971): 1048–62.

24. Observers have often commented that people sometimes justify their own pathologies by using political arguments. See the classic studies of Harold Lasswell, *The Psychopathology of Politics* (Chicago: University of Chicago Press, 1932), p. 77; and Gabriel Almond, *The Appeals of Communism* (Princeton: Princeton University Press, 1954). While this may be true, and in many research settings it is difficult to separate out whether this is occurring, in the present study every attempt was made to determine what factor was really causing the subject's violent actions. Thus in those cases where a subject claimed that violence was stimulated

by a desire to release the frustration and anger associated with feelings of deprivation, care was taken to ensure a high degree of confidence that this was the actual cause.

25. Two examples might be the Irish Catholics in Northern Ireland and the French Canadians of Quebec. For the French Canadians, see Pierre Vallierer's *Les Nègres blancs d'Amerique* [White niggers of America] (Montreal: Editions Parti Pris, 1968).

26. This tendency is also recorded by the Ira Henry Freeman biography of an African-American gang leader in Brooklyn, New York. See Carl Joyeaux (pseud.), *Out of the Burning: The Story of a Boy Gang Leader* (New York: Crown, 1960), pp. 102–4.

27. In the course of this research, 267 cases were observed of one gang attacking others to gain control over a new territory for purposes of material improvement and/or growth in membership.

28. Interestingly, this effort on the part of the leadership to test willingness to follow orders is remarkably similar to the pioneering experiments concerning obedience to authority reported in Milgram, *Obedience to Authority*.

29. See Short and Strodtbeck, "Why Gangs Fight," in Short, ed., *Gang Delinquency and Delinquent Subcultures*, p. 247, 250–51.

30. This is similar to the assertions made by Simmel and elaborated by Coser concerning the role social conflict plays in group cohesion (Simmel, *Conflict;* Coser, *Functions of Social Conflict*, pp. 87–110).

31. As with all the cases reported in this book, I was able to observe the entire process that Lizard described, from the time of internal conflict and economic stagnation to the leadership's decision to attack the rival gang as a way to unify the organization and the war and the internal cohesion that resulted from the war. The strategy to engage in violence in order to save the organization proved to be successful in this case.

32. I was with the gang when it attacked the two residents who had failed to inform it that the police were on patrol (which had resulted in two members being arrested). I was also present to observe the organization's decline and ultimate collapse as a result of the community's withdrawal of support.

33. The case of the El Rukns gang in Chicago. See the *Chicago Tribune*, 3, 4, 6, 7 November 1987, for articles on the conspiracy trial involving the El Rukns gang.

34. These patterns I observed are also reported in the *San Francisco Chronicle*, 4 September 1988, and Vigil, *Barrio Gangs*, p. 135.

35. The incident recorded here is very similar to the Michael Farmer incident, in which a young crippled boy was beaten to death by members of a gang who thought he was a member of a gang that had been attack-

ing them. The incident was reported in the New York papers, a special CBS television documentary by Edward R. Murrow, and Yablonsky, *The Violent Gang*, pp. 9–25.

36. These types of incidents occur frequently in Los Angeles, and a significant number of people who were not members have become fatalities. The African-American gangs in Los Angeles do not seem to be taking any steps to avoid these occurrences, and this is a prime indication that they, as organizations, are out of control. Without a reversal of this trend, they will wither away as effective organizations.

37. Many combat veterans of the Vietnam War describe the tension and fear they experienced during certain operations as precipitating factors in their excessive use of violence in situations that did not merit such a response. See Phillip Caputo, *A Rumor of War* (New York: Ballantine Books, 1978).

38. Holding the organization's directives to blame for one's use of violence is a familiar rationalization, also reported by Hannah Arendt in connection with Nazi German society and government in *Eichmann in Jerusalem: A Report on the Banality of Evil* (New York: Viking, 1963).

39. Vigil also reports this to have occurred with the Chicano gangs he studied, and he relates this type of violence to vendettas (see Vigil, *Barrio Gangs*, p. 131).

40. See Thrasher, *The Gang*. See also Fagan, "Social Organization of Drug Use and Drug Dealing among Urban Gangs," which uses a typology of gang organizations and relates it to various types of violent activity.

41. The organization is able to avoid chaos because in nearly every gang that employs this type of structure, there is a code that states that an individual member can get into trouble, but that if this causes problems for the organization that member will be severely punished. This has a tendency to establish a modest amount of control.

42. Their notion of violence differs slightly from the axiom advanced by specialists in international relations concerning the use of war in achieving objectives, which is that nation-states usually embark on war when they have exhausted all other forms of diplomatic maneuvers to achieve their objectives (see W. W. Kulski, *International Politics in a Revolutionary Age* [New York: Lippincott, 1964]). Gangs on the other hand, never exhaust all the potential alternative strategies before they resort to violence. They may try some alternative strategies and then resort to physical force; or they may simply intellectually consider these strategies, decide they will not work, and then proceed immediately to the strategy of physical force.

Chapter Six

1. For a good example see Yablonsky, *The Violent Gang.*
2. For a good example see Thrasher, *The Gang.*
3. Suttles, *Social Order of the Slum;* Bloch and Niederhoffer, *The Gang;* Miller, "Lower Class Culture as a Generating Milieu of Gang Delinquency."
4. Some studies have suggested that the reaction of the local community to gangs is dependent on the type of community involved—that is to say, communities experiencing poverty (and what many of these studies often refer to as social disorganization) or a change in ethnic composition may be more tolerant of gangs (see Curry and Spergel, "Gang Homicide, Delinquency and Community"). There were twenty-seven communities included in the present study, and although all were low-income communities, there was variation in the level of both socioeconomic and physical (buildings and grounds) deprivation, as well as in their ethnic composition. However, I found that neither of these two conditions (the level of poverty in the community, or whether it was ethnically stable) was critical in determining how the gang and the community would interact.
5. For a similar finding, see Ruth Horowitz, "Community Tolerance of Gang Violence," *Social Problems* 34 (December 1987): 437–49.
6. See Sally Engle Merry, *Urban Danger: Life in a Neighborhood of Strangers* (Philadelphia: Temple University Press, 1981); Lee Rainwater, *Behind Ghetto Walls: Black Family Life in a Federal Slum* (Chicago: Aldine Press, 1970); Suttles, *Social Order of the Slum.*
7. For a similar observation, see Gerald D. Suttles, *The Social Construction of Communities* (Chicago: University of Chicago Press, 1972), p. 200.
8. Vigil also reports this; see his *Barrio Gangs,* pp. 131–32.
9. This concern on the part of parents to protect females until they are married or old enough to move from the area corroborates the findings reported in the studies by Suttles, *Social Order of the Slum,* pp. 226–28; and Horowitz, *Honor and the American Dream,* pp. 116–17.
10. See Suttles, *Social Construction of Communities,* pp. 189–229.
11. What usually happened when the court ruled in favor of the tenants was that the landlords would provide heat for a short time and then shut it off again. The residents would have to begin the legal fight all over again while still being without heat. This is not an isolated event, but happens often in the Bronx and in sections of Manhattan and Brooklyn.
12. Some people charge purchases until their payday. Of course, the store owner charges them interest on the loan. However, for those peo-

ple, the store owner's loan books were used to prove that they had purchased the oil.

13. It turned out that the rumors were correct. The syndicate did want to open both a brothel and a drug house on the block.

14. These findings concerning Irish gangs are in part consistent with those of Short and Strodtbeck, in that the Irish community is likely to encourage the gangs to use force to repel those groups (mainly nonwhite groups) who they believe present a threat. See Short and Strodtbeck, *Group Process and Gang Delinquency*, pp. 112–14. For a more recent example, see Ida Susser, *Norman Street: Poverty and Politics in an Urban Neighborhood* (New York: Oxford University Press, 1982), pp. 121–24.

15. This has been true of business, political, and military organizations. See Albert O. Hirschman, *Exit, Voice and Loyalty: Responses to Decline in Firms, Organizations, and States* (Cambridge, Mass.: Harvard University Press, 1970). The successful guerrilla campaigns in Vietnam and Cuba, which were able to adopt an offensive posture, might also be compared to those in Bolivia and Namibia, which were forced to remain defensive-oriented. Also consider the successful campaigns of the Union Army as opposed to those of the Confederacy in the American Civil War after 1863.

16. *Crew* is a term applied to a small group of individuals who band together to undertake armed robberies and muggings.

17. See Suttles, *Social Order of the Slum*, p. 230, for corroborating evidence on the impact of rumors in gang fights.

18. Vigil reports that Chicano gang members ride into "enemy territory" writing graffiti on the walls and run quickly out of the area because they know they will be attacked by the local gang (*Barrio Gangs*, pp. 130–32).

19. Leonard W. Doob, *Patriotism and Nationalism: Their Psychological Foundations* (New Haven: Yale University Press, 1964), p. 6.

20. For supporting evidence, see Vigil, *Barrio Gangs*, p. 131.

21. There are a significant number of studies documenting the fact that social status for low-income residents is based on criteria established within the low-income neighborhood. See Elliot Liebow, *Tally's Corner: A Study of Negro Streetcorner Men* (Boston: Little, Brown, 1967); Hannerz, *Soulside;* Willis, *Learning to Labor;* Jay Macleod, *Ain't No Making It: Leveled Aspirations in a Low-Income Community* (Boulder, Colo.: Westview Press, 1987); Suttles, *Social Order of the Slum*.

22. Interestingly, two years later, a new gang formed with a portion of its membership (much of the leadership core) coming from the old gang, and it was able to reestablish a working relationship with the community.

23. In an anti-gang sweep, the police patrol through the community and pick up, detain, and sometimes arrest known or probable gang members. See Los Angeles Times, 9 April 1988, Metro section, p. 1, and 11 April 1988, Metro section, pp. 1, 8.

24. Crack is a derivative of cocaine and comes in the form of a "rock," which is burned and snorted. It is much more addictive than cocaine and can be purchased for as little as one dollar a hit. Its street value is similar to that of Angel Dust, and it can produce erratic and violent behavior on the part of those who are under its influence. See Eric Lichtblau and Gaylord Shaw, "Crack: It's Not Just a 'City Drug,' " Los Angeles Times, 5 April 1988, pt. 1, pp. 1, 20, 22.

25. The homicide rate for gangs in Los Angeles for the past four years has been very high. See Malcolm W. Klein and Cheryl L. Maxson, "Street Gang Violence," in Neil Alan Weiner and Marvin E. Wolfgang, eds., Violent Crime, Violent Criminals (Newbury Park, Calif.: Sage, 1989), pp. 198–234.

26. See the Los Angeles Times, 7 April 1988, Metro section, pp. 1, 8.

27. Vigil also reports that the Chicanos he studied were involved in drive-by shootings; see his Barrio Gangs, pp. 133–35.

28. See Bob Baker, "Gang Rule: Living in a Battle Zone," Los Angeles Times, 10 April 1988.

29. See Bob Pool, "Police Call Gang Sweep a Success: 1453 Are Arrested," Los Angeles Times, 12 April 1988, pt. 2, pp. 1, 4.

30. John Hagar, a lawyer of the American Civil Liberties Union, is reported to have criticized the police operations (Los Angeles Times, 15 April 1988, pt. 3, p. 4).

31. The NAACP did speak out against the police crackdowns (Los Angeles Times, 15 April 1988), but few community leaders followed suit immediately.

32. The gang's conscious decision to embrace this type of structure calls to mind the issues that Arthur M. Okun describes as being present for larger modern states like the United States (see Okun, Equality and Efficiency: The Big Trade Off [Washington, D.C.: Brookings Institution, 1975]).

33. See Hobsbawm, Primitive Rebels, p. 7.

Chapter Seven

1. Of course, it was assumed, by Thrasher at least, that the political bosses were corrupt and that they constituted one element in adult organized crime. Thus, the gangs' involvement with the political machine

was a form of socialization into adult criminal activity. See Thrasher, *The Gang,* pp. 313–36.

2. It must be understood that in Thrasher's analysis there was a direct link between corrupt political machines, the Mafia, and the gang. This is because for Thrasher the gang was not simply an adolescent organization; rather, there were different kinds of gangs, some of which were feeder organizations for the Mafia and had young adults in them. See Thrasher, *The Gang,* pp. 281–312.

3. The work of Suttles would have to be included in this group of studies concerning the gang and politics (Suttles, *Social Order of the Slum,* pp. 119–22). Horowitz's work also describes the relationship of the residents she studied to local politics, but omits describing any relationship between gangs and politics (Horowitz, *Honor and the American Dream,* pp. 209–18, 225).

4. Under the term *politician,* I include both incumbents and candidates running for public office.

5. There are volumes of material depicting the classic political machine, including Harold Gosnell, *Machine Politics: Chicago Model* (Chicago: University of Chicago Press, 1937); Gustavus Meyers, *The History of Tammany Hall* (New York: Boni & Liveright, 1917); Amy Bridges, *A City in the Republic: Antebellum New York and the Origins of Machine Politics* (New York: Cambridge University Press, 1984); Riordan, *Plunkitt of Tammany Hall;* and Joseph F. Dineen, *The Purple Shamrock: The Honorable James Michael Curley of Boston* (New York: Norton, 1949). On the decline of the machine, see also Theodore Lowi, "Machine Politics—Old and New," *The Public Interest,* no. 9 (Fall 1967): 83–92.

6. This comment was recorded longhand on notepaper, not tape-recorded.

7. The street-level politician will be discussed in detail in a later section of this chapter.

8. The case of Chicago mayor Jane Byrne is a case in point. It was reported that her organization had solicited the El Rukn gang to do political organizing for her on the South Side of Chicago. She categorically denied any contact, even though there was evidence that representatives of her organization had made some type of contact. See the *Chicago Tribune,* 5 February 1983.

9. This quotation was taken longhand, not tape-recorded.

10. While only nine gangs were able to negotiate the use of property as payment for their political services, these nine were involved in numerous arrangements throughout the period of the study.

11. This movement to develop a civic culture type of city grew out of the anti-machine reform political movements that occurred throughout

the first half of the twentieth century in the United States. See Richard
Hofstadter, *The Age of Reform* (New York: Vintage Books, 1955); and
Edward Banfield and James Q. Wilson, *City Politics* (New York: Vintage
Books, 1966), pp. 138–50.

12. For a statement of the concept of civic culture and some empirical
tests of it, see Gabriel Almond and Sidney Verba, *The Civic Culture* (Boston: Little, Brown, 1965).

13. Gangs in reform cities like Los Angeles are most likely to be characterized by politicians as demons that must be eliminated if American
society is to maintain its character. Gangs, therefore, are similar to those
other objects that have been identified as political and social demons
threatening our American way of life. For an analysis of the demons
that permeate American political culture, see Michael Paul Rogin,
Ronald Reagan, the Movie: And Other Episodes in Political Demonology (Berkeley: University of California Press, 1987).

14. The cooperation of the community was dependent on whether the
street-level politician could indicate to the community that he or she was
concerned with the youth of the community, crime and violence, and
economic development. The politician needed the gangs because the gangs
sometimes could influence the community in terms of what candidate to
vote for, and because they could be used in the politician's electoral campaign.

15. For the community, the proposed project would have meant a
large number of homes would have been removed and the residents displaced. For the politician, the project's removal of residents meant that
he would lose his electoral base of support and face the possibility of
losing the next election.

16. Conversely, the leadership of the gang would not have contact
with the politician, but with the people running his office. However, in
the case of street-level politicians, the gangs usually dealt directly with
them.

17. The concept of street-level bureaucrats was first developed by
Michael Lipsky. See his "Toward a Theory of Street-Level Bureaucracy,"
in Willis Hawley and Michael Lipsky, eds., *Theoretical Perspectives on
Urban Politics* (Englewood Cliffs, N.J.: Prentice-Hall, 1976), pp. 196–213.

18. Quotation recorded longhand while talking to the respondent,
not tape-recorded.

19. There were times when the leadership of a particular gang was
having difficulty securing money through the gang's various business
ventures. At those times, a disgruntled faction would begin to emerge
within the gang, and the leadership would attempt to ward off any po-

tential challenge to their authority by trying to secure more recreational activities for the general membership.

20. Quotation taken longhand, not tape-recorded.
21. Quotation taken longhand, not tape-recorded.
22. Quotation taken longhand, not tape-recorded.
23. Quotation taken longhand, not tape-recorded.
24. Quotation taken longhand, not tape-recorded.
25. Quotation taken longhand, not tape-recorded.
26. It should be understood that the increase in planned field trips varied within and between cities. However, despite variations in the number of field trips that were planned by the recreation departments, all of the gangs that made an effort to have the number increased experienced relative success in those efforts.
27. It is not the concern of this study to analyze the effectiveness of the various governmental agencies' efforts to manage their assorted job-training programs, therefore the names of the specific government departments/agencies are not provided.
28. At some basic level the residents of all the communities I studied believed that social programs were a direct response to social unrest. Interestingly, this is a proposition advanced by Frances Fox Piven and Richard A. Cloward in *Regulating the Poor* (New York: Vintage Books, 1972).
29. For an excellent discussion of the role of street-level bureaucrats in facilitating referrals for gang members or in assisting the acquisition of services, see Irving Spergel, *Street Gang Work: Theory and Practice* (Garden City, N.Y.: Anchor Books, 1967), pp. 163–74.
30. The act of client aggressiveness is a strategy that street-level bureaucrats are sensitive to and one in which they are likely to give the client what they want. See Jeffrey Manditch Prottas, *People Processing: The Street-Level Bureaucrat in Public Service Bureaucracies* (Lexington, Mass.: Lexington Books, 1979), pp. 108–9.
31. For the street-level bureaucrat, it is the calculation of potential benefits that brings his or her operational meaning of the term *prudence* very close to that employed by Edmund Burke. See Louis I. Bredvold and Ralph G. Ross, eds., *The Philosophy of Edmund Burke* (Ann Arbor: University of Michigan Press, 1960), pp. 35–42.
32. I interviewed thirty-four high-ranking bureaucrats within various local government bureaucracies charged with providing services that gang members received. In addition, I interviewed sixty street-level bureaucrats over the more than ten years of this study.
33. Of the ninety-four government bureaucrats interviewed in the three cities, thirty-four were administrators of policies involving gangs.

Of these thirty-four, ten were from Boston and twelve each were from New York and Los Angeles. Of the ninety-four government bureaucrats, sixty were street-level bureaucrats involved with the task of implementing policy.

34. Quotation taken longhand, not tape-recorded.

35. Quotation taken longhand, not tape-recorded.

36. See Michael Lipsky's discussion of the general differences between street-level bureaucrats and managers in *Street-Level Bureaucracy: Dilemmas of the Individual in Public Services* (New York: Russell Sage Foundation, 1980), pp. 18–23.

37. First, not all of the funding comes from government sources. Some funding comes from church organizations, while other money comes from funds established by private business organizations, but the overwhelming majority is from government. Some of the government funding is from local government, but again there are agencies that get money from the state and federal governments as well. For a good description of such an organization, see Charles N. Cooper, "The Chicago YMCA Detached Workers: Current Status of an Action Program," in Malcolm W. Klein, ed., *Juvenile Gangs in Context: Theory, Research, and Action* (Englewood Cliffs, N.J.: Prentice-Hall, 1967), pp. 183–93.

38. Quotation taken longhand, not tape-recorded.

39. For an excellent example of this, see Robert Woodson, ed., *Youth Crime and Urban Policy: A View from the Inner City* (Washington, D.C.: American Enterprise Institute for Public Policy Research, 1980), the proceedings of a conference sponsored by the American Enterprise Institute in Washington, D.C., in May 1980.

40. See ibid.; Moore, *Homeboys*, pp. 129–48.

41. Quotation taken longhand, not tape-recorded.

42. There have been some successes in modifying violent gang behavior and retarding gang growth, but the number of successful agencies has been small in relation to the number actively working in low-income communities. For a discussion of the success of a few programs, see Robert L. Woodson, *A Summons to Life: Mediating Structures and the Prevention of Youth Crime* (Cambridge, Mass.: Ballinger Publishers, 1981), pp. 45–107.

Chapter Eight

1. Interestingly, most sociological studies of gangs likewise depict an antagonistic power relationship in which the goal of the criminal justice system is the elimination of gangs. It is not possible to name all the studies that have described the police and gang as antagonists. Recent repre-

sentative examples include Vigil, *Barrio Gangs,* pp. 141–48; Alfredo Mirande, *Gringo Justice* (South Bend, Ind.: University of Notre Dame Press, 1987); Hagedorn, *People and Folks,* p. 31.

2. The data in the present study tend to substantiate James Q. Wilson's assertion that what politicians permit in the realm of police behavior is an important factor in explaining police behavior. See his *Variations in Police Behavior* (Cambridge, Mass.: MIT Press, 1968), pp. 143–44.

3. Most people approved of the LAPD's use of the battering ram to destroy identified "crack houses."

4. In 1988 the LAPD undertook a number of operations similar to those conducted in war. It even used the military term *sweep* to identify these operations. In addition, the police had the support of the city council, which was willing to spend a great deal of the taxpayers' money for these activities because council members believed there was little opposition to such a policy. See the *Los Angeles Times,* 8, 9, 11, 12, 13 April 1988.

5. Quotation taken longhand, not tape-recorded.

6. When gangs shoot at police officers, it is usually not done to injure or kill them, but rather to send a message to change their behavior.

7. This point was brought to light in the 1988 motion picture *Colors.* The wise, prudent older police officer (played by Robert Duvall) is in an argument with the gung-ho younger rookie (played by Sean Penn) over whether they should arrest a couple of young gang members who have a small amount of drugs on them or wait and see if they will eventually lead them to the main suppliers. In an effort to convince the younger officer of the need to be prudent, Duvall uses a parable. He says: "There was these two bulls who were on this hill. The young bull says to the older bull, let's run down the hill there and fuck a cow. And the older bull retorts back, let's walk down the hill and fuck all the cows!"

8. See Erving Goffman, *Interaction Ritual: Essays in Face-to-Face Behavior* (Garden City, N.Y.: Anchor Books, 1967), pp. 5–45.

9. Philadelphia was one of the first cities to use such a program. It was known as the Crisis Intervention Network and was directed by Bennie Swans.

10. The LAPD feared that the Intervention Units would be a "watchdog organization" over it, criticizing and attempting to expose police inadequacies or irregularities in an effort to maintain the units' own legitimacy (and existence).

11. It was easy for the police to say that the intervention team needed direct assistance or that they were unable to stabilize the situation. This could be used to justify police use of force.

12. Quotation taken longhand, not tape-recorded.

13. In a very real sense these organizations are, like the social organizations discussed in chapter 8, dependent on gangs.

14. This is to say, not that the courts (i.e., judges and prosecuting attorneys) do not want to strengthen social control by eradicating gangs, but that they find themselves unable to do so.

15. This was also true of gangs that had adopted the influential organizational model, where one person, or a small group, governs the organization. In those gangs, the membership simply elected an individual who aspired to be an "influential" as interim leader until the original leader(s) were released from prison. See chapter 3 for a description of the influential model of gang leadership.

16. Juveniles receive lesser sentences for nonviolent crimes. In recent years the courts have instituted harsher sentences for those involved in violent crime. Nonetheless, even for violent crime, the sentences are generally less harsh (depending on the type of violent crime) than they would be if they were adults. However, it must be emphasized that gangs attempted to use juveniles more for nonviolent actions because they knew the sentences would be less severe for these crimes.

17. Both New York and California have modified their laws to permit juveniles who have been involved in violent crime to be tried in adult courts.

18. The key phrase here is "juvenile and adult gang members" because it is not as nagging a problem in most other crime-related areas. Yet, in the case of the gangs, where there is a desire to curb an organization rather than individuals per se, it presents some internal obstacles toward that goal.

19. The officials that I refer to here are judges, parole officers, and prosecuting attorneys.

20. Actually California has attempted to circumvent this problem by enacting new legislation that is directed squarely at gangs. The legislature has passed the Anti-Gang Street Terrorism Act, which is designed to severely restrict the activity of gangs by making it against the law to be in a gang. The constitutionality of this law will likely be tested in the courts because its potential for abuse is quite high.

21. See Moore, *Homeboys,* pp. 106–10.

22. Deadly and other gang members' response to being labeled "program resistant youth" is to resist the labelers by making them defensive about their assertions. See Erving Goffman, *Stigma: Notes on the Management of Spoiled Identity* (Englewood Cliffs, N.J.: Prentice-Hall, 1963).

23. On this point, it is worth looking at the literature on thought reform. The efforts of many governments to reeducate their citizens with

a new set of political values are very similar to efforts to get gang members (and perhaps those labeled criminals in general) to view their activities (gang participation) as counterproductive to society. For the classic works on thought reform, see Robert Jay Lifton, *Thought Reform and the Psychology of Totalism* (Chapel Hill: University of North Carolina Press, 1989); or Edward Schein's *Coercive Persuasion* (New York: Norton, 1961). It should also be noted that governments like that of Vietnam established concentration camps after the war for independence had been won in order to reeducate and/or confine those who had been opponents of the new regime.

24. See Moore, *Homeboys,* p. 102, who also found this to be an important factor. In this regard, gangs have managed to neutralize the impact of certain characteristics that Erving Goffman attributes to "total institutions" like prisons. See Goffman, *Asylums: Essays on the Social Situation of Mental Patients and Other Inmates* (Garden City, N.Y.: Anchor Books, 1961), pp. 1–124, but esp. pp. 14–35.

25. Gangs have been able to establish social control within the prisons and create an underground economy. See Moore, *Homeboys,* pp. 114–16, who found this as well. In addition, prison officials have frequently increased a prisoner's term upon finding out that the prisoner has been involved in a violent incident and is a member of a gang. They do this in an effort to deter gang-initiated violence in the prisons.

26. The interviews of gang members coincide with the accounts of other people who have been in prison. See Jean Harris, *Stranger in Two Worlds* (New York: Zebra Books, 1987), pp. 295–436. Goffman calls "institutional practices" what I am labeling procedures. See his *Asylums,* p. 94.

27. Of course, it is possible, if the gang member is a juvenile, that he may have had contact with the parole officer in the latter's capacity as a juvenile court intake officer. For a good discussion of the role of the parole officer as a juvenile court intake officer, see Arnold Binder, Gilbert Geis, and Dickson Bruce, *Juvenile Delinquency: Historical, Cultural, Legal Perspectives* (New York: Macmillan, 1988), pp. 290–91.

28. Quotation taken longhand, not tape-recorded.

29. Some of these illegal acts would be associating with people forbidden under the terms of their parole and conspiracy to commit (that is, planning) or actually participating in some illegal behavior.

30. It is their belief that their involvement can be concealed through the number of other gang members involved.

31. There are many athletes who have some attributes of what I have called the defiant individualist character. This is not extraordinary, because many of these athletes are from the same socioeconomic areas as

gangs and had the same drive to get themselves out of those areas. The difference is that they saw their ticket out as being through professional athletics instead of illegal activities. It is very important to point out that although society applauds this avenue to success, the probability of success is much less than through crime.

Chapter Nine

1. Vigil and Hagedorn mention the media, but they do not attempt to analyze the relationship between gangs and the media. The main point advanced by both studies is that media coverage has created negative images of gangs. See Hagedorn, *People and Folks,* pp. 23–24, 156; and Vigil, *Barrio Gangs,* pp. 40, 124.

2. By stating that these news or current affairs shows assume one of three formats, I do not mean to suggest that in adopting one of the formats they exclude the other two. I simply mean that while all three may be attempted, one will be utilized as the primary organizing format. Thus, for example, a local news show may want its news to provide understanding and be entertaining, but its primary objective and emphasis (as a format) will be on reporting the news.

3. Todd Gitlin uses the term the "routine of journalism." See his important analysis of the media's impact on mass movements in *The Whole World Is Watching: Mass Media in the Making and Unmaking of the New Left* (Berkeley: University of California Press, 1980), p. 4.

4. Quotation taken longhand, not tape-recorded.

5. Quotation taken longhand, not tape-recorded.

6. See Gitlin, *The Whole World Is Watching,* p. 35, for a discussion of the importance of deadlines in keeping the story of an event simple.

7. The amount of contact that a reporter has with gang members varies from no contact whatsoever on the part of television anchors to very limited amounts on the part of newspaper reporters.

8. By arguing that the gang-related story serves as a "hook" to secure more readers, listeners, and viewers to the news, I do not mean to suggest that the gang-related story is the only one used by media officials to do that. There are usually a number of stories used to catch and hold audience interest.

9. See Herbert J. Gans, *Deciding What's News: A Study of CBS Evening News, NBC Nightly News, Newsweek and Time* (New York: Random House, 1980), p. 218.

10. Ibid., p. 219.

11. The same incident that Murrow reported on was also used by Yablonsky (in his book *The Violent Gang*) to analyze the phenomenon

of gangs. Intriguingly, Yablonsky and Murrow came to opposite conclusions. One might explain this by saying that one is a trained sociologist (Yablonsky) and the other is a trained journalist (Murrow). One might also be prejudiced and conclude that Yablonsky, because of his training, is more likely to be accurate. Yet my research indicates that Murrow's conclusions offer a more accurate picture of the gang and the dynamics that led to the death of Michael Farmer than do Yablonsky's. However, this has less to do with the method of investigation and more to do with the analytic abilities of Murrow.

12. There have, of course, been many documentaries done on gangs, but I have chosen to focus on these three programs because they represent examples of the format utilized to present the general public with an understanding of the gang phenomenon.

13. See Herbert J. Gans, *Deciding What's News,* p. 168, for a discussion of the "peg" in the news industry.

14. See ibid., pp. 146–81.

15. For example, in the television documentary "Our Children: The Next Generation," Dan Medina at one point says: "The excitement of violence in the street has become a new spectator sport for many." This is followed by a number of very short scenes (a few seconds each) of gang violence. Then he says: "It is that excitement that is the greatest recruiting tool for L.A. County gangs. Violence, status, money, and women are the hooks that fill the ranks." One moment he is talking about the excitement of violence as the catalyst for gang violence and then in an instant we are offered three other factors as influencing agents (status, money, and women). No evidence is presented and no explanation is offered. As a result, status, money, and women are all incorporated into violence.

16. Again in the television documentary "Our Children: The Next Generation," early in the show, Medina says that in addition to the victims of gang violence, the families of gang members are also victims and goes on to say, "It is these families who are meeting to do something about it [the violence]." Then later in the program, in an attempt to create balance, he shows some parents who are not doing anything about the fact that their children are in a gang. Finally, at the end of the program, he concludes that one of the main reasons gang violence is continuing is that families are not living up to their responsibilities. The problem is that in attempting to present both parents who are trying to do something and others who appear to be doing nothing, without any evidence about the differences, audiences are left on their own to reconcile what appear to be two conflicting statements.

17. A variety of problems are encountered when using other people's observations. Two of the more general ones are: (1) that the observations

made by another person in another context are not valid for the case being reported; and (2) that the observations of the other person(s) are themselves inaccurate.

18. Of course, these decisions are greatly influenced by the professional considerations mentioned above as to what makes a good story, such as issues of clarity, balance, and so on.

19. In fact, this reporter's take on gangs was not new. It was like many others that had been done before. This quotation was recorded in longhand, not tape-recorded.

20. In speaking of "so-called experts," I am not suggesting that the people solicited to be on the panel lack expertise. While not all of the guests are experts on the topic being examined, many do have expertise in other areas and a good many have expertise on the subject being discussed. I use the phrase "so-called experts" to emphasize that it is the host of the program that presents the guests in this manner, not necessarily the guests themselves.

21. Of course, sometimes this method becomes too successful and the host loses control. This did not occur on the topic of gangs, but on "Geraldo," the moderator, Geraldo Rivera, lost control of a discussion between white supremacists and African-Americans, resulting in a physical altercation in which Rivera himself received a broken nose.

22. Along with motion pictures could be included those movies made for television and those segments in television series that use the subject of gangs for their themes. Such television series as "Hill Street Blues," "L.A. Law," "Cagney and Lacey," and "The Mod Squad" all had episodes devoted to gangs.

23. Other contemporary movies like *Fort Apache, The Bronx* also have characterized gangs in this manner. In fact, even the early Bowery Boys movies characterized the members as social misfits or losers, albeit lovable ones.

24. In *The Warriors* and *Colors*, it is made blatantly obvious that the values of those who are in gangs are anathema to those of the greater society. However, this is also the message in *West Side Story*, even though it is presented in a more subtle manner. In *West Side Story*, everything good (i.e., the "good values") is represented in the characters of Maria and Tony. The bad values are represented by gang members, regardless of whether they are white or Puerto Rican, and emotionally emphasized in the slaying of Tony and the torment of Maria over his death. In fact, the movie characterizes Tony's death in the symbolism of Christ and the Crucifixion. Tony is sacrificed so that the gangs (Jets and Sharks) can come together humanly (which they do symbolically in carrying his body away together) and Maria, like the blessed Virgin, mourns his sacrifice.

25. *Fort Apache, the Bronx* is a film about the South Bronx in New York City. The movie does have gangs in it, but its main focus is on crime in this particular slum community and the police officers who must patrol it. *Colors,* of course, is focused on the gangs of Los Angeles, but is also about the community in which they live.

26. All of the four movies that I have mentioned contain scenes that represent the community in this light. *West Side Story* has its gentle store owner who wants to help but is impotent to curb violent gang activity. *Colors* has a community meeting scene in which the members of the community meet with the police to develop a strategy; in the process of the meeting, all decorum breaks down and the meeting drifts into complete chaos.

27. In a sense, some influential academic books unintentionally help to reinforce the idea that poor communities have a different morality than the rest of society. See Suttles, *Social Order of the Slum,* pp. 4–6, 223–34.

28. Michael Paul Rogin's book *Ronald Reagan, the Movie* is the best treatment of this tendency on the part of Americans to be concerned with the social and political demons that threaten their society.

29. There were various criticisms of these movies. *The Warriors* was even criticized by members of a gang writing in a quarterly magazine called *Youth-at-Large* published by the Inner City Roundtable of Youth, Inc. / ICRY organization. The end of the review/criticism says: "It [the movie] made these invented demon-youths, as well as the youths of ICRY, appear to have no human function or feeling, neither family nor friend, consciousness or conscience, ambitions or anything remotely associated with life goals as we know them. . . . So just as a general statement, we didn't think very much of "The Warriors"—and we're the Warriors" (their emphasis). See *Youth-at-Large* 1, no. 2 (December 1979): 10, 21. In addition, the gang youths writing in this publication vindicated Sol Yurick, the author of the novel *The Warriors* on which the movie was based, saying the book was not like the movie.

30. An example of this would be the comments of a young gang member in the television documentary "Our Children: The Next Generation," who says when asked why he believes that he and his fellow gang members will not be hassled by another gang, "We have three hundred and fifty-seven reasons why nobody will fuck with us." This is a play on the fact that they have a pistol that shoots a .357 size bullet. Another example was seen in a segment on CBS's "60 Minutes" (done by Dan Rather) where a Chicano gang member shoots himself in the foot to show how macho he is.

31. This interview was recorded longhand and not tape-recorded.

32. For a discussion of the idea that nonwhite women entrap upright white men, see Winthrop D. Jordan, *White over Black: American Attitudes toward the Negro, 1550–1812* (Baltimore: Penguin Books, 1969), pp. 150–51.

Conclusion

1. On American attitudes toward inequality, see James R. Kluegel and Eliot R. Smith, *Beliefs about Inequality: Americans' Views of What Is and What Ought to Be* (Hawthorne, N.Y.: Aldine de Gruyter, 1986).

2. This particular view is advanced by Yablonsky in his *The Violent Gang*, but it colors the media's portrayal of gangs as well.

3. This was also found to be true of Mafia members. See Pino Arlacchi, *Mafia Business: The Mafia and the Spirit of Capitalism* (London: Verso, 1986); and Peter Lupsha, "Individual Choice, Material Culture and Organized Crime," *Criminology* 19 (May 1981): 3–24. In a sense, Arlacchi's and Lupsha's findings, as well as my own, would tend to reinforce some of the points made by Bell in his "Crime as American Way of Life," in *End of Ideology*.

4. Recent works on the role of individualism in American culture include Robert N. Bellah, Richard Madsen, John M. Sullivan, Ann Swidler, and Steven M. Tipton, *Habits of The Heart: Individualism and Commitment in American Life* (Berkeley: University of California Press, 1985); and Herbert J. Gans, *Middle Class Individualism: The Future of Liberal Democracy* (New York: Free Press, 1988).

5. In a sense, this allowance for individual needs resembles the point that Herbert Marcuse makes about industrial political systems: industrial systems allow discontent and then utilize the fact that they allow it to legitimize the present political order. See Marcuse, *One-Dimensional Man: Studies in Ideology of Advanced Industrial Society* (Boston: Beacon Press, 1970).

6. See Orlando Patterson, *Slavery and Social Death: A Comparative Study* (Cambridge, Mass.: Harvard University Press, 1982).

7. See the work of William Julius Wilson, *The Truly Disadvantaged: The Inner City, the Underclass and Public Policy* (Chicago: University of Chicago Press, 1987); also see the essays in *The Ghetto Underclass: Social Science Perspectives*, the volume he edited for *The Annals of the American Academy of Political and Social Science* 501 (January 1989). Other relevant work includes MacLeod, *Ain't No Makin' It*; Sullivan, *Getting Paid.*

8. See Ruth Horowitz, "Masked Intimacy and Marginality: Adult Delinquent Gangs in a Chicano Community," *Urban Life* 11, no. 1 (April

1982): 3–26; Hagedorn, *People and Folks,* pp. 110–28; Vigil, *Barrio Gangs.*

9. For a discussion of the fears associated with perceived urban dangers, see Sally Merry's description in *Urban Dangers.*

10. For the role that the Little League plays in socializing boys into their roles in society, see Gary Allen Fine, *With the Boys: Little League Baseball and Preadolescent Culture* (Chicago: University of Chicago Press, 1987).

11. See Bredvold and Ross, eds., *The Philosophy of Edmund Burke,* pp. 35–42.

Bibliography

Almond, Gabriel. *The Appeals of Communism*. Princeton: Princeton University Press, 1954.

Almond, Gabriel, and Sidney Verba. *The Civic Culture*. Boston: Little, Brown, 1965.

Arendt, Hannah. *Eichmann in Jerusalem: A Report on the Banality of Evil*. New York: Viking, 1963.

Arlacchi, Pino. *Mafia Business: The Mafia and the Spirit of Capitalism*. London: Verso, 1986.

Asbury, Herbert. *The Gangs of New York: An Informal History of the Underworld*. Garden City, N.Y.: Garden City Publishing Co., 1927.

Baker, Bob. "Gang Rule: Living in Battle Zone." *Los Angeles Times,* 10 April 1988.

Banfield, Edward C. *The Moral Basis of a Backward Society*. Glencoe, Ill.: Free Press, 1958.

———. *The Unheavenly City Revisited*. Boston: Little, Brown, 1974.

Banfield, Edward, and James Q. Wilson. *City Politics*. New York: Vintage Books, 1966.

———. "Political Ethos Revisited." *American Political Science Review* 65 (December 1971): 1048–62.

Bell, Daniel. "Crime as an American Way of Life: A Queer Ladder of Social Mobility." In *The End of Ideology: On the Exhaustion of Political Ideas in the Fifties*. Cambridge, Mass.: Harvard University Press, 1988.

Bellah, Robert N., Richard Madsen, John M. Sullivan, Ann Swidler, and Steven M. Tipton. *Habits of the Heart: Individualism and Commitment in American Life*. Berkeley: University of California Press, 1985.

Binder, Arnold, Gilbert Geis, and Dickson Bruce. *Juvenile Delinquency: Historical, Cultural, Legal Perspectives*. New York: Macmillan, 1988.

Bloch, Herbert A., and Arthur Niederhoffer. *The Gang: A Study in Adolescent Behavior*. New York: Philosophical Library, 1958.

Bredvold, Louis I., and Ralph G. Ross, eds., *The Philosophy of Edmund Burke*. Ann Arbor: University of Michigan Press, 1960.

Bridges, Amy. *A City in the Republic: Antebellum New York and the Origins of Machine Politics*. New York: Cambridge University Press, 1984.

———. "Becoming American: The Working Classes in the United States before the Civil War." In Ira Katznelson and Aristide R. Zolberg, eds., *Working Class Formation: Nineteenth Century Patterns in Western Europe and the United States*, pp. 157–96. Princeton: Princeton University Press, 1986.

Campbell, Anne. *Girls in the Gang*. New York: Basil Blackwell, 1987.

Caputo, Phillip. *A Rumor of War*. New York: Ballantine Books, 1978.

Carley, Demetrius. *Urban Government*. Englewood Cliffs, N.J.: Prentice-Hall, 1976.

Christie, Richard, and Florence L. Geis. *Studies in Machiavellianism*. New York: Academic Press, 1970.

Cloward, Richard A., and Lloyd B. Ohlin, *Delinquency and Opportunity: A Theory of Delinquent Gangs*. New York: Free Press, 1960.

Cohen, Albert K. *Delinquent Boys: The Culture of the Gang*. Glencoe, Ill.: Free Press, 1955.

Coleman, Richard P., and Lee Rainwater. *Social Standing in America: New Dimensions of Class*. N.Y.: Basic Books, 1978.

Cooper, Charles N. "The Chicago YMCA Detached Workers: Current Status of an Action Program." In Malcolm W. Klein, ed., *Juvenile Gangs in Context: Theory, Research, and Action*. Englewood Cliffs, N.J.: Prentice-Hall, 1967.

Coser, Lewis A. *The Functions of Social Conflict*. New York: Free Press, 1956.

———. *Continuities in the Study of Social Conflict*. New York: Free Press, 1967.

Crawford, L. Y. "Groups, Gangs and Cohesiveness." In James F. Short, Jr., ed., *Gang Delinquency and Delinquency Subcultures*. New York: Harper & Row, 1968.

Curry, G. David, and Irving A. Spergel, "Gang Homicide, Delinquency and Community." *Criminology* 26, no. 3 (August 1988): 381–406.

Dahl, Robert A. *A Preface to Democratic Theory*. Chicago: University of Chicago Press, 1956.

Dahrendorf, Ralf. *Life Chances: Approaches to Social and Political Theory*. Chicago: University of Chicago Press, 1979.

Des Pres, Terrence. *The Survivor: An Anatomy of Life in the Death Camps.* New York: Oxford University Press, 1976.

Dexter, Lewis A. "Court Politics: Presidential Staff Relations as a Special Case of a General Phenomenon." *Administration and Society* 9, no. 3 (November 1977): 267–304.

Dexter, Lewis Anthony. *Representation vs. Direct Democracy in Fighting about Taxes: Conflicting Notions of Sovereignty, Legitimacy, and Civility in Relation to a Tax Fight, Watertown, Massachusetts, 1953–59.* Cambridge, Mass.: Schenkman, 1981.

Dineen, Joseph F. *The Purple Shamrock: The Honorable James Michael Curley of Boston.* New York: Norton, 1949.

Doob, Leonard W. *Patriotism and Nationalism: Their Psychological Foundations.* New Haven: Yale University Press, 1964.

Fagan, Jeffery. "The Social Organization of Drug Use and Drug Dealing among Urban Gangs." *Criminology* 27, no. 4 (November 1989): 633–70.

Fanon, Franz. *Wretched of the Earth.* New York: Grove Press, 1965.

Fine, Gary Allen. *With the Boys: Little League Baseball and Preadolescent Culture.* Chicago: University of Chicago Press, 1987.

Fromm, Erich. *Escape from Freedom.* New York: Avon, 1965.

Fromm, Erich, and Michael Maccoby. *Social Character in a Mexican Village.* Englewood Cliffs, N.J.: Prentice-Hall, 1970.

Gans, Herbert J. *Deciding What's News: A Study of CBS Evening News, NBC Nightly News, Newsweek and Time.* New York: Random House, 1980.

———. *Middle Class Individualism: The Future of Liberal Democracy.* New York: Free Press, 1988.

Gitlin, Todd. *The Whole World Is Watching: Mass Media in the Making and Unmaking of the New Left.* Berkeley: University of California Press, 1980.

Goffman, Erving. *Asylums: Essays on the Social Situation of Mental Patients and Other Inmates.* Garden City, N.Y.: Anchor Books, 1961.

———. *Stigma: Notes on the Management of Spoiled Identity.* Englewood Cliffs, N.J.: Prentice-Hall, 1963.

———. *Interaction Ritual: Essays in Face-to-Face Behavior.* Garden City, N.Y.: Anchor Books, 1967.

Gosnell, Harold. *Machine Politics: Chicago Model.* Chicago: University of Chicago Press, 1937.

Hagedorn, John M. *People and Folks: Gangs, Crime and the Underclass in a Rustbelt City.* Chicago: Lakeview Press, 1988.

Hamilton, Alexander, John Jay, and James Madison. *The Federalist Papers.* New York: Modern Library, 1937.

Harris, Jean. *Stranger in Two Worlds*. New York: Zebra Brooks, 1987.

Hechter, Michael. *Internal Colonialism: The Celtic Fringe in British National Development, 1536–1966*. Berkeley: University of California Press, 1975.

———. *Principles of Group Solidarity*. Berkeley: University of California Press, 1987.

Hirschman, Albert O. *Exit, Voice, and Loyalty: Responses to Decline in Firms, Organizations, and States*. Cambridge, Mass.: Harvard University Press, 1970.

Hobsbawm, E. J. *Primitive Rebels: Studies in Archaic Forms of Social Movements in the 19th and 20th Centuries*. New York: Norton, 1959.

Hofstadter, Richard. *The Age of Reform*. New York: Vintage Books, 1955.

Horowitz, Ruth. *Honor and the American Dream: Culture and Identity in a Chicano Community*. New Brunswick: Rutgers University Press, 1983.

Horowitz, Ruth, and Gary Schwartz. "Honor, Normative Ambiguity and Gang Violence." *American Sociological Review* 39 (April 1974): 238–51.

Ianni, Francis A. J. *Black Mafia: Ethnic Succession in Organized Crime*. New York: Simon & Schuster, 1974.

Jordan, Winthrop D. *White over Black: American Attitudes toward the Negro, 1550–1812*. Baltimore: Penguin Books, 1969.

Josephson, Matthew. *The Robber Barons: The Great American Capitalists, 1861–1901*. New York: Harcourt, Brace & World, 1962.

Joyeaux, Carl [pseud]. *Out of the Burning: The Story of a Boy Gang Leader,* by Ira Henry Freeman. New York: Crown, 1960.

Katz, Jack. *The Seduction of Crime: Moral and Sensual Attractions in Doing Evil*. New York: Basic Books, 1988.

Katz, Daniel, and Robert L. Kahn, *The Social Psychology of Organization*. 2d ed. New York: Wiley, 1978.

Keiser, R. Lincoln. *The Vice Lords: Warriors of the Streets*. New York: Holt, Rinehart & Winston, 1979.

Klein, Malcolm W. *Street Gangs and Street Workers*. Englewood Cliffs, N.J.: Prentice-Hall, 1971.

Klein, Malcolm W., and L. Y. Crawford. "Groups, Gangs and Cohesiveness." In James F. Short, Jr., ed., *Gang Delinquency and Delinquency Subcultures*. New York: Harper & Row, 1968.

Kluckholn, Florence, and Fred Strodtbeck. *Variations in Value Orientation*. Evanston, Ill.: Row & Petersen, 1961.

Kluegel, James R., and Eliot R. Smith. *Beliefs about Inequality: Ameri-*

cans' Views of What Is and What Ought to Be. Hawthorne, N.Y.: Aldine de Gruyter, 1986.

Kochman, Thomas. *Black and White Styles of Conflict*. Chicago: University of Chicago Press, 1981.

Kornhauser, Ruth Rosner. *Social Sources of Delinquency: An Appraisal of Analytic Models*. Chicago: University of Chicago Press, 1978.

Kulski, W. W. *International Politics in a Revolutionary Age*. New York: Lippincott, 1964.

Lasswell, Harold. *The Psychopathology of Politics*. Chicago: University of Chicago Press, 1932.

Lichtblau, Eric, and Gaylord Shaw. "Crack: It's Not Just a 'City Drug.' " *Los Angeles Times*, 5 April 1988, pt. 1, pp. 1, 20, 22.

Liebow, Elliot. *Tally's Corner: A Study of Negro Streetcorner Men*. Boston: Little, Brown, 1967.

The Life and Tragic Death of Jesse James, the Western Desperado, by "(one who dare not now disclose his name)." Cliffside Park, N.J.: Barclay & Co., 1886.

Lifton, Robert Jay. *Thought Reform and the Psychology of Totalism*. Chapel Hill: University of North Carolina Press, 1989.

Lipset, Seymour Martin. *Political Man: The Social Bases of Politics*. Expanded ed. Baltimore: Johns Hopkins University Press, 1981.

Lipset, Seymour Martin, Martin A. Trow, and James S. Coleman. *Union Democracy: The Internal Politics of the International Typographical Union*. New York: Anchor Books, 1956.

Lipsky, Michael. "Toward a Theory of Street-Level Bureaucracy." In Willis Hawley and Michael Lipsky, eds., *Theoretical Perspectives on Urban Politics*. Englewood Cliffs, N.J.: Prentice-Hall, 1976.

———. *Street-Level Bureaucracy: Dilemmas of the Individual in Public Services*. New York: Russell Sage Foundation, 1980.

Lowi, Theodore. "Machine Politics—Old and New." *The Public Interest*, no. 9 (Fall 1967): 83–92.

Lupsha, Peter. "Individual Choice, Material Culture and Organized Crime." *Criminology* 19, no. 1 (May 1981): 3–24.

Lupsha, Peter, and K. Schlegel. "The Political Economy of Drug Trafficking: The Herrera Organization (Mexico and the United States)." Paper presented at a meeting of the Latin American Studies Association, Philadelphia, 1979.

McClelland, David C. *The Achieving Society*. New York: Free Press, 1961.

MacCloud, Jay. *Ain't No Making It: Leveled Aspirations in a Low Income Community*. Boulder, Colo.: Westview Press, 1987.

Machiavelli, Niccolò. *The Prince and the Discourses*. New York: Modern Library, 1950.

Marcuse, Herbert. *One-Dimensional Man: Studies in Ideology of Advanced Industrial Society.* Boston: Beacon Press, 1970.

Marx, Karl. *The Economic and Philosophical Manuscripts of 1844.* 4th rev. ed. Moscow: Progress Publishers, 1974.

Matza, David. *Delinquency and Drift.* New Brunswick, N.J.: Transaction Books, 1990.

Merry, Sally Engle. *Urban Danger: Life in a Neighborhood of Strangers.* Philadelphia: Temple University Press, 1981.

Merton, Robert K. *Social Theory and Social Structure.* New York: Free Press, 1968.

Meyers, Gustavus. *The History of Tammany Hall.* New York: Boni & Liveright, 1917.

Michels, Robert. *Political Parties.* Glencoe, Ill.: Free Press, 1949.

Mieczkowski, Thomas. "Geeking Up and Throwing Down: Heroin Street Life in Detroit." *Criminology* 24 (November 1986): 645–66.

Milgram, Stanley. *Obedience to Authority.* New York: Harper & Row, 1974.

Miller, Walter B. "Lower Class Culture as a Generating Milieu of Gang Delinquency." *Journal of Social Issues* 14, no. 3 (Fall 1958): 5–19.

———. "White Gangs." *Trans-Action* 6, no. 10 (September 1969): 11–26.

———. *Violence by Youth Gangs and Youth Groups as a Crime Problem in Major American Cities.* Washington, D.C.: Department of Justice, 1975.

———. "Gangs, Groups and Serious Youth Crime." In David Shichor and Delos H. Kelly, eds., *Critical Issues in Juvenile Delinquency.* Lexington: Lexington Books, 1980.

Mills, C. Wright. *White Collar: The American Middle Class.* New York: Oxford University Press, 1951.

Mirande, Alfredo. *Gringo Justice.* South Bend, Ind.: University of Notre Dame Press, 1987.

Moore, Joan W. *Homeboys: Gangs, Drugs, and Prisons in the Barrios of Los Angeles.* Philadelphia: Temple University Press, 1978.

———. "Isolation and Stigmatization in the Development of an Underclass: The Case of Chicano Gangs in East Los Angeles." *Social Problems* 33, no. 1 (October 1985): 1–12.

Moore, Joan, Diego Vigil, and Robert Garcia. "Residence and Territoriality in Chicano Gangs." *Social Problems* 31 (December 1983): 182–94.

New York City Youth Board. *Reaching the Fighting Gang.* New York: New York City Youth Board, 1960.

Okun, Arthur M. *Equality and Efficiency: The Big Trade Off.* Washington, D.C.: Brookings Institution, 1975.

Parsons, Talcott, ed., *Max Weber: The Theory of Social and Economic Organization.* New York: Free Press, 1969.

Patterson, Orlando. *Slavery and Social Death: A Comparative Study.* Cambridge, Mass.: Harvard University Press, 1982.

Piore, Michael J. *Notes for a Theory of Labor Market Stratification.* Working Paper no. 95. Cambridge, Mass.: Massachusetts Institute of Technology, 1972.

Piven, Frances Fox, and Richard A. Cloward. *Regulating the Poor.* New York: Vintage Books, 1972.

Pool, Bob. "Police Call Gang Sweep a Success: 1453 Are Arrested." *Los Angeles Times,* 12 April 1988, sec. II, pp. 1, 4.

Pressman, Jeffrey L., and Aaron Wildavsky. *Implementation: How Great Expectations in Washington Are Dashed in Oakland; or, Why It's Amazing That Federal Programs Work At All, This Being a Saga of the Economic Development Administration as Told by Two Sympathetic Observers Who Seek to Build Morals on a Foundation of Ruined Hopes.* Berkeley: University of California Press, 1973.

Prottas, Jeffrey Manditch. *People Processing: The Street-Level Bureaucrat in Public Service Bureaucracies.* Lexington, Mass.: Lexington Books, 1979.

Rainwater, Lee. *Behind Ghetto Walls: Black Family Life in a Federal Slum.* Chicago: Aldine Press, 1970.

———. *What Money Buys: Inequality and the Social Meanings of Income.* New York: Basic Books, 1974.

Riordan, William L. *Plunkitt of Tammany Hall.* New York: Dutton, 1963.

Rogin, Michael Paul. *Ronald Reagan, the Movie: And Other Episodes in Political Demonology.* Berkeley: University of California Press, 1987.

Schein, Edward. *Coercive Persuasion.* New York: Norton, 1961.

Short, James F., Jr. "Introduction." In Frederic Thrasher, *The Gang,* abridged ed., xxi–xxii.

Short, James F., Jr., and Fred L. Strodtbeck. *Group Process and Gang Delinquency.* Chicago: University of Chicago Press, 1965.

———. "Why Gangs Fight." In James F. Short, ed., *Gang Delinquency and Delinquent Subcultures,* pp. 246–56. New York: Harper & Row, 1968.

Simmel, Georg. *Conflict.* Trans. Kurt H. Wolff. Glencoe, Ill.: Free Press, 1955.

Slotkin, Richard. *The Fatal Environment: The Myth of the Frontier in the Age of Industrialization, 1800–1890.* New York: Atheneum Press, 1985.

Spergel, Irving A. *Racketville, Slumtown and Haulberg*. Chicago: University of Chicago Press, 1964.

———. *Street Gang Work: Theory and Practice*. Garden City, N.Y.: Anchor Books, 1967.

———. "Violent Gangs in Chicago: In Search of Social Policy." *Social Services Review* 58, no. 2 (June 1984): 199–225.

Sullivan, Mercer. *Getting Paid: Youth Crime and Work in the Inner City*. Ithaca, N.Y.: Cornell University Press, 1989.

Susser, Ida. *Norman Street: Poverty and Politics in an Urban Neighborhood*. New York: Oxford University Press, 1982.

Suttles, Gerald D. *The Social Order of the Slum: Ethnicity and Territory in the Inner City*. Chicago: University of Chicago Press, 1968.

———. *The Social Construction of Communities*. Chicago: University of Chicago Press, 1972.

Tatum, Stephen. *Inventing Billy The Kid: Visions of the Outlaw in America, 1881–1981*. Albuquerque: University of New Mexico Press, 1982.

Thrasher, Frederic. *The Gang: A Study of 1303 Gangs in Chicago*. Chicago: University of Chicago Press, 1928.

Vallierer, Pierre. *Les Nègres blancs d'Amerique* [White niggers of America]. Montreal: Editions Parti Pris, 1968.

Vigil, James Diego. *Barrio Gangs: Street Life and Identity in Southern California*. Austin: University of Texas Press, 1988.

Weber, Max. *Economy and Society: An Outline of Interpretive Sociology*. Edited by Guenther Roth and Claus Wittich. Berkeley: University of California Press, 1978.

Whyte, William Foote. *Street Corner Society*. Chicago: University of Chicago Press, 1943.

Willis, Paul E. *Learning to Labor*. New York: Columbia University Press, 1977.

Wilson, James Q. *Variations in Police Behavior*. Cambridge, Mass.: MIT Press, 1968.

Wilson, William Julius. *The Truly Disadvantaged: The Inner City, the Underclass and Public Policy*. Chicago: University of Chicago Press, 1987.

———, ed. *The Ghetto Underclass: Social Science Perspectives*. Annals of the American Academy of Political and Social Science 501 (January 1989).

Wolfinger, Raymond. "Why Political Machines Have Not Withered Away and Other Revisionist Thoughts." *Journal of Politics* 34 (May 1972): 365–98.

Woodson, Robert L. *A Summons to Life: Mediating Structures and the*

Prevention of Youth Crime. Cambridge, Mass.: Ballinger Publishers, 1981.

———, ed. *Youth Crime and Urban Policy: A View from the Inner City.* Washington, D.C.: American Enterprise Institute for Public Policy Research, 1980.

Yablonsky, Lewis. "The Delinquent Gang as a Near-Group." *Social Problems* 7 (Fall 1959): 108–17.

———. *The Violent Gang.* New York: Macmillan, 1966.

Youth-at-Large 1, no. 2 (December 1979): 10, 21.

Index

Adolescent gangs. *See* Gangs, urban
African-American gangs. *See* Black gangs
Agencies, official. *See* Authorities; Criminal justice system; Parole officers; Police
Alcohol, illegal: as gang business, 120
Alcohol abuse: in urban gangs, 133–34
Ambition: and gang violence, 165, 168, 176; and individual violence, 143–44, 154–55, 157
Appalachian white gangs, 309
Arson: as gang business, 123–24, 157
Asbury, Herbert, 3
Asian gangs, 7, 10, 11
Authorities: cooperation with research, 15, 16–17; "defiant individualism" and confrontation with, 26–27, 28, 280; and gang violence, 176; interaction with gangs, 1, 15, 19, 23. *See also* Criminal justice system; Parole officers; Police
Automobile parts, stolen: as gang business, 121–22

Banfield, Edward: *The Moral Basis of a Backward Society*, 24
Black gangs, 7–8, 10, 11, 84–85, 89, 91, 93; and dress codes, 83
Block, Herbert, 4
Boston: nature of politics in, 216–17; political character of police chief in, 253–54
"Brotherhood ideology": and gang organization, 86–87, 148
Bureaucrats: attitudes toward gangs, 242–43; gang leadership pressures, 236–37; gang-related goals of, 234; gangs'

strategies in dealing with, 241–42, 250; nongovernment bureaucrats as resources for, 245–46; personal ambitions, 243–44; prudent-exchange relationships with gangs, 33–34, 216, 233–35, 240–41, 242–43, 245, 249, 250, 318–19; strategies in dealing with gangs, 242–45, 250
Bureaucrats, nongovernment: as advocates for gangs, 248–49; dependent-exchange relationships with gangs, 246–49, 250–51, 319; effectiveness in controlling gang behavior, 249; gangs as advocates for, 246–48; as resources for government agencies, 245–46; sources of, 246
Burke, Edmund, 321
Business activities of gangs. *See* Gang business

Capitalism. *See* Entrepreneurial spirit
Caucasian gangs. *See* White gangs
Central American gangs, 7, 11, 81
Chicano gangs, 46, 86, 100; age stratification in, 72–73; attitude toward imprisonment, 116; characteristics of, 115, 134–35, 316; as consumption-oriented, 134–35; cultural and family constraints in, 71–72, 100, 135; and dress codes, 83–84; drug abuse in, 133; and formal codes of conduct, 78; gang business in, 115, 116; gang organization in, 70–75, 76–78; honor within, 142, 143, 145; "influential" leadership model in, 76–78; multi-generational traditions in, 46–47, 52, 115, 140,

373

145; compared to respect, 141–42,
145; individual violence in defense of,
142, 151–52, 155, 158
Horowitz, Ruth, 45, 79

Ideology, social: and gang organization,
84–86, 114
Immigration: and urban gangs, 2
Imprisonment: Chicano gangs and, 116;
and failure of rehabilitation, 273–76;
gangs and, 61, 115–16, 265–66; gangs'
attitudes toward, 271–76; and status,
272–73. *See also* Prison gangs
Individual: criminal justice system and,
264, 265; gang-joining and the, 37, 38–
39, 313; gang organization and the, 5,
18, 22, 23, 100, 135–36. *See also*
"Defiant individualism"
Individual violence: and ambition, 143–
44, 154–55, 157; and attacks on community members, 151–52, 157; and
attacks on noncommunity members,
153–57; in defense of honor, 142,
151–52, 155, 158; and "defiant individualism," 141, 176; and development of reputation, 142–44; drug abuse
as cause of, 147; fear as cause of, 151–
53; within the gang, 141–48; misinterpreted as gang violence, 140, 141;
and poor diet, 146–47; as result of
frustration and anger, 145–47, 156–
57; as skill-testing, 144–45, 155–56;
and sleep deprivation, 147; as status-
seeking, 138–39; over women, 145–
46, 152. *See also* Gang violence
Initiation rites, 11–12, 50
Institutional agents. *See* Authorities;
Criminal justice system; Parole officers; Police
Irish gangs, 7, 10–11, 42, 46, 52, 55, 56–
57, 84–86, 100, 166–67, 309; characteristics of, 75–76, 115, 316; as
consumption-oriented, 134–35; and
dress codes, 83; drug abuse in, 82, 133;
economic resentment by, 159; gang
business in, 115, 116; gang organization in, 75–77; links with adult social
clubs, 75–76, 115, 121, 135, 181, 188–
89, 218–19; multi-generational traditions in, 181, 315; and political tradition, 218–19, 220–21; and resistance
to social and racial community integration, 190–91; transitional nature of,
75
Irish social clubs: and links with Irish

gangs, 75–76, 115, 121, 135, 181,
188–89, 218–19
Italian gangs, 10, 309

Jamaican gangs, 7, 11
Job-training programs, government: and
gangs, 238–40, 313, 320; low-income
communities' favor of, 239
Juvenile courts. *See* Criminal justice system

Katz, Jack, 38
Keiser, R. Lincoln, 86
Klikas: in Los Angeles Chicano gangs, 71–
74
Kornhauser, Ruth, 21

Latino gangs, 7, 10, 11, 55, 84; age stratification in, 128; drug abuse in, 80–
82; gang business in, 125. *See also*
Chicano gangs
Law enforcement. *See* Authorities; Parole
officers; Police
Legal representation: for gangs, 266–67
Libya, 165
Lipset, Seymour Martin: *Union Democracy*, 88–89
Loan sharks: urban gangs and, 186–87
Los Angeles: Crisis Intervention Units in,
260–63; gang business in, 115, 116;
gang organization in, 70–75; gang wars
in (1987–88), 170–72, 205–6, 290–
91; low-income community conditions
in compared to east coast, 9; mutual
antipathy between gangs and politicians in, 223–24; nature of politics in,
216–17, 223–25; political character of
police chief in, 254; political role of
gangs in, 224
Low-income communities: attitudes toward money in, 106–7; competitiveness in, 24, 26, 103–4, 139, 315; and
criminal justice system, 269; distrust of
police in, 183–85, 206, 257; favor of
government job-training programs in,
239; formal standing of gangs in, 179;
frustration in, 182–83, 315; gang
membership in, 7–9; housing in, 8–9;
lack of opportunity and "social death"
in, 45, 315; in motion pictures about
gangs, 301, 309; physical dangers in,
44–45, 183–85, 312, 317; real estate
development in, 188–90, 230–31; relations with police, 255–58; social re-

Compositor:	Maple-Vail Book Mfg. Group
Text:	10/13 Sabon
Display:	Sabon
Printer:	Maple-Vail Book Mfg. Group
Binder:	Maple-Vail Book Mfg. Group